From
Brezhnev
to
—— Gorbachev ——

About the Book and Author

From 1982 to 1985, the period on which this book focuses, the Soviet Union was governed by a succession of ailing old men—Brezhnev, Andropov, and Chernenko—who, supported by an equally elderly Politburo, were often physically incapable of controlling and directing the bureaucratic state machine and party organization. This unprecedented situation precipitated a secret and bitter power struggle within the top Soviet leadership between two main factions: the Chernenko apparatchiks, who had risen to power under Brezhnev and owed their positions to him; and the supporters of Andropov, including the younger, more dynamic, and power-hungry members of the party elite, who had been advocating fairly bold reforms to deal with the grave social and economic problems facing the USSR.

Dr. Hazan provides a detailed analysis of this hidden power struggle as he examines the final years of Brezhnev's reign and the brief ascendancies of Andropov and Chernenko. These rapid changes led to the demise of the old guard in the Politburo and the emergence of a new breed of leader in Mikhail Gorbachev, culminating in the final consolidation of his power at the 27th CPSU Congress. Drawing on an extensive range of primary sources and using vivid examples of how the factions exploited the gigantic propaganda machine of the Soviet mass media, the author looks behind the Kremlin's walls to explore the essence of Soviet politics. The book describes the power base of each of the recent Soviet leaders and analyzes the steps they took to consolidate their positions and tighten controls over the bureaucracy and the military.

Baruch A. Hazan teaches at the Institute of European Studies, Vienna, Austria. He is the author of *The East European Political System* (Westview, 1985), *Olympic Sports and Propaganda Games* (1982), and *Soviet Impregnational Propaganda (1982)*.

From
Brezhnev
to
___ Gorbachev ___
Infighting
in the Kremlin

Baruch A. Hazan

Westview Press / Boulder and London

To my parents,
Amely and Albert Hazan,
and to
Sara and David Goldstein

Copyright © 1987 by Westview Press, Inc.

Published in 1987 in the United States of America by Westview Press, Inc.; Frederick A. Praeger, Publisher; 5500 Central Avenue, Boulder, Colorado 80301

Library of Congress Cataloging-in-Publication Data
Hazan, Barukh, 1942–
    From Brezhnev to Gorbachev.
    Includes index.
    1. Soviet Union—Politics and government—1982–
2. Elite (Social sciences)—Soviet Union. 3. TSK KPSS.
Politbiuro. I. Title.
DK288.H39 1987   320.947   86-13267
ISBN 0-8133-0368-0

Printed and bound in the United States of America

The paper used in this publication meets the requirements of the American National Standard for Permanence of Paper for Printed Library Materials Z39.48-1984.

10   9   8   7   6   5   4   3   2   1

Contents

Preface

This book should not be considered a definitive assessment of the power struggle in the Kremlin but merely a description and analysis of a number of crucial stages in this process. Since I have had no access to inside information on the discussions within the Politburo and the Central Committee or on the developments in the Kremlin, my study has been almost entirely based on the official Soviet discourse—speeches, articles, party and governmental announcements, reports on the movement of the Soviet leaders, and so on. Consequently, the Soviet mass media—national and regional newspapers and journals, radio, television, and TASS—are the main sources used in the study. I have deliberately avoided the use of other works dealing with related issues or with the period covered by this study, not because I regard these works as inferior in any way but simply because my intention was to base the study on the available Soviet primary sources.

The correct assumption by many authors that all officially published material in the Soviet Union is subject to rigorous censorship has often led to the conclusion that such sources cannot serve as a reliable basis from which to analyze political developments in the Soviet Union, unless of course the authors engage in the notorious practice of "reading between the lines." This conclusion, however, is not necessarily correct. Throughout the period discussed in this study republican leaders have effectively used the republican press to indicate their attitudes toward a new leader or their position on a particular issue. Careful comparative analysis of the releases by the Soviet regional press often provides revealing insights into the political scene. The same applies to various articles ostensibly dealing with historical subjects or theoretical issues or discussing events in Lenin's life or past periods of Soviet history. These are often charged with strong allegorical meaning in relation to current developments in the Kremlin, indicating dissenting opinions or a new approach. Although such sources cannot compare to those available to students of Western political systems (official protocols, interviews, open statements of the leaders, memoirs), they certainly serve as alternative and often surprisingly reliable sources of information on the issues engaging the attention of the Soviet leaders at a particular period and on the leaders' positions in the power struggle.

Naturally, a study that relies almost exclusively on official sources suffers from unavoidable limitations. It is difficult and sometimes even impossible to establish a connection between a certain journalist and a particular leader or a group of leaders (luckily, this is not the case with the republican press); in most cases it is impossible to find sufficient corroboration of conclusions reached from an analysis of the open sources. Finally, authors constantly run the risk of making too much of the available material and using it as a basis for broad generalizations. Even though I have tried to avoid this temptation, I am painfully aware of the limitations of this type of analysis and the problems that it poses. Nevertheless, I hope that this book provides an accurate, though limited, analysis of one of the most turbulent and unusual periods of Soviet political life.

Baruch A. Hazan

——— Acknowledgments ———

In the autumn of 1963, having obtained a short furlough from the Israeli Army, I went to register at the Hebrew University of Jerusalem, without having any clear idea of what I really wanted to study. Since I had been born in Bulgaria and lived there until the age of fourteen, I was proficient in the Bulgarian and Russian languages, and accordingly formed the vague intention of studying in a field connected with the USSR or Eastern Europe. However, I had no concrete plans. Having one or two hours free before registration, I made my way to the library of the Department of Political Studies. The first book that I pulled out at random from the shelf dealt with Soviet foreign policy and was published by one Frederick Praeger. So was the second and most of the books that I subsequently perused. I therefore formed a clear impression that the field of Soviet studies was inseparably connected with the name of Frederick Praeger. When I left the library, I still had no clear idea about my field of study but was nevertheless sure of one thing—sooner or later, I wanted to write a book that would be accepted for publication by Frederick Praeger.

This is not my first book to be published by Mr. Praeger's house. Two years ago he salvaged a project—a research study on East European governments—which had almost failed to see the light of day when another publisher went out of business. However, this is the first of my books to be written from the very outset for Westview Press and, in fact, the first to be suggested by Mr. Praeger himself. As such, it represents the fulfillment of a common idea that had been in the back of both our minds for several years.

Although Mr. Praeger shares the credit for the book's conception, he cannot also share the blame for the mistakes and inaccuracies that have inevitably crept into the text. These are my very own, and I offer my apologies to the reader in advance.

Several of my students at the Vienna Institute of European Studies and my office colleagues were of great help during the preparation of the manuscript. Chris Campbell, Heidi Boenisch, Alison Doughtie, and Kim Olson helped me in preparing the footnotes, whereas Mariana Heindl, Joe Fabijan, and John Macleod were of invaluable assistance with their deep knowledge of the Soviet political scene, as well as with their good humor and forbearance. Ms. Janet Kovacs, the librarian of the Institute of European Studies in Vienna, was very helpful in finding material, especially when I was losing all hope with obscure names and titles. The preparation of the manuscript's final version would have been much more difficult without the help of my friend and colleague Robert Mackenzie. I also wish to express my deep gratitude to the staff of Westview Press, especially to Susan L. McEachern, Jeanne E. Campbell, and Pat Peterson, who turned the work of publishing the book into a real pleasure for me. Finally, on the home front, I must as always thank Helen, Ramona, Iris, and Dorly, who by their patience and understanding managed to create the right atmosphere at home for me to conduct my research.

B.A.H.

1

Introduction

The thorny issues of leadership and of leaders' succession have plagued many generations of Marxists. Karl Marx and Friedrich Engels treated almost all political leaders, both historical figures and their own contemporaries, with open contempt, repeatedly stressing that the issue of leadership could only be analyzed in terms of the specific historical circumstances and that leaders were actually produced by history itself. Paraphrasing Claude-Adrien Helvétius, Marx asserted that every social epoch needs its own great men, and when it does not find them, it invents them.[1] He thus implied that all leaders are replaceable but failed to explain just how leaders are thrown up by the historical process.

Development of the Communist Concept of Leadership

The negative attitude of Marx and Engels toward leaders affected their analysis of the leadership of the proletarian revolution. In this context they reiterated their aversion to individual leaders: They pointed out that collective leadership had initiated and implemented all important historical acts, maintained that the only genuine revolutions are those without leaders, and denounced "any personality cult."[2] Marx even went further. He concluded that the proletariat has no need for leaders; in fact they often, as in the case of the Paris Commune, can "hamper real action" instead of inspiring it.[3]

Engels later significantly modified this view, holding that even in the supposedly leaderless Communist society a number of organizations, such as industrial enterprises, would still require persons to coordinate planning and other activities;[4] thus he provided the modern leaders of the Communist world with some ideological justification for their existence. Nevertheless, Marxist teaching provides no guidelines for the selection or replacement of leaders in the Communist society, leaving Marxist disciples with the task of developing the ideological justification for the existence of Communist leaders.

1

Georgiy Plekhanov qualified Marx's theory that leaders were the product of historical circumstances. Plekhanov asserted that, although leaders are powerless to alter the course of history—which is determined by independent forces—"influential leaders can change the individual features of events and some of their particular consequences."[5] Plekhanov further asserted that leaders, though limited in range and effectiveness by material circumstances, "by virtue of the particular traits of their character, can influence the fate of society."[6] He praised men who "see further than others and desire things more strongly than others," thus possessing qualities that "make them capable of serving the great social needs of their time."[7]

Lenin further clarified the leadership issue presented in Marx's writings and offered a completely new view on the role of the leader in the revolution. He did not share Marx's contempt for leaders. On the contrary, doubting the abilities of the proletariat and fearing its tendency to act spontaneously and therefore in a misdirected and dangerous manner, Lenin stressed the important role of the party leadership in controlling and directing the action of the proletariat. According to Lenin, even if the working class were defeated and the party dispersed, as long as a leadership cadre survives eventual victory is assured.[8]

Lenin charged the leaders of the proletariat with many tasks: to educate the proletariat, to raise the level of its consciousness through agitation and propaganda, and to lead it toward victory by acting as mass mobilizers, organizers, and strategists and by stimulating heroic actions that would serve as the motive force for a revolutionary chain reaction. The "spark" concept was one of Lenin's favorite ideas: The leaders were to provide the spark to ignite the combustible social material and thus set off a general explosion, whereas the Russian Revolution was to serve as the spark that would initiate a worldwide conflagration.[9]

Only after the victory of the Russian Revolution and the establishment of the Communist regime in the Soviet Union did the inadequacy of Marx's views on leadership become clearly apparent. The emergence of a Communist power created a new world situation and demonstrated that Marx's doctrine on leadership was totally unrealistic. Instead, Lenin and his successors developed the theory of the "dictatorship of the proletariat" to explain the form of the Communist state. The term *dictatorship* implied an authoritarian political system, the leadership of which was not limited by legal or constitutional constrictions or indeed by public opinion, and a regime in which coercion and physical and mental terror were the accepted instruments of government. In this system, the basic goal remained the achievement of communism through rapid industrialization and radical social transformation. However, the role of the masses in this process was to be strictly passive: They were expected obediently to implement the plans of leaders whom they did not have the power to appoint or remove. Indeed, strict discipline, a rigid hierarchy, and an extensive system of paternalism in all areas of life became the main characteristics of this regime.

The authoritarian political structure was headed by a small group of leaders that enjoyed a complete monopoly of the decisionmaking process and ensured the implementation of their decisions through an elaborate bureaucratic apparatus, assisted by propaganda, agitation, terror, and coercion. Consequently, the leaders of the dictatorship of the proletariat quickly acquired a special status for themselves. In total disregard of Marx's dictum, Marx himself and the Soviet leaders became the subjects of unprecedented personality cults, which for Lenin (up to the present) and Joseph Stalin (until his death) carried with them quasi-religious adulation. Surprisingly, these personality cults, which encompassed to varying extents all Soviet leaders, became an element of continuity in the Soviet political system.

In the seven decades of its existence, the Soviet regime has often relied heavily on ideological formulations and justifications to justify actions that offended international law or the accepted norms of human and international behavior. However, questions of leadership in general or succession in particular were not decided on an ideological basis. Instead, they were usually determined by a political struggle that had little relation to Marxism but much in common with the succession struggles in other dictatorial regimes. Personal ambition, collusion, ruthlessness, and political skill, as well as the ability to generate support at the right moment among the state organs, were the factors that determined the outcome of the succession struggle in the USSR.

Toward the end of his life, Lenin perceived the dangers posed by his own and perhaps future successions in the USSR. Being well aware of the tremendous ideological gap in this area, he tried to deal with the problem by preparing his "Testament." In it he evaluated the positive and negative qualities of the top Soviet leaders of his time. He stopped short of recommending anyone as his heir but nevertheless voiced concern regarding the immense power that Stalin had accumulated through his position as general secretary of the Communist Party of the Soviet Union (CPSU) Central Committee and the manner in which he might exploit this power. Lenin called for Stalin's removal on the grounds that he was too rude and capricious and not sufficiently loyal or polite. Stalin's supporters had the "Testament" suppressed: It was published in the USSR only in 1956 and had no influence on the succession struggle. Ironically, Stalin emerged as Lenin's heir. The whole affair established the precedent that the succession issue in the USSR would be solved by a power struggle in which the leaders' personalities had a decisive influence. This proved to be the main characteristic of Soviet leadership and its succession during the subsequent decades of Communist rule.

Features of Soviet Leadership
and Succession

Individual, not Collective, Leadership

Although the Soviets claimed to have collective leadership (a huge propaganda effort is invested in creating the impression that individual leadership does not and can not exist in the USSR), Soviet history shows that, except during very brief periods following Stalin's death and Nikita Khrushchev's ouster, the Soviet political system has essentially been dominated by a single leader. The problem of the specific position or positions to be occupied by this leader developed some years after the establishment of the Communist regime and was solved in different ways during subsequent Soviet history. In his "Testament," Lenin did not discuss the official institutions of the top leadership (except for proposing an increase in the membership of the Central Committee); he dealt with the actual personalities of the top Soviet leaders of his time. The "Testament" was concerned with the future leader, not with future collective leadership. It evaluated not the different ideological positions of the leaders but their personal characters. Thus in the very political system that by definition rejects the existence of personal leadership, the issue of first succession was approached in purely personal terms and was eventually solved through a violent power struggle in which the winner, Stalin, employed physical terror against opponents and allies alike to acquire and consolidate his power. Nevertheless, although Stalin (commonly cited as the classic all-powerful single leader of the Communist state) set the pattern followed by his successors (each according to his abilities), Lenin first perceived the succession in the USSR in purely personal terms.

Significance of the Post of General Secretary

Lenin held the post of chairman of the Council of People's Commissars (Sovnarkom), equivalent to that of prime minister. Although already acknowledged as the founder and leader of the Soviet state, he held no official party office; yet because of his personality and charisma, as well as his role in directing the October Revolution, he was the undisputed leader of the USSR. Stalin, who followed him, used the office of general secretary of the Central Committee to generate the power and support necessary to ensure his own election. From his election to the general secretaryship (during Lenin's lifetime) to his death, Stalin never relinquished this post, making it the mainstay for the political leadership of the USSR and a necessary prerequisite for any person aspiring to become the top leader. Indeed, at the time of Lenin's death, Stalin showed no interest in assuming Lenin's official position as Sovnarkom chairman to demonstrate that he was Lenin's true successor. He had already invested the office of general secretary with such power that he did not need another official post to assert himself as the new Soviet leader. During World War II and subsequently, Stalin took over the chairmanship of the Council of Ministers, a move copied by Khrushchev after 1958. However, in neither case did these additional offices alter the fact that the post that served as the source and proof of the top leader's power was that of general secretary of the CPSU Central Committee.

Use of Central Committee as a Legitimizing Body

Nikita Khrushchev increased even further the importance of the office of general secretary. He was astute enough to acquire the post of general secretary for himself. He eased Georgiy Malenkov out of this post only a few days after Stalin's death, giving Malenkov the post of chairman of the Council of Ministers, from which he could be subsequently ousted without difficulty. Lacking Stalin's charisma, he made skillful use of the party apparatus as an instrument for communicating and implementing his programs. Khrushchev's approach was most evident in the brilliant manner in which he used the Central Committee in 1957 to banish the "antiparty group"—establishing a precedent for using the Central Committee as the ultimate legitimizing authority in the Kremlin power struggle. In October 1964 Leonid Brezhnev and his supporters used the Central Committee as the means for the public ousting of Khrushchev himself. The CPSU Central Committee played the same legitimizing role during the 1982–1985 successions. Although the real decision on the successions of Yuriy Andropov, Konstantin Chernenko, and Mikhail Gorbachev was clearly made by the Politburo, in all three cases the Central Committee officially legitimized the Politburo decision.

Khrushchev introduced a further novelty into the Kremlin power struggle. After ridding himself of Lavrentiy Beria, Stalin's ruthless KGB chief, who made an unsuccessful bid for the leadership, he ended the use of physical terror in the power struggle among the Soviet leaders; no longer would lethal consequences befall the losers, as they did in Stalin's time. The fact that Chernenko gained supremacy in his second attempt demonstrated that after 1953 a failure in the succession struggle did not necessarily represent a lethal blow to the defeated side.

The Triple Crown

Brezhnev, obviously fond of the external symbols of power and status, added to his official posts the chairmanship of the USSR Supreme Soviet Presidium, a position that he held from 1977 until his death in 1982. From that point until the ascent of Gorbachev, the acquisition of the "triple crown" (the posts of general secretary of the CPSU Central Committee, chairman of the USSR Supreme Soviet Presidium, and chairman of the Defense Council) provided the ultimate and visible proof that the new leader had established himself. In both Andropov and Chernenko's cases (see Chapters 2, 3, and 4) the election to the post of chairman of the Supreme Soviet Presidium signaled the end of the succession struggle or at least of its most crucial stage.

Gorbachev's rise to power changed this pattern. Although apparently adding the post of chairman of the Defense Council[10] to his position as general secretary, he declined the post of chairman of the Supreme Soviet Presidium, explaining that he intended to devote himself to party work; instead he initiated the election of Andrey Gromyko to this post (Chapter 7). Thus Gorbachev abandoned one feature of the Soviet succession but strengthened another, namely, the supremacy of the office of general secretary.

The Age Question

Soon after Gorbachev's ascent, many observers remarked that his relative youth (fifty-four years, the youngest man in the Politburo) might indicate a change toward a more youthful top leadership. This interpretation is correct only if Gorbachev's age is being compared to those of Andropov and Chernenko at their successions or to Brezhnev's at the time of his death. Although Gorbachev was much younger and more vigorous than Andropov and Chernenko, who succeeded as old men in poor health, both Lenin and Stalin were in their forties when they came to power whereas Khrushchev (fifty-nine years) and Brezhnev (fifty-seven years) were little older than Gorbachev. Thus, in the so-called pattern relating to the age of the Soviet leader, Andropov and Chernenko, not Gorbachev, were the exceptions.

The Personality Cult

The cult of personality was an integral component of the tenure of all the Soviet leaders before Gorbachev. The cult surrounding Lenin seemed to develop from his natural charisma; however, his heirs, Stalin, Khrushchev, and Brezhnev, each promoted a specific cult, which not only served to inflate the leader's ego through mass adulation but also had clear political goals, such as strengthening his image vis-à-vis his colleagues, supporters, and opponents, blocking and neutralizing criticism from below, delaying his decline, and counteracting the effects of any political, economic, and social failures. Although Andropov and Chernenko did not have enough time to develop their own cults, each possessed some of the necessary preattributes. Andropov, the former KGB (Committee for State Security) chief had developed the image of being an innovator, strict disciplinarian, and ascetic; Chernenko lacked Andropov's qualities and track record, but he inherited Brezhnev's apparatus almost intact and, given time, would have had little difficulty in using it to foster his own personality cult.

Gorbachev has many positive qualities—charm, eloquence, an image of sincerity, and a populistic aura—which could easily form a basis for developing his own personality cult. However, from the very beginning of his tenure, and especially during the 27th CPSU Congress (Chapter 8), he publicly expressed his aversion to the practice of adulating the leader. Of course, he may resort to the device of a cult at a later stage. Sooner or later Gorbachev will have to show some concrete results in his foreign and domestic policies. This situation could become acute for him after the nuclear reactor disaster at Chernobyl, which is likely to seriously hamper the implementation of his ambitious agricultural plans and further strain the Soviet foreign currency reserves by necessitating increased food purchases from the West. A properly developed personality cult could effectively shield Gorbachev from criticism prompted by disappointed expectations.

Death—Prime Force in the Succession

The Soviet succession is a party issue, decided by a small group of party leaders (the Politburo and Central Committee Secretariat, with the apparent consent of the top KGB and Soviet Army leaderships), who use a party instrument—the Central Committee—to anoint the leader of the largest country in the world. In the cases of Andropov and Chernenko (Chapters 3 and 4) the Central Committee was also used to decide their elections as chairmen of the Supreme Soviet Presidium, an example followed later in the election of Gromyko (Chapter 8). The three rapid successions during the 1982–1985 period formalized and institutionalized the party procedure for electing the new leader. They also confirmed another important feature—that death is the motive force for the succession in the USSR. Here too Marx proved to be wrong: Not historical circumstances but death and the Politburo create the new Soviet leader.

Because the election of the new leader is conducted in great secrecy by a small group whose decision is later ratified by the Central Committee, the succession procedure, lacking any constitutional or legal foundation, would appear to create uncertainty regarding the leader's possible removal at any time and make his position precarious throughout his tenure. Instead, the Politburo members, well aware that every succession could jeopardize their positions, prefer to activate the procedure only when it becomes absolutely necessary (when the leader dies). The Politburo has not yet developed an honorable procedure for retiring old leaders (although Gorbachev may have taken the first steps in his treatment of the prominent members of Brezhnev's faction, described in Chapter 8) or an accepted procedure for legally terminating the tenure of a leader whose programs and policies have failed. Khrushchev was the only Soviet leader ousted as a result of a plot conceived by Politburo members; all other Soviet leaders have died in office. Even when the leader was no longer in full control of his mental and physical faculties (all Soviet leaders who died in office seemed to have reached this stage toward the end of their lives), the Politburo preferred to wait until his death. In the early 1980s, every additional day of Brezhnev's life created fresh embarrassments for the CPSU; during Andropov's and Chernenko's prolonged and conspicuous absences from public view, Politburo members were unable to do anything except await the leaders' deaths.

Power Struggle Based on Personalities

Finally, the Soviet succession is decided by a political struggle or rather a struggle for the use of power. In democratic regimes this struggle take the form of a contest between different leaders or parties, involving the candidates' personalities and political platforms, and it is resolved by free and democratic elections. In contrast, in the USSR the succession struggle takes the form of infighting between individual leaders, backed by small factions, within a small and secretive party organ. The issues assume importance only after the succession or even after the initial period of consolidation. Furthermore, the Soviet political and economic system does not lend itself to radical reform because any significant change can undermine the power of the party—the very body deciding on the changes.

Accordingly, real issues play little if any role in the actual succession struggle. The choice is between different figures, all of whom freely employ the trite slogans of increased productivity, higher efficiency, and stricter discipline to further their candidacies. Each leader involved in the 1982–1985 successions had favorite issues with which he was identified: Andropov was noted for his campaign against alcoholism and for stricter discipline; Chernenko, for better contacts with the people; and Gorbachev, for increased material incentives for improving productivity and quality of production and a certain measure of decentralization in planning, in addition to the issues supported by Andropov. However, these issues did not seem to be mutually exclusive. It is difficult to see how any Soviet leader could object to any of them, except for the issue of planning decentralization. Furthermore, there is no evidence that these issues played any role in the actual process of deciding the succession. If so why was Chernenko's candidacy rejected in November 1982 but approved in February 1984? If Gorbachev's platform prompted the Politburo to approve his election in 1985, why did it fail to produce a similar result in 1984 after Andropov's death?

To the outside observer with no firsthand knowledge of the Politburo's deliberations, the three successions appear to have been decided on purely personal terms, the decisions in each case representing the outcome of the political maneuvering of two opposing factions in the Politburo in a period of fierce infighting. In all three cases the control of a majority in the Politburo was the crucial factor in deciding the succession. In Chernenko's succession, neither faction seemed to enjoy a clear majority, which evidently led to a compromise deal—the election of Chernenko to the general secretaryship with the understanding that

Gorbachev would become his undisputed successor. The unusual speed with which Gorbachev assumed office after Chernenko's death supports this hypothesis (see Chapter 6).

Stages of the Power Struggle

A mistake often made is to focus solely on two stages of the power struggle—acquiring power and losing it. Between these two stages lie a number of additional stages, namely, those of consolidating and then expanding power, using power, maintaining it, and sharing or delegating it. All of these phases are reflected in different degrees in the 1982–1985 infighting in the Kremlin. The stage of losing power clearly cannot be analyzed in the present study because the first leaders of the USSR involved in the 1982–1985 successions lost their power as a result of death.

Brezhnev's Long Reign

The various stages of Brezhnev's long tenure (1964–1982) demonstrate the gradual development of the power struggle. During this period he expanded his power and then ingeniously protected it by sharing part of it with lower-level officials. Brezhnev was a pragmatic leader who quickly perceived the importance of institutionalized and regularized methods of government. A possible reason for Brezhnev's approach, apart from his personal character, is that his crucial role in organizing Khrushchev's overthrow would naturally make him very wary upon taking office himself and anxious to prevent the same fate. After consolidating his position as unquestioned leader, Brezhnev protected his power by delegating some of the decisionmaking to lower officials in the party pyramid, usually the leaders of state agencies and local party organizations; this approach resulted in a new form of collective leadership.

The outcomes of this policy were twofold. First, the system devised by Brezhnev guaranteed his own power and security by granting similar power and security to his supporters. Since the lower-level officials clearly recognized Brezhnev as the source of their security, they regularly and openly expressed their support for his policies, acclaiming every new program or initiative that he put forward. This naturally led to the development of the Brezhnev personality cult, which in its latter stages reached preposterous proportions. Second, the CPSU apparatus and the local party and state officials who benefited most from this situation became paragons of conservatism, acting only to preserve the established order, which fully corresponded to their own selfish interests. They became the main factor ensuring the continuation of Brezhnev's rule—sharing responsibility for policy implementation, enjoying un-precedented personal power and security, and opposing any demands for change from other groups in the Soviet political system. The prevailing view clearly was, "What is good for me is good for the country, and the man who made this all possible must continue to lead the country and the party as long as possible."

In the later stages of his tenure Brezhnev perfected his system of protecting his power by extending it to the Politburo itself. The appointment of Nikolay Tikhonov as chairman of the Council of Ministers and the meteoric rise of Chernenko from an unremarkable middle-level official to full membership in the Politburo and to the post of secretary in charge of cadres and ideology (usually held by the heir apparent in the USSR) made them the core of Brezhnev's faction. The faction also included Kazakhstan's first secretary Dinmukhamed Kunayev, Viktor Grishin, first secretary of the Moscow City CPSU Committee, and possibly also Vladimir Shcherbitskiy, first secretary of the Ukrainian party organization. This faction successfully blocked any initiatives that might jeopardize or curb Brezhnev's and its own power. Thanks to the efforts of his Politburo faction and the support of the nomenklatura, Brezhnev was able to protect his power to the very end, although the conservatism thus generated developed into a debilitating stagnation in all areas of Soviet political and economic life.

Andropov's Brief Tenure

The power enjoyed by the nomenklatura and by Brezhnev's faction in the Politburo was delegated power, and its source lay in Brezhnev's own person. Once Brezhnev was dead, much of their power was lost. Consequently, the Brezhnev faction failed to ensure Chernenko's success in his first bid for the succession (Chapter 2). However, its members evidently retained enough of their former power to keep their seats in the Politburo. Andropov inherited only limited power, curbed by the continuing existence in the Politburo of Brezhnev's faction. Thus Andropov successfully acquired power by his election as general secretary but still faced the subsequent and crucial stages of the power struggle—consolidating, expanding, and protecting his power (Chapters 2 and 3). The infighting throughout Andropov's tenure related to the subsequent stage of expanding power at the expense of those who had shared it for years with Brezhnev.

Andropov's tenure was too short and he was in too poor health for him to achieve significant successes in his struggle against the remnants of Brezhnev's political neofeudalism. He was unable to remove a single member of Brezhnev's faction from the Politburo or to significantly diminish the power of the nomenklatura. Furthermore, Andropov's death deprived his faction in the Politburo of much of its power, making it too weak to ensure Gorbachev's election as the next general secretary (Chapter 4). Thus the pattern of the development of the power struggle after Brezhnev's death repeated itself.

Chernenko's Second Chance

The most vulnerable period for the recipients of delegated power appears to be immediately after the demise of their leader. After a while, they are able to reorganize and seek their own independent sources of power. Thus, after Andropov's death Brezhnev's faction proved successful in what they had failed to achieve two years before— ensuring the election of their candidate, Chernenko, to the general secretaryship of the CPSU Central Committee. However, the power of the old Brezhnev faction was far from absolute. Its success was compromised by the novel deal accompanying Chernenko's election: that he should share his power not only with his own supporters but also with his main rival Gorbachev and his faction. The main ingredient of the deal (described in Chapter 4) seemed to be that Gorbachev was given extensive power in the areas of cadres and ideology, a clear pointer to his future ascent to the post of general secretary.

Chernenko, after his election, could be expected to engage in the subsequent stages of the power struggle and attempt to expand and protect his power at the expense of the rival faction. During the first phase of his tenure evidence indicates that he did begin to work in this direction (Chapter 4). However, his declining health, as well as the serious limitations to his power and authority imposed by the deal with Gorbachev's faction, prevented him from advancing beyond the stage of merely acquiring some degree of power. Chernenko's election to the chairmanship of the USSR Supreme Soviet Presidium (Chapter 4) and to the chairmanship of the Defense Council (Chapter 5) cannot be regarded as evidence of his expanding his power. The triple crown was merely the outward proof of his acquisition of supreme power, a concept established by Brezhnev. It is logical to assume that in his deal with Gorbachev Chernenko bargained for these visible symbols of total power in exchange for surrendering to Gorbachev the supervision of the vital party areas of cadres and ideology and, apparently, promising him the future succession.

Gorbachev's Election

Accordingly, Gorbachev's unprecedentedly swift election as general secretary, only hours after Chernenko's death, was not a surprise but merely the execution of the tacit agreement. Therefore, the first stage of the power struggle—acquisition of power—presented no problems for Gorbachev. However, given Gorbachev's relative youth and good health, he clearly would engage energetically in the subsequent stages of the struggle, striving to expand his power. Gorbachev's first priorities were to deprive the nomenklatura of the power it had acquired by delegation and to oust Brezhnev's old allies from the Politburo. Success in these actions was essential before he could begin to implement his new policies. Within a relatively short period, Gorbachev had ousted many of Brezhnev's feudal supporters and deprived others of much of their power; he then installed people of his own mold into key positions in the party and state apparatus (Chapters 7 and 8).

This struggle was not easy. Although many members of the Brezhnev old guard were gently eased into overdue retirement and others unceremoniously ousted, two of Brezhnev's closest allies, Kazakhstan's Kunayev and the Ukraine's Shcherbitskiy, generated enough independent support to survive unscathed the congresses of both their respective republican party organizations and the 27th CPSU Congress, retaining their seats in the Politburo. (Gorbachev's obvious exasperation at this failure is described in Chapter 8.) In December 1986, nine months after the congress, Gorbachev succeeded in ousting Kunayev from his post as first secretary of the Kazakh party organization and, subsequently, at the January 1987 Central Committee plenum, from his membership in the Politburo. The survival of Shcherbitskiy indicates that although Gorbachev successfully consolidated his power, the embers of the last power struggle still glow in the Kremlin and that Gorbachev, who has already expanded his power and apparently delegated parts of it to his supporters in the Politburo, is still very much involved in the task of protecting his power. Gorbachev must be painfully aware that the surviving powerful elements of Brezhnev's faction and products of his era, who still occupy positions of influence in the party apparatus, may be able to undermine his power, especially if his economic and foreign policies misfire. The Soviet Army, still underrepresented in the Politburo, and the KGB, which was subjected to open criticism at the beginning of 1987 because of the illegal arrest of a journalist in the Ukraine, could also develop into potential centers of opposition. Clearly the latest power struggle in the Kremlin is not over; it merely entered a new stage.

2

Succession in the USSR: Brezhnev's Twilight and Death

The death of the leader is never officially forewarned in the USSR. The totalitarian essence of the Soviet society precludes any reports on the health of the leaders or explanations for their frequent absences from the political scene, which are often the results of their advanced ages and fragile constitutions. Thus, even though Lenin suffered in agony for at least two years before his death, the Soviet press provided false and reassuring reports on the progress of his "recovery," and only a few people were aware of his real condition. (In the early 1920s it was still possible to report on certain aspects of the leaders' lives, something that later became tabu.) Consequently, although the fact of Lenin's illness was generally known, his death came as a devastating shock for the entire country.

The announcement of Stalin's death came as a bolt from the blue. It surprised not only the world at large but also other Soviet leaders. Nevertheless, they recovered quickly and plunged into a period of fierce infighting, the reverberations of which continued well after the 20th CPSU Congress of 1956. Brezhnev was reportedly ailing for so many years (here *reportedly* refers only to reports in the Western mass media) that his immortality eventually became a plausible possibility. In any event, his death, only a few days after the 1982 October Revolution anniversary parade, which he attended, was at least mildly surprising.

At least until Brezhnev's death the Soviets lacked a genuine and recent precedent, let alone an established pattern, for the behavior of the top party and state institutions at the time of the leader's death. The observance of Lenin's death, only a few years after the October Revolution and following a relatively long period of personal inactivity, hardly set a pattern. Furthermore, the long period of bloodshed, during which Stalin did away with foes and allies alike, is one that the CPSU would like to forget and certainly does not provide an accepted precedent or pattern.

Thus, during Brezhnev's tenure, Stalin's death in 1953 provided the most recent precedent, but hardly a pattern, for accepted official behavior at the time of the leader's death. Stalin's lieutenants had lived for decades in fear in the tyrant's shadow, awaiting their own turn in the grim merry-go-round of bloody purges. Stalin's style was secretive and conspiratorial and was based on suspicion and hatred toward all. Under such a leader, the main concern of the Politburo members was to survive. In this context, it is difficult to imagine the leaders making any specific plans or preparations for the event of Stalin's death. Since there was no official and established pattern, and since during the thirty years of his rule Stalin obliterated the dividing lines between party and state posts (assuming both the party and governmental leadership for long periods), at the time of his death it was unclear whether the party or state organs would provide the better base for the new leader to consolidate his power. This lack of clarity partly explains why Georgiy Malenkov become premier. This was the post held by Lenin, and Lenin had never been the first secretary of the Central Committee.

The situation in 1982 was quite different. The all-pervading atmosphere of fear that dominated the Stalin period no longer existed. The members of the Politburo, who felt quite secure in their positions, had seen the disappearance of charismatic leaders, the consolidation of Khrushchev and his subsequent ousting, the rise of Brezhnev, the ousting of President Nikolay Podgorniy, as well as the expulsion or demotion of scores of lesser leaders. They had actively participated in the orderly and regular functioning of the Soviet party and state organs and were confident in their ability to use these organs for the orderly selection of a new leader, thus effecting a legal and well-organized transition of power to the successor. Furthermore, Brezhnev's steadily worsening health had prepared them for the inevitable. Thus, the prospect of the transition was viewed with relative calm and confidence. Nevertheless, their ability actually to implement the transition and establish a pattern was yet to be tested; the events surrounding Stalin's death and Khrushchev's ousting served as a historical background for the imminent changeover.

Succession After Stalin's Death

The first indication in March 1953 that a transition of power was imminent was the TASS (Telegraph Agency of the Soviet Union) announcement at 0815 Moscow time on 4 March 1953 that Stalin had suffered a stroke during the night of 1–2 March.[1] Some fifteen minutes later, Radio Moscow repeated the earlier TASS announcement and carried a medical bulletin on Stalin's condition. On the same day (4 March) *Pravda* carried a "Government Report," signed by the Central Committee and the Council of Ministers and dated 3 March, stating the occurrence of the stroke and describing Stalin's condition.[2] The report contained an appeal to the people to demonstrate "the greatest unity and solidarity, firmness of spirit, and vigilance in these difficult days."[3] In addition, a separate medical bulletin on Stalin's condition was issued, signed by the top Soviet medical authorities, including the minister of health. The lack of "material response" to the treatment was noted.[4]

On the following day, 5 March, *Pravda* carried a further bulletin on Stalin's condition accompanied by an editorial on the importance of maintaining the unity of the party and the people, which paraphrased the Central Committee's report of the previous day.[5]

At 0630 Moscow time on 6 March 1953 the Soviet radio, quoting a TASS report of 0430 Moscow time, announced the death of Stalin.[6] The *Pravda* issue of the same day carried the official announcement by the CPSU Central Committee, Council of Ministers, and Presidium of the Supreme Soviet that Stalin had passed away.[7] In addition to a medical bulletin on the causes of death, *Pravda* also carried an announcement of the appointment of a funeral commission, headed by Nikita Khrushchev and including as members Lazar Kaganovich, Nikolay Shvernik, Marshal Aleksandr Vasilevskiy, Nikolay Pegov, General Pavel Artemyev, and Mikhail Yasnov.[8]

The first announcement of the transition of power was issued by Radio Moscow at 2030 Moscow time on 6 March. It quoted a decision reached at a joint meeting of the CPSU Central Committee, the USSR Council of Ministers, and the Presidium of the Supreme Soviet and announced the initial allocation of posts in the new leadership. Its main features were the appointment of Malenkov as first secretary of the CPSU Central Committee and premier, the abolition of the Bureau of the Presidium of the Council of Ministers, the reduction of the membership of the Central Committee Presidium from thirty-seven to fourteen members, and the release of Khrushchev from the post of first secretary of the Moscow City party organization, to allow him to concentrate on his duties as Central Committee secretary.[9]

On the following day, 7 March, *Pravda* published the official decision on the initial leadership assignments, yet another editorial on the need for unity, and various information related to the funeral, the period of mourning, the results of the autopsy, and the governmental decree on the placing of Stalin's body in Lenin's Mausoleum.[10]

On 8 March *Pravda* commenced the work of boosting Malenkov's prestige. It carried a picture of Malenkov and Stalin together, as well as a photograph of the honor guard at Stalin's lying-in-state, which included Malenkov, Beria, Khrushchev, Nikolay Bulganin, Kliment Voroshilov, and Kaganovich. A further editorial on unity reassured the people that the party "is strengthening the Soviet army, navy, and intelligence organs so as to be constantly prepared to deal a crushing blow to any aggressor."[11]

The *Pravda* issue of 10 March was completely devoted to Stalin's funeral, carrying photos and the texts of the speeches of Premier Malenkov and First Deputy Premiers Beria and Vyacheslav Molotov. An obviously doctored picture dated 1950 showed Malenkov alone with

Mao Tse-tung.[12] The other participants in the original photograph had been removed in an evident attempt to enhance Malenkov's image.

On 14 March 1953 a Central Committee plenum, the first since Stalin's death, approved a reshuffle of the leadership. Malenkov resigned from the post of first secretary of the CPSU Central Committee, retaining only his position as head of government. The composition of the secretariat as approved by the plenum was as follows: Khrushchev (first secretary), Mikhail Suslov, Petr Pospelov, Nikolay Shatalin, and Semen Ignatiev. On 16 March *Pravda* reported that a 15 March session of the Supreme Soviet had approved the new government and that on behalf of the Central Committee, the Council of Ministers, and the Presidium of the Supreme Soviet Khrushchev had nominated Marshal Kliment Voroshilov for the chairmanship of the Supreme Soviet Presidium. The report further stated that Beria had nominated Malenkov for the post of prime minister and that Malenkov, after approval of his appointment by the Supreme Soviet, had announced the list of the members of the Council of Ministers.[13] The CPSU Central Committee plenum of 14 March was not reported by *Pravda* until 21 March—a week after the plenum had taken place.[14]

This power transfer in fact ended the first stage of the transition. However, the infighting, which was to continue for many years, was only in its initial stages. Indeed, as early as 16 April 1953 *Pravda* disclosed that a succession struggle was in progress by carrying a major article on the subject of collective leadership. The article stressed the importance of "collective experience" and "reaching collective decisions on all important questions of party work," as against one-person decisions, which "always, or almost always, are one-sided decisions."[15]

Transition After Khrushchev's Ousting

Although Stalin's death and the events following it could be considered a partial though distant precedent, Khrushchev's ousting in October 1964 clearly resulted from a plot among his colleagues in the Politburo. The latter, however, attempted to present the transition as a normal affair prompted by a simple request from Khrushchev to be relieved of his duties for health reasons. (Incidentally, this formula has often been used in the USSR to provide a semihonorable face-saving route for certain leaders to leave the political scene. However, the extent to which this formula was to be employed during the first months of Gorbachev's tenure gives the impression that the health of scores of Soviet leaders and various officials dramatically deteriorated during those months.)

The only common denominator between the successors of Stalin and Khrushchev was their apparent attempt to dissociate themselves from the previous leader by criticizing his style and policies and by offering a new style of leadership and a new order of policy priorities. On a more practical level, the transition after Khrushchev's ouster was characterized by a period of ostensible harmony, with no signs of the power play intrigues and outright struggle that marked the period immediately following Stalin's death.

The first indication of important developments to follow was the lack of any reference to Khrushchev in the 15 October morning edition of *Pravda*. The mystery was deepened by a report on a meeting in Moscow between Cuban President Fidel Castro and Anastas Mikoyan and Podgorniy, from which Khrushchev was absent.[16]

The first official announcement of Khrushchev's removal was a TASS dispatch in its English and Russian services at 2000 Moscow time on 15 October, reporting that on 14 October a CPSU Central Committee plenum had accepted Khrushchev's request to be relieved from his posts of first secretary of the CPSU Central Committee and chairman of the USSR Council of Ministers "in connection with his advanced age and the deterioration of his health" and had elected Leonid Brezhnev as first secretary. The dispatch also reported that on 15 October the Supreme Soviet Presidium had accepted Khrushchev's resignation from the chairmanship of the Council of Ministers and had appointed Kosygin to replace him.[17] Although it has never been officially confirmed, Central Committee Secretary Mikhail Suslov is said to have delivered a sharp speech at the plenum, detailing a long list of charges against Khrushchev. In addition, the plenum reportedly had adopted a "secret resolution" prohibiting future party leaders from holding the post of chairman of the Council of Ministers.[18]

Pravda of 16 October carried on its front page the announcements of the leadership changes, together with the photographs of Brezhnev and Kosygin. An editorial on the following day listed the charges against Khrushchev without actually naming him.

> The Leninist party is an enemy of subjectivism and drifting in communist construction. Hare-brained scheming, immature conclusions, and hasty decisions and actions divorced from reality, bragging and phrase-mongering, commandism, and unwillingness to consider the achievements of science and practical experience are alien to it. The construction of communism is a live, creative undertaking, which does not tolerate armchair methods, personal decisions, and disregard for the practical experience of the masses. (*Pravda,* 16 October 1964)

The editorial informed readers that the party and state were "taking all measures to strengthen the defense potential of the country and safeguard the integrity of its borders."[19]

During the succeeding days the Soviet media carried extensive reports on the activities of the new leaders, clearly hinting at Brezhnev's superiority over Kosygin. Thus *Pravda* of 20 October 1964, publishing the speeches in the ceremonies honoring the Voskhod space crew, carried Brezhnev's on page 2 and Kosygin's on page 3. Nevertheless, editorials continued to stress the need for a collective leadership and hinted at the perils of the personality cult.

On 16 November at 2400 Moscow time, TASS International Service announced that a CPSU Central Committee plenum, which had taken place earlier that day, had annulled Khrushchev's 1962 reform of party structure. In addition, the plenum elected Petr Shelest and Aleksandr Shelepin members and Petr Demichev a candidate member of the CPSU Central Committee Politburo (then called the Presidium). Eight candidate members of the Central Committee were promoted to full membership. Several members were dismissed: Frol Kozlov, who had apparently opposed Brezhnev, was dropped from the Politburo and the Secretariat "because of illness"; Polyakov lost his position as Central Committee secretary; and Khrushchev's son-in-law Aleksey Adzhubey was expelled from the Central Committee for "errors" in his work.[20]

The next day *Pravda* carried the announcement of the changes and the report on the Central Committee plenum. Commentary on these came on the following day, 18 November, in an editorial entitled, "Loyalty to the Leninist Principles of Organization." The editorial explained the need to merge the industrial and agricultural party organizations, pointing out that the 1962 reform had been carried out "without due preparation."[21] The editorial marked the end of the power play's first act; however, Brezhnev was yet to consolidate his power and assert his authority among the top leadership of the CPSU.

This brief review of the succession game's initial stages should not be considered a comprehensive analysis of all the factors, elements, and stages of Soviet succession in the period before the death of Brezhnev. However, it has been suggested that the infighting within the Kremlin after Stalin's death lasted until December 1959, when a CPSU Central Committee plenum approved Khrushchev's proposal to reduce the numbers of Soviet ground troops by one-third, an act that enabled Khrushchev to implement various measures of his foreign policy program, presented at the 21st CPSU Congress earlier that year.[22] And in the same vein, the political succession following Khrushchev's ousting lasted until November 1971, when a Central Committee plenum endorsed Brezhnev's foreign policy initiatives and comprehensive program, presented earlier that year at the 24th CPSU Congress.[23]

The tenures of Andropov and Chernenko were too brief to serve as examples of leadership transition. Furthermore, both leaders were ailing much of the time during their periods of office, and their declining health was the reason for prolonged absences from public view. Both proved incapable of removing their main opponents from the Politburo, and they never achieved the status enjoyed by Khrushchev and Brezhnev after their consolidation. Gorbachev, on the other hand, being relatively young and robust, seems to be well on his way toward achieving final and undisputed power in a much shorter period than did either

Khrushchev or Brezhnev. In any event, the period between 1981 and 1986 was characterized by almost continuous infighting over Brezhnev's succession, beginning while Brezhnev was still alive and lasting until the 27th CPSU Congress in February-March 1986.

Possible Successors to Brezhnev

The constantly changing circumstances, uncertainty of timing, lack of reliable information, and the very nature of the totalitarian society render any serious attempt to establish the identity of the heir meaningless. The cases of Leon Trotsky and Georgiy Malenkov are illustrative, as was Chernenko's frustrated attempt to inherit the leadership from Brezhnev after the death of his patron. Furthermore, a person who is informally identified as the most likely successor invariably seems to become a conspicuous target for attacks. The special position he enjoys during the final period of his patron's life may well become a liability after his protector's death. In addition, the unofficially designated heirs often tend to annoy the leaders by their very presence—another factor making their positions precarious. In short, attempting to determine the identity of the likely successor is a risky and frustrating venture, and the developments following the death of the top leader tend to invalidate all speculations and predictions.

Nevertheless, Sovietologists were not deterred from attempts to determine the identity of Brezhnev's successor, even though among the top party leaders no clearly qualified candidates were evident who were in good health and had had comprehensive experience in all areas of party life and in the conduct of both domestic and foreign policies. Furthermore, for many years Brezhnev had avoided appointing well-qualified, relatively young officials to top positions, reducing still further the circle of possible successors. In October 1982, excluding Brezhnev himself, seven of the twelve full members of the Politburo were seventy or more years old, and 40 percent of the Central Committee members were sixty-five years or older.[24]

Analysts of Soviet affairs generally agree that a successor in the USSR must be a member of the Politburo or the Secretariat of the CPSU Central Committee. (Table 2.1 lists members of the groups from 1979 to 1986.) In addition, during the last years of Brezhnev's rule, these analysts generally agreed that Chernenko was the heir designated by Brezhnev; the opinions of the other members of the CPSU Politburo could be guessed but not substantiated.

Careful scrutiny of the qualifications of the other members of the Politburo showed that all of them were rather unlikely prospects in the succession game. At the beginning of 1982 the CPSU Politburo conained thirteen members in addition to Brezhnev. Andrey Kirilenko, a member of the Politburo and the Secretariat, was for many years considered the leader most likely to succeed Brezhnev. However, time

TABLE 2.1   Membership of the CPSU Central Committee Politburo and Secretariat

	December 1979	August 1982	August 1983	November 1984	June 1985	March 1986
Andropov, Yuriy Vladimirovich	M	M, S	M, G			
Brezhnev, Leonid Ilich	M, G	M, G				
Chernenko, Konstantin Ustinovich	M, S	M, S	M, S	M, G		
Gorbachev, Mikhail Sergeyevich	C, S	M, S	M, S	M, S	M, G	M, G
Aliyev, Geydar Ali Rza Ogly	C	C	M	M	M	M
Biryukova, Aleksandra Pavlovna						S
Chebrikov, Viktor Mikhaylovich				C	M	M
Demichev, Petr Nilovich	C	C	C	C	C	C
Dobrynin, Anatoliy Fedorovich						S
Dolgikh, Vladimir Ivanovich	S	C, S	C, S	C, S	C, S	C, S
Grishin, Viktor Vasilyevich	M	M	M	M	M	
Gromyko, Andrey Andreyevich	M	M	M	M	M	M
Kapitonov, Ivan Vasilyevich	S	S	S	S	S	
Kirilenko, Andrey Pavlovich	M, S	M, S				
Kiselev, Tikhon Yakovlevich		C				
Kosygin, Aleksey Nikolayevich	M					
Kunayev, Dinmukhamed Akhmedovich	M	M	M	M	M	M
Kuznetsov, Vasiliy Vasilyevich	C	C	C	C	C	
Ligachev, Yegor Kuzmich				S	M, S	M, S

Name	1	2	3	4	5	6	7
Masherov, Petr Mironovich	C						
Medvedev, Vadim Andreyevich					M		S
Nikonov, Viktor Petrovich				S	M	S	S
Pelshe, Arvid Yanovich	M	S	M			S	
Ponomarev, Boris Nikolayevich	C	S	C	S	C	S	C
Rashidov, Sharaf Rashidovich	C		C				S
Razumovskiy, Georgiy Petrovich						C	
Romanov, Grigoriy Vasilyevich	M	S	M	S	M	S	
Rusakov, Konstantin Viktorovich		S		S	S	S	
Ryzhkov, Nikolay Ivanovich		S		S	S	S	M
Shcherbitskiy, Vladimir Vasilyevich	M		M		M		M
Shevardnadze, Eduard Amvrosyevich	C		C		C		M
Slyunkov, Nikolay Nikitovich						C	C
Sokolov, Sergey Leonidovich					C		C
Solomentsev, Mikhail Sergeyevich	C		C		M		M
Solovyev, Yuriy Filipovich							C
Suslov, Mikhail Andreyevich	M	S		S			
Talyzin, Nikolay Vladimirovich							C
Tikhonov, Nikolay Aleksandrovich	C		M		M	M	
Ustinov, Dmitriy Fedorovich	M		M		M	M	
Vorotnikov, Vitaliy Ivanovich			C		M		M
Yakovlev, Aleksandr Nikolayevich						M	S
Yeltsin, Boris Nikolayevich						S	C
Zaykov, Lev Nikolayevich					S	C	M
Zimyanin, Mikhail Vasilyevich		S		S	S	S	S

M = Politburo member; G = general secretary; C = Politburo candidate member; S = secretary did not work in his favor: By the beginning of 1982 Kirilenko, several months older than Brezhnev, was apparently no longer in the general secretary's good graces.

Mikhail Suslov, born in 1902,[25] had been a Politburo member since 1952 and a Central Committee secretary since 1948.[26] Although his age of seventy-nine excluded him from the circle of possible successors, he was considered a key figure in determining Brezhnev's successor. However, his death in January 1982 prevented his participation in the crucial stages of the succession infighting.

Latvia's representative in the Politburo, Arvid Pelshe, born in 1899[27] and a Politburo member since 1966,[28] was clearly too old. His ornamental presence at the top of the party leadership carried no political weight.

Viktor Grishin, first secretary of the CPSU Moscow City organization, was an interesting figure. Born in 1914, he became a candidate member of the Politburo (then called the Presidium) in 1961. In 1967 he became first secretary of the CPSU Moscow gorkom and in 1971, a full member of the Politburo. From 1965 to 1967 he had been chairman of the All-Union Central Council of Trade Unions.[29] Although he enjoyed the backing of the powerful Moscow party organization and was a suitable age for consideration, Grishin lacked any significant foreign policy experience and had never worked in the Central Committee Secretariat. In 1982 he was a figure to be reckoned with but hardly a candidate to replace Brezhnev. Had Brezhnev died several years earlier, Suslov, Grishin, and, most of all, Kirilenko would have been leading candidates; however, by the beginning of 1982 it was too late for them.

Vladimir Shcherbitskiy, first secretary of the Ukraine, had been a member of the Politburo since 1971. He had never held a post in the Secretariat and had never worked in Moscow.[30] His power base lay in the Ukraine, and his personal weight in Moscow was rather small. Possibly an important ally (or a dangerous foe), Shcherbitskiy was not a candidate to inherit from Brezhnev.

Similar characteristics were shared by Grigoriy Romanov, born 1923, first secretary of the CPSU Leningrad City Organization and Politburo member since 1976;[31] and by Dinmukhamed Kunayev, born 1912, first secretary of the Kazakh Communist Party Central Committee and Politburo member since 1971.[32] Although Romanov was to play a prominent role in the power game in its later stages, at the start of 1982 both he and Kunayev seemed provincial figures, remote from the real center of power in Moscow.

Yuriy Andropov, born 1914, and Marshal Dmitriy Ustinov, born 1908, were two key figures whose support (or opposition) could have been crucial. After all, no one could expect either to gain the position of general secretary or to consolidate himself in this position without the approval and support of the KGB and the Soviet Army. Andropov, the powerful and feared leader of the KGB, had been a full member of the Politburo since 1973.[33] He had some previous experience in the

Central Committee Secretariat, where between 1962 and 1967 he was the secretary responsible for liaison with the socialist countries' Communist and workers parties.[34] In addition, one could assume that the head of the KGB and former ambassador to Hungary possessed vast experience in international affairs. On the other hand, the very feature that made him so powerful—his leadership of the KGB—disqualified him from succeeding Brezhnev (or so it appeared at the beginning of 1982). That position seemed to place a stigma on its holder and ban him from ever becoming general secretary. However, since KGB support was regarded as vital in gaining the post of general secretary, Andropov was one of the most interesting and important figures in the Politburo.

Marshal Dmitriy Ustinov was in a position similar to that of Andropov. A full Politburo member since 1976 when he succeeded the deceased Marshal Andrey Grechko as minister of defense,[35] he had been a candidate member for eleven years (1965–1976) and a Central Committee secretary in charge of the military industry.[36] No matter how important Soviet Army support is in the infighting in the Kremlin, its chief is normally not a candidate. Furthermore, at the beginning of 1982 Marshal Ustinov was already seventy-four years old and in poor health. His area of specialization was rather narrow, and he was regarded as an important figure in the game but not as a likely candidate.

Andrey Gromyko, born 1909, Politburo member since 1973 and minister of foreign affairs since 1957,[37] was the third Politburo member expected to play a prominent role in the forthcoming succession. His experience lay exclusively in foreign affairs, and the Ministry of Foreign Affairs was his sole power base. A very authoritative figure enjoying worldwide prestige, Gromyko seldom bothered to conceal his contempt of Chernenko and was considered a major opponent to Chernenko's possible election. Undoubtedly Gromyko's role in determining the successor would be a decisive factor.

Prime Minister Nikolay Tikhonov, born 1905, full member of the Politburo since 1979 and chairman of the Council of Ministers since 1980,[38] was, together with Chernenko, Brezhnev's closest ally. Too old to be a candidate himself, he was expected to throw his personal weight behind Chernenko and facilitate his election.

This left only two other members of the Politburo—Mikhail Gorbachev and Konstantin Chernenko. Mikhail Gorbachev was the junior member of the Politburo. An apparent protégé of Suslov, he reportedly had been brought by Suslov to Moscow from Stavropol where he had been first secretary of the Stavropol kraykom from 1970 to 1978.[39] He became a Central Committee secretary in charge of agriculture (1978), a candidate member of the Politburo (1979), and a full member (1980).[40] At the start of 1982 he was an unknown factor with little personal weight. In fact, no one in Moscow has benefited from being in charge of the disaster area of Soviet agriculture. Still, Gorbachev appears to have managed to remain unscathed during several catastrophic years for Soviet agriculture. Ability to survive is always an important asset in the Kremlin. In addition, Gorbachev's positions as full member of the Politburo and Central Committee secretary, as well as his age (born 1931), certainly qualified him as a possible future contender, but by no means was he a serious candidate to succeed Brezhnev. This was not the case with Konstantin Chernenko; indeed, at the beginning of 1982 Chernenko apparently was Brezhnev's own choice for his successor.

Chernenko as Heir Apparent

Konstantin Ustinovich Chernenko was born on 24 September 1911 in Novoselevo (then Bolshaya Tes), in Krasnoyarsk kray.[41] He graduated from the Moscow Higher Party School in 1945 and from the Kishinev Pedagogical Institute in 1953. A Russian of peasant origin, his career had been spent largely in staff positions within the CPSU bureaucracy. A party member since 1931, Chernenko had been secretary of the Krasnoyarsk kraykom (1941–1943); secretary of the Penza obkom (1945–1948); and chief of the Propaganda Department of the Moldavian Communist Party Central Committee (1948–1956). In 1956 he was elected to full membership of the Moldavian Central Committee. From 1956 to 1960 Chernenko was the chief of the Mass Agitation Work Section of the CPSU Central Committee Propaganda and Agitation Department. From 1960 to 1964 he was chief of the Secretariat of the USSR Supreme Soviet Presidium. In 1965 he was appointed chief of the CPSU Central Committee General Department. Between 1966 and 1971 Chernenko was a candidate member of the CPSU Central Committee and in 1971 became a full Central Committee member. In 1976 he was elected CPSU Central Committee secretary, apparently in charge of administration, a post that included responsibility for security and order within the party apparatus and information and documentation. During 1977-1978 Chernenko was a candidate member of the Politburo and a full member from 1978.[42]

Chernenko's Early Career

Chernenko's career prior to 1982 had two basic characteristics. First, he had never headed a nationwide party organization or even a party organ at the union republic level. Thus he had never had an opportunity to develop either a regional or professional power base. On the other hand, his long service in the Central Committee apparatus helped him establish excellent personal contacts in the party and state apparatus.

The second, more interesting characteristic—his connection with Brezhnev—proved to be the sole base for Chernenko's bid for the leadership. He worked under Brezhnev in Moldavia in the 1950s, and Brezhnev promoted him to key positions of increasing responsibility.[43] During the final period of Brezhnev's life, Chernenko was constantly at his side, serving as his link with the outside world, his closest aide, and a certain contender in the power game for Brezhnev's succession. When the 26th CPSU Congress opened on 23 February 1981, the 4,994 Soviet delegates and 123 delegations from 109 countries[44] saw an old and obviously ailing Brezhnev, who had great difficulty in reading his relatively short speech. The live relay from the congress opening lasted for only a few minutes; some six minutes after Brezhnev started reading his speech the live relay ended, and an announcer read the rest of his speech. During the few minutes that Brezhnev was seen, he stumbled occasionally, could not pronounce many words, and in general was a pitiable figure.

At the 26th CPSU Congress the CPSU top leadership demonstrated that it was primarily interested in self-preservation and in avoiding any decision that might jeopardize the balance of power inside the Kremlin. Indeed, the 1981 Politburo was an astonishingly precise reflection of the 1981 Soviet society—inept, inert, stagnated, old, and afraid of change. Nevertheless, the Congress also reflected Brezhnev's solid position at the top of the party, as well as his vast power and undisputed authority. He succeeded in achieving the promotion of his son Yuriy Brezhnev, first deputy minister of foreign trade, and of his son-in-law Lt. Gen. Yuriy Churbanov, deputy minister of the interior, to candidate membership of the Central Committee. Furthermore, he succeeded in promoting S. K. Tsvigun, KGB first deputy chairman and reportedly Brezhnev's brother-in-law, to full membership of the CPSU Central Committee.[45]

A number of Brezhnev's personal aides and advisers were also promoted. Andrey Aleksandrov-Agentov was promoted to full membership of the CPSU Central Committee, and Anatoliy Blatov to the status of candidate member of the CPSU Central Committee. Brezhnev's foreign policy advisers—Vadim Zagladin, Nikolay Inozemtsev, and Georgiy Arbatov—were also elected full members of the CPSU Central Committee.[46]

Chernenko's Ties to Brezhnev

During the Congress Chernenko's special position was also demonstrated. Upon becoming CPSU Central Committee secretary in charge of industry, Brezhnev had transferred Chernenko to the party's central apparatus in Moscow, appointing him head of the Mass Agitation Section of the CPSU Central Committee's Agitation and Propaganda Department.[47] In 1960 Brezhnev became chairman of the USSR Supreme Soviet Presidium, and Chernenko took over the post of head of the Secretariat of the Presidium of the USSR Supreme Soviet. After the ousting of Khrushchev in 1964, Brezhnev, then the newly installed general secretary, appointed Chernenko head of the CPSU Central Committee General Department. Chernenko remained in this post for twelve years, simultaneously serving as Brezhnev's private secretary

TABLE 2.2   Ranking of Soviet Leaders at May Day and October Revolution
Parades

May 1979	November 1979	May 1980	November 1980
1. Brezhnev	Brezhnev	Brezhnev	Brezhnev
2. Kosygin	———[1]	Kosygin	Tikhonov
3. Suslov	Suslov	Suslov	Suslov
4. Kirilenko	Kirilenko	Kirilenko	Kirilenko
5. Grishin	Grishin	Grishin	Pelshe
6. Gromyko	Pelshe	———[2]	Grishin
7. Pelshe	Gromyko	Gromyko	Gromyko
8. Chernenko	Chernenko	Chernenko	Chernenko
9. Andropov	Andropov	Andropov	Andropov
10.		Tikhonov	Gorbachev

[1] Kosygin was absent; *Pravda*, 8 November 1979.
[2] Pelshe was absent; *Pravda*, 2 May 1980.

and chief of cabinet.[48] Although Chernenko was virtually unknown in
the West until his appointment as Central Committee secretary in 1976,
close observers of Soviet affairs were accustomed to the constant
presence of the stocky, taciturn Siberian, who became Brezhnev's
shadow. Even during his meteoric rise (1976–1978), Chernenko continued to serve as Brezhnev's secretary and closest aide.

At the 26th CPSU Congress, the special nature of the close relationship
of Chernenko and Brezhnev became patently obvious. Chernenko was
constantly at Brezhnev's side, hovering over him, helping him with
his duties, physically assisting him, and generally serving as a combination nanny, personal aide, link with the other Politburo members, right
hand, and chief of cabinet—the very role that everyone had been used
to seeing him perform for years. At that time the venerable Suslov was
still enjoying a higher status than Chernenko; however, the other Central
Committee secretary who was also a Politburo member—Kirilenko—
was clearly outranked by Chernenko.

Chernenko's status at the Congress was incompatible with his previous
position in the semiofficial ranking chart of the Soviet leadership,
prepared by Kremlinologists on the basis of the leaders' positions at
public events (see Table 2.2). From May 1979 to November 1980
Chernenko regularly ranked eighth or ninth at the May Day and October
Revolution anniversary parades, which are commonly recognized as
precise instruments for measuring the status of the various leaders.

Despite Chernenko's relatively low position prior to 1981, the pointers
to his ascent following the 26th Congress were too numerous to be
ignored. In December 1980 Chernenko represented the CPSU at the

2nd Congress of the Cuban Communist Party,[49] a very special honor: The head of the CPSU delegation to the congress of another ruling Communist party had almost invariably been a very senior Central Committee secretary. In fact Brezhnev himself and Suslov frequently attended the congresses of the fraternal parties as heads of the CPSU delegation. (The only recent case in which the CPSU delegation has been led by a Politburo member of relatively low status was in March-April 1981, when Shcherbitskiy led the CPSU delegation to the 12th Bulgarian Communist Party Congress.[50]) In April 1980 Chernenko's collected works were published, a further sign of his enhanced status, and finally, on 22 April 1981 he delivered the main address at the annual Lenin Day celebration.[51]

Chernenko's Elevated Status

On 1 May 1981 Chernenko's elevated status was evident from the official lineup at the Red Square parade. Only Brezhnev, Tikhonov, and Suslov outranked Chernenko, who shared the fourth position with Kirilenko, whose career was evidently on the wane.[52]

A comparison of the celebrations of the birthdays of Chernenko and Kirilenko, which took place in September 1981, confirmed the pointers that Chernenko's career was on the rise. The entire Politburo was on hand on 24 September 1981, when Chernenko's seventieth birthday was celebrated—an apparent attempt, orchestrated by Brezhnev, to enhance Chernenko's image as a leading member of the CPSU Politburo. After awarding Chernenko the gold star of Hero of Soviet Labor, Brezhnev described him as a "restless man," always trying to "do more." Chernenko's "creatively bold approach" was also pointed out by Brezhnev.[53] Chernenko himself did not waste the opportunity and thanked Brezhnev for his "constant support."[54] All in all, it was an impressive ceremony, indicative of Chernenko's elevated status.

In contrast, the treatment that Kirilenko received on his seventy-fifth birthday was lukewarm, though correct from the protocol viewpoint. He was awarded the October Revolution Order—an appropriate distinction. However, the bestowal of the order was marred by the restrained announcement by the leading Soviet organs, which contained only minimal praise.[55] Furthermore, the leading party and state organs very conspicuously refrained from greeting Kirilenko on his birthday and new honor. In fact, even though Kirilenko was still officially the number four person in the Soviet top leadership, his treatment on his birthday was the same as that accorded to junior members of the leadership. Against the background of Kirilenko's birthday celebration, Chernenko's stood out as a most lavish affair.

In addition to the Hero of Socialist Labor award, Chernenko's prestige was accentuated by the publication of his article, "The Leninist Strategy of Leadership," in *Kommunist,* no. 13, September 1981.[56] The article advocated closer relations between the leaders and the masses and was clearly associated with one of Chernenko's central ideas—the encouragement of workers to write letters to party and state organs as a means of communication between the party and the masses. Incidentally, in September-October 1981 almost all Soviet newspapers carried articles on the importance of workers' letters, an additional sign of Chernenko's growing prominence.

Meanwhile, Chernenko remained constantly in a position of high visibility, attending every important (and televised) political event. Occasionally, as during the 6 November 1981 Kremlin ceremony marking the October Revolution anniversary, he sat at Brezhnev's right, a position previously occupied by Suslov.[57] Furthermore, his attendance at some of these meetings clearly demonstrated his expanding areas of responsibility. On 28 October 1981 Chernenko received the Yugoslav ambassador to the USSR;[58] before this, the reception of foreign ambassadors was the exclusive prerogative of Brezhnev (as chairman of the Supreme Soviet Presidium) and of Gromyko as foreign minister.

Another indication of Chernenko's enhanced personal prestige and political status was the identification of his personal aide in the press— a privilege never accorded the other senior Central Committee secretaries Suslov and Kirilenko. Chernenko's aide V. V. Pribytkov was identified as such in *Pravda* of 27 October 1981 and 27 November 1981. Chernenko continued to meet various foreign delegations visiting the USSR. On 26 November he met a Nicaraguan delegation led by Humberto Ortega, Nicaragua's minister of defense.[59] During this meeting new facets of Chernenko's areas of responsibility were disclosed that represented an obvious infringement of Defense Minister Ustinov's status; until that meeting he had met the defense ministers of other countries.

When Chernenko could not find appropriate occasions for even more public exposure, he created events. Thus on 23 November he visited his RSFSR (Russian Soviet Federated Socialist Republic) Supreme Soviet constituency.[60] Such meetings are not held routinely in the USSR; usually there is a special reason behind such meetings and on such occasions most of the Politburo members hold similar meetings. No other USSR leader held such a meeting in the second half of 1981. Since nothing of any consequence occurred at the meeting, it appears to have been an engineered event, aimed at providing Chernenko with additional mass media coverage.

When Leonid Brezhnev celebrated his last birthday on 18 December 1981, Chernenko acted as master of ceremonies. At the televised Kremlin ceremony he sat directly behind Brezhnev, apart from the other Politburo members. Throughout the ceremony he assisted in running of the event, helped Brezhnev with his duties, and guided him throughout the activities.[61]

On the following day (19 December) a reception was held in the Kremlin in Brezhnev's honor. Brezhnev used the occasion to share his thoughts on the future of the party leadership. Without naming anyone,

Brezhnev stressed the need for maintaining the unity of the Politburo and ensuring continuity after his departure from the scene. He asserted that no major political changes were to be expected after his departure and indicated that he would continue to lead the party as long as he "possessed the strength to do so."[62]

Additional televised ceremonies during November and December 1981 continued to confirm the fact that Chernenko was serving as Brezhnev's righthand man. Thus the televised celebration of the October Revolution anniversary[63] and the 4 December public meeting marking the fortieth anniversary of the battle of Moscow[64] demonstrated Chernenko's physical proximity to Brezhnev and his de facto position as heir apparent. However, against this background it became painfully evident that Brezhnev was incapable of officially anointing Chernenko as his heir. Apparently, the majority of the Politburo members opposed any official step aimed at institutionalizing Chernenko's de facto status as Brezhnev's successor. Therefore, although unable to overcome the opposition of the Politburo, Brezhnev continued to show signs of favoritism toward Chernenko. When *Izvestiya* of 15 December 1981 prepared a full-page layout dedicated to Brezhnev's seventy-fifth birthday, containing various photographs of the leader, Chernenko figured prominently in a 1973 picture showing him standing next to Brezhnev as he signed an official document. No other Politburo member was accorded such an honor.[65]

Chernenko as Number Two

In 1982 the balance of power within the Politburo was drastically changed. On 25 January Mikhail Suslov died. A member of the Politburo and a Central Committee secretary for many years, Suslov was the most powerful and eloquent voice of conservatism in the Politburo and the unofficial second secretary of the Central Committee in charge of ideology and the world Communist movement. He had also been a major obstacle in Chernenko's path toward assuming Brezhnev's position.

Suslov had resented both Chernenko's rise and his status as the heir apparent. He had supported Andrey Kirilenko, who like Suslov himself had climbed from one party rank to the next in the CPSU hierarchy to reach one of the most prominent positions in the Politburo. Suslov regarded Kirilenko as a suitable successor for Brezhnev, and he openly supported Kirilenko's candidacy. Brezhnev and Chernenko saw that the removal of Kirilenko was a vital precondition for Chernenko to be established as the heir apparent and unofficial number two person in the Soviet leadership and that this would be difficult as long as Suslov was alive. However, upon Suslov's death, Kirilenko's career clearly entered a steady decline whereas Chernenko proceeded quickly to consolidate his position.

Already on 28 January 1982, at Suslov's lying-in-state, the Soviet television and press showed Chernenko as number two in the official lineup, preceding Tikhonov and Kirilenko.[66] This was a precedent, because although serving for many years as Brezhnev's righthand man, Chernenko had never officially occupied the number two position. His promotion was accompanied by an apparent demotion of Central Committee Secretary Kirilenko, at least in status. Not only had Chernenko moved ahead of him in the official lineup, but his name appeared out of alphabetical order—after the names of Grishin, Pelshe, and Chernenko—in the announcement concerning Suslov's funeral commission.[67] Perhaps in an attempt to dispel any doubts that this slight was intentional, on 30 January *Pravda* relisted the names of the commission's members, with Kirilenko's name once again out of order and way down the list.[68]

Suslov's funeral on 31 January provided additional evidence of Chernenko's enhanced status. The Soviet television program that broadcast a live relay of the funeral showed Chernenko sharing the limelight with Brezhnev and Premier Tikhonov, ahead of Kirilenko.

Soon more signals confirmed Chernenko's new standing. The most striking evidence was the fact that he led the CPSU delegation to the congress of the French Communist party, which opened on 3 February.[69] Maintaining relations with the major European Communist parties had been one of Suslov's major responsibilities; the selection of Chernenko to lead the CPSU delegation to the French Communists' congress was a clear indication that some of Suslov's prerogatives and responsibilities had been handed over to Chernenko.

Undermining of Brezhnev's Authority

Signs of a different nature, which became apparent immediately after Suslov's funeral, seemed to indicate that the death of the old secretary had triggered a new and possibly decisive stage in the succession game. In February various Western sources reported that an investigation of several cases of alleged corruption and bribery was taking place in Moscow. Soon the name of Brezhnev's daughter, Galina Churbanova, was involved in the affair. According to the stories in circulation, a top circus administration official, Anatoliy Kolevatov, a personal friend of Churbanova, had allowed performers to make trips abroad on the condition that they brought back for him high-value goods, easily disposable at outrageous prices on the Moscow black market.[70] When $200,000 and diamonds valued at more than $1 million were found in his apartment, he claimed that they belonged to Brezhnev's daughter.[71] Other picturesque characters with comic-book names and nicknames, such as Boris the Gipsy, were arrested, and the rumor factory continued to work overtime. It was hinted that Boris the Gipsy (Boris Buryatiya, a high-living Bolshoy Opera singer) had in his apartment a stash of diamonds belonging to Brezhnev's daughter, whose lover he was alleged to be.[72]

Galina Churbanova's husband was Lt. Gen. Yuriy Churbanov, deputy minister of internal affairs in charge of domestic security matters. This could have been the connection to the KGB. When on 19 January KGB deputy chief Semen Tsvigun died from a "long and difficult illness" if *Pravda* of 20 January is to be believed, various rumors connected his death with the scandal involving Brezhnev's family. According to some, Tsvigun committed suicide, and others even stated that he had been killed. It is a fact that Brezhnev did not sign Tsvigun's obituary and that Tsvigun was not buried in the Novodevochy Convent, where prominent figures of his rank are normally interred.

Exactly how Tsvigun's suicide or murder or natural death was connected with the other rumors concerning the ill-doings of Brezhnev's family has never been clarified. However, the scandal doubtless eroded further the leader's authority. Even *Pravda,* managed by Viktor Afanasyev (who was later associated with Andropov and Gorbachev), permitted publication of a commentary, based on a "reader's letter" and dealing with personal morals. The commentary succinctly stated: "The psychological characteristics of the family and its convictions are reflected as in a mirror in the characters of their children."[73] The insinuation was obvious.

The rumors were accompanied by articles and interviews in the Soviet press, clearly of an allegorical nature, evidently aimed at undermining Brezhnev's authority. On 1 March 1982 *Pravda* carried an interview with the well-known circus clown Yuriy Nikulin. The byline itself (a byline is a rare phenomenon in *Pravda*) evoked certain associations. The name of the interviewer was Galina Kozhukhova. Was the name intended to suggest the theme of the interview? Although Nikulin ostensibly spoke about the Soviet circus (dwelling on the need to appoint "more unselfish and fully dedicated people" and condemning the artist "who rushes to work as the administrator of his own successes, strives at once to organize for himself trips that are more interesting, and to obtain decorations more rapidly"[74]) one could easily interpret the interview as an allegory relating to Brezhnev, especially since everyone was aware of the leader's penchant for decorations, such as the gold stars dangling from his lapels.

Certain magazines even joked at Brezhnev's expense. For example, *Avrora,* the organ of the Leningrad Writers' Union, carried on page 75 of its December 1981 issue (the month in which Brezhnev celebrated his seventy-fifth birthday) a caricature of a fictional superman-poet (unmistakably resembling Brezhnev), beneath which was the following caption: "The respect for his talent is so great that the majority of the people think that he is already dead. . . . It is hard to believe that he will die some day. Apparently, he himself thinks that he will never die. . . ." Bearing in mind that some months previous Brezhnev had acquired literary fame by publishing his memoirs and receiving the Lenin Prize for Literature, the caricature of the poet-superman, the page number, and the date of the publication all combined to produce an unbelievable affront, which apparently passed unpunished. It is impossible to imagine how an action like this could have occurred in the USSR, especially in Romanov's Leningrad, without open support from highranking leaders and the cooperation of the censorship organs.

Anyone believing that the interview and the caricature were coincidences had the chance to learn the opposite from an article in *Pravda* of 12 March. The article ostensibly concerned a party official Klavdiy Svechnikov, whose biography in *Pravda* astonishingly closely paralleled Brezhnev's own career. The story describes the ousting of Svechnikov from his post of party secretary at a state farm, amid rumors of corruption and because of "reasons of health." However, in truth scheming bosses eager to hush things up had decided to silence him. At the end of the story, loyal party members at the state farm rebel against their superiors and force Svechnikov's reinstatement. As *Pravda* stressed, Svechnikov had been unanimously elected by his party committee; the implication was that the committee alone could determine the fate of the secretary.[75] Was this really a report on an obscure party secretary named Svechnikov or another allegory, this time inspired by Brezhnev's clan? Had Brezhnev been asked to resign by certain Politburo members? Was Brezhnev making it clear that if forced to step down for reasons of health he and his supporters would contest the decision and defend his right to continue in his position, since he had been unanimously elected by the Central Committee? Was he indicating that only the Central Committee, and not certain Politburo members, could remove him from the helm? Nothing can be proved, but the signs were unmistakable: The struggle for Brezhnev's succession was on, infighting was taking place in the Kremlin, and all means and devices were going to be employed in the interval until Brezhnev's death or removal from the political arena. Finally, it seemed that certain Politburo members acted as sources of rumors associated in one way or another with Brezhnev personally and with the succession issue.

Chernenko's Supporters and Detractors

Meanwhile, an important question remained unanswered: Who would replace the deceased Suslov as Central Committee secretary? Chernenko was already a Central Committee secretary and since Suslov's death had assumed some of the latter's responsibilities. He was also the clear choice of Brezhnev to succeed him. However, Brezhnev had proved incapable of attaching some official recognition to his preferred heir. Furthermore, Chernenko clearly did not enjoy the backing of many Politburo members: To the majority he symbolized the declining authority of the party's top organs vis-à-vis the regional party apparatus— a direct result of Brezhnev's practice of delegating power. Those Politburo members who headed key organs of official state power, such as Foreign Minister Gromyko and Defense Minister Marshal Ustinov, did not bother to conceal their contempt for Chernenko, who had no experience whatever in their areas of control. Other Politburo members, such as Andropov, who had his own plans regarding Brezhnev's succession, and Kirilenko, who rightly blamed Chernenko for his own career setback, had obvious personal reasons for disliking Brezhnev's protégé. Thus, although clearly Brezhnev's favorite and the heir apparent, Chernenko could not count on much support among his Politburo colleagues. On the other hand, no other contender for Brezhnev's succession had come forth. Since the combined posts of Politburo member and Central Committee secretary seem to be a vital precondition for any contender, and Kirilenko's career was fading and Gorbachev's was at its dawn, the important question after January 1982 was, "Who will be appointed Central Committee secretary to fill the position left vacant by Suslov?" The answer to this question could give a clear indication as to the identity of the leader who would face Chernenko in the struggle when the time came.

The period of uncertainty dragged on. Various names, mentioned in speculations disseminated in the West, disappeared as soon as they were published. The fact however remained: No new Central Committee secretary was appointed. At that time Politburo member Vladimir Shcherbitskiy, the Ukraine party chief, decided to fire several ranging shots in the infighting game, perhaps to enhance his image as a leader of national caliber. He accomplished this by publishing numerous articles and interviews within a short period dealing with almost all important issues in the domestic and international fields and by identifying himself with Chernenko's views. This approach was first evident in a 14 February *Pravda* interview, in which he stressed the need for leaders to pay closer attention to public opinion—Chernenko's pet theme. Virtually paraphrasing Chernenko, Shcherbitskiy asserted that the party cannot exist without the "most solid links" with the masses and criticized leaders who "divorce" themselves from the people and disregard their interests. Letters from workers were described as a "very important channel" of information from below (another profound thought of Chernenko), and higher party organs were urged to be more forthcoming in giving information to lower party organizations.[76] A similar article encompassing the same ideas was published by the trade union daily paper *Trud* on 23 March. What made these two publications more bizarre was the fact that Shcherbitskiy had never before addressed these issues, which apparently had suddenly attracted his attention after Chernenko seemed to have firmly assumed the number two position after Suslov's death. Furthermore, in a major speech in the Dnepropetrovsk election district, Shcherbitskiy went out of his way to publicize his concern for defense in an apparent attempt to appear as a champion of military interests. Among other things, he praised the pamphlet, "Whence the Threat to Peace," published by the USSR Ministry of Defense.[77] Shcherbitskiy also appealed for "strengthening the country's might" and expressed support for Poland's martial law.[78]

In two articles in *Kommunist,* no. 1, January 1982, and *Voprosy Istorii* no. 1, January 1982, Shcherbitskiy strongly denounced Ukrainian nationalism and "artificial attempts" to impose the Ukrainian language on the people. (This was one of his favorite topics.) Apparently frustrated by his prolonged period of service in the Ukraine, at the periphery of real power, Shcherbitskiy was committing himself to Chernenko, hoping to reap the fruits after Chernenko's succession.

Meanwhile, Brezhnev was ailing. One never knew whether he would appear at events that required his attendance or, if he did appear, whether he would be able to perform his duties. Concern over his ability to fulfill his role apparently forced the cancellation of the planned live broadcast of the 16 March 1982 opening session of the USSR Trade Union Congress. Moscow's *Weekly Television and Radio Program Guide* on 10 March announced a live relay from the opening session, to be broadcast both on radio and TV. This announcement was repeated by almost all the USSR dailies on 12 and 13 March. However, on 13 March *Pravda* and *Izvestiya* published a new schedule that made no mention of a live broadcast. Eventually, a one-hour recording of Brezhnev's speech was broadcast in the afternoon by the radio and television. Last-minute concern with Brezhnev's ability to read his speech appeared to cause the cancellation. (Apparently those responsible for the cancellation remembered Brezhnev's poor performance at the 26th CPSU Congress, when the live relay of his speech was cut off after several embarrassing minutes.) At several televised public events Brezhnev appeared frail and insecure and obviously in pain. Many rumors concerning his health and intentions circulated, some probably instigated by certain Politburo members. According to one (which later proved true), by late March Brezhnev had successfully survived a blood clot on the brain, a brain hemorrhage, and a heart attack. The rumors were so persistent that Nikolay Blokhin, the cancer specialist of the USSR Academy of Sciences, was obliged to state officially that Brezhnev was "vacationing, simply enjoying a normal holiday."[79]

Andropov's Enhanced Status

Another rumor (which proved false) maintained that Brezhnev was going to retire toward the end of the year and that he would be replaced by Andropov. French radio even ventured the opinion that the rumor had been spread by Andropov's men, whereas the German Press Agency quoted a "spokesman of the USSR Ministry of Foreign Affairs," who denied the rumor.[80]

The public appearances of the KGB chief Yuriy Andropov have always been watched with interest: His attendance or absence and his apparent attitude toward different leaders could provide clues to the interim situation of the infighting.

On 22 April 1982 the annual celebration of Lenin's birthday took place. The main address at the Kremlin celebration was read by Yuriy Andropov. His speech was the first clear and public indication that he had entered the maneuvering for the succession and that he opposed

Brezhnev's faction. Andropov's selection to address the meeting did not in itself qualify him as a contender; after all, he had already served as a speaker at the same ceremony in 1976.[81] The contents of his address plainly showed Andropov's political colors and intentions. After stressing that Lenin's teachings "cannot tolerate stagnation," Andropov called for "boldness and flexibility" in solving the country's problems. He criticized centralism by implication, noting that Lenin believed that "socialism is not created by orders from above." His sharpest remarks, however, were reserved for the area of private morals. Pointing out that life in the USSR was improving by the day, Andropov stated:

> But this does not mean that we are totally free of shortcomings and problems, of phenomena against which consistent and resolute struggle must be waged. For example, cases of embezzlement, bribery, red tape, lack of respect for the individual, and other antisocial phenomena still do occur—and cause legitimate revulsion among the Soviet people. It does not matter whether they have come down to us from the past or are brought in from abroad by parasites who batten onto certain short-comings in our development. If such phenomena do exist, they stand in our way. It is the duty of every Communist and every citizen to battle against them. The Soviet people fully support the measures which the party is taking to eradicate them.[82]

Andropov's enhanced status was already indicated two weeks before his unorthodox address at the Lenin Day celebration. On 8 April, with Brezhnev, Ustinov, and Chernenko, he signed the obituary for the deceased Marshal Pavel Rotmistrov.[83] Until then, Andropov had customarily only signed obituaries that were also signed by all other Politburo members. Now he appeared in very exclusive company, indicating a special status. His speech at the Lenin Day celebration and subsequent events confirmed this assumption.

Azerbaijan's party boss, Geydar Aliyev, an entrepreneur, was one of the first to interpret the signs correctly. An article in *Bakinskiy Rabochiy* (republic newspaper of Azerbaijan) of 2 May 1982 on the May Day parade in Moscow Andropov's picture appeared in the fourth position, immediately after those of Brezhnev, Tikhonov, and Chernenko, although at the parade Andropov had occupied his usual eighth place in the official lineup of leaders.[84] No other republic newspaper made a similar alteration. Similarly, in November 1979 *Bakinskiy Rabochiy* had ranked Chernenko ahead of Kirilenko,[85] before Chernenko had moved up in his standing in Moscow—thus demonstrating Aliyev's sharp eye and keen political sense.

The major newspapers of the Soviet republics, such as *Pravda Ukrainy, Pravda Vostoka, Bakinskiy Rabochiy,* and *Kazakhstanskaya Pravda,* often serve as reliable sources of information concerning the stands of the relevant republican party secretaries on topical issues. The republican newspapers enjoy a certain measure of independence because they lack the broad international exposure of the Moscow-based central Soviet newspapers, the contents of which are coordinated and closely scrutinized before publication, usually resulting in a uniform approach. This independence comes through mainly in relation to internal republican affairs, and the newspapers tend to fall under the influence of the particular republican party organization and its leadership. Accordingly, differences in the newspapers' treatment of major events such as Andropov's election as general secretary (Chapter 2), clearly reflect the positions of the republic leaders on these matters. In the present context, therefore, *Bakinskiy Rabochiy* must be regarded as a semiofficial organ for expressing the views of Aliyev, Azerbaijan's party boss.

Meanwhile Chernenko was extremely active: claiming Suslov's mantle as chief ideologist, attending different public events, and generally making an obvious effort to be in the center of the public eye. In an article in the CPSU's ideological organ *Kommunist,* no. 6, April 1982, Chernenko indicated that he supported the introduction of new ideas for solving the country's problems. He repeatedly stressed "creativity" and "flexibility," emphasizing, however, that the party should not deviate from basic principles. Many of the thoughts expressed in the article and even some key concepts ("boldness," "flexibility," and so forth) were identical to thoughts and concepts contained in Andropov's 22 April address. They both condemned overreliance on administrative methods in solving the country's problems, rejected the idea of pluralism in Soviet society, and refused to blame the country's problems on the heritage of the past.[86] This remarkable concern with the same subjects can be interpreted in several ways. Perhaps the very same issues were the focus of attention of the Politburo, and both Chernenko and Andropov were looking for an additional forum to air their views. Or perhaps both felt that the issues of flexibility, change, and ideological purity were destined to play a key role in the succession struggle. Or perhaps it was merely coincidental that the two main contenders (as Andropov had clearly entered the succession struggle) were expressing similar views on identical topics at more or less the same time.

The answer to the question, "Who will replace Suslov as Central Committee secretary?" could also help to answer the question, "Who will inherit from Brezhnev?" or "Who is the other contender?" The answer was provided by the 24 May 1982 plenum of the CPSU Central Committee, which elected Andropov CPSU Central Committee secretary.[87] As an immediate result Andropov assumed some of Suslov's responsibilities, which had previously been handled by Chernenko.[88] These responsibilities mainly related to the ideological sphere, whereas Chernenko apparently proceeded to concentrate on the armed forces, border troops, and so on. His participation in purely military events, such as the 11 May 1982 conference of Army party secretaries[89] and the 27 May 1982 fiftieth anniversary of the formation of the border troops,[90] seemed to suggest this. Also in 1982 the second edition of his work *Questions of the Work of the Party and Government Apparatus* was published (Moscow: Politizdat, 1982), in an obvious attempt to claim competence in economic affairs. At the same time, the KGB appeared to remain under Andropov's control. Although he had been compelled to resign after his election as Central Committee secretary, his successor Vitaliy Fedorchuk, an old Andropov crony, who was appointed on 26 May,[91] certainly protected Andropov's power base in the secret police.

Andropov's appointment was of course based on a previous Politburo decision. It can be assumed that the decision was not unanimous and was adopted only after a bitter fight in which Chernenko was in the minority. Several sources also assumed that the decision was adopted while Brezhnev was still recovering from his heart attack and so could not participate in the Politburo meetings.[92] There was one indication of a deal among Politburo members that resolved the crisis surrounding Andropov's appointment: Vladimir Dolgikh, a secretary of the CPSU Central Committee, was appointed candidate member of the Politburo by the same Central Committee plenum that elected Andropov Central Committee secretary.[93] Dolgikh, who was then fifty-eight years old, stemmed from the same Krasnoyarsk party organization as Chernenko (who appeared to be his patron), and his promotion seemed to be intended, at least partly, to balance Andropov's election.

Relative Positions of Chernenko and Andropov

Chernenko's status did not appear to be affected by Andropov's election. During the June 1982 visit of Gustav Husak to Moscow, Chernenko played a leading part in the ceremonies, and on 2 June received from Husak the highest CSSR (Czechoslovak Socialist Republic) order to mark his seventieth birthday in September 1981.[94] Three weeks later, *Pravda* lavishly praised Chernenko's book on party work.[95] In June at a plenum of the Krasnoyarsk party organization Chernenko read a speech that was reported by all Soviet dailies, as well as by TASS and Soviet radio and television.[96] He also spoke at a Central Committee conference with officials from the agro-industrial complexes,[97] thus clearly demonstrating his active involvement in various fields of party work. His status and power were further demonstrated by his success in appointing two journalists closely affiliated with him to important posts: Vladimir Kasyanenko as chief editor of *Voprosy Istorii KPSS*[98] and Yevgeniy Sklyarov as editor in chief of *Problemy Mira I Sotsializma*.[99] Thus Andropov's election as Central Committee secretary did not seem to affect Chernenko's status as de facto second secretary. Furthermore, the ever-expanding range of his activities during summer 1982 suggested that he no longer had a specific area of responsibility within the Politburo but maintained a general oversight of party and state affairs.

The unusually wide range of Chernenko's activities and his high public visibility helped obscure Andropov's new role in the leadership and even to reduce the impact of Andropov's promotion. At the same time, Andropov was maintaining a relatively low profile, probably preparing for the real battle that would take place only after Brezhnev's death. Nevertheless, there were several interesting aspects of his behavior, the primary one being his consistent avoidance of participating in events in which Brezhnev or Chernenko played the major role. Despite his wide experience in relations with the East European countries, Andoprov was absent from the 2 June Kremlin ceremony at which Gustav Husak honored Chernenko on his seventieth birthday.[100] However, he did attend the 31 May ceremony in Moscow at which Vietnam's leader Le Duan awarded an honor to Brezhnev.[101]

Andropov did seem to have assumed some responsibility in the areas of foreign affairs and culture. On 26 June, together with Central Committee secretary Boris Ponomarev, he met the Indian Communist party leader Rajeswara Rao.[102] In the past Suslov and Ponomarev had usually dealt with the leaders of nonruling Communist parties. In addition, Andropov played a central role during the 21–23 June visit to the USSR of Grisha Filipov, then chairman of the Bulgarian Council of Ministers.[103] Against the background of Filipov's visit his curious absence from the negotiations with Husak became even more conspicuous. One can assume that the prominent role Chernenko played during Husak's visit precluded any active participation by Andropov. Some additional points in the succession game were scored by Andropov when on 24 June he represented the Politburo and spoke on its behalf at the celebration marking the 1,500th anniversary of the city of Kiev.

Andropov's involvement in the area of culture was signaled when on 1 June he signed the obituary of the prominent Moscow actor Boris Chirkov, which was also signed by Brezhnev, Grishin, and Chernenko.[104] On the other hand, he did not sign a 23 June obituary for an economic specialist, which was signed by Brezhnev, Chernenko, Grishin, Kirilenko, Tikhonov, and Ustinov.[105] Since senior Central Committee secretaries usually sign all important obituaries, it seems that, despite his promotion, during summer 1982 Andropov's status had not changed greatly. He apparently had received some new areas of responsibility, but as long as Brezhnev remained alive Chernenko continued clearly to outrank Andropov.

An interesting development, which could have been connected with Andropov's ascent, was the increased visibility of Mikhail Gorbachev. Since such visibility in the USSR usually implies enhanced status and since the signs began to appear soon after Andropov's election, it can be assumed that the two developments were related. In fact in summer 1982 Gorbachev took part in events and activities clearly outside his previous area of responsibility—Soviet agriculture. The most notable among them was his active involvement in the talks with the Bulgarian

Premier Grisha Filipov.[106] In addition, Gorbachev represented the Politburo at the 18 June opening in Moscow of the USSR anniversary exhibition, "In a United Family."[107] On 25 June he took part in a plenum of the All-Union Trade Union leadership,[108] another event that did not require his presence. On the other hand, his major address on the food program in Yaroslavl on 16 June[109] was more within his area of responsibility, as was his participation in a 4 June Aeroflot conference dealing with the role of civil aviation in the transport of agricultural products.[110]

The signs indicating Gorbachev's intensified activity were confirmed when on 23 July Sergey Medunov, an old Brezhnev crony and first secretary of the CPSU Krasnodar Kray Committee, was removed from his position at a plenum of the CPSU kraykom, attended by Central Committee Secretary Ivan Kapitonov, and replaced by the USSR ambassador to Cuba, Vitaliy Vorotnikov.[111] Gorbachev, who in the 1970s was the CPSU secretary at neighboring Stavropol, apparently viewed Medunov as a competitor and according to at least two sources[112] had prepared an extensive dossier on him, listing his crimes and involvement in corruption, which he later submitted to Andropov during a visit to the area. Previous attempts to remove Medunov had failed, mainly because of the protection afforded by Brezhnev. In summer 1982 Brezhnev was evidently too weak, both physically and politically, to save Medunov. Thus his removal seems to have been a well-orchestrated Andropov-Gorbachev production.

Toward the end of September Brezhnev, obviously feeling better, decided to orchestrate a show of his own and demonstrate that he was still at the helm. He traveled to Baku in Azerbaijan, where on 26 September he presented the Azerbaijan Soviet Socialist Republic (SSR) with the Order of Lenin. Brezhnev began reading his speech, which was televised in Moscow, and continued for several minutes. Suddenly, Brezhnev's aide Andrey Aleksandrov-Agentov and Azerbaijan's first secretary Geydar Aliyev were seen to become agitated and leave their seats. After offstage consultations, Aleksandrov appeared at Brezhnev's side with what appeared to be a different speech. Brezhnev, apparently not understanding what was happening, tried to push his aide aside, and after seconds of evident confusion during which Aleksandrov could clearly be heard saying, "Leonid Ilich, I implore you . . . ," the aide succeeded in whisking away the original speech and replacing it with another. Brezhnev, clearly stunned, stammered, "It was not my fault, Comrades, I shall start all over again," and began to read the new text. The audience, obviously relieved at the return to normality, burst into applause. The live relay ended there, and the second speech was read on the radio by an announcer.[113] The show of strength had misfired, and the frailty and evident inability of Brezhnev to function properly had been publicly exposed live on television. Brezhnev may have originally begun reading a speech that was not intended for public dissemination.

The infighting in the Kremlin, which during summer 1982 could no longer be concealed, also influenced the behavior of certain republic leaders. Shcherbitskiy of the Ukraine had committed himself earlier in the year, by openly associating himself with Chernenko's ideas on closer relations between the leaders and the masses, the importance of worker's letters, and so on. Although most other republic leaders were evidently awaiting the results of the struggle, two decided to make their moves before the final outcome was clear, taking a calculated risk that they would be rewarded as a sign of gratitude after the success of the leader they supported.

Azerbaijan's Geydar Aliyev made his move on 2 May 1984, when *Bakinskiy Rabochiy* "promoted" Andropov to fourth place in the leadership standing. Aliyev had served previously as the KGB chief of the republic, directly under Andropov, before becoming the republic party secretary in 1969. The timing of the move—May 1982, well before Andropov's election as Central Committee secretary later that month—left no doubt that Aliyev had laid his bet on Andropov. This farsighted decision did not escape Andropov's notice. Aliyev was the first to be rewarded after Andropov's ascent to the post of general secretary.

Unlike Aliyev, and somewhat surprising in view of later developments, Georgia's party boss Eduard Shevardnadze decided to choose Chernenko. Speaking at a meeting of party workers on 3 May 1982, Shevardnadze lavishly praised "the great theoretical and practical work" accomplished by Chernenko in "developing party democracy and strengthening party primary organizations."[114] Although Shevardnadze had cited Chernenko's writings and speeches before, this was the first time that he had praised him generally, probably indicating his conviction that Chernenko had achieved a new status in the leadership.

Both Shcherbitskiy and Shevardnadze made their moves before Andropov had been elected secretary of the CPSU Central Committee. Afterward, like all other republican party leaders (but perhaps with a greater measure of apprehension), they strictly refrained from any public display of allegiance and awaited the final results of the succession struggle before making a further public expression of support.

Late summer 1982 was a relatively quiet period in the succession struggle. The summer vacation interim seemed only a partial reason. Andropov, for instance, made his last public appearance on 31 August 1982,[115] then disappeared from view until 27 October[116] when he took part in a military conference in the Kremlin. His absence may possibly have made the succession struggle less acute. However, Chernenko and surprisingly Brezhnev were rather active in October and the beginning of November. In mid-October Novosty Press Agency republished a book by Chernenko, the second revised edition of his work *The CPSU and Human Rights.*[117] In the book, Chernenko compared the protection of human rights in the USSR and in the United States, stressing that "the rights and freedom of the Soviet citizens are not simply proclaimed by the USSR Constitution, but are guaranteed by economic, political, and legislative means."[118]

Brezhnev's Final Days

On 27 October an unusual military conference was held in the Kremlin. The only reason for the conference seemed to be to provide a forum at which the USSR party and state leadership could reassure the Soviet Army that it intended to keep its commitment to maintain a strong defense. The uncertain domestic situation, which could be reflected in the USSR's foreign policy, was undoubtedly causing concern in the Army, and the leadership wanted to give some assurances. In his conference speech, Brezhnev explained that the leadership remained committed "to strengthening the defenses of the country," stressing that "it would be inadmissible to lag behind" Western military technology, and stating, "I constantly handle matters of consolidating the Army and Navy in the performance of my official duties, so to say."

He further added,

Everyone sees that the Soviet Armed Forces are a powerful factor for peace and security, a reliable means of curbing aggressive forces. And the people spare nothing to keep them always up to the mark. We equip the armed forces with the most advanced weapons and military hardware. The party Central Committee adopts measures to meet all your needs. . . .

The Soviet Army should be up to the mark in all respects: equipment, structure, and methods of training. It should correspond to the requirements of the present time.

Care for the soldier and officer, for the conditions of the troops, has always been and remains in the focus of attention of our party and the Soviet state."[119]

The conference proved very instructive in indicating the ranking of the Soviet leadership. It was Andropov's first public appearance since 31 August and the first public event at which Soviet television ("Vremya" program on 27 October) showed him sitting with Chernenko since his election as Central Committee secretary in May. At the conference the leaders sat in the following order: Andropov, Chernenko, Brezhnev, Ustinov, Tikhonov, and Gromyko. Seated next to Brezhnev, Chernenko clearly demonstrated his superior status as compared to Andropov. This actually reflected the situation that had emerged in September and October, during which Andropov was not reported to have taken part in any public event (whether because of illness or an attempt to keep a very low profile) whereas Chernenko continued his intensive and highly visible activities.

On the day following the conference, Chernenko flew to Tbilisi to present the city with the Order of Lenin. He utilized the ceremony to point out his close relationship with Brezhnev and flattered Shevardnadze.

Dear Comrades, we have a duty to the capital of Georgia, Tbilisi, Leonid Ilich Brezhnev said to me the other day in conversation. The city has been awarded the Order of Lenin, the 65th anniversary of October is drawing near, and it would be a good thing to present the award before the holiday. I myself had hoped to have time to come and present the order to the city, but the preparations for the Supreme Soviet session and for the party Central Committee plenum and other urgent affairs just would not let me leave Moscow even for a short time. It would be a good thing if you were just to fly to Georgia, Leonid Ilich continued, and present the order to the city of Tbilisi. The Republic, as you know, is interesting. The party organizations work energetically and creatively. A good tone for everything is set by Eduard Amvrosyevich Shevardnadze. Convey to him and, of course, to all the other comrades, my best wishes and greetings.[120]

Brezhnev himself seemed to be making an extra effort to improve Chernenko's chances, as well as the position of his other major ally in the Politburo, Premier Tikhonov. In a Kremlin ceremony on 2 November 1982, Brezhnev awarded the Order of Lenin and a second gold medal of Hero of Socialist Labor to Tikhonov.[121] Since Tikhonov was born on 14 May 1905,[122] there did not seem to be any routine reason for honoring him, aside from boosting his prestige. Brezhnev spoke in warm, rather personal terms, stressing Tikhonov's "rich experience, his rare capacity for work and self-denial in his labor, his firm party principles, all of which are qualities for which he has been known—not just for one decade—and help him to cope successfully with his difficult tasks."[123] In a way, Brezhnev was once again publicly endorsing one of his allies in the Politburo in a manner reminiscent of campaigning for a candidate.

Brezhnev took an active part in the events marking the sixty-fifth anniversary of the October Revolution. He attended the 5 November festive meeting in the Kremlin's Palace of Congresses, at which Viktor Grishin delivered the main address.[124] Brezhnev walked unaided, but the Soviet television showed no closeup shots of him. What could clearly be seen, however, was that Chernenko still outranked Andropov. He sat on Brezhnev's right, and Moscow's mayor Vladimir Promyslov sat on his left. Tikhonov sat next to Promyslov, and Andropov—clearly in the fourth position—next to Tikhonov.[125] The same ranking was shown some two hours later during the festive concert. Brezhnev (this time assisted by an aide) was flanked by Tikhonov and Chernenko, and Andropov appeared in his usual fourth place.[126]

The day of 7 November 1982 was bitterly cold. Brezhnev, wearing a heavy overcoat and tinted sunglasses, attended the Red Square military parade.[127] The ordeal continued for more than two hours, during which Brezhnev, impassive and obviously feeling ill, stared apathetically at the parade. Tikhonov and Chernenko flanked him, and the Soviet camera operators repeatedly focused on to the leading trio.[128] Incidentally,

Kirilenko and Pelshe did not attend the parade or the other events connected with the anniversary.[129]

The parade was just the beginning of a long day. Immediately after, the Soviet party and state leadership gave a reception for the anniversary, at which Brezhnev (flanked by Tikhonov and Chernenko) spoke.[130] His speech was brief (about 500 words), as were all his speeches during the last period of his life, and contained the standard banalities on the USSR peace policy, "international imperialism," "detente and peace," as well as the usual warning. "We shall do the utmost to see to it that those who like military ventures should never take the land of the Soviets unawares, that the potential aggressor should know: A crushing retaliatory strike will inevitably be in for him. Our might and vigilance will cool, I think, the hot heads of some imperialist politicians."[131]

Soviet radio altered its regular programming in the evening of 10 November by broadcasting somber classical music, a customary prelude to the official announcement of the death of an important leader. Kirilenko, who had not been seen in public for several weeks, could not have merited such an observance; the same could be said for Pelshe, who had failed to attend the Moscow October Revolution anniversary parade. Little doubt surrounded the identity of the deceased. At 11:00 A.M. Moscow time, the chief television news announcer Igor Kirilov read simultaneously on the Soviet television and radio the following announcement in a dramatic voice, choked by tears:

> The Central Committee and the Communist Party of the Soviet Union, the Presidium of the USSR Supreme Soviet, and the Council of Ministers of the USSR inform with deep sorrow the party and the entire Soviet people that Leonid Ilich Brezhnev, general secretary of the CPSU Central Committee and president of the Presidium of the USSR Supreme Soviet, died suddenly at 0830 A.M. on 10 November, 1982.
>
> The name of Leonid Ilich Brezhnev, a true continuer of Lenin's great cause and an ardent champion of peace and communism, will live forever in the hearts of the Soviet people and the whole of progressive mankind.[132]

Observers noticed that more than twenty-four hours had passed between the official time of Brezhnev's death and the time of the announcement. This delay, combined with the lack of another official announcement on the election of a new general secretary, meant that the Politburo could not agree on the successor. Brezhnev had died and with him perhaps an important period of Soviet history. However, the infighting relating to the election of a successor, which had begun long before Brezhnev's death, apparently continued relentlessly after his demise.

3

Andropov Succeeds:
Rudimentary Consolidation

Two days after Brezhnev's death and one day after the announcement of his death, the CPSU had a new general secretary. Yuriy Andropov was "unanimously" elected at a 12 November plenum of the CPSU Central Committee, on the proposal of Konstantin Chernenko, who had been "instructed" or "entrusted" to do so by the Politburo.[1] This necessarily implies that the Central Committee plenum had been preceded by a Politburo meeting, in which, according to some sources, representatives of the Soviet Army took part and which chose Andropov in preference to Chernenko.[2] However, the bare facts available tell us no more. What really occurred at the enlarged and prolonged Politburo meeting or at the Central Committee plenum must remain a subject of rumor and speculation. Naturally, this ambiguity did not deter many authors from interpreting the events, and several rather detailed accounts describe conjecture of what occurred, who said what, and who voted for whom. At least there can be no doubt that Chernenko—Brezhnev's own heir designate—was a candidate and that the Politburo had to make a choice between him and Andropov.

According to Iliya Zemtsov, an observer of the Kremlin, who quoted "reports from Moscow by George Kennan, Hedrick Smith, and Serge Schmemann, carried by the *New York Times* on 13, 14, 15, 17, 18 and 30 November 1982,"[3] at the Politburo meeting Chernenko first proposed Premier Tikhonov as general secretary. Tikhonov declined, referring to his advanced age (seventy-seven), and in turn proposed Chernenko as a candidate, emphasizing the latter's close relations with Brezhnev. Five members of the Politburo—Ustinov "on behalf of the Army," Grishin "in the name of the party apparatus," and Romanov, Gromyko, and Shcherbitskiy "by pointing to the complex international situation and the difficult economic conditions"—insisted on the appointment of Andropov. Citing this information, Zemtsov concluded that Andropov was elected by a vote of 6 to 5, or perhaps 6 to 4 with Gorbachev abstaining, on the basis of "other" reports (which Zemtsov does not specify). Finally, Zemtsov stressed that "Kirilenko and Pelshe are known to have been absent."[4]

Zemtsov's account and similar attempts to present the final score of the Politburo voting without quoting any reliable sources can hardly be taken seriously for a simple mathematical reason: If Kirilenko and Pelshe did not take part in the Politburo meeting that elected Andropov, only ten full Politburo members were left to cast their votes. All the Soviet sources reporting on the various proceedings on 12 and 14 November list only ten Politburo members attending the events relating to Brezhnev's lying-in-state. This number is given in the radio[5] and television[6] reports of the 12 November visit of the party and state leaders and on the honor guard formed by them by Brezhnev's coffin, the television report on the similar honor guard on 14 November,[7] and the television coverage of the funeral itself.[8] The ten names that appear in all these reports were Andropov, Gorbachev, Grishin, Gromyko, Kunayev, Romanov, Tikhonov, Ustinov, Chernenko, and Shcherbitskiy. Thus the score could only have been 6 to 4; 7 to 3, and so on, but certainly not 6 to 5. (Theoretically, Pelshe could have cast his vote by proxy, but no one has mentioned this possibility.)

Although subsequent developments seemed to confirm the assumption that Ustinov, Gromyko, Gorbachev, Romanov, and possibly Shcherbitskiy sided with Andropov, whereas Tikhonov and Kunayev stood with Chernenko, Grishin's position remains unclear. He had close relations with Chernenko toward the end of the latter's life, which could suggest that he was the fourth man in Chernenko's camp (if the final result of the vote was 6 to 4, not 7 to 3). Thus, we can argue on the basis of personal relations and political developments after Andropov's election that the votes of Politburo members were split between Andropov and Chernenko; five members (Ustinov, Gromyko, Gorbachev, Romanov, and Shcherbitskiy) apparently sided with Andropov whereas three (Tikhonov, Kunayev and Grishin) supported the candidacy of Chernenko.

Another question is, Why was Andropov selected? A surfeit of hypotheses and speculations, which must be treated with great caution, has also surrounded this issue. The issue cannot simply be brushed aside by suggesting that in the USSR the heir apparent is predestined to failure. The quasi-psychological explanation that Chernenko was rejected because of the "fear of another Brezhnev" is not supported by any hard evidence. Why not assume that the majority of Politburo members simply considered Andropov better qualified for the post of general secretary? In the author's opinion his higher qualifications, added to his superior experience and better record in different areas and his keen political acumen, helped him to gain the support of such powerful pressure groups as the Soviet Army and facilitated the formation of a solid coalition with a majority vote in the Politburo, against which Chernenko had no chance. Years of active involvement in foreign policy (and especially in East European affairs) and party work (as Central

Committee secretary) and his deep involvement in domestic affairs as KGB chief must have convinced the other party leaders that he was far better equipped for the job than Chernenko. Furthermore, since it is logical to assume that the head of the KGB is also a member of the Defense Council, Andropov had the opportunity to develop a good working relationship with the Soviet Army, which proved helpful when the successor was to be elected.

Against this impressive record, Chernenko's qualifications seemed rather slight. His experience in such vital areas as foreign policy and military affairs was negligible. Even in such areas as party organizational work, in which he was considered by some to have solid experience, his record was unimpressive. For example, during the last five years of Brezhnev's life, Chernenko was not only the heir apparent but also the Central Committee secretary in charge of personnel. In retrospect, he obviously failed to utilize this crucial position to build support and improve his chances. Thus, during those five years only fifteen of the seventy-one obkom first secretaries were replaced, and even many of the fifteen newly appointed secretaries seemed to have close links with other leaders rather than with Chernenko.[9] Lacking experience in vital areas and unable to utilize his position to build up support, Chernenko seems to have relied solely on his personal relationship with Brezhnev. If Brezhnev himself had had the say in the appointment of his successor, this approach would have been sufficient to secure Chernenko's election. However, the past record shows that Soviet leaders have never succeeded in influencing the selection of their immediate successor, simply because their death necessarily preceded the election of the heir.

The Politburo's decision to elect Andropov was only the first bitter pill that Chernenko had to swallow. In an obvious attempt to demonstrate the unity and cohesion of the party leadership, the Politburo "entrusted" Chernenko with proposing Andropov at the 12 November Central Committee plenum.[10] Naturally, speculation was rife about this plenum also. One commentator described it as "almost certainly a rump meeting, consisting of three groups: elected members working in Moscow (chiefly government, not party officials); selected members who happened to arrive three days early in Moscow to attend a plenum long scheduled for 15 November; and selected members who had been summoned to Moscow after Brezhnev died."[11] The same commentator suggested that the "haste with which its organizers convened this rump plenum seems to have been designed to squelch politicking and has intimations of a coup."[12] Even if one ignores the lack of any evidence or source supporting this statement, a Central Committee plenum convened forty-eight hours after the leader's death could not accurately be termed "hasty" or "rump."

Another researcher supplied details about the "fight put up by Chernenko's supporters" at the plenum,[13] maintaining that in the first vote the Central Committee members split between Andropov and

Chernenko, and only the second ceremonial vote provided the unanimity cited by the Soviet press.[14] No evidence or source has been cited to support this thesis. The official announcement on the plenum's decision speaks of "unanimous support."[15] Whether or not this reflects the true picture must remain a matter of conjecture.

Nevertheless, Chernenko's speech at the plenum did include passages that could be interpreted as attempts to recall his close relations with Brezhnev, with reference to his good fortune "to be together with Leonid Ilich, to listen to him in person, to experience directly the keenness of his mind, his resourcefulness, and his love of life,"[16] and implicitly warning Andropov not to impose his will on the Politburo: "Now it is twice, thrice as important to conduct party matters collectively."[17]

Having elected Andropov, the leadership could concentrate on the other important matter that had to be dealt with—the burial of Leonid Brezhnev. At the funeral Chernenko had to swallow the third bitter pill. He was denied the honor of eulogizing his patron and protector and had to listen to Andropov and Ustinov, the very persons most responsible for the rejection of his candidacy, eulogizing the person who had wanted him to be the successor. The ceremony, which would become familiar to Soviet citizens and indeed the whole world during the next two and a half years through the televised funerals of Andropov and Chernenko, was solemn and impressive. In his eulogy, Andropov exalted Brezhnev, promised to do everything "to increase the cohesion of the great community of socialist states," and warned "the forces of imperialism" that "a crushing rebuff to any attempt of aggression" was awaiting them.[18]

After paying due respect to Brezhnev's memory, Marshal Ustinov predictably declared: "The Soviet Armed Forces, raised and educated by the Communist Party, are and will continue to be a mighty factor of peace and security of the peoples, they are constantly ready to defend the inviolability of our borders and the peaceful work of the Soviet people, to discharge with honor their patriotic and international duty."[19]

The routine speeches of Academician Anatoliy Aleksandrov, president of the USSR Academy of Sciences,[20] and the Moscow worker Viktor Pushkarev,[21] contained nothing important or memorable. No reverberations of the power struggle that accompanied Andropov's election could be discerned in the speeches. Thus a page of Soviet history was closed: A new leader was elected, and a new era began.

Characterization of Andropov's Tenure

Although the transfer of power after Brezhnev's death took place amid an impressive display of collective unity and smooth efficiency, several important conclusions, which were to characterize the entire period of Andropov's tenure, could readily be drawn.

Chernenko as the Big Loser

Brezhnev's position and strength had been Chernenko's main and apparently sole power base, and during his tenure Chernenko enjoyed a position second only to that of his mentor. Even after Andropov's election in May 1982 to the CPSU Central Committee Secretariat, Chernenko did not lose his prominence and continued to be viewed as Brezhnev's obvious successor and to be accorded a preeminence unequaled by any other Politburo leader apart from Brezhnev. Chernenko's position of prominence was obvious during October and the beginning of November. Furthermore, some republican leaders and even certain East European states, such as Czechoslovakia and Bulgaria, treated him as a leader with a special status. His prominence was further evinced when the two major Czechoslovakian newspapers *Rude Pravo* and Bratislava's *Pravda* on 30 October carried extensive excerpts from Chernenko's 29 October Tbilisi speech, even though Eastern European papers usually only reprinted local speeches of the general secretary. Against this impressive background, it is only natural to consider Chernenko, the candidate not elected, the main loser in the succession drama.

Challenges to the Election of Andropov

Although to the public's eyes the transition took place smoothly and with dignity, several facts suggest that Andropov's election was achieved only after fierce and bitter infighting in the Politburo. The substantial delay between Brezhnev's death and the official announcement suggests that the Politburo could not immediately agree on a successor and that the decision was reached only after protracted debate. It can be taken for granted that Chernenko claimed the post for himself.

The delay in Andropov's selection indicates that Chernenko had some support among the Politburo members and that his faction succeeded in temporarily delaying Andropov's election. The conclusion was obvious: Andropov was to face harsh realities in his new position. He had to neutralize quickly the influence of Chernenko's faction, perhaps by ousting some of his supporters from the Politburo, and he risked becoming permanently indebted to those who had facilitated his own election. In short, he had to assert his authority among both friends and foes if he was to survive as general secretary. This meant that the infighting was not over and that Andropov had won a battle but certainly not the war. In fact it was impossible to define clearly where the succession battle ended and the fight of consolidation of Andropov's power began; both battles formed part of the same prolonged infighting, waged by the same actors on the same political stage. The first act was over; the show went on.

Role of the Soviet Army

The striking prominence accorded to Defense Minister Ustinov during the funeral of Brezhnev and the lying-in-state ceremonies suggested the crucial role of the military in Andropov's succession. Ustinov was the only Politburo member other than Andropov to deliver a eulogy at the funeral. The spectacle of the spokesman for the military establishment delivering a eulogy, while Prime Minister Tikhonov and former crown prince Chernenko remained in the background, signaled the singular new status and power position of Ustinov. During the funeral he appeared in the fourth position after Andropov, Tikhonov, and Chernenko[22]—a higher position than ever before.

The question arises, Why did the army decide to throw its support behind Andropov? Policy differences between Chernenko and Andropov could hardly be seen as significant (both had essentially advocated détente and arms control negotiations). Perhaps, a partial answer was contained in Chernenko's unorthodox speech in Tbilisi on 29 October.

> But if Washington is unable to rise above primitive anticommunism and if it continues a policy of threat and diktat, that is fine, we are strong enough and we can wait. Neither sanctions nor warlike poses frighten us. We believe in reason. We believe that sooner or later—and the sooner the better—reason will prevail and the danger of war will be averted.[23]

Perhaps this ill-timed statement—that the Soviet Army was already "strong enough" to counter any threat from the United States—antagonized the military and caused it to transfer its support to Andropov, who had no such blemish on his public record. Furthermore, his long experience (more than fifteen years) as head of the KGB evidently increased Andropov's standing with the military. Chernenko had no military record to speak of. He was painfully aware of this shortcoming, and in 1984, after finally attaining the coveted position of CPSU Central Committee secretary general, he made an obvious attempt to produce a military record of sorts, disclosing previously unpublished information on his service in the border guard troops.

Andropov was aware of the importance of the Soviet Army's support and also apparently conscious of the military's reaction to Chernenko's speech in Tbilisi. In his acceptance speech at the 12 November 1982 Central Committee plenum, he expressed the view that the "invincible might" of the Soviet Armed Forces was the best means of preserving peace.[24]

Andropov's Unprecedented Background

Yuriy Andropov was the first chairman of the KGB to be elected general secretary of the CPSU Central Committee. The previous general secretaries were politicians who belonged to the party apparatus and who made use of this apparatus to further their careers, acquiring their principal experience in organizational affairs and different branches of the economy. Their experience in conducting foreign policy came later when they were already serving as top party leaders. Andropov was a leader of a different ilk. Although it is safe to assume that as head of the KGB he had amassed some experience in economics and in domestic politics, his main asset was his extensive experience in foreign affairs. Indeed, most of his career had been in the fields of security and foreign affairs.

His lack of a conventional grounding in party organizational work was expected to be a disadvantage as he strove to increase his personal power within the party (assuming that he had time to work toward this goal). He had never headed any party organization and had even less of an organizational base in the party than Chernenko. Thus in many areas of his activity as general secretary he would have to rely heavily upon advisers. This reliance on advisers, in addition to his dependence on his Politburo allies, as well as his uncomfortable awareness of the constantly watchful eyes of his Politburo opponents who followed his every move, considerably restricted Andropov's freedom of action and choice of alternatives. However, the new general secretary did have significant power base that could serve as the main instrument for Andropov to consolidate his position and assert his power.

Andropov's Power Base

Yuriy Vladimirovich Andropov was born on 15 June 1914 in Nagutskaya, now situated in Stavropol kray.[25] Son of a railroad employee, Andropov graduated from the Rybinsk Water Transportation Tekhnikum in 1936. He attended the Petrosazovsk University but failed to graduate. From 1951 to 1953 he attended the Higher Party School in Moscow.

His political career commenced at the Rybinsk Water Transportation Tekhnikum, where he became secretary of the local Komsomol organization in 1936. In 1937 he was elected secretary of the Yaroslavl obkom of the Komsomol, and in the following year he became first secretary of that body.

In 1939 Andropov was accepted into the party and in the following year was appointed first secretary of the Karelo-Finnish Komsomol Central Committee. He remained in this post until 1944. It has been suggested that during his Karelian period Andropov was brought into contact with Otto Kuusinen, who may have played an important part in promoting Andropov's career.[26]

After the war Andropov remained in Karelia as second secretary of the Petrozavodsk Gorkom of the Communist party, a post he held from 1944 to 1947. In 1947 he was elected second secretary of the Karelo-Finnish Communist Party Central Committee. At this point his career really took off. In 1950 he was elected a deputy in the USSR Supreme Soviet Council of Nationalities and immediately became a member of its Foreign Affairs Commission. In 1951 he joined the CPSU Central Committee apparatus, apparently working in a section of the International Department.

In 1953 Andropov began his career as an international official when he joined the USSR Ministry of Foreign Affairs, occupying a post in the Fourth European Department, in charge of Polish and CSSR affairs. During the same year he was appointed counselor and then chargé d'affaires at the Soviet Embassy in Budapest. Between 1954 and 1957 he was Soviet ambasssador to Hungary and thus found himself personally involved in the Soviet invasion of Hungary in November 1956.

In the following year Andropov returned to Moscow and became head of the CPSU Central Committee Department for Liaison with Communist and Workers' Parties of the Socialist Countries, holding this post until 1967. No doubt Nikita Khrushchev, then party chief, was instrumental in recalling Andropov to Moscow, and Andropov sided with Khrushchev in his struggle against the "dogmatists" within the party.[27] During this period Andropov developed his relationships with a number of close associates and advisers who formed a group of consultants that followed him in all his subsequent posts.

In 1961 Andropov became a full member of the CPSU Central Committee and in the following year Central Committee secretary in charge of liaison with the socialist countries' Communist and Workers' parties. Andropov remained as Central Committee secretary until 1967. During this period relations between him and Suslov were rather strained, and Suslov may have had a hand in, or at least welcomed, Andropov's removal from the Central Committee Secretariat in 1967.[28] In any event, it was hardly a coincidence (especially in the USSR, where coincidences are rarely permitted to happen) that Andropov rejoined the Secretariat in May 1982 after Suslov's death. Perhaps the old priest of ideological purity succeeded in blocking not only Chernenko's but also Andropov's career.

When Andropov was transferred to the KGB in 1967, it seemed that his party career would suffer a setback. After all, the post of KGB chief is very often the final stage of a political career in the USSR. The post seems to place a stigma on its holders and almost invariably disqualifies them from subsequently holding any other important position. This was not the case with Andropov. He evidently remained the party's man in the KGB, totally subordinating the KGB to the will of the party. Naturally, his loyalty to the party leadership was properly rewarded. After remaining a candidate member of the CPSU Central Committee Politburo for six years, in 1973 Andropov was promoted to full Politburo membership.

Andropov remained KGB chief until his election for the second time as Central Committee secretary in May 1982. He utilized his leadership of the KGB by turning the latter into a personal stronghold—manipulating promotions, appointing allies, and ousting opponents. His election to the post of KGB chief was accompanied by the election of three deputy heads: Semen Tsvigun, Brezhnev's ill-fated brother-in-law; Georgiy Tsinev, Brezhnev's old crony from Dnepropetrovsk, and Viktor Chebrikov, the then current head of the KGB, who in 1967 was merely a junior party official from Brezhnev's power base of Dnepropetrovsk. Apparently Brezhnev, not intending to leave the new KGB chief too much room for independent maneuver, set up a network of control and report around Andropov. However, Andropov not only knew the rules of the game but also how to play. He used his first two to three years as KGB chief to consolidate his position and then began to expand his power base within the organization. Since the mid-1970s Andropov had managed to more than double the number of deputy chairmen of the KGB, bringing in his own appointees while undercutting the power of Brezhnev's protégés. The case of Vladimir Kryuchkov was typical. He was a third secretary at the Soviet Embassy in Budapest when Andropov was ambassador. When Andropov returned to Moscow to become head of the Central Committee Department for Liaison with Communist and Workers' Parties of the Socialist Countries, Kryuchkov also joined that department. Clearly, Andropov had brought in a loyal supporter, a practice he continued later when he took over the KGB.

The enhanced importance of the KGB under Andropov, as well as the increased number of deputy heads, was reflected in the lists of delegates to the 25th and 26th CPSU Congresses. Appended to the stenographic reports of the two congresses, these lists identified only five KGB deputy chairmen in 1976 (S. Tsvigun, G. Tsinev, V. Chebrikov, V. Pirozhkov, and N. Yemokhonov), whereas in 1981 the number rose to ten (the five mentioned plus V. Lezhepekov, M. Yermakov, S. Antonov, G. Grigorenko, and V. Kryuchkov).

The appointments in the KGB leadership after the mid-1970s strengthened Andropov's position. An overwhelming majority of the top KGB personnel had been appointed by him, so that when Andropov left the KGB in May 1982 the Committee for State Security remained one of the most solid components of his power base.

By the same token, it might be assumed that Andropov had a number of close allies in the Central Committee Department for Liaison with Communist and Workers' Parties of the Socialist Countries. At least one valued associate from his days in that department—Central Committee Secretary Konstantin Rusakov—could be considered a source of vital support. Rusakov was a deputy head of the department under Andropov (1964–1965) and then first deputy head (1965–1968).[29] After Andropov's transfer to the KGB Rusakov succeeded him as departmental head and remained in this post until 1972.[30] Some of the top officials of the Department for Liaison with Communist and Workers' Parties of the Socialist Countries owed their positions and therefore their allegiance to Rusakov or even to Andropov, thus providing the new general secretary with an additional and badly needed element in his power base.

Andropov's team of advisers and consultants provided additional support. Predictably, his association with most of them began many years before his election as general secretary and even before his appointment as KGB head. One of the most important among them was Fedor Burlatskiy, head of the Philosophy Department of the CPSU Central Committee's Institute of Social Sciences. Almost twenty years before Andropov's election as general secretary, he was identified by *Pravda* as a section head of an unidentified Central Committee department (the Liaison Department is rarely specifically identified in the Soviet press), who traveled with Andropov to Hungary.[31] Andropov could certainly count on Burlatskiy for support in the field of ideology.

Georgiy Arbatov, who is the current director of the Institute for the USA and Canada at the USSR Academy of Sciences, was another valuable member of the consultants' group. From 1964 to 1967 he held a "responsible post (or posts) in the CPSU Central Committee apparatus,"[32] which might have been in Andropov's own department but was certainly in one dealing with foreign affairs. In 1967 he was appointed to the directorship of the institute,[33] a post which he currently holds. Both Burlatskiy and Arbatov cooperated with Otto Kuusinen in preparing the manual, *Fundamentals of Marxism-Leninism*.[34] It can be safely assumed that Andropov's association with Burlatskiy and Arbatov began a good thirty years before he became general secretary. Furthermore, Arbatov's profound knowledge of U.S. affairs and his personal involvement in various negotiations between the USSR and the United States made him an invaluable adviser on foreign policy issues.

A further member of the team was Aleksandr Bovin. *Pravda* of 24 September 1964 mentioned him as a member of an Andropov-led delegation, describing him as a "responsible official" of an unspecified Central Committee department. *Pravda* of 31 October 1969 mentioned him again, this time as "leader of a group of consultants," again from an unidentified Central Committee department, who accompanied Rusakov on a trip to the CSSR. Since at the time Rusakov was head of the Central Committee Department for Liaison with Communist and Workers' Parties of the Socialist Countries, it was reasonably certain that Bovin also belonged to that department. When Andropov was elected general secretary, Aleksandr Bovin was a senior political commentator of *Izvestiya,* a post he held for several years, and also a prominent television and radio personality, often taking part in the important "Round Table" Sunday radio program, which is frequently used by the Soviet leadership to launch new ideas or proposals.

Oleg Bogomilov, in 1982 head of the Institute of Economics of the World Socialist System at the USSR Academy of Sciences, and Viktor Sharapov, identified in November 1982 as an "aide to the general secretary,"[35] were two other members of Andropov's team of advisers.

Bogomilov apparently had broad experience in economics, whereas Sharapov, having served as a correspondent in the United States, Canada, and Vietnam, could provide useful analyses of foreign policies. Since *Kommunist,* no. 10, July 1982, mentioned him as the editor of a reprint of Andropov's 22 April 1982 Lenin Day speech, it may be assumed that Sharapov had contributed to the foreign policy sections of various speeches made by Andropov.

Even though none of the advisors and consultants mentioned enjoyed very high standing within the party (except for Party Secretary Rusakov) or held any important government post, they proved useful. They provided Andropov with valuable advice in the areas of economics and foreign policy, and they built support for him at various levels of the party apparatus, thus serving as key elements in his power base.

Andropov as General Secretary— Mixed Signals

The first signals regarding the strength of Andropov's position were confusing. Indeed, the CPSU Central Committee plenum, which was held on 22 November 1982 and the USSR Supreme Soviet Session of 23–24 November both produced conflicting indications of Andropov's strength. The most important decisions adopted by the Central Committee plenum were to relieve Kirilenko of his duties as Politburo member and Central Committee secretary "because of the state of his health and in connection with his personal request"[36] and to elect Geydar Aliyev full member of the Politburo and Nikolay Ryzhkov CPSU Central Committee secretary.[37]

Kirilenko's ousting was a fait accompli long before Andropov's election as general secretary and thus had nothing to do with Andropov's position, Kirilenko's appearance at Brezhnev's funeral as a private citizen, rather than with the Politburo, confirmed the previous signs that he had been ousted. The strongest evidence of this fact was the absence of his portrait in the line of Politburo members' pictures in Red Square, displayed on 4 November 1982 for the October Revolution anniversary ceremonies. His last public appearance had been on 31 August, when he greeted Brezhnev on his return from the Crimea (together with all the other Politburo members),[38] and after that date he had not taken part in any official event. Thus Kirilenko's removal from the Politburo had occurred well before Brezhnev's death, and he certainly played no part in the succession process. A further confirmation of Kirilenko's noninvolvement in the infighting was the manner in which the Central Committee plenum committee reported his retirement and especially the restrained praise accorded him by Andropov: "The general secretary of the CPSU Central Committee Yuriy Brezhnev pointed out that Comrade A. P. Kirilenko had been working actively for many years in the local party bodies and in the CPSU Central Committee, and we do justice to his services to the party and the country."[39]

The appointments of Aliyev and Ryzhkov were much more important. It has already been noted that Andropov was in an unenviable position in the Politburo. Surrounded by opponents and powerful leaders to whom he was indebted for his appointment, he urgently needed the support of people affiliated with or indebted to him in the Politburo. Naturally, he looked first for such support to his main power base—the KGB. Aliyev, a candidate member of the Politburo since 1976, had been associated with the KGB, in all its previous incarnations, since 1941. Between 1964 and 1967 he was deputy chairman of the KGB in Azerbaijan and from 1967 to 1969, chairman of the KGB in that republic. In addition, he held the rank of major general in the KGB.[40] His credentials indicated a close personal association with Andropov; he was exactly the sort of man Andropov needed in the Politburo. Whether the other Politburo members were happy with the promotion of a second KGB general is another matter. Indeed their approval or disapproval was immaterial; the important thing was that Andropov succeeded in achieving the promotion of his candidate.

The election of Nikolay Ryzhkov could also be considered a victory for Andropov, not so much because of any special affiliation with Ryzhkov, who seems to have been a protégé of the ousted Kirilenko, but because Ryzhkov's elevation blocked the promotion of Central Committee Secretary Vladimir Dolgikh to full Politburo membership. Dolgikh was born in Ilanskoye, Krasnoyarsk kray,[41] Chernenko's own home area, and thus was presumably his protégé. In fact, Dolgikh's election to Politburo candidate membership at the May 1982 Central Committee plenum, which elected Andropov Central Committee secretary, was considered at the time to be a counterbalance to Andropov's election. Dolgikh almost immediately took over Kirilenko's responsibility for the supervision of planning and economic policy and appeared to be well on his way to achieving full Politburo membership after the removal of Kirilenko.[42] Instead, the 22 November Central Committee elected Nikolay Ryzhkov Central Committee secretary, thus blocking the advance of Chernenko's man. Accordingly, the election of the apparently nonpolitical industrial expert Nikolay Ryzhkov to the depleted Secretariat can be considered a further success for Andropov.

On 23 November Chernenko's faction had demonstrated its powerful influence when the USSR Supreme Soviet failed to elect a new chairman. The plenum adopted the 1983 plan and budget, which had been approved the previous day by the Central Committee plenum,[43] and appointed Geydar Aliyev first deputy chairman of the Council of Ministers.[44] This was clearly another victory for Andropov. Now Aliyev could supervise the activities of the then seventy-seven-year-old Premier Tikhonov, Chernenko's closest ally in the Politburo.

On the other hand, the first Supreme Soviet session since Brezhnev's demise adjourned without electing a new chairman of its presidium.

The election of Andropov as a mere member of the Supreme Soviet Presidium[45] was a formal matter and a poor recompense for not electing him chairman of the Supreme Soviet Presidium. Since this is a highly visible post, its protracted and unprecedented vacancy suggested that the leadership was unable to arrive at a decision, and this failure to agree on a candidate could be intepreted as a setback for Andropov.

The praise contained in the speech of KGB Chief Vitaliy Fedorchuk, when presenting a draft law on the USSR state border, was a poor solace for Andropov. Officially expressing the KGB's satisfaction with Andropov's election, Fedorchuk noted:

> The Border Guard troops, all the Chekists, like all the Soviet people, received the unanimous election of Comrade Yuriy Vladimirovich Andropov—a very close cofighter of Leonid Ilich Brezhnev—as general secretary of the CPSU Central Committee with a feeling of profound satisfaction and complete approval.
>
> We all know Yuriy Vladimirovich Andropov as a talented leader and organizer and a politician of the Lenin school, possessing a broad perspective and great perspicacity, a profound perception of problems and a wise circumspection when taking decisions.
>
> In his 15 years working at the post of chairman of the USSR KGB, Comrade Yuriy Vladimirovich Andropov played a prominent role in the steady implementation of the party's line of fully restoring and consolidating Leninist principles in the work of the state security organs and of further developing those principles in conformity with the present stage of communist building and the development of statehood and democracy.[46]

The 22 November Central Committee plenum and the 23–24 November Supreme Soviet session, as well as the related Politburo meeting that preceded them, were settings for the first round of infighting following the death of Brezhnev. There were no clearcut results. Both opponents gained some points in anticipation of more decisive rounds in the future.

Toward the end of the year the new lineup of the party leadership crystallized: Andropov, Tikhonov, Chernenko, Ustinov, Gromyko, and Grishin. It reflected the remarkable rise of the military–foreign policy establishment in the Politburo. The heads of the KGB and of the defense and foreign ministries were co-opted into the Politburo only in 1973, and for long after tended to hold low positions in the ranking. Now the former KGB head ranked first, the defense minister fourth, and the minister of foreign affairs fifth. Together they represented a major force in the eleven-person Politburo. Jointly with Aliyev they formed the core of Andropov's faction, which is not to suggest that their common denominator was anything more than a common interest in checking Chernenko and his group and in protecting their own power from encroachment. Furthermore, Andropov's dependence on his allies appeared significantly to limit his options in military and foreign affairs, leaving him somewhat more leverage in the area of economics on which he seemed to concentrate his attention during the first stage of his tenure.

Republican Support

An important indication of the relative strength of the leader is the extent to which the republican leaders are willing to commit themselves openly to him. No wonder, therefore, that the attention of Sovietologists has not focused exclusively on the Kremlin but has also taken account the public statements of the party leaders of the republics. In the semifeudal system of the CPSU, the latter form some of the most important vassals whose support is essential to the leader.

The first republican leader to go on record with a tribute to Andropov was the Georgian first secretary Eduard Shevardnadze. In his 17 November speech in Tbilisi,[47] he devoted twelve paragraphs to Andropov. He referred to the "Politburo headed by Yuriy Vladimirovich Andropov." The controversial concept (throughout the years the Soviet press had repeatedly maintained that no one heads the Politburo) became accepted only from the mid-1970s, when Brezhnev rose above his colleagues. Significantly, Shevardnadze did not refer to the collective leadership in his speech.

Shevardnadze had good reason to be the first publicly to elevate Andropov to the rank of Politburo head. He had to atone for what in retrospect became a flagrant case of backing the wrong horse, when during the presuccession period he fawned on Chernenko during the latter's visit to Tbilisi in October 1982. For three days the local paper *Zarya Vostoka* echoed Shevardnadze's enthusiasm and devoted almost all its coverage to Chernenko's visit. Photos, articles, and commentaries relating to the visit filled the newspaper. With characteristic flattery, Shevardnadze called Chernenko "particularly dear to Tbilisi" and "the most respected person in the city" and made him an honorary citizen of Tbilisi.[48]

By being the first to refer to Andropov as the "head of the Politburo," Shevardnadze was indicating that the adulation of Chernenko in October was already a thing of the past, that his political pragmatism lay above any personal relations with, or preference for, Chernenko, and that he offered his loyal services to the new leader.

The second republican leader to hail Andropov was the Ukraine party boss Vladimir Shcherbitskiy. He praised Andropov as a "great organizer, talented leader, and warm-hearted person," who "has made and is continuing to make a great contribution to increasing the power and international prestige of our motherland and to strengthening the socialist community, and who firmly defends the revolutionary Marxist-Leninist ideology and its purity."[49] Like Shevardnadze, Shcherbitskiy was attempting to secure his position after having previously been in the front ranks of Chernenko's supporters; his 23 March 1982 article in *Trud* still marred his political record. Therefore, there can hardly be any doubt as to why Shevardnadze and Shcherbitskiy, the two leaders with "pro-Chernenko deviations" in their past, were the first publicly to commit their support to Andropov.

The third republican leader to commit himself publicly was Kirgizia's Turdakun Usubaliyev. He praised Andropov as a "staunch Communist" with "great experience in party and state work" and called him "leader of our Leninist party." He also made reference to the Politburo "headed by Andropov."[50]

However impressive this show of support may be, there were also certain signs of less than enthusiastic support for Andropov. For example, the praise coming from Kazakhstan's Dinmukhamet Kunayev ("a firm Leninist, a selfless fighter for the ideals of Communism, and a talented organizer and political leader"),[51] Leningrad's Romanov ("an indisputable political and state leader who skilfully directs the diverse tasks dictated by the CPSU's Leninist course"),[52] Estonia's Valter Vayno, and Azerbaijan's Kyamran Bagirov was comparatively lukewarm, not going beyond the rather standard rhetoric employed by Chernenko when proposing Andropov for the post of general secretary at the 12 November 1982 plenum and by Grishin when putting forward Andropov's name at the 23 November Supreme Soviet session.[53]

All the republican Central Committees held plenums between 29 November and 9 December 1982. These were perfect opportunities for the republican secretaries to come out with public endorsements of Andropov. Yet many of them failed to do so. Viktor Grishin (Moscow), Sharaf Rashidov (Uzbekistan), Tikhon Kiselev (Belorussia), Semen Grossu (Moldavia), Pyatras Grishkayvichus (Lithuania), Rakhman Nabiyev (Tadzhikistan), and Karen Dermichyan (Armenia) refrained from personal praise of Andropov; at most they made favorable comments on Andropov's speech at the 12 November 1982 special Central Committee plenum. Some republican leaders referred either directly or indirectly to the concept of collective leadership. For example, Belorussia's Kiselev spoke of the Central Committee's "leading core," which "was formed under the benign influence" of Brezhnev and of the "invincible collective wisdom and will of the party."[54] Latvia's Avgust Voss spoke of the unity around the "tested and true leading core of the party, the Politburo."[55] Turdakun Usubaliyev's comments echoed the others: He too stated that "the leading core of our party, the Politburo, was formed under the decisive influence of Leonid Ilich Brezhnev."[56]

Some of the republican secretaries' speeches were surprisingly revealing. They disclosed that, emulating the quasi-feudal manner of Brezhnev, Andropov had already begun exploiting his newly won power by allocating material resources to local leaders to solicit their political support. Thus Usubaliyev revealed that on 23 November he had had a private conversation with Andropov and that Andropov had "recently ordered the appropriate government organs to allocate to Kirgizia additional aid for its agriculture."[57] Similarly, Romanov disclosed that on 1 December he too had had a private talk with Andropov on the subject of accelerating work on the construction of flood-prevention structures in Leningrad and that Andropov had promised to obtain the aid required from the appropriate government organs.[58]

The formula "head of the Politburo" had served as an indicator of Brezhnev's status. During the early period of his tenure, the prevailing concept was "collectivity." Indeed, the concept was embodied in the ruling troyka—Brezhnev, Kosygin, and Podgorniy. In 1969 Brezhnev's crony Dinmukhamed Kunayev was the first to use the tell-tale formula in his own fief of Kazakhstan. After Andropov's election as general secretary, it was only natural for Sovietologists to analyze the use of the concept as a method of determining attitudes toward the new leader. As pointed out, some republican leaders found no difficulty in "promoting" Andropov to the head of the Politburo whereas others held back.

The motives for using or refraining from the formula seemed to vary. For instance, the leaders of Belorussia and the Baltic republics who had refrained from using it were the last to join the Brezhnev cult, and their aloofness toward Andropov may have reflected their relative independence and aversion to servility. Some of those who did use this formula, such as the Central Asian and Transcaucasian leaders, had been in the forefront in the boosting of Brezhnev's prestige, and their behavior may simply have reflected their penchant for sycophancy toward the boss. However, for certain Politburo members, resistance to the use of the formula appeared to reflect political motivation rather than personal disposition. Kazakhstan leader Kunayev, Leningrad's Romanov, and the Uzbek leader Rashidov had lavished praise on Brezhnev and used the formula "the Politburo headed by Brezhnev." However, they showed restraint in praise of Andropov when chairing the local meetings in their power base areas, which elected the Politburo (in absentia) to the honorary presidiums. Their attitude could only be interpreted as one of "wait and see," that is, of avoiding total commitment while waiting to see whether Andropov would indeed succeed in consolidating his position. All in all, the simple and unpretentious style adopted by Andropov made the formula "head of the Politburo" meaningless or at least not as important and revealing as it had been in Brezhnev's time.

Andropov's Style and Priorities

Andropov did not appear to attribute much importance to formal or external signs of power and much preferred an informal, semipopulistic style, as practised by Khrushchev. A typical example of this style was his unannounced and apparently unexpected visit to Moscow's Sergo Ordzhonikidze Machine Tool Plant on 31 January 1983. Andropov toured the plant, chatted with the workers, and finally informally addressed the entire collective.[59] The visit was in fact a well-orchestrated (and well-publicized) event aimed at enhancing the new leader's open and populistic style, and it reflected Andropov's growing confidence, which in turn apparently reflected his growing power. The latter was indicated by a quickening in the pace of new personnel appointments toward the end of the year.

The most important new political appointment before the end of the year was the replacement of KGB Chief Vitaliy Fedorchuk by his first deputy Viktor Chebrikov.[60] In spite of the simultaneous appointment of Fedorchuk to the post of minister of internal affairs and his promotion to the military rank of Army general,[61] this move appeared to actually represent a demotion for Fedorchuk. Since both Fedorchuk and Chebrikov had long been associated with Andropov as his deputies, a simplistic explanation of Fedorchuk's fall out of favor seems inadequate. It appeared that Andropov wanted a close collaborator as minister of internal affairs at a time when the anticorruption drive initiated by him was accelerating. In any event, there could be no mistake in interpreting the removal of the former minister of internal affairs Nikolay Shchelokov. He had been closely linked with Brezhnev since his Moldavian days, probably implying a similar association with Chernenko. Clearly, he was among the first to pay the price of associating with the loser in the succession struggle.

The appointments of Mikhail Kapitsa and Viktor Komplektov as deputy ministers of foreign affairs[62] seemed to reflect Andropov's foreign policy priorities. The men had specialized in Chinese and U.S. affairs, respectively, and their promotions were apparently devoid of political connotations relating to the power struggle.

A more interesting case was the appointment of Nikolay Slyunkov as the Belorussian party leader to replace the deceased Tikhon Kiselev.[63] Both the appointee and the haste in replacing Kiselev were surprising. Although he was a Belorussian, Slyunkov had worked in Moscow since 1974 as deputy chairman of Gosplan (the State Planning Committee). He had a reputation as an effective manager and promoter of technological innovations but had had very little experience in party work in Belorussia (merely a brief stint as head of the Minsk City party committee). The appointment therefore deviated from Brezhnev's policy of recruiting top-level republican officials from the ranks of the local leadership. Slyunkov's predecessor Kiselev had been chairman of the Belorussian Council of Ministers and briefly (1978–1980) deputy chairman of the USSR Council of Ministers before becoming first secretary of the Belorussian Central Committee.[64] With the exception of the former Azerbaijan first secretary Aliyev, who had made his career in the republic's KGB apparatus, all the republican first secretaries appointed under Brezhnev had long records of party service in their republics and had previously held important republican party or state positions.

The appointment of Slyunkov was announced on 13 January 1983,[65] the day of Kiselev's funeral and only a day after the announcement of his death. Normally, the Kremlin takes about two weeks to replace a deceased republican party boss. Kiselev's appointment, for example, was announced twelve days after Petr Masherov's death on 4 October 1980.[66] The death of Tadzhikistan's First Secretary Dzhabar Resulov was announced on 5 April 1982; his successor was appointed fifteen days later.[67] The rapid and unexpected choice of Slyunkov as Belorussian first secretary seemed to indicate that by January 1983 Andropov already had enough power and authority to settle personnel matters decisively and speedily.

The most important appointment during the first six months of Andropov's tenure was that of Gromyko as first deputy chairman of the Council of Ministers.[68] This was the second appointment of a first deputy premier since Andropov came to power. As with the appointment of Aliyev to the same post four months previous, Andropov's probable motive was to counterbalance the influence of Tikhonov within the government: Significantly, the decision to appoint Gromyko was made while Tikhonov was visiting in Yugoslavia.[69] An interesting aspect of the appointment was the 1953 precedent of appointing the minister of defense (then Nikolay Bulganin) first deputy chairman of the Council of Ministers, to serve in this post simultaneously with the foreign minister (then Vyacheslav Molotov).[70] Andropov only promoted Gromyko. Did this indicate strained relations with Ustinov or an attempt by the general secretary to assert his authority among the powerful Politburo members to whose support he owed his position? Various pointers, such as Ustinov's absence from several important events (e.g., the 9 July 1983 celebration of the fortieth anniversary of the Battle of Kursk)[71] and the appointment of Romanov as Central Committee secretary (an appointment that seemed to encroach upon Ustinov's areas of responsibility), did indicate a certain tension in relations between Andropov and Ustinov.

More appointments clearly reflecting Andropov's influence followed. In March 1983, the Novosti chief Lev Tolkunov was made editor-in-chief of *Izvestiya*.[72] He had joined Andropov's staff in the Central Committee East European Countries Department in 1957 and by 1963 had risen to the post of first deputy head of that department; he was Andropov's second in command. His replacement as Novosti chief, Pavel Naumov, had also worked in the CPSU Central Committee apparatus and had worked in *Pravda* as head of the department dealing with East European affairs (during the period that Andropov headed the analogous department in the Central Committee). On 13 April 1983 *Izvestiya* announced the appointment of Yuriy Batalin as the new head of the State Committee for Labor and Social Problems, a post presumably considered important by Andropov because of the emphasis he had been placing on labor discipline in his proposals for reviving the Soviet economy.

On 10 April 1983 *Izvestiya* announced the appointments of Sergey Afanasyev as minister of heavy and transportation machine building and of Oleg Baklanov as minister of general machine building.

The *Sobraniye Postanovleniy Pravitelstva*, no. 7, 1983 (Collected Decrees of the USSR Government), pp. 141–144, officially noted the appointment of no less than six new deputy ministers in various economic ministries. These, as well as other new appointments in the republics, seemed to indicate that by April 1983 Andropov was already in a position to initiate sweeping changes in the structure of different ministries. Moreover, another appointment showed that Andropov had managed to extend his influence even over the party apparatus, which previously had been Chernenko's stronghold. On 29 April 1983 Yegor Ligachev was promoted from his post as head of the CPSU Tomsk obkom to the post of head of the Central Committee Party Organizational Work Department,[73] where he replaced Central Committee Secretary Ivan Kapitonov. The appointment hinted that Ligachev was heading toward the Secretariat, and this soon became a fact. Ligachev had been first secretary of the Tomsk obkom since 1965.[74] Although no relations between Andropov and Ligachev are known, the fact that the appointment was made when Chernenko was apparently ill (he had been absent from public view since 30 March) indicates that Chernenko was probably not even consulted about the appointment. It seems plausible that the Ligachev appointment was aimed at counterbalancing the CPSU apparatus officials, many of whom had been associated with Brezhnev and Chernenko, with someone from the periphery who was not associated with the two leaders.

Thus, by May 1983 Andropov seemed to have succeeded in strengthening his position, asserting his authority, and rallying enough support in the party and state apparatus to initiate and carry through substantial personnel reshuffles, at least in selected areas of the administration. In retrospect, most of the appointments and demotions made prior to May 1983 appear to have been in connected with Andropov's drive for more efficiency in the economy and stronger labor discipline. Few of the appointments and demotions (e.g., Gromyko, Ligachev, and possibly Aliyev) had political connotations. In May 1983 Andropov still occupied only one of the three posts previously held by Brezhnev: He was general secretary of the CPSU Central Committee but not yet chairman of the Defense Council or chairman of the Supreme Soviet Presidium. He was unable to remove his opponents from the Politburo, and only in the case of Tikhonov was he able to curb an opponent's authority by appointing two additional first deputy premiers, Gromyko and Aliyev. From October 1980 until Aliyev's appointment, Tikhonov had only a single deputy, Ivan Arkhipov, who was not a Politburo member but was an old ally of Brezhnev. By May 1983 Tikhonov had two full Politburo members as first deputies, which clearly lessened his power and authority. However, Tikhonov continued as chairman of the Council of Ministers, and together with Chernenko, Kunayev, and apparently Grishin formed an effective bloc vote in the Politburo capable of checking and even foiling Andropov's moves. Where it counted most—in the Politburo and the Secretariat—Andropov was not able to achieve much through personnel reshuffling. Depite all expectations, Ryzhkov was not elected a full member of the Politburo, and even Slyunkov was not given Belorussia's automatic seat among the candidate members of the Politburo.

In a different vein, Andropov succeeded in cultivating a populistic image of a leader devoted to strengthening discipline, improving production efficiency, and remedying the diverse social maladies of the Soviet people, such as alcoholism. This image was carefully promoted not only by unusual events such as his 31 January visit to the Sergo Ordzhonikidze plant but also by various articles and interviews describing him as a leader of a different breed. In one such interview, given to the Stockholm paper *Dagens Nyheter* on 27 February, Aleksandr Bovin, one of Andropov's closest associates and a prominent radio and television commentator, dwelled extensively on the "purely human difference" between Brezhnev and Andropov, promising that 1983 would be "an optimistic and youthful year."[75]

By May 1983 the signals indicating Andropov's power and authority were somewhat mixed. Although blocked by Chernenko's group from introducing any major personnel changes in the Politburo or the Secretariat and from obtaining the post of chairman of the Supreme Soviet Presidium and the chairmanship of the Defense Council, he had generated sufficient power to initiate personnel changes at the ministerial and lower levels and to project the image of a new type of leader, devoted to steady serious work, to improving the Soviet economy, and to combating various social weaknesses.

Chernenko as a Defeated Rival— Mixed Signals

Chernenko appeared to have quickly recovered from his humiliation following Brezhnev's death. He remained much in public view, attending major cultural and scientific events. For example, on 3 December 1982, together with the Moscow First Secretary Grishin, he attended a joint plenum of the Writers' Union, Artists' Union, Cinema Workers' Union, and other creative arts organizations,[76] and on 8 December 1982 he was the only full Politburo member to attend a session of the Academy of Sciences.[77] Furthermore, the Andropov regime adopted some policies that had been espoused in the past by Chernenko. In particular, the 10 December 1982 announcement of the Politburo concerning the value of citizens' letters[78] echoed Chernenko's virtually single-handed efforts of recent years to force the party and state bureaucracies to be more responsive to such letters. In addition, *Pravda*'s editorial of 6 December concerning work with the cadres used Chernenko's term *glasnost* to refer to the open approach to personnel appointments, involving "wide publicity." During the celebrations marking the sixtieth anniversary of the USSR, Chernenko appeared second only to Andropov. He opened the ceremonies on the first day and on most occasions could be seen at Andropov's side.[79]

On 5 January the "Vremya" program of the Soviet television showed Chernenko stepping in front of the other leaders to greet Andropov on the latter's return from the Warsaw Pact meeting in Prague.[80] Chernenko was also singled out for special praise in the new installment of Brezhnev's memoirs signed to print on 20 December and published in the January 1983 issue of *Novyy Mir*. Moreover, an article of his on nationalities policy was published in the December 1982 issue of *Problemy Mira I Sotsializma,*[81] and in late November he was awarded the honorary position (formerly held by Suslov) of head of the USSR Supreme Soviet Foreign Affairs Commission.[82] Finally, on 27 December, together with Boris Ponomarev, he met a delegation of the Argentinian Communist party.[83] All this showed that Chernenko retained at least some of his former prominence.

However, unmistakable signs of his diminished authority and re-stricted room for action also appeared. For the first time since 1976, Chernenko did not participate in the Soviet delegation to the Warsaw Pact summit, a biennial affair, which in January 1983 was held in Prague.[84] Furthermore, he appeared to be virtually excluded from taking part in high-level meetings with foreign leaders. It will be remembered that before Brezhnev's death Chernenko had regularly participated with Brezhnev in meetings with foreign leaders and had played an increasingly active role in foreign affairs. For example, in 1982 alone Chernenko in the company of Brezhnev and other leaders met Wojciech Jaruzelski, Gustav Husak, Erich Honecker, Thruong Chihn (of Vietnam), Muham-mad Ali Nasir (of the People's Democratic Republic of the Yemen), and Mengistu Haile Mariam (of Ethiopia). In February 1982 he traveled to France to attend the Congress of the French Communist party and met with Marchais. After Brezhnev's death these leaders and numerous others paid visits to Moscow and met Andropov but without Chernenko being present.

Toward the end of the year it became apparent that Andropov had succeeded in maneuvering Chernenko out of some important positions that the latter had previously controlled. The supervision of the party's organizational apparatus (Chernenko had been Brezhnev's "organiza-tional" secretary—a vital position concerned with the delicate issue of personnel), as well as the supervision of intraparty communication, the police, and the military, were no longer in Chernenko's hands. He was appointed chairman of the Supreme Soviet Foreign Affairs Com-mission, but this appointment was largely ceremonial, as disclosed by

Chernenko's absence from the really important meetings with foreign leaders. By the end of the year Chernenko's only field of supervision was ideology, an area that had been commanded by Suslov for so many years. This development was indicated both by Chernenko's increased participation in various cultural events and by his appointment as head of the Foreign Affairs Commission, a post that had been held by Suslov for many years.

January marked a low ebb in Chernenko's fortunes. He did not appear in public for several weeks and was not reported present at the 17 January opening of the Artists' Union Congress[85] or at the 29 January Central Committee conference on propaganda work,[86] even though both events fell within his areas of supervision. Chernenko's book, *The Vanguard Role of the Communist Party,* published in February 1983, received minimum publicity, a glaring depature from the customary practice. The first review of the book was in *Voprosy Istorii KPSS,*[87] a journal that had played an active part in boosting Chernenko's prestige during the last stage of Brezhnev's life. The magazine featured the review very prominently and even attempted to present the book as an original new work rather than a collection of Chernenko's previously published pronouncements. In a transparent attempt to remind everyone that Chernenko was supposed to be the chief party ideologist, the review stressed the importance of the book as an ideological text, describing the publication as an "important event in the ideological-political life of the party."[88] Other reviews appeared somewhat later, suggesting that editors' hesitation was eventually overcome by pressure from Chernenko's faction.

Another book by Chernenko, *Asserting the Leninist Style in Party Work,* published in April, fared somewhat better. Soviet television promptly reported its publication, noting rather dryly that "the book contains works from the 1981-82 period,"[89] and *Pravda* gave it a positive review in an extensive, though unattributed, article.[90]

The fact that the Soviet press failed to unequivocally and vociferously praise the words of the Central Committee secretary in charge of ideology was a clear indication of Chernenko's ambiguous status during this period. However, the varying treatment of Chernenko's works in the different newspapers and journals does not imply that the central press was joining in the succession struggle and indicating its preferences. More likely individual journalists, whose careers had been advanced by different leaders, were acting in accordance with their political loyalties and sympathies. A famous example of such action was when Alexsey Adzhubey, Khrushchev's son-in-law and *Izvestiya's* chief editor, in October 1964 managed to publish the announcement of Khrushchev's "retirement" one day later than *Pravda.* This postponement did not indicate *Izvestiya's* own stance on the matter but only the personal attitude of Adzhubey. Other instances of the involvement of leading Soviet journalists in the succession struggle are given in Chapter 3 (the case of the absence of *Izvestiya*'s chief editor Lev Tolkunov) and in Chapter 6 (Bugayev's and Chikin's articles in *Kommunist*).

Chernenko was not seen in public from 30 March through April, again missing important events such as the 18 April 1983 Agricultural Conference (at which Andropov made a speech and which was attended by virtually all party leaders from the national, republican, and regional levels)[91] and the regular 22 April Lenin Day meeting. Since the Soviet newspapers continued regularly to publish obituaries signed by Chernenko, and since his book was mentioned on Soviet television in April and later well reviewed in *Pravda,* Chernenko's absence evidently was not the result of political disgrace or tacit removal from office. However, when he failed to attend the 1 May parade in Moscow[92] persistent rumors concerning his ousting began to appear in the Western mass media. Ignoring the fact that Chernenko's portrait did appear among those in Red Square,[93] France Press news agency commented on 1 May: "Konstantin Chernenko, who ranks second in the Soviet hierarchy, was believed by observers here to be in serious difficulties, because of his absence from the traditional May Day celebrations today in Red Square."[94]

The rumors and speculations apparently prompted sources close to Chernenko to report several days later that he had resumed at least part of his official duties:

> Konstantin Chernenko, the virtual No. 2 of the Soviet Communist Party, who was reportedly ill for over a month, has recovered sufficiently to deal with some of his duties, the Central Committee Secretariat told Agence France Press today.
>
> The Secretariat said that Mr. Chernenko, who is 71, had officially returned to his office, but worked there three hours a day to check incoming business.[95]

Soon after, on 1 June, at the funeral of Politburo member Arvid Pelshe,[96] Chernenko appeared in his customary third place in the official leadership lineup, after Andropov and Tikhonov. The "slight cold" reported by the Western media on the basis of Moscow leaks and rumors[97] was evidently over. The observers eagerly awaited the upcoming Central Committee plenum and Supreme Soviet session scheduled for mid-June, at which a major showdown between the two rival factions was expected to take place.

The Press—Mixed Signals

Mixed signals indicating the relative status and strength of the leaders were not the only pointers to continuing instability at the top. Another sign was the different, at times discrepant themes selected by the central newspapers for their editorials, in particular immediately after 12 November 1982 when the Central Committee plenum elected Andropov general secretary. Both Chernenko and Andropov spoke at the plenum. Although their speeches appeared to be similar (both relatively brief speeches focused on Brezhnev's death), each included themes not mentioned by the other.

The key sentences in Andropov's speech must have sounded attractive to those giving a high priority to defense.

> We know very well that one cannot obtain peace from the imperialists simply by asking for it. Peace can be defended only by relying on the invincible might of the Soviet armed forces. As a party and state leader and chairman of the USSR Defense Council, Leonid Ilich paid unceasing attention to keeping the country's defense capability at the level of current requirements.[98]

Although Chernenko did not directly contradict Andropov, he hinted at different priorities. He stressed peaceful coexistence and domestic issues to the point of observing that defense "depended on economic development." He further added: "Our policy objectives will continue to be the welfare of the people and the preservation of peace on earth."[99] Chernenko had words of approval for the country's "well-considered" socioeconomic program and its "broad and concrete peace program." He then added that "detente, disarmament, resolution of conflicts, and elimination of the threat of nuclear war are the tasks that face us ahead." Both speeches appeared in the press on 13 November, and quotations from them (without attribution) began appearing in editorials on 14 and 15 November.

Krasnaya Zvezda's editorial on 14 November was virtually "Andropov writ large." The major emphasis of Andropov's speech was elaborated and its implications spelled out. The editorial noted "attempts of aggressive imperialist circles to disrupt peaceful coexistence" and concluded that "one cannot obtain peace from the imperialists simply by asking for it. Peace can be defended only by relying on the invincible might of the Soviet armed forces." This was a direct, though unattributed, quotation from Andropov's speech. However, *Pravda, Sovetskaya Rossiya,* and *Selskaya Zhizn* ignored Andropov's statement on the importance of defense. *Pravda*'s editorial on 14 November focused on domestic policy issues while mentioning foreign policy objectives in distinctly unbellicose terms. All major republican newspapers and some central newspapers reprinted this editorial.

In addition to ignoring Andropov's emphasis on defense, some papers chose to quote Chernenko, though mostly without attribution. *Sovetskaya Rossiya* on 14 November used Chernenko's precise words: "Detente, disarmanent, resolution of conflicts, and elimination of the threat of nuclear war are the tasks that face us ahead." *Izvestiya* of 15 November quoted Chernenko's statement that "our policy objectives will continue to be the welfare of the people and the preservation of peace on earth." The same paper also quoted Chernenko's statement implying that economic development had a higher priority than defense. (However, the *Izvestiya* editor-in-chief was soon after replaced by Andropov's long-time associate Lev Tolkunov.) There were other similar inconsistencies. For example, *Pravda* refrained from extolling Andropov, and the *Krasnaya Zvezda* editorial surprisingly advocated collective leadership, a theme raised by no other newspaper.

A possible explanation of the discrepancies between the editorials of November 14 and 15 (and similar discrepancies following the June 1983 Central Committee plenum, and even during the first period of Gorbachev's tenure in March-June 1985) is that there was no single authoritative document to provide thematic guidance. (Observation of the behavior of the Soviet press over the years indicates that the authors of editorials select their themes from a common set of authoritative documents, usually from the pronouncements of top party leaders.) The lack of such documents throughout November was a clear sign of instability within the top leadership.

Another piece of evidence pointing to unrest at the top was the editorial of *Kommunist,* no. 18, December 1982, signed to press on 14 December. Touching upon themes and using codewords that have traditionally indicated disagreement within the party leadership, it signaled that a struggle, probably based on personal rivalry, was in progress in the Kremlin. The editorial warned that disunity in the party is apt to weaken the Soviet state, a prospect "realized by the USSR's enemies." The same editorial stressed that Lenin always fought "uncompromisingly against any manifestations of cliquishness or factionalism in the party." It quoted the resolution of the 10th Party Congress (in 1921), which prohibited the formation of factions within the party and demanded the "unconditional, immediate expulsion" of all violators of this prohibition.[100]

The editorial could be interpreted as being directed against Chernenko (long identified with ideological inflexibility and an obvious target of any criticism related to factionalism) or simply as an effort to head off potential opposition when Andropov was about to consolidate his power. Some ideas expressed in the editorial could be construed as evidence in favor of the latter interpretation. "Careerism" and "affinity with the class enemies" were mentioned as vices that had developed within the inner circles of the party, and notice was served that the party statutes include all provisions necessary for "ridding the party's ranks of wayward and corrupt elements" and improving the "quality of its membership." Although it is impossible to prove that Andropov himself was behind the press references to factionalism, it is logical to assume that these articles were aimed against Chernenko and his faction, and therefore inspired, if not orchestrated, by Andropov's men. After all, Andropov was the general secretary, and consequently any accusations of factionalism could only be directed against those who contested his supremacy.

The theme was immediately taken up by other Soviet media. *Pravda* of 21 January carried an article by A. Sovokin, doctor of historical sciences, entitled "Ilich's Great Feat: On the 60th Anniversary of V. I. Lenin's Last Words." Being on very safe ground (quoting Lenin) the article was even more revealing and indicative than the *Kommunist* editorial:

> Lenin demanded the adoption of the necessary measures against the possibility of a split in the party, which the enemies of Soviet power were hoping for.
>
> Lenin's ideas about the party's unity, collective leadership and the party's leading, guiding role in building socialism and communism in our country retain their significance to this day.[101]

Valentin Chikin, who often appeared as the author of important and well-informed articles, went one step further in his piece "January Monologue," published by *Sovetskaya Rossiya* on 21 January. He quoted Lenin's explicit words: "I believe that such a thing is necessary to enhance the Central Committee's prestige [by increasing the size of the Central Committee], for serious work on improving our apparatus and to prevent conflicts between small sections of the Central Committee for assuming excessive significance." At this point Chikin contributed his own thoughts: "Concern for 'stability' is all-important. Which of our enemies does not gamble on a split and on serious disagreements within the party? History has many sad lessons."[102]

The theme persisted, despite the signs of Andropov's consolidation. Three months later Chikin published an article (*Kommunist,* no. 6, April 1983) entitled, "V. I. Lenin: 'These Are the Lofty Tasks of Which I Am Dreaming.'" Extensively drawing upon his previous *Sovetskaya Rossiya* article and reproducing entire passages including the key sentence on "stability," Chikin pointed out that "while confined to bed by illness and on strict medical instructions," Lenin continued his work. After dwelling on the importance of stability and the danger of splits, Chikin outlined the preferred image of the Communist leader, once again safely basing his ideas on Lenin's own words:

> Vladimir Ilich was very concerned for the authority of the Communist, particularly the leader. Of course, this is a special authority, but it is never created by titles or decrees, but is formed of its own accord by the natural process of life. Lenin was always impressed by the ideal of the leader and comrade before whose superiority you bow down in the knowledge that he will always understand and, in turn, wants to be understood.[103]

Gorbachev—The Third Man

While observers of the power struggle in the Kremlin were focusing their attention on the moves of the two major stars—Andropov and Chernenko—a third man was waiting in the wings, Mikhail Sergeyevich Gorbachev, who was slowly but steadily and persistently acquiring prominence and power. Although the youngest member of the Politburo (born on 2 March 1931 in Privolnoye, Stavropol kray),[104] Gorbachev possessed the major asset essential for advancement to the very top: He was a member of both the Politburo and the Secretariat. Furthermore, although he was originally responsible for agriculture, under Andropov he expanded his areas of involvement.

Gorbachev's enhanced position was clearly evident at the end of 1982. He was a major figure at the 21 and 22 December celebrations marking the sixtieth anniversary of the founding of the USSR,[105] chairing one of the ceremonial meetings and thus sharing the status of Chernenko, Tikhonov, and Ustinov. On 7 January 1983 he attended a meeting of senior party officials, at which Andropov's campaign for strengthening discipline was launched.[106]

It soon became obvious that Gorbachev frequently acted as a second secretary under Andropov or even as a vigorous and trusted deputy for Andropov, whose health was steadily declining. Gorbachev involved himself in areas unrelated to his official field of specialization—the agro-industrial complex. For example, on 20 March he signed the *Pravda* obituary of Sergey Postovalov, deputy chairman of the CPSU Control Committee; on 13 April 1983 he signed the obituary of a high army officer, Colonel General Pavel Yefimov[107] and on 2 June a *Pravda* obituary of a cultural figure, the theater and film actress Liliya Berzina. Usually such obituaries are signed only by the most senior leaders (if the rank of the deceased merits this) and by those active in the deceased's former area of specialization. Since Gorbachev had never been active in military and cultural affairs, and since Andropov and Chernenko were the only other senior leaders to sign all three obituaries, the implication was unmistakable: Gorbachev had joined the ranks of the chosen and had become a person to be reckoned with in the power game.

There were other indications of his enhanced power and prestige. On 10 February 1983 *Pravda* carried a substantial article by Gorbachev on agricultural matters. The article was immediately reprinted by the leading newspapers of most of the Soviet republics. On 19 March 1983 Gorbachev chaired an important all-union conference of party agricultural officials,[108] and on 18 April he spoke at a Central Committee conference on agriculture.[109] The conference was attended by the entire Politburo (except for Chernenko, who was suffering from a "slight cold"), a fact that accentuated Gorbachev's newly acquired prominence.

Gorbachev was again selected to deliver the main address at the 22 April 1983 public meeting in Moscow marking the 113th anniversary of the birth of V. I. Lenin.[110] Since Chernenko was still absent, Gorbachev basked in the public light free of any competition, under Andropov's benevolent gaze. Gorbachev demonstrated considerable diplomatic skill— by quoting both Andropov and Brezhnev—and touched upon the subject of developing closer relations between the party and the masses—a favorite subject of Chernenko, without mentioning him by name.[111]

One area in which Gorbachev had no record was foreign policy. To rectify the situation, in May 1983 he was sent to Canada as the leader of a USSR Supreme Soviet delegation. There for the first time he displayed the qualities that in 1984-1985 became his hallmark—so-phistication, a quick wit, ability to answer unpleasant questions and, most of all, a solid, quiet, and impressive presence. These qualities were most evident at his 17 May meeting with the Canadian Parliament Standing Committee on External Affairs and National Defense, many of whose members were hostile to him. While handling critical and even belligerent questions with assurance, knowledge, and even aggressiveness, he displayed charm and good humor and eventually impressed both the Canadian parliamentarians and the mass media.[112]

Gorbachev's special status became even clearer after Andropov's disappearance from public view in August. However, as early as in April Vadim Zagladin, then the first deputy chief of the CPSU Central Committee International Department, stated in an interview for *Le Monde* that one should not concentrate on the succession of Brezhnev by Andropov but on the replacement of Brezhnev, Suslov, and Kirilenko by Andropov, Chernenko, and Gorbachev, thus indicating the extraordinary status of the other two top leaders.[113] This remark might also have implied the formation of a form of collective leadership in the USSR. If so, it certainly was a strange collective that included two bitter rivals—Andropov and Chernenko—each warily watching and trying to block the moves of the other and a young ambitious leader regarded as heir apparent by Andropov and as a potential rival by Chernenko. However, the most significant aspect of Zagladin's comment was the elevation of Gorbachev to equal status with Andropov and Chernenko. Zagladin, who enjoyed excellent sources of inside information, was evidently predicting the future course of the Soviet power allotment.

Thus, even before the critical June 1983 Central Committee plenum and Andropov's disappearance in August, Mikhail Gorbachev had already acquired a special position and extraordinary importance, which were to grow in the months to come. Nevertheless, as long as Chernenko was active and his faction remained powerful enough to block many of Andropov's moves, Gorbachev was not yet a full-fledged contender in the power game but more the player in the wings, awaiting (with confident certainty) his opportunity.

4

Andropov's Eclipse:
Ruling by Remote Control

April and May were months of quiet consolidation of Andropov's power; they included no events favoring Chernenko's cause and the latter remained out of public view. He made a public appearance on 30 March at a Marx centennial celebration at the Bolshoy Theater in Moscow[1] but then disappeared until the end of May. Andropov, although in no better health than Chernenko, took full advantage of Chernenko's absence. On 9 May 1983 *Pravda* carried an article by Marshal Ustinov in commemoration of the victory of World War II, which contained an astonishing reference to Andropov as the "chairman of the USSR Defense Council." In fact, Andropov's appointment to that post had never been officially announced. Nevertheless, in what may have been a hint at Andropov's long-standing membership on the Council, Ustinov pointed out that Andropov "had already had a direct part in determining military policy for many years."[2]

On 1 June Chernenko reappeared in public for Pelshe's funeral. The lineup at the funeral seemed to indicate the enhanced status of Ustinov and Gromyko, who alternated as fourth and fifth in rank, following Andropov, Tikhonov, and Chernenko. However, all important inferences about possible status changes had to be put off until the forthcoming Central Committee plenum and Supreme Soviet sessions; during them the appointments to the vacancy in the Politburo and the chairmanship of the Control Committee (which had been headed by Pelshe since 1966)[3] would be made and whether Andropov would finally be elected chairman of the USSR Supreme Soviet Presidium would be determined. The anticipation was even keener in view of the reports of Andropov's deteriorating health, which could no longer be concealed. In his public appearances in May and June Andropov was noticeably pale, frail, and on occasion visibly in pain. He was almost constantly assisted when walking, and the trembling of his hands was painful to watch.

The Plenum

The plenums of the CPSU Central Committee merely approve the decisions previously adopted by the Politburo. Therefore, the communiqué on the regular weekly Politburo meeting published on 10 June, four days before the Central Committee plenum was scheduled to open, was eagerly anticipated. The communiqué turned out to be disappointing. According to the published text, the Politburo had reviewed the "results of the Soviet-Finnish talks which took place in Moscow during the official visit of Mauno Koivisto, president of the Finnish Republic"; "information about the conversation Yuriy Andropov, general secretary of the CPSU Central Committee, had with the notable political and public figures, Averell and Pamela Harriman"; "the progress of the public discussion of the draft law of the USSR on work collectives"; "the construction and putting into operation of atomic heat supply stations in 1983–1990"; and "Andrey Gromyko's account of the results of his conversations with Fernando Moran, minister of foreign affairs of Spain."[4] There was no hint that any personnel or organizational issues had formed part of the Politburo's deliberations.

Ostensibly, the CPSU Central Committee plenum that convened on 14 June was to deal with "questions of the ideological and mass political work of the party."[5] However, what is known in the party parlance as organizational matters—personnel changes—drew the attention of observers. A further matter of interest was whether the power play in the Kremlin would be reflected in any way in the plenum's proceedings. The contradictory indications of Chernenko's status and Andropov's position, as well as the relative standings of the other leading members of the Politburo, were expected to be partially clarified.

Surprisingly, the opening address at the plenum was delivered by Chernenko. The very fact that he had been assigned to deliver the major address challenged the view that his position was precarious. It now appeared that the months of absence from public view and the persistent rumors of his downfall had failed to affect his status. A second surprise was Chernenko's efforts to demonstrate his loyalty to Andropov by trying to curry favor with him at the very beginning of his speech:

> The decisions of the November 1982 plenary meetings of the Central Committee of the CPSU, which continued the line of the 26th Party Congress and confirmed the continuity of its domestic and foreign policy, are supported by all the people. The working people of the Soviet Union ardently approve the activity of the CPSU Central Committee, and of its Politburo headed by General Secretary of the Central Committee Yuriy Vladimirovich Andropov.[6]

The recognition of Andropov as "head of the Politburo" appeared in the resolution adopted at the close of the plenum:

> Having heard and discussed the report of Comrade K.U. Chernenko, member of the Political Bureau, secretary of the CPSU Central Committee, the plenary meeting of the CPSU Central Committee points out that the ideological and political situation in the country is characterized by the further cohesion of Soviet people around the Communist Party of the Soviet Union, its Central Committee, and the Political Bureau of the Central Committee with Yuriy Vladimirovich Andropov at the head.[7]

Since the expression "head of the Politburo" could not have been used unintentionally (although the title is informal and unofficial and in itself implies no additional power, its use is an accurate criterion for evaluating the strength of the general secretary), and since Chernenko's status was clearly reflected at the plenum by his selection to deliver the main report, it might be assumed that some kind of a deal had been worked out between the two Kremlin factions.

Andropov himself delivered a report on the second day of the plenum. His report, like Chernenko's, contained no indications of the situation prevailing in the Politburo. He focused on the future ideological work of the party, strongly emphasizing the importance of the new edition of the party program, "which is being prepared on decisions of the 26th Congress, and which is to play an exceptionally important role for ideological work and for the party's entire work in general."[8] Andropov did not hesitate to criticize some of the ridiculous aspects of the old party program adopted under Khrushchev in 1961 (which spoke of the Soviet Union's overtaking the U.S. standard of living within twenty years), although he refrained from specifying them: "Much of what is recorded in the program has already been fulfilled. At the same time, some of its provisions, and this must be said straightforwardly, have not withstood in full measure the test of time because they contained elements of separation from reality, of anticipating things, and of unjustified detailedness."[9]

Furthermore, when speaking about the use of radio and television for propaganda purposes, Andropov did not refrain from mentioning his opponent's name: "All this was mentioned at length both in Comrade Konstantin Ustinovich Chernenko's report and in the debate."[10] This reference strengthened the impression that a deal, or perhaps merely a cease-fire, had been reached between the two factions.

The most eagerly awaited result of the plenum was the report on the personnel changes at the top. At noon on 15 June, the second day of the plenum, the full list of the changes was published:

> The plenum of the CPSU Central Committee elected member of the Political Bureau of the CPSU Central Committee Grigoriy Romanov secretary of the CPSU Central Committee.

The plenum of the CPSU Central Committee endorsed Mikhail Solomentsev, alternate [candidate] member of the Political Bureau of the CPSU Central Committee, as chairman of the Party Control Committee at the CPSU Central Committee.

The plenum of the CPSU Central Committee elected Vitaliy Vorotnikov alternate member of the Political Bureau of the CPSU Central Committee.

The plenum of the CPSU Central Committee promoted to full membership the following alternate members of the CPSU Central Committee: Sergey Akhromeyev, first deputy chief of the General Staff of the USSR Armed Forces; Boris Balmont, minister of the Machine-Tool Building and Instrument-Making Industry; Vyacheslav Kochemasov, ambassador extraordinary and plenipotentiary of the USSR to the GDR; Vasiliy Cherdintsev, a grain combine operator of the collective farm "Rassvet" in the Orenburg region, and Vitaliy Shabanov, deputy defense minister of the USSR.

The plenum of the CPSU Central Committee excluded Nikolay Shchelokov and Sergey Medunov from the CPSU Central Committee for mistakes they had made in their work.[11]

The first obvious conclusion was that Andropov was again unable to add any new full members to the Politburo, which after Pelshe's death contained only eleven full members. Indeed, the fact that Aliyev had been the only full member to be added to the Politburo since 1980 clearly demonstrated the great difficulty in reaching a consensus on the election of new full members to that body.

A further conclusion related to Chernenko's power. The personnel changes approved by the plenum demonstrated that he was unable to protect Brezhnev's former protégés. The two members of the Central Committee expelled by the plenum, Medunov and Shchelokov, had been associated with Brezhnev and therefore almost certainly with Chernenko.[12] Both men had been disgraced following investigations apparently conducted by the KGB into alleged instances of personal corruption. Sergey Medunov was first secretary of the Krasnodar kray before his removal in July 1982; Nikolay Shchelokov was replaced as minister of foreign affairs on 17 December 1982.[13] Their ousting from the Central Committee indicated that the investigation of their activities had continued even after their dismissal from their other posts and that Chernenko had been powerless to help them either during the investigations or at the plenum itself. Thus their ousting, when no new full members were being elected to the Politburo, suggested a deadlock between the two factions or rather their approximately equal strength, at least during the period of the plenum.

Another interesting result of the plenum was the promotion of two military men—Marshal of the USSR Sergey Akhromeyev, a first deputy chief of General Staff, and Army General Vitaliy Shabanov, deputy minister of defense for armaments—to full membership of the Central Committee. The simultaneous appointment of two military figures to the Central Committee was not a routine matter; it indicated that

Andropov was already repaying his debt to the military for their support in November 1982 when he was elected general secretary. In the same vein, the election to the Central Committee of Vyacheslav Kochemasov, the USSR ambassador to the German Democratic Republic (GDR), was a clear case of promoting an old associate. During the late 1950's Kochemasov had been an assistant to Andropov in the Central Committee's Socialist Countries Department.[14]

The election of Vitaliy Vorotnikov as candidate member of the Politburo was a clear demonstration of Andropov's confidence in him. Vorotnikov had been sent by Brezhnev to Cuba as ambassador, after having held the post of first deputy premier of the RSFSR (Russian Soviet Federated Socialist Republic) from 1975 to 1979. In July 1982 he was recalled from Cuba and sent to Krasnodar to rectify the situation created there by Medunov's transgressions. His election to the Politburo (as a candidate member) indicated that Vorotnikov could soon expect to be transferred to more responsible posts. On 28 June *Pravda* reported Vorotnikov's appointment as chairman of the RSFSR Council of Ministers. His career was evidently blooming.

Mikhail Solomentsev's election to the chairmanship of the Party Control Committee seemed to have no apparent connection with the power play in the Kremlin because Solomentsev himself was not a major figure and because of the very nature of the post. The position of Party Control Committee chairman carries little personal influence; indeed it had been held for more than twenty years by Pelshe, one of the less powerful Politburo members.

The most interesting new personnel change was the promotion of Politburo member Grigoriy Romanov to the post of Central Committee secretary. Romanov was one of the younger members of the Politburo and certainly one of the more ambitious. He had no known connections with Andropov or Chernenko, and Leningrad—his political fortress— was not one of the party centers that had hailed Andropov as "head of the Politburo" immediately after Brezhnev's death. There had been no previous indications that Romanov was due for promotion: No change had been noted in his semiofficial position in the leadership lineup, and no known new duties had been assigned to him. The areas of supervision that he would be allocated in his new capacity of Central Committee secretary had yet to be seen.

The Supreme Soviet Session

The 14–15 June plenum of the CPSU Central Committee provided only partial and inconclusive answers about the relative strength of the two Kremlin factions. After the plenum the attention of observers was concentrated on the USSR Supreme Soviet session, which convened on 16 June. The crucial questions were whether, after seven embarrassing months, the USSR would finally have a new president and whether the person chosen would be Andropov.

Andropov as Supreme Leader

The session opened on 16 June. Immediately following the formal approval of the agenda, the first item of which was the election of the new chairman of the Supreme Soviet Presidium, the floor was given to Chernenko.[15] Chernenko clearly was not going to be elected chairman of the presidium (since he could hardly propose himself); again he seemed about to propose Andropov for a post that he dearly wanted himself. Chernenko's first sentence dispelled all doubts:

> Comrade Deputies: The CPSU Central Committee, the USSR Supreme Soviet Presidium, and the Councils of Elders of the Soviet of the Union and the Soviet of Nationalities of the Supreme Soviet introduce for your consideration a proposal for the election of Comrade Yuriy Vladimirovich Andropov, general secretary of the CPSU Central Committee, as chairman of the USSR Supreme Soviet Presidium.

After waiting for the applause to subside, Chernenko continued:

> Comrades, this question was considered at the Central Committee plenum. In an atmosphere of complete unanimity, the plenum considered it justifiable that Comrade Yuriy Vladimirovich Andropov, general secretary of the CPSU Central Committee, should also hold the post of chairman of the USSR Supreme Soviet Presidium. [Applause] The CPSU Central Committee Politburo and the Central Committee plenum proceeded on the assumption that the rise in the Communist Party's leading and guiding role in the life of Soviet society and in our domestic and foreign policy is completely accepted by people here and abroad as proof of the indivisibility of the authority of the party and state, as an expression of the unity of mind and will of the party and the people.[16]

Thus Chernenko had confirmed that the Politburo and the Central Committee were responsible for the real decision, which he asserted was "proof of the indivisibility of party and state"; in other words, the concentration of the two posts in the same hands was considered a necessity, at least at that stage. No answer was offered to the obvious question of why this decision—demonstrating "the unity of mind and will of the party and the people"—was delayed for seven months.

A few hours later, Soviet television carried a report on the proceedings of the session. Soviet viewers saw a very frail Andropov, who rose to his feet unassisted but was evidently unable to walk without help. Accordingly, he read his acceptance speech while standing by his chair rather than on the central podium.[17] In a weak, low voice Andropov said:

Esteemed Comrade deputies. Allow me, from the bottom of my heart, to express to you warm gratitude and thanks for the great confidence that you have shown in me in electing me chairman of the USSR Supreme Soviet Presidium. I take your decision as an expression of confidence in our Leninist Communist Party, of which I have been a member for more than 40 years and to whose ideals I consider myself devoted.

Allow me to assure you that, in occupying the post of chairman of the Supreme Soviet Presidium, I will apply all my efforts, all my knowledge, and all my experience to justify your great confidence with honor.[18]

Incidentally, the decision to elect Andropov chairman of the USSR Supreme Soviet was naturally unanimously adopted by the Supreme Soviet deputies.[19]

Andropov's election closed the circle. He had now assumed the three posts held by Brezhnev—general secretary, chairman of the Defense Council, and chairman of the Supreme Soviet Presidium. His preeminence was now officially confirmed. However, the limited changes at the top of the party showed that, though the top posts were his, Andropov had still not generated sufficient power to resolve the deadlock within the Politburo and that Chernenko, despite his repeated humiliation, still had enough power to cause difficulties for Andropov. Chernenko's role at the Central Committee plenum and the Supreme Soviet session, though clearly subordinate to Andropov's, was prominent enough (as one of the two main speakers at the plenum and the person proposing Andropov at the Presidium session) to confirm his continuing power and influence. In addition, apparently on the basis of a behind-the-scenes deal between the two rivals, Chernenko had established himself as the arbiter of Soviet ideology and thus the full-fledged successor of Suslov, whereas Andropov became the supreme party and state leader. Although it was questionable whether Chernenko's ambitions were satisfied, for the time being this had to be enough.

Nevertheless, the idyllic situation in the Kremlin was more apparent than real, as evinced by the strange behavior of the Soviet press during the course of the two meetings. In a manner that by Soviet standards is extremely unusual, some newspapers, among them the Army daily *Krasnaya Zvezda* of 18 June 1983, carried on their front pages photographs of the Soviet leaders at the Supreme Soviet session in an order that deviated from that presented by *Pravda* and *Izvestiya* of 17 June. Although the party and government media organs showed Chernenko ranking third, the Army newspaper, as well as some local papers, had him in fifth place, assigning the third position to Defense Minister Marshal Ustinov. The photos showing Chernenko ranking third were all dated 17 June, whereas the pictures in *Krasnaya Zvezda* and the other newspapers that ranked him fifth were undated. This discrepancy could be explained by assuming that the different newspapers selected photos from different sessions of the Supreme Soviet proceedings or had simply caught Chernenko at a moment when he had temporarily changed his seat; however, since in the Soviet press little is left to chance, this hypothesis is hardly satisfactory.

The lengthy editorials of 19 June dealing with the Central Committee plenum provided even clearer evidence of the continuing efforts to undermine Chernenko's standing. *Pravda's* first edition on 19 June carried an editorial that focused on Andropov's speech at the plenum and completely ignored Chernenko's address, not even mentioning the fact that he had delivered a major report. Chernenko's faction reacted immediately, and the second edition of the same day was revised to include a brief reference to Chernenko's speech at the plenum. However, other newspapers continued to ignore him. *Selskaya Zhizn* of the same day failed to mention Chernenko and his speech, whereas *Krasnaya Zvezda* gave the title of the speech without specifying who had delivered it. *Izvestiya* and *Sovetskaya Rossiya* did refer to Chernenko, but most of the local press (except the Leningrad and Belorussian papers) reprinted on 21 June the first *Pravda* 19 June editorial (the version that ignored Chernenko).

Too many discrepancies occurred between November 1982 and June 1983 for them to have been inadvertent. The lack of unanimity could possibly be attributed in part to Chernenko's protracted absence in April and May 1983. More likely, however, a deliberate attempt was made to downgrade and perhaps even humiliate him; otherwise the discrepancies would not have appeared with such consistency. Although such an apparent lack of coordination in the coverage of Chernenko had been noticeable in the Soviet press on several previous occasions, disparities in the treatment of the same subjects as were apparent in the coverage of Chernenko are very unusual in a totalitarian society. They can only be explained by the hypothesis that Chernenko and his faction continued to enjoy some influence and power and as a result retained control of a part of the Soviet press, along with sections of the party apparatus; they thus were capable of preventing Andropov from imposing his will in all areas. The influence of Chernenko's faction was certainly evident in the Politburo, where Andropov proved unable to oust any of Chernenko's supporters, let alone Chernenko himself, thus making Chernenko the first unsuccessful contender for the primacy who retained his post. Although he no longer enjoyed the status he had had under Brezhnev and his areas of responsibility were limited to the field of ideology, he nevertheless remained a Politburo member and a Central Committee secretary.

July 1983 was Andropov's last full month of real activity. The general secretary evidently felt stronger because he had meetings with a Hungarian delegation led by Janos Kadar, with FRG Chancellor Helmut Kohl and Foreign Minister Hans-Dietrich Genscher, and with delegations from the French and Portuguese Communist parties. At least one foreign leader—Helmut Kohl—reported in interviews for West German[20] and Soviet television[21] that his meetings with Andropov had been valuable and that they were "frank and direct political conversations, without any diplomacy. One could say that this was man-to-man talk, that is, we spoke clearly, and we both greatly value this. . . . I met a man who, as the Germans say, hits the mark with his arguments."[22]

Gorbachev was also active during this period. He played a prominent part during Kadar's visit, accompanying him on a tour of the Moscow Likhachev Vehicle Plant, and separately received Ferenc Havasi, secretary of the Hungarian Party Central Committee.[23] Several days prior to the Hungarian delegation's visit he represented the Soviet leadership at the ceremony in Kursk to commemorate the fortieth anniversary of the famous World War II battle.[24] In his address on the occasion,[25] he expressed his approval and support for Andropov's appointment to the chairmanship of the USSR Supreme Soviet Presidium:

> The Soviet people welcomed with great enthusiasm the election of Yuriy Vladimirovich Andropov, general secretary of the CPSU Central Committee, as chairman of the USSR Supreme Soviet Presidium. This corresponds with the supreme interests of the party and the state and will help enhance our party's leading and guiding role, will help the more successful solution of the tasks of communist building and of strengthening peace on earth.[26]

Gorbachev represented the Central Committee Secretariat at the 21 June Leningrad CPSU obkom plenum, at which L. Zaykov was elected first secretary to replace Romanov, who had been elected Central Committee secretary by the Central Committee June plenum.[27] This event underscored Gorbachev's involvement in organizational matters and showed that his areas of responsibility were still expanding.

Andropov's Career Fades

As July drew to its end, so did Andropov's career. On 29 July a public meeting in Moscow marked the eightieth anniversary of the Second Congress of the Russian Social Democratic Labor Party. In its first report on the meeting TASS stated: "In the presidium of the celebration meeting were Yuriy Andropov, the general secretary of the CPSU Central Committee and president of the Presidium of the USSR Supreme Soviet, and other Soviet leaders."[28] Some two hours later TASS, in a correction to the first version, gave a list of the names of the attending leaders that did not include Andropov's, but it added: "The honorary presidium consisting of the Politburo of the CPSU Central Committee with Yuriy Andropov as its head was enthusiastically elected."[29] On the following day, *Pravda* repeated that Andropov had been elected to the honorary presidium, "consisting of the CPSU Central Committee Politburo headed by Comrade Yuriy Vladimirovich Andropov."[30] The explanation seems obvious: Andropov was scheduled to attend, as stated in the first TASS report, but failed to show up, probably for health reasons, so that TASS was obliged to correct its initial version.

Soon after, Andropov resumed some of his regular activities. For example, on 17 August he received William Winpinsinger, president of the International Association of Machinists and Aerospace Workers (USA) and made a detailed presentation of USSR foreign policy.[31] On the following day, 18 August, he received a group of visiting U.S. Democratic senators led by Claiborne Pell and gave another presentation of Soviet foreign policy.[32] According to *Pravda* of 30 September 1983, on the previous day Andropov had met a delegation from South Yemen, led by Muhammad Ali Nasir. In contrast to the normal practice, the newspapers carried no photos of the meeting nor was its location disclosed. Thus, Andropov's meeting with the U.S. senators was his last official public appearance.

A few days earlier on 15 August, when attending a Kremlin meeting with party veterans, Andropov (perhaps sensing that the end was approaching) delivered an unusual speech—his farewell to his public political life. Frail and pensive, Andropov said:

> Nevertheless, age is age and a veteran's transfer to a well-earned rest is linked to the change in normal living standards. Withdrawal from activity in a pursuit one loves is not simple. With age, illness lies in wait for a person, and at times all this is accompanied by difficult spiritual tribulations. Even the most complete society is not capable of banishing all this completely, but wherever they occur both spiritual tribulations and material difficulties can be alleviated. This we must do.[33]

Although at the time the speech drew relatively little attention, it was in fact a unique document, comparable in some ways to Lenin's "Testament." Andropov, the hardened Chekist, was bidding farewell to his generation but in a different way from Lenin. Exploiting the fact that he was addressing a sympathetic audience whose members were of similar age to himself and many of whom no doubt suffered similar ailments, Andropov made these highly personal and unprecedented remarks. Unlike Lenin, he did not evaluate the personal qualities of his fellow Politburo members nor did he make any recommendations. Instead, he expressed sorrow that he had not been granted time to accomplish his plans and hope that others would complete his task.

Ostensibly, Andropov was making a general statement on the problems of old age. However, those who knew that since February he had been undergoing regular kidney dialysis (as stated in the medical bulletin on his death) sensed that he was speaking about himself. He implied that a new succession was approaching and stressed that "each generation is in some ways stronger than the previous one, knows more and sees farther."[34] This speech, not the 17 and 18 August meetings with U.S. visitors, should be seen as Andropov's final important policy act as the supreme leader. Incidentally, Gorbachev played a prominent part at the party veterans meeting, both serving as chairperson and delivering a short opening address.[35]

From August 1983 to February 1984 the USSR was a country without a leader. The infighting intensified in the Kremlin, and Chernenko, after a prolonged period of diminished public activity, emerged once more in the center of political developments. Nevertheless, obvious efforts were made by members of the Andropov faction, with the support of the Soviet media, to create the impression that Andropov was still at the helm. Andropov continued to be referred to as "head of the Politburo" by other leaders and to sign telegrams and obituaries. Quotations from his writings were included in all major speeches by leading Soviets. At least some leaders were clearly taking great pains to obfuscate the fact of Andropov's absence from public view.

On 30 October *Pravda* carried Andropov's "Reply to the Appeal of the Third International Congress 'World Physicians for the Prevention of Nuclear War.'" In this item Andropov felt compelled to explain his absence:

> It is with great attention and interest that I read the message passed on to me a few days ago, addressed by your authoritative forum to the leaders of the Soviet Union and the United States. Regrettably, a cold prevented me from meeting you personally in Moscow, but I would like to share with you some of my ideas in connection with your message.[36]

On 17 November Gorbachev met U.S. businessperson John Crystal and conveyed to him "the oral answer of President of the Presidium of the USSR Supreme Soviet Yuriy Andropov to the editor of the *Des Moines Register* newspaper, in which Yuriy Andropov thanked the author of the address for the invitation to visit the State of Iowa."[37]

On 27 October *Pravda* carried an "interview" with Andropov, in which he made a new proposal concerning the INF[38] negotiations.[39] The interview was reprinted by *Izvestiya*[40] and many other Soviet newspapers and reported by TASS[41] and Soviet radio[42] and television.[43] In December, Andropov signed the obituary of film director Grigoriy Aleksandrov,[44] and on 22 December he reportedly signed the decision of the Supreme Soviet Presidium on the composition of the electoral commission for the Supreme Soviet elections.[45]

These reports, as well as numerous other telegrams, greetings, and letters signed by Andropov, represented phantom appearances. He remained physically absent from even the most important events, such as the celebrations of the October Revolution anniversary and the December Central Committee plenum. Incidentally, the major roles in the revolution celebrations seemed to be very carefully allocated by the Politburo members so as to preserve a balance between the two factions. For example, Romanov delivered the main address at the 5 November festive meeting at the Kremlin Palace of Congresses,[46] whereas Marshal Ustinov was the speaker at the traditional 7 November parade on Red Square,[47] and Tikhonov spoke at the 7 November Kremlin reception.[48]

Even before the October Revolution anniversary events, after the cancellation of a scheduled visit by Andropov to Bulgaria, the foreign press agencies began to speculate on the seriousness of his condition.[49] When Andropov failed to attend the October Revolution events, the Kremlin felt obliged to explain his absence and to indicate when he could be expected to resume his duties. On 5 November Leonid Zamyatin, head of the International Information Department of the CPSU Central Committee, told foreign reporters in Moscow, "Soviet leader Yuriy Andropov caught a cold ten days ago, but that his condition was not serious." Zamyatin added, however, that Andropov would probably not attend the military parade for the anniversary of the October Revolution and that the final decision would be made by Andropov's doctors.[50] On 7 November, Andropov's son Igor, who was taking part in the preparatory meeting for the Helsinki Conference on European Confidence and Security, told journalists that "his father's health is not poor."[51]

On 23 November, *Moskovskaya Pravda* carried a report on a speech made by Moscow party boss Viktor Grishin at the Krasnyy Proletariy Plant.

> V. V. Grishin announced that the day before he had talked with Comrade Yuriy Vladimirovich Andropov, general secretary of the CPSU Central Committee and chairman of the USSR Supreme Soviet Presidium, and that, in particular, he had told him about today's political day.
>
> Yuriy Vladimirovich Andropov asked him to convey ardent greetings to the workers and employees of the Krasnyy Proletariy Plant and wished them great successes in their work to fulfill the plans for 1983 and the entire 5-year plan.[52]

From time to time Soviet sources leaked to foreign newspapers and even officials "reports" converning Andropov's imminent return to regular duties. A typical example was the statement of Peter Boenisch, Federal Republic of Germany (FRG) government spokesperson, who on 3 December told *Bild Am Sontag* that he had information that the "Soviet state and party leader Yuriy Andropov will probably be able to resume his official duties next week. The Federal Government has information that, happily, the health of Soviet General Secretary Andropov has improved. The Soviets told me that Andropov will probably resume his official duties on 10 December."[53]

Certain ludicrous reports also circulated, such as the sensational news published in the London *Daily Express,* which stated that according to "KGB sources in Moscow," Andropov "has been shot in the arm after an amazing Kremlin confrontation with Yuriy Brezhnev, the son of his late predecessor. Andropov is said to be recovering from the shooting, but the effects of the wound—and the difficulties of explaining away a damaged arm—have kept him out of action for some 10 weeks."[54] Such a report indicates the extent to which Andropov's long absence had attracted the attention of the world media and inflamed the imaginations of certain journalists.

Chernenko Resurfaces

The reports on Andropov's improving health and imminent resumption of duties were evidently inspired by his supporters in the Politburo. At the same time there were indications that Chernenko's faction was exploiting the situation to increase its power and regain lost positions. Several statements published in Andropov's name during September-November 1983 appear to have been intended to create the impression that Soviet affairs were now being managed by collective leadership. Andropov's customary use of the first person in articles was replaced by phrases emphasizing that the expressed views were those of the Soviet leadership. These statements did not directly undermine Andropov's official position and authority; nevertheless, they were indicative of a new situation in the Kremlin. For example, Andropov issued an official, personal statement on U.S. foreign policy, the KAL airliner incident, and the INF talks on 28 September, entitled, "Statement of Yu. V. Andropov, general secretary of the CPSU Central Committee and chairman of the USSR Supreme Soviet Presidium." It stated, "The Soviet leadership deems it necessary to inform the Soviet people, other peoples, and all who are responsible for determining state policy of its assessment of the course pursued in international affairs by the current U.S. Administration."[55]

Two months later, in a further personal statement on the beginning of the deployment of U.S. missiles in Western Europe, again entitled "Statement of Yu. V. Andropov, general secretary of the CPSU Central Committee and chairman of the USSR Supreme Soviet Presidium," Andropov reportedly stated: "The leadership of the Soviet Union has already apprised the Soviet people and other peoples of its assessment of the present U.S. Administration's militarist course and warned the U.S. Government and the Western countries which are at one with it about the dangerous consequences of that course."[56]

After long months of almost complete silence and political inertia, Chernenko emerged again into the limelight, publishing several major articles and receiving various foreign delegations. An important article on the CPSU's ideological work was published in the October issue of *Kommunist*[57] (immediately after his 28 September statement on U.S. foreign policy that began with the words "The Soviet leadership . . .") , and a second article dealing with the ideological foundations of the CPSU's international activities appeared in the November issue of *Problemy Mira I Sotsializma*.[58] A third article, devoted to human rights, was released by Novosti Press Agency and reprinted in most East European newspapers.[59]

Chernenko's meetings with foreign delegations were even more revealing. For months he had been virtually excluded from meetings with foreign visitors, whereas during Andropov's lengthy absence his renewed involvement with foreign delegations clearly showed his extended responsibilities. For example, on 19 October he met a delegation of the Czechoslovak Communist Party Central Committee led by Jan Fojtik, Central Committee secretary and candidate Politburo member, and discussed issues relating to ideological and mass political work.[60]

On 24 October Chernenko and Ponomarev met a delegation from the Unified Socialist party of Mexico led by P. Gomez, secretary general of the party Central Committee. During the talks, the deployment of nuclear missiles in Western Europe and "the increasingly brazen interventionist actions by the United States and its satellites against Nicaragua" were condemned.[61]

Between 27 and 30 November Chernenko hosted a delegation of the Hungarian party Central Committee led by G. Aczel, Politburo member and Central Committee secretary, and discussed with the Hungarian guests matters concerning "ideology, science, culture, education, and mass political work."[62]

Finally, on 19 December 1983 Chernenko met Lionel Soto Prieto, member of the Secretariat of the Cuban Communist Party Central Committee. This time the talks were not restricted to matters of ideology, culture, and mass political work but dealt with "strengthening Soviet-Cuban cooperation, as well as topical international problems."[63]

During the celebrations to mark the sixty-sixth October Revolution anniversary Chernenko utilized Andropov's absence and drew attention to himself both at the 5 November festive meeting in Moscow and at the 7 November Red Square parade.

Factional Struggle Intensifies

Andropov's prolonged absence from the public scene was becoming a source of embarrassment to the Kremlin leaders, who were still doggedly referring to his "slight cold." In addition, Andropov's absence must have increased tension within the Politburo and exacerbated the struggle between the two factions. This was illustrated by an unusual article in the *Izvestiya* issue of 15 November 1983, which ostensibly dealt with a recently published book entitled, "A Bullet in the Heart of the Revolution," which described the 30 August 1918 attempt on Lenin's life by Fanny Roid-Kaplan. The paper had no logical reason to review the book: The assassination attempt against Lenin is a subject very seldom mentioned in the Soviet press. It seems reasonable to assume that the book review was somehow related to Andropov's prolonged absence and represented a by-product of the Kremlin infighting. Suggesting that the subject was "highly topical even today," the review stressed that because the information on Lenin's condition had been made public, it had not given rise to great public concern. An example of the 1918 press treatment was included:

> *Krasnaya Zvezda* wrote in its 12 September 1918 issue: "Comrade Lenin's health is entirely satisfactory. Comrade Lenin has been allowed to sit up and read. The patient is fully abreast of all political news. ... He is joking a great deal with those around him and is confident that he will be out of bed in the next few days." Several days later, asked how he felt, Vladimir Ilich answered: "Couldn't be better. Time for work!"[64]

The inclusion of this example could be interpreted as an implied criticism of the manner in which Andropov's own absence had been handled and a veiled but insistent demand for the publication of information on his true condition. The article also pointed out that a full disclosure of the patient's true condition was not imperative but that a "white lie" about the leader's health was acceptable under such circumstances:

> The doctors expressed "their extreme amazement at the endurance and patience of Vladimir Ilich Lenin, who did not make the slightest sound even when submitting to the terribly painful dressing of the wound." It is to be supposed that when the doctors treating him, literally a few hours after the assassination attempt, confidently said that Ilich has a strong constitution, that Ilich will live, this was said not for the sake of a white lie—fully permissible, not to be condemned, and salutary in such cases—but really with profound conviction and on the basis of observation of the wounded man's reaction.[65]

The intelligent reader could detect many other hints and indications in the article, but the main idea was clear: The leader is very sick, more information on his condition is to be disclosed, but bear in mind that you will probably not be told the entire truth because it is more bitter than you are permitted to know.

Izvestiya's editor Lev Tolkunov was Andropov's man. From 1957 to 1962 he worked under Andropov in the Central Committee Socialist Countries Department, where he became Andropov's deputy. His appointment as *Izvestiya* editor-in-chief earlier in 1983[66] had been arranged by Andropov. It is inconceivable that he would publish an article clearly serving the interests of Andropov's opponents and fueling the rumors about Andropov's condition. But then Tolkunov does not appear to have been in Moscow at the time of the review's publication. Japan's *Asahi Shimbun* of 13 November reported on a 12 November meeting between Tolkunov and Japanese news reporters, during which Tolkunov informed the journalists that Andropov "only had a cold," that "he was continuing to execute his duties," and that he would resume normal functions "in a few days."[67] Since this optimistic briefing had nothing in common with the inauspicious article on the assassination attempt on Lenin, it can be inferred that Tolkunov's absence from the USSR had been exploited by Andropov's rivals to plant the article, which hinted at the true gravity of Andropov's condition. Incidentally, according to the *Washington Post* of 23 November, another political commentator, Georgiy Arbatov, head of the United States and Canada Institute and a close associate of Andropov, had stated on 10 November in Tokyo that Andropov was to resume his duties "in four to five days."

This was not the only article that signaled the intense political maneuvering inside the Kremlin. Fedor Burlatskiy, a leading Soviet political commentator, suggested in *Literaturnaya Gazeta* of 23 November 1983 that Soviet military leaders dissented from the views of the CPSU leadership on the issue of the deployment of U.S. missiles in Western Europe and in fact were applying considerable pressure on the leadership to respond decisively to the U.S. challenge. Displaying a critical attitude toward the military, Burlatskiy implied that civilian leaders (in general) must never allow the military to influence sensitive political decisions. He attributed little value to the generals' judgment, saying "it was not worth a penny."[68]

Political-Military Tension

The strong probability of tension between political and military leaders had become evident even earlier, after the shooting down of the South Korean Boeing 747 on 1 September. The first response came from the military, in the person of Chief of Staff Marshal Nikolay Ogarkov, who explained to the world the USSR's reasons for shooting down the aircraft. The political leadership reacted only on 29 September 1983, when *Pravda* commented on the incident. Furthermore, statements made by Soviet diplomats stationed abroad and especially an 18 September British Broadcasting Company (BBC) interview with *Pravda* editor Viktor Afanasyev, clearly indicated that the Soviet political leadership disagreed with the military on the issue of the airliner's destruction and that the decision to destroy the airliner was taken at the military level, without consultation with political leaders.

Haunted by Andropov's illness and harassed by the growing infighting and the increasing political involvement of the military, the Soviet leadership displayed further signs of confusion and indecision in foreign affairs, indicating the temporary absence of an authoritative decision-making center. For example, a broad international propaganda campaign was organized against the deployment of U.S. missiles in Western Europe. This operation was routine, carried out by the well-oiled machine of the Soviet propaganda apparatus, and thus did not require a special decision.

In issuing actual initiatives or concrete political proposals, however, the Kremlin displayed an amazing paralysis; in fact on one occasion the situation bordered on the grotesque, reflecting the leadership's inability to act. On 27 October Andropov (in absentia, naturally) made a proposal concerning the Intermediate-Range Nuclear Forces (INF) negotiations, according to which the USSR offered to reduce to 140 the number of SS-20 missiles deployed in the European part of the Soviet Union.[69] On 19 November in a *Volksstimme* (the organ of the Austrian Communist party) interview Viktor Afanasyev, the editor-in-chief of *Pravda,* was questioned on the fact that the USSR had offered to limit its "missile systems" in the European part of the USSR to 120. On the very same day Marshal Ustinov, the Soviet defense minister, writing in *Pravda,* stated that "the USSR agrees to leave only 140 SS-20 missiles in the European part of the USSR."[70] Earlier, rumors had circulated in the West that the chief Soviet negotiator at the INF talks, Yu. Kvitsinskiy, had informally proposed to his U.S. counterpart Paul Nitze that the USSR would reduce its missiles deployed on its European territory to 120 but insisted that the final number should be suggested by the United States in the form of a compromise proposal. On 21 November the USSR minister of foreign affairs indignantly denied the rumor, attributing the new offer to "the U.S. side."[71] Against the background of the conflicting statements by Afanasyev and Ustinov, the situation became farcical.

This situation prompted many Western observers and analysts to conclude that affairs in Moscow were actually being managed by the military. The abundance of articles published in the last quarter of 1983 by various Soviet military figures, as well as statements on USSR foreign policy made by military personnel, were interpreted by the *Washington Post* as indications of the growing political weight of the Soviet military. Stressing that Marshal Ogarkov had explained to the world the shooting down of the South Korean airliner and Marshal Ustinov had announced that the rate of deployment of Soviet missiles in the CSSR and GDR would increase, the *Washington Post* concluded that the armed forces, dissatisfied with the situation in the Kremlin, had assumed a "stronger role in political affairs" and had become "the one clear voice" in Moscow.[72] The *Christian Science Monitor* went even further, suggesting that "military men may now be in the driver's seat in the Soviet Union."[73] Against this background it seems certain that the 23 November article by Burlatskiy in *Literaturnaya Gazeta* represented the reaction of the political leadership, or at least of a section of it, to the increasing involvement of the military in political affairs.

Succession Struggle

Andropov's faction, led by Gorbachev, was also alert to the possibilities for exploiting Andropov's indisposition and scrambling for a better position in the impending leadership struggle for Andropov's succession. In late October a "spokeswoman of the CPSU Central Committee Main Department" informed reporters in Moscow that "Konstantin Chernenko has resigned from his post as head of the Main Department of the CPSU Central Committee."[74] Since such announcements are seldom (if ever) made in the USSR and certainly not by a spokeswoman, and bearing in mind Chernenko's increased activity in the latter part of 1983, the report seems to have been intended to undermine Chernenko's authority and embarrass him at a crucial stage of the infighting. In addition, a decision on the date of the regular Supreme Soviet session was finally made. This decision had been repeatedly postponed, perhaps in the hope that Andropov would recover sufficiently to take part. Although such sessions must be announced at least thirty days in advance[75] and the session traditionally had to take place before the close of the year, the date of the session was announced by *Pravda* only on 2 December 1983: The session was set for 28 December, and it was to be preceded by a Central Committee plenum.

Perhaps the most important development in December and January related to the infighting was the marked increase in personnel appointments. Some sixteen party members at the oblast and kray levels were replaced, whereas only three such changes had been made since August when the accountability-election meetings at the kraykom and obkom levels began.[76] Other important changes included the appointment of Boris Shcherbina as deputy chairman of the USSR Council of Ministers[77] and the appointments of Y. Sizenko as USSR minister of the meat and dairy industries[78] and of Igor Belousov as minister of shipbuilding.[79] Several deputy ministers were also appointed, and Nikolay Kruchina was made CPSU Central Committee administrator of affairs.[80] Although this last sensitive post had become vacant early in September, three months were needed to agree on the new appointee. Scores of other officials at the republican and local levels were also appointed.

Not all the new appointments could be traced to particular leaders in the Politburo, although Gorbachev's hand could be seen in many. For example, Nikolay Kruchina had worked under Gorbachev in the Central Committee Department of Agriculture, as also had Yuriy Belov, who on 30 January was elected second secretary of the Tadzhik Central Committee.[81] Vladimir Kalashnikov, who on 4 January was elected first secretary of the agriculturally very important Volgograd kray,[82] had worked previously with Gorbachev when the latter was first secretary of the CPSU Stavropol Kray Committee.[83]

Despite the importance of the new appointments and the indications of Gorbachev's strength, the 26-27 December Central Committee plenum was expected to produce clearer evidence of the two factions' relative strength. The plenum and the following Supreme Soviet session were convened to approve new appointments at the highest party and state level, including filling vacancies in the Politburo—appointments of immense importance on the eve of the approaching succession.

Andropov's faction appears to have more effectively exploited the available opportunities during the weeks preceding the Central Committee plenum and Supreme Soviet session. Gorbachev made a well-publicized visit to his power base of the Stavropol kray from 23 to 26 October. He toured industrial plants and kolkhozes, held meetings with local party organizations, and spoke at a meeting with members of his constituency in Ipatovo. He did not fail to refer to

> Comrade Yuriy Vladimirovich's instructions for deepening the intensification of production in all sectors, ensuring the unconditional fulfillment of the Food Program, improving the style and methods of economic management, strengthening labor discipline, further boosting the people's prosperity, and safeguarding peace under the conditions of the unrestrained arms race, unleashed by imperialism.[84]

Additional points were scored by Andropov's faction when a 14 December Central Committee decree sharply criticized violations and abuses in the Moldavian Communist party organization,[85] accusing it of "operating on the basis of inertia," "inclining toward bureaucracy" in its leadership methods, and failing to "analyse" in depth various economic processes. Although the decree fitted into the campaign against corruption and for discipline initiated by Andropov, no other reason was apparent, apart from an attack on Chernenko, for singling out the leadership of a republic long associated with the political careers of Brezhnev and his right-hand man.

Finally, on the very eve of the party plenum and the presidium session, Gorbachev received much needed international exposure by heading the CPSU delegation to the 10th Congress of the Portuguese Communist party.[86] On 16 December he read the CPSU greetings message to the Congress, in which he paid several tributes to Andropov, recalling his statements of 28 September and 24 November, his warning against the threat of a nuclear war, and his position on the deployment of U.S. missiles in Western Europe.[87] Andropov's speeches and statements were obviously used by Gorbachev to give an aura of authority to his own statements. The visit to Portugal achieved the expected results. The congress evoked unusual interest because of the doubt concerning the reelection of the veteran leader of the Portuguese Communists, Alvaro Cunhal, and because of developments within the Spanish Communist party, which under the leadership of Gerardo Iglesias was manifesting pronounced Eurocommunist tendencies in contrast to the loyal Portuguese Communist party. Observers were curious to see whether any signs of Eurocommunism would become evident at the Portuguese congress, and accordingly the event was extensively covered by the foreign press.

The CPSU Central Committee plenum opened on 26 December. The main items on its agenda were the draft plan and budget for 1984. However, two other issues focused observers' attention: Would Andropov attend the plenum? What personnel changes would be adopted? The first issue was quickly settled: Andropov made one of his phantom appearances. He did not attend the plenum in person but sent a speech to be read to the Central Committee members. The first paragraph of the speech attempted to explain the rather unusual circumstances surrounding the whole affair:

> Dear Comrades, I deeply regret that because of temporary causes I will not be able to attend the session of the plenum. But I have attentively studied all the materials that form the basis of the plan for the coming year. I gave them much thought and was preparing to speak and outline some of my considerations. That is why I am sending the text of my speech to the members and candidate members of the CPSU Central Committee.[88]

The answer to the question concerning the personnel changes was contained in the "Information Report" published at the end of the plenum's first day:

> The plenary meeting of the CPSU Central Committee examined organizational questions.
> The plenary meeting of the Central Committee made Comrades V. I. Vorotnikov and M. S. Solomentsev, who were candidate members of the CPSU Central Committee Politburo, full members of the CPSU Central Committee Politburo.
> The Central Committee plenum elected CPSU Central Committee member V. M. Chebrikov to candidate membership of the CPSU Central Committee Politburo.
> The plenary meeting of the Central Committee elected member of the CPSU Central Committee Ye. K. Ligachev secretary of the CPSU Central Committee.[89]

The personnel changes made it plain that Andropov's illness and prolonged absence had not affected the strength of his faction. On the contrary, the new appointments showed that Andropov's supporters had the upper hand. Both Vorotnikov and Ligachev had already been promoted in summer 1983. Vorotnikov had been sent by Brezhnev to Cuba as ambassador in 1979, and in 1982, while Brezhnev was still alive, he was recalled and appointed first secretary of the Krasnodar kraykom, where he promptly purged party officials associated with Medunov (and implicitly with Brezhnev and Chernenko). Ligachev had already headed the CPSU Central Committee Cadres Department before his election as Central Committee secretary, and in this post he had worked closely with Gorbachev in organizing and supervising the local accountability-election meetings for the local party committees and later the election campaign for the USSR Supreme Soviet.

Chebrikov's political colors were plain to see. Having been Andropov's deputy in the KGB for many years, he now headed the KGB and apparently enjoyed the full support of his former boss. Solomentsev's loyalty was unclear. His political career had been blocked for years by Brezhnev, who refused to promote him from his candidate membership of the Politburo, a post to which Solomentsev had been elected in 1971.[90] Originally a protégé of Brezhnev's opponent Frol Kozlov, he had no apparent reason to support Chernenko. On the other hand, there was no clear evidence that he had any association with the Andropov-Gorbachev faction. His promotion seemed to balance that of Vorotnikov. It should be noted that Vorotnikov inherited Solomentsev's post of chairman of the RSFSR Council of Ministers when Solomentsev was elected chairman of the CPSU Control Committee following the death of Pelshe.

Even if Solomentsev's loyalty was unclear in December 1983, his promotion did not alter the fact that three more leaders clearly linked with Andropov and his faction had been promoted whereas none of Chernenko's faction and no Army personnel had been elected. (There had been speculations in some Western newspapers that USSR Army Chief of General Staff Marshal Ogarkov, who as a result of his exposure after the downing of the South Korean Boeing airliner and because of his outspoken articles and statements had become a prominent public figure, would be elected a candidate member of the Politburo.) Thus, the new appointments made by the December 1983 Central Committee Plenum fitted into the general pattern of the continued advancement of Andropov's and Gorbachev's people, which had become very noticeable in November-December 1983. Gorbachev's special position was also pointed up as he was the only Central Committee secretary to speak at the plenum.

The 28-29 December USSR Supreme Soviet session was an anticlimax. As expected, Andropov failed to make an appearance.[91] The Supreme Soviet adopted the 1984 plan and budget, as well as a resolution "on the International Situation and the Foreign Policy of the Soviet State,"[92] in a generally unmemorable session.

In late December and January Andropov continued to make phantom appearances, signing the decision on the composition of the USSR Electoral Commission,[93] signing a decree awarding an honor to Lt. Gen. F. Bokov,[94] answering an appeal for disarmament made by a French antiwar organization,[95] signing an obituary for Central Committee Secretary P. Ponomarenko,[96] and even registering for the upcoming Supreme Soviet elections.[97] Even in February, only a few days before his death, the press reported that Andropov signed a decree honoring TASS Deputy Director G. Shishkin.[98] Other leaders continued to invoke Andropov's name, to quote his statements in their speeches and even to greet various groups on his behalf. For example, on 12 January Vladimir Dolgikh, Central Committee secretary and Politburo candidate member, "conveyed with a special feeling and satisfaction heartfelt congratulations and best wishes from Comrade Yuriy Vladimirovich Andropov" to the workers of the Siberian town of Novokuznetsk.[99]

In January signs indicated that Chernenko had extended his influence to new areas. On 16 January he together with Tikhonov signed the obituary of Vladimir Leontyev[100] and on 25 January the obituary of Mikhail Lesechko,[101] who had both been well-known economic figures. Chernenko previously had seldom signed obituaries of economic figures and certainly not with his name listed out of alphabetical order (as on these occasions), indicating his improved status within the leadership. During Andropov's tenure Chernenko had almost exclusively signed only the obituaries of prominent persons in the fields of ideology and culture. Furthermore, on 23 January the Soviet press announced the publication of an enlarged edition of Chernenko's speeches and articles.[102] *Pravda* of 8 February reviewed the book, concentrating on Chernenko's writings in the area of ideology and conspicuously ignoring his works on other subjects.

Thus, on the eve of Andropov's death, the two factions involved in the infighting were scrambling to improve their positions for the coming critical days. Gorbachev, who had emerged as Andropov's right-hand man and who, according to the Western media, had been a daily visitor to Andropov's bedside in the clinic where he was being treated,[103] concentrated on the promotion of his own people to extend his control in the field of cadres and added some much needed international exposure to his political persona. Chernenko was also increasing his influence, protecting his positions, and consolidating his central place in the Soviet leadership. Having astonishingly quickly recovered from the bitter disappointment of not succeeding Brezhnev, he had survived politically under Andropov (a remarkable feat) and was now preparing for something that no previous top Soviet leader had ever been offered— a second bid for the supreme post of general secretary of the CPSU Central Committee.

5

The Second Chance: Chernenko Succeeds, the Twofold Decision

Andropov made his last public appearance at the 18 August 1983 meeting with the U.S. senators. By September his condition had become so grave that he had to enter the hospital, and in October one of his kidneys was reportedly removed. From that time on, Andropov was confined to the premises of the Kuntsevo governmental hospital, usually hooked up to a dialysis machine. Thus, during these months the general secretary ruled the country in absentia through his adjutants in the Politburo who owed their positions to him and primarily through the agency of Mikhail Gorbachev.

Stalemate in the Politburo

Gorbachev's own position in the Politburo was undoubtedly strengthened by the appointments Andropov had made during his brief tenure. Nevertheless, Chernenko still remained the senior secretary, both in years of service as a Politburo member and Central Committee secretary and in terms of seniority in the official hierarchy. This fact could not be altered by Andropov during his short periods of normal activity and certainly not by Gorbachev, who merely acted as Andropov's proxy. Paradoxically, Chernenko's position was further strengthened by Andropov's absence from the daily scene. When it became clear that Andropov would never return to normal work and that the policies he had initiated were being implemented by his youthful adjutants headed by Gorbachev, many party bureaucrats whose own positions and comfortable way of life were endangered by these policies found solace in the dream of turning the clock back to the Brezhnev era through the agency of Chernenko. Andropov had rocked the boat too much for their taste.

In the fifteen months of Andropov's tenure as general secretary there had been a turnover of over one-fifth of the Moscow-based members of the Council of Ministers, more than one-fifth of the regional party secretaries, and over one-third of the departmental heads in the CPSU Central Committee. At the time of Andropov's death, the total complement of full and candidate members of the Politburo and the Central Committee secretaries numbered twenty-three. Just over one-sixth of these had been promoted to their posts during Andropov's rule, and exactly one-quarter of the Politburo's full members had obtained their positions during the same period.[1] Thus, after fifteen months many Central Committee members and other high state and party officials were feeling the heat in the kitchen and wistfully dreamed of prolonging their careers (and accompanying privileges) under Chernenko, especially when the choice for the new leader evidently lay between him and Gorbachev, a ruthlessly efficient, young, dynamic, and unpredictable administrator who was totally committed to Andropov's reforms.

Consequently, during the final weeks of Andropov's life Chernenko, who as senior secretary had been chairing the weekly Politburo meetings, grew confident that the majority of supporters within the Politburo commanded by Andropov would almost certainly dissipate upon Andropov's death. He anticipated that some members of Andropov's faction, finding themselves abruptly deprived of their main source of strength, would switch their support to Chernenko, especially in view of the predominantly pro-Chernenko atmosphere prevailing in the Central Committee as a whole.

During the last weeks of Andropov's life a stalemate developed in the Politburo: Its members seemed either unwilling or unable to reach decisions on any issues of import as they awaited with trepidation Andropov's inevitable death and the ensuing leadership struggle. Apparently, however, they reached one decision: to hint at the impending demise of the general secretary. Since the Politburo could not or would not indicate the true state of Andropov's health, it resorted to the previously employed allegory based on Lenin's death—somewhat of an idée fixe in the last months of Andropov's tenure.

From 20 through 23 January 1984 *Izvestiya* published a four-part series on Lenin's final days: "Refusing to Succumb," "Farewell," "Death," and "Memory." The series was full of ominous phrases, apparently meant to warn the Soviet people of what lay ahead:

> When a man departs forever, crossing the threshold into eternity, much of what has happened toward the end of his life—his last words, meetings, and gestures—acquire with the passage of time a special, and at times fateful meaning. One of Lenin's last official letters began with the following words: "I have now finished winding up my affairs and can depart with an easy mind."[2]
>
> Even after 12 December, when illness approached irreversibly and he was finally tied to his bed, Vladimir Ilich continued to think about business. He still hoped to speak at the 10th All-Russian Congress of the Soviets and was not afraid to look a few months ahead and think of what he would say to the delegates of the 12th Party Congress. . . . He was not fated to do this.[3]

The latter passage evoked memories of Andropov's inability to attend the December 1983 Central Committee plenum and Supreme Soviet session and suggested a parallel between 1924 and 1984. The readers immediately understood the similarity between Lenin's last days in his dacha in Gorki and Andropov's ordeal in the Kuntsevo hospital. The Soviet leadership was informing the people that Andropov's next appearance would be in the Moscow House of the Trade Unions, where traditionally dead leaders lay in state.

However, while the Politburo was obliquely conveying this message to the masses, it was unable to reach any decision on the succession as long as the leader remained alive. All the members knew that Andropov's death was imminent. For this reason, the postponement of Defense Minister Marshal Ustinov's visit to India was announced on 4 February.[4] Nevertheless, the Politburo meeting of 2 February, which almost certainly was the forum in which this postponement was decided, reportedly dealt only with routine matters, such as Soviet-Spanish relations, the pledges of various workers collectives, and the improvement of consumer services.[5]

Andropov's Legacy

When on 10 February 1984 Soviet radio and television canceled scheduled programs and began broadcasting solemn symphonic music, the citizens of the USSR knew what announcement was about to be made. After 176 days of absence from public view, Yuriy Andropov was about to make his last appearance. At 1430 Moscow time Igor Kirilov, the chief Soviet television announcer, appeared on the screen suitably clad in a somber black suit, with Andropov's portrait, draped in a red-black ribbon, on the wall behind him, and made the expected announcement: At 1650 on the previous afternoon, Yuriy Andropov's heart and kidney had finally given up the struggle.[6] The former KGB chief, who had come to the helm of state too late and in too poor health to leave a lasting record, had finally died. Although obviously a transition leader, Andropov nevertheless opened the road for such young and dynamic leaders as Gorbachev, Ligachev, Vorotnikov, and Ryzhkov to reach the top of the Soviet political hierarchy, and now they must drive through the reforms initiated by their dead patron.

During Andropov's fifteen-month tenure the following main developments were advanced:

1. Andropov unleashed an attack against the conservative elements in the party apparatus—the holders of power delegated by Brezhnev. Aware that no attempt to change the Soviet system could succeed as long as the conservative nomenklatura members held their positions, Andropov initiated extensive personnel changes, replacing about one-fifth of the oblast and kray party secretaries and a similar percentage of the Moscow-based members of the Council of Ministers. He also

brought G. Romanov to Moscow and effected his election as a Central Committee secretary, thereby complicating the future succession struggle. Andropov added Y. Ligachev to the secretariat and, only weeks before his death, succeeded in promoting Chebrikov and Vorotnikov to the Politburo. However, despite these successes Andropov was unable to remove any of the prominent Brezhnevists from the Politburo. Chernenko, Tikhonov, Kunayev, Shcherbitskiy, and Grishin all retained their positions, providing a constant reminder of the limitations of Andropov's power.

2. Andropov succeeded in promoting Gorbachev to one of the top positions in the Soviet leadership. During Andropov's tenure Gorbachev rose from the position of a junior Politburo member and secretary in charge of agriculture to become perhaps the most powerful member of Andropov's faction, controlling the crucial area of cadres; he was obviously equipped to claim Andropov's post after the latter's demise. The developments following Andropov's death—when Gorbachev effectively challenged Chernenko and forced him to share his power—demonstrated Gorbachev's true strength.

3. Andropov started several extensive campaigns: to eliminate corruption at all levels (including at the very top), to strengthen discipline, and to combat alcoholism. He also initiated a number of tentative, cautious measures aimed at changing aspects of the Soviet economic system and party life. Most of these initiatives did not develop beyond the embryo stage because of the effective resistance of the nomenklatura, assisted by the Brezhnevists in the Politburo, and because of Andropov's own declining health, which curbed his activities and forced him to absent himself for long periods from public view. Nevertheless, the first assault against stagnation and corruption shook the party apparatus, and the political climate changed as many party officials felt their secure positions, acquired under Brezhnev, threatened. They focused their hopes on Chernenko as an instrument for reviving Brezhnevism without Brezhnev and a means for preserving their privileges. Although their hopes were briefly fulfilled, the respite proved only temporary. After only fourteen months, Gorbachev came to power and immediately took on the task of continuing Andropov's policies with much greater vigor. Accordingly, although Andropov was unable to carry his plans through fruition, it is probably true to say that he profoundly influenced the policies and methods employed by Gorbachev today.

Chernenko's Succession amid Strife and Hesitation

When Chernenko was reported to be the head of Andropov's funeral commission,[7] observers might have expected that he would quickly and smoothly be elected general secretary of the CPSU Central Committee, thus completing a second leadership transition within fifteen months. The initial signs indicated that events were following the pattern established following Brezhnev's death. The announcement of Andropov's death was made on the following day (exactly as in Brezhnev's case), and the official plans for the funeral and the composition of the funeral commission were announced a few hours later. It was reasonable to expect that an extraordinary Central Committee plenum would be called for 11 February and would promulgate the official announcement of Chernenko's appointment because such plenums were speedily convened after the deaths of Stalin and Brezhnev. However, the same Politburo meeting that decided the composition of the funeral commission set the date for the Central Committee plenum, 13 February,[8] thus creating the longest interregnum in Soviet history. The hours and then the days dragged on, but no announcement came.

In the period between Andropov's death and the convening of the plenum, various signs suggested confusion, vacillation, and tension within the leadership. This confusion was particularly striking given the official announcement on Andropov's death: "Andropov had developed serious kidney problems in February 1983 and his condition took a serious turn for the worse in late January 1984."[9] In other words, Andropov's death was not unexpected, and the Politburo had had ample time and opportunity to settle the succession question before his death. However, the postponement of the plenum and the evident state of indecision showed that the Politburo had *not* dealt with this vital issue and was encountering great difficulties in resolving it. Signs indicated that the Politburo was in almost continuous session in an attempt to break the deadlock and decide on a new leader. Thus, when the leadership of the Ministry of Defense met on 10 February to mark Andropov's death, Marshal Ustinov was not present;[10] since he had participated in the similar ceremony for Brezhnev[11] and had been present at all the other events relating to Andropov's last rites attended by the other Politburo members, his absence can only be explained by a prior, much more important engagement.

Vladimir Shcherbitskiy, party leader of the Ukraine, was not among the Politburo members who on 11 February paid their respects at Andropov's bier.[12] His presence in Moscow became evident only on 13 February, when the evidently exhausted Politburo members came once more to pay their respects at Andropov's lying-in-state. Dinmukhamed Kunayev, an old Brezhnev crony and an important member of Chernenko's faction, also failed to attend the first Politburo visit to the bier on 11 February.[13] In retrospect, his absence appears to be significant and somehow connected with the power game in the Politburo; otherwise one cannot explain the painstaking efforts of the Soviet press on the following day to create the impression that Kunayev did in fact attend the ceremony. Press photographs purportedly taken during the ceremony showed Kunayev standing on the right of Chernenko. This deception was clearly deliberate: In the photo in *Pravda*[14] Kunayev is the only person among the leaders whose shadow is not visible on the left, whereas his face—unlike any others in the photograph—has a shadow on the right. *Izvestiya* botched the job even more. The thin white line separating Kunayev from the other Politburo members clearly indicates where the doctoring was performed. Finally, the Soviet television report on the leaders' first visit to Andropov's bier on 11 February clearly showed that Kunayev was absent.[15]

The Soviet press reflected the confusion in the Politburo in other ways. For example, both the official address of the main party and state organs to the Soviet people on Andropov's death[16] and *Pravda*'s 16 February editorial, "The People and the Party are United," were grudging in their praise of Andropov. Indeed, the editorial actually dealt with Andropov only in the first three paragraphs and devoted the remainder of the text to the party, its leadership of the Soviet people, and its policies.[17] The message was clear: The less than generous assessment of Andropov's period in office seemed to indicate that Andropov's successes resulted not from his personal merits but from the collective party leadership.

In contrast, *Sovetskaya Rossiya* on 13 February carried an article by Valentin Chikin, a committed supporter of Andropov's reforms, which reminded readers of "Andropov's constructive boldness which sometimes seemed surprising."[18] Chikin strongly recommended that the new leader should continue Andropov's initiatives. More than a year previously the same Chikin, when ostensibly describing Lenin's concern for the age and health of the Central Committee members, had implied that the present position gave rise to similar concern and called for the infusion of young blood into the top party leadership.[19] These and other signs, together with the atmosphere of uncertainty, indicated that the Politburo's deliberations on succession were plagued with contention and vacillation.

The Plenum—A Twofold Decision?

The CPSU Central Committee extraordinary plenum, which elected Chernenko CPSU Central Committee general secretary, was held on the morning of 13 February, and by 1113 GMT TASS was already issuing its communiqué. The communiqué (subsequently reprinted in all Soviet newspapers) praised Andropov in much warmer terms than the previous address of the Soviet leadership and the 13 February *Pravda* editorial.

> The plenary meeting of the Central Committee noted that the Communist Party of the Soviet Union, the entire Soviet people had suffered a grievous loss. An outstanding leader of the Communist Party and the Soviet State, and ardent patriot, Leninist, and tireless fighter for peace and communism had passed away.

Holding, on assignment by the Party, the most important posts in the
Party and the State, Yuriy Andropov devoted all his energy, knowledge
and great experience to the implementation of the Party's policy, to
strengthening its ties with the masses, to enhancing the Soviet Union's
economic and defense might.[20]

The communiqué also praised Andropov's "attention to the realization
of the course outlined by the 26th CPSU Congress and subsequent
plenary meetings of the CPSU Central Committee," as well as his
"profound contribution" to developing relations with and and strengthening the "unity and cohesion" of the socialist community.[21] Turning
to the election of Chernenko, the communiqué continued:

> On instructions of the Political Bureau of the Central Committee, a
> speech on this question was made by Member of the Political Bureau
> of the CPSU Central Committee, Chairman of the USSR Council of
> Ministers Nikolay Tikhonov. He proposed to elect Konstantin Ustinovich
> Chernenko General Secretary of the CPSU Central Committee.
> The plenary meeting unanimously elected Konstantin Chernenko Gen-
> eral Secretary of the CPSU Central Committee.[22]

Finally, the communiqué reported Chernenko's acceptance speech but
did not mention if any other speeches were made at the plenum.
  The choice of Tikhonov to make the nomination indicated a victory
for the old guard, and the content of Tikhonov's speech revealed the
extent of the victory. After mandatory (and somewhat cursory) praise
of Andropov, stressing that his "great personal contribution" was the
result of "collective experience,"[23] Tikhonov dwelled on Chernenko's
merits: his "wealth of experience" and his gifts as a "talented organizer,"
"ardent propagandist," and "staunch fighter for the implementation of
the policy of our great party." He described Chernenko as a "true
associate of such leaders of the Leninist type as Leonid Brezhnev and
Yuriy Andropov" (the first mention of Brezhnev's name after a long
period of oblivion) and emphasized Chernenko's "ability to inspire
people by his energy and creative approach to any matter, the ability
to rally comrades for harmonious team work." Tikhonov did not fail
to mention Chernenko's "active part in shaping the strategic lines of
our peaceful foreign policy" and to recall "how much time Konstantin
Chernenko devotes to questions relating to strengthening the country's
defense capacity, to equipping the Armed Forces with modern technology, and to the ideological upbringing of the personnel of the Army
and the Navy."[24]
  The lavish and largely undeserved praise of Chernenko, and the fact
that Tikhonov completely disregarded the issue of collective leadership,
confirmed the triumph of the old guard. Tikhonov's message was:
"We've won!" In contrast, when Chernenko nominated Andropov for
the same supreme post in November 1982, he was far more moderate

in his praise of the nominee and repeatedly stressed the importance of collective leadership.[25]

This time, in his acceptance speech Chernenko showed more generosity toward his deceased rival, praising him more fully and carefully stressing the importance of unity at all party levels:

> The unity of their ranks is the source of the inexhaustible strength of the Soviet Communists. This strength fully manifests itself when, as Lenin said, "all of us, as members of the Party, act as one man." The Leninist Central Committee of the CPSU and its leading core—the Political Bureau of the Central Committee—act precisely thus, in concord and unity. This makes it possible to take thoroughly-weighed, well-considered decisions, leading to the consolidation of the alliance of the working class, the peasantry and the intelligentsia, of fraternal friendship of the peoples of the USSR.[26]

On 14 February all the Soviet newspapers published the "information report" on the Central Committee plenum and the texts of the speeches of Tikhonov and Chernenko. No reference was made to any other speeches being made at the plenum. However, two days later, when a brochure containing the plenum's proceedings was published, it became clear that a third speech had been delivered—a "closing speech" by Mikhail Gorbachev. Some Soviet journals, such as the *Novoye Vremya* issue of 17 February, did not carry Gorbachev's speech, even after the appearance of the pamphlet on the plenum's proceedings, whereas others, such as *New Times,* no. 8, February 1984, and *Kommunist,* no. 3, February 1984 (signed to press on 15 February), did publish it. The unusual content of Gorbachev's speech, as well as the unusual manner in which it was handled by the media, indicates that something out of the ordinary must have taken place at the Politburo meetings preceding the plenum and possibly at the plenum itself. Because of its importance the brief speech is reprinted in its entirety.

Speech by Mikhail Gorbachev, Political Bureau Member and Secretary of the CPSU Central Committee

Comrades!

We are completing the work of the Extraordinary Plenary Meeting of the Central Committee, convened at a crucial moment in the life of the Party and the people. The Plenary Meeting has proceeded in an atmosphere of unity and cohesion. Questions relating to the continuity of leadership have been resolved with a great sense of responsibility to the Party and the people.

The Plenary Meeting has shown that the Party will continue its advance along the Leninist course charted by the 26th CPSU Congress and the November 1982 and December 1983 Central Committee Plenums. This was particularly vividly manifested in the unanimous election of Comrade Konstantin Ustinovich Chernenko to the post of General Secretary of the

CPSU Central Committee, and in the full support of the propositions and conclusions on questions of the domestic and foreign policy activities of the Party and the State which were advanced in his speech at today's Plenary Meeting of the CPSU CC.

Allow me on behalf of the Political Bureau to express confidence that the members of the Central Committee and all participants in the Plenary Meeting, on returning to their localities, to their Party organizations, will act in the spirit of unity and cohesion, high exactingness and responsibility that has marked the present Plenary Meeting of the Central Committee of the Party.

We wish you every success in your work.

The Plenary Meeting is hereby declared closed.[27]

The very fact that Gorbachev was called upon to speak at the plenum indicates the unexpected prestige that he had acquired. On the other hand, the way in which the speech was handled suggests an attempt to diminish, or even completely obscure, the importance of his role. The content of Gorbachev's speech, especially his emphasis on "unity and cohesion" at the beginning and end of the speech, implies that good reason existed for his call for party unity and that the decision to elect Chernenko was adopted (presumably by the Politburo itself) only after a long session of bitter infighting—the exact opposite of "unity and cohesion." These facts naturally suggest a number of important questions: How exactly was the decision reached by the Politburo? Why was it adopted (and why was Chernenko chosen)? And, perhaps most important, was Chernenko's selection the only important decision concerning the succession taken by the Politburo?

While Andropov remained alive, his faction enjoyed a majority in the Politburo; however, his death not only shifted the balance but also apparently affected the unity of the coalition assembled around him. After his death twelve full (voting) members remained in the Politburo: Konstantin Chernenko (seventy-two years), Nikolay Tikhonov (seventy-eight), Mikahil Solomentsev (seventy), Dinmukhamed Kunayev (seventy-two), Viktor Grishin (sixty-nine), Vladimir Shcherbitskiy (sixty-six), Andrey Gromyko (seventy-four), Dmitriy Ustinov (seventy-five), Mikhail Gorbachev (fifty-two), Grigoriy Romanov (sixty-one), Geydar Aliyev (sixty), and Vitaliy Vorotnikov (fifty-seven). Theoretically, Andropov's faction seemed to have a majority even after the death of its patron. Only Tikhonov and Kunayev could be identified with certainty as supporters of Chernenko. Viktor Grishin also almost certainly sided with Chernenko. On the other hand, Gorbachev enjoyed the support of Aliyev, Vorotnikov, Gromyko, and Ustinov. (This conjecture is based on the opposition of Ustinov and Gromyko to Chernenko in 1982 and on Andropov's promotion of Aliyev and Vorotnikov.)

These alliances would give a division of 4 to 5, with queries surrounding the positions taken by Romanov (promoted to Central Committee secretary under Andropov), Solomentsev (promoted to full Politburo membership during Andropov's rule after having been kept a candidate Politburo member for twelve years under Brezhnev), and Shcherbitskiy, the unpredictable Ukraine party leader. One wonders why at least two of them transferred their allegiance to Chernenko: A possible explanation is that Andropov's faction disintegrated after the death of its leader, and some of its members saw the succession struggle as an opportunity to further their own careers by shifting their support to Chernenko.

On the other hand, Chernenko's faction remained united around its candidate. Romanov, a shrewd, pragmatic and ambitious politician, who regarded himself as a potential future candidate for the supreme post, owed nothing to the old guard, which had kept him in Leningrad. Brought to Moscow by Andropov in June 1983, he no doubt counted on the future support of Andropov's faction. Realizing his inability to effectively challenge Chernenko (or indeed Gorbachev) at that particular moment, he probably preferred to cooperate with Gorbachev. A split in Andropov's faction between the supporters of Gorbachev and Romanov seems implausible because in such a case Chernenko's victory would have been faster, easier, and, what is most important, complete. It seems much more likely that Solomentsev and Shcherbitskiy voted for Chernenko, thus producing the 6 to 6 stalemate that led to the wrangling and confusion during the period between the death of Andropov and the Central Committee plenum.

Taking this hypothesis one step further, it is reasonable to assume that once Gorbachev's faction realized that it no longer commanded a majority in the Politburo and that the decision would probably be made in the Central Committee, where Chernenko enjoyed a clear majority, it changed its strategy. Its members agreed to Chernenko's election as general secretary (amid a public show of unity) but demanded (and apparently obtained) a high price—the acceptance of Gorbachev's special status as their heir apparent. It is questionable whether all the Politburo members, especially those who cherished their own plans and ambitions, considered themselves bound by such a decision in the long term. However, at the time this solution may have appeared an acceptable way of breaking the stalemate.

Several facts can be cited in support of this hypothesis. When the Politburo members visited Andropov's bier for the first time on 12 February, Gorbachev occupied an inferior position in the leadership lineup, far down the line from the senior members of the Politburo.[28] However, only two days later (after the presumed dual decision of the Politburo) when the Politburo members came again after the Central Committee plenum to pay their respects at Andropov's bier, Gorbachev stood on one side of Chernenko (with Tikhonov on the other).[29] Furthermore, at Andropov's funeral Gorbachev's newly acquired prominence was demonstrated beyond any doubt: He was one of the leading pallbearers (the other being Chernenko).[30] In the semiofficial but usually very precise Kremlin protocol, this was a certain sign that Gorbachev had been accorded a special status. Later, however, during the ceremonial of the funeral when the Politburo members took their places on the tribune of the Lenin Mausoleum, Gorbachev resumed his former, inferior position in the lineup[31] and remained in this position even in subsequent official events, such as Chernenko's speech on 1 March, on the eve of the Supreme Soviet elections.[32] However, these signs of resistance to his new status gradually disappeared in the later phase of Chernenko's tenure.

A second question is, Why was Chernenko chosen? Why was an obviously sick, unconfident, unqualified, and incompetent seventy-two-year-old man, whose age at his election exceeded by ten years the average lifespan of Soviet men, selected to lead the USSR? His infirmity was painfully visible during Andropov's funeral when he was unable to keep his hand still in salute for more than a few seconds and his voice betrayed his respiratory problems. His uncertainty was embarrassingly demonstrated by his constant reliance on other Politburo members for guidance.

Paradoxically, Chernenko's advanced age seemed to some degree to facilitate his election to the general secretaryship. The old party leadership or at least most of the old leaders were opposed to electing a young dynamic leader like Gorbachev, who would continue Andropov's policy of rejuvenating the leadership and thus would endanger their own positions. After the atmosphere of uncertainty prevailing during Andropov's tenure, Chernenko's election was a step toward restoring the security of individuals' tenure at the top of the party hierarchy. Old, infirm, and perhaps unqualified, Chernenko represented everything the old members of the apparatus wanted: security for their positions, predictability, and renewed "trust in the party cadres" (those appointed by Brezhnev). To a large degree, Chernenko was the party apparatus's answer to Andropov's reforms and insurance against similar calamities occurring with Gorbachev. Their consciences were clear because Gorbachev was recognized as the heir apparent. Thus Chernenko's election was not merely an extension of their secure and quiet life but also a contract between two generations, a promise for the future, and an excellent compromise solution for the present.

In this context, one cannot help but detect some irony in Gorbachev's final words at the Central Committee plenum, when he expressed "confidence that the members of the Central Committee and all participants in the Plenary Meeting, on returning to their Party organizations, will act in the same spirit of unity and cohesion, high exactingness and responsibility that has marked the present Plenary Meeting of the Central Committee of the Party."[33]

Chernenko's Power Base

Chernenko's political life had been spent in Brezhnev's shadow, in a succession of apparatus posts to which he had been appointed by his patron. Although he had never headed a regional party organization, Chernenko for seventeen years had managed the CPSU Central Committee General Department,[34]—basically a backroom job, removed from the limelight. However, that position allowed him to supervise the party bureaucracy and dispense various favors, such as appointments and promotions inside the party apparatus. Chernenko utilized this position to develop a vast support network within the party machine that proved invaluable in February 1984. This bastion of Chernenko's power became the main target of Andropov's personnel reforms, and, therefore, with Andropov's death the party apparatus naturally saw in Chernenko a chance for restoring job security and accordingly gave him their unreserved support. Chernenko was aware of the importance of his power base, and in his acceptance speech he flatteringly addressed the territorial and regional party secretaries at the plenum:

> The first secretaries of the territorial and regional Party committees are taking part in the work of the Plenum. I would like to address you specially, Comrades. The Central Committee knows well how broad is the range of your obligations, your concerns. It knows how much depends on you in the solution of our current, immediate and strategic tasks. The Political Bureau of the Central Committee is convinced that you will do everything necessary to ensure stable rates of industrial production growth, successful implementation of the Food Programme, development of labor activity of the masses, as well as to implement the measures directed at raising people's well-being and, consequently, at enhancing the Party's vanguard role.[35]

The new general secretary could also rely for support on several regional party organizations. Born in Krasnoyarsk, Chernenko spent the early stages of his Komsomol and party career in the Krasnoyarsk kray, where he held posts in the regional agitation and propaganda party department and headed the Institution for Party Education.[36] Later in his career, like other top Soviet leaders (such as Gorbachev with the Stavropol kray), Chernenko retained his local connection, launching his campaign on the importance of letters to party and state officials in Krasnoyarsk in July 1978 and paying frequent visits to the region.

Chernenko spent a substantial part of his career in Moldavia where he headed the Propaganda and Agitation Department of the Moldavian Communist Party Central Committee from 1948 to 1956[37] and where his connection with Brezhnev was established. Furthermore, since 1966 Chernenko had represented Moldavia in the USSR Supreme Soviet, and consequently many of his election speeches were delivered in that republic. Chernenko apparently played an important part in the appointment of the former first secretary of the Moldavian Communist party, Ivan Bodyul, as deputy chairman of the USSR Council of Ministers on 19 December 1980.[38] Not surprisingly, Bodyul was one of the first highranking Soviet officials to "retire" after Gorbachev's election on 30 May 1985.[39]

Additional support from the territorial organizations was probably available from Kazakhstan (Kunayev's fortress) and, surprisingly, Georgia. In his election speech on 21 February 1984 in the Tbilisi Leninskiy Raykom, Shevardnadze—always alert to changes at the top and quick off the mark where favor was to be curried—suddenly remembered Chernenko's October 1982 visit to Tbilisi (an event never mentioned by him during Andropov's tenure) and said:

> Our republic warmly recalls Comrade K. U. Chernenko's visit to Georgia in October 1982 and his meetings and conversations with members of the Central Committee Bureau, the aktiv of the Georgian Communist Party, workers of Tbilisi's Dimitrov Aviation Plant, other labor collectives, and representatives of our capital's intelligentsia and young people. Konstantin Ustinovich's advice, wishes, and instructions have formed the basis of many achievements in the republic.
>
> Konstantin Ustinovich Chernenko had a big role in the elaboration and adoption of the well known CPSU Central Committee resolutions on the Georgian party organization in recent years. Some of them were adopted on his initiative. For this reason the special gratitude, recognition, respect, and love that he enjoys among Georgia's working people, are perfectly natural.[40]

Naturally, Shevardnadze also referred to Chernenko as the "head of the Politburo."[41]

Last, the old guard of the Politburo, Tikhonov, Kunayev, Grishin, and Shcherbitskiy, were Chernenko's allies and supporters. Their support was based on more than their obvious common denominators—age and connection with Brezhnev; they also were bound by joint interest and self-preservation. During his relatively brief tenure Andropov succeeded in changing one-third of Kazakhstan's regional first secretaries and nine of the Ukraine's twenty-five regional first secretaries and in revealing several corruption scandals in Moscow (such as the case of the manager of the Gastronom No. 1 store), which were bound to have an adverse effect on Grishin's status.[42] In addition, Tikhonov, who was to celebrate his seventy-ninth birthday on 14 May 1984, had few reasons to welcome Andropov's campaign to rejuvenate the party leadership, a campaign to which Gorbachev was also committed.

Although Chernenko's sources of power were relatively clear, the centers of opposition or dissent were more complex. Marshal Ustinov and Foreign Minister Andrey Gromyko did not support Chernenko at the time of Brezhnev's death. Chernenko's relations with the Army had been a subject of speculation, and observers pointed out Chernenko's somewhat lukewarm attitude toward the Army's needs. The attitude of the military toward General Secretary Chernenko was a matter of great interest in the weeks following his election. Foreign Minister Gromyko seldom bothered to conceal his contempt of Chernenko. Would he change his attitude now that Chernenko was the elected party leader? Finally, what stance would be adopted by the young guard in the

Politburo, who were closely associated with Andropov and Gorbachev? Were they going to cooperate with the new party leader? Was Gorbachev going to collaborate with Chernenko (confirming that an interfactional contract existed) or would he try to undermine the moves of his rival to consolidate his position? The first weeks of Chernenko's rule were widely expected to provide some answers to these questions.

Chernenko—Attempts to Consolidate

Chernenko's attempts to consolidate his position were accompanied by the establishment of Gorbachev as number two in the Soviet leadership. Gorbachev's new status was underscored by the reverse order of the election speeches in the 1984 USSR Supreme Soviet election campaign (a reliable indicator of the leaders' relative positions, explained in Appendix A).

Other indications of Gorbachev's improved status followed. Gorbachev (together with Chernenko, Romanov, Tikhonov, and Ustinov)[43] signed the obituary for Marshal Pavel Batitskiy and the one for Sergey Trapeznikov, the head of the CPSU Central Committee Science and Educational Institutions Department.[44] Chernenko was the only other leader to sign the latter obituary. Since in the past Gorbachev had had little responsibility in the military and educational fields and had no known family relationship with the deceased, his signing of the obituaries suggested an enhanced status and expanded areas of responsibility. Since this development followed the (assumed) deal between the two factions, Gorbachev's ascent could be interpreted, paradoxically, as part of Chernenko's own consolidation, showing that the deal was working.

Nevertheless, other signs implied that some friction was still present at the top. For one thing, the military showed little enthusiasm for Chernenko's election. *Krasnaya Zvezda, Izvestiya,* and *Pravda* of 16 February carried editorials on the CPSU Central Committee 13 February plenum. *Pravda* and *Izvestiya* used Tikhonov's speech at the plenum as a source of inspiration and repeated almost verbatim its praise of Chernenko. In contrast, *Krasnaya Zvezda* had no praise for Chernenko and dryly noted his election, adding that he had spoken at the plenum. A week later the same paper removed all doubt about its bias in a 23 February editorial dealing with the Day of the Soviet Armed Forces: The newspaper referred to the 13 February Central Committee plenum without even mentioning Chernenko's name. (On the very same day in 1983 and 1982 *Krasnaya Zvezda* had mentioned Andropov and Brezhnev, respectively.) In a *Pravda* article published on the same day, Marshal Ustinov dissented from the line followed by the Soviet media since Chernenko's election (confining its verbal attacks to Western circles rather than to the United States or President Reagan); he sharply attacked the United States and stressed that "its policy is pushing toward a nuclear catastrophe" and "disregarding generally accepted norms of international law."[45] Only ten days previously during his acceptance speech, Chernenko had not mentioned the United States, so Ustinov's *Pravda* article was a clear sign of dissent. His line was supported in a 21 February *Krasnaya Zvezda* article by Warsaw Pact chief Marshal Kulikov, who echoed Ustinov's concern over U.S. policy and implied an urgent need for the USSR defense machine to be reinforced to combat the heightened U.S. militarism.

Krasnaya Zvezda was not alone in its snub of the new general secretary: The younger Soviet leaders, who had obtained their promotions from Andropov, had few kind words for Chernenko. Romanov,[46] Vorotnikov,[47] and Ryzhkov[48] included in their speeches much warmer words for Andropov than for Chernenko, failing to give the latter even the customary routine epithets such as "outstanding party and state figure." On the other hand, the speeches of the leaders linked with Chernenko were full of adulation. His main allies, Tikhonov[49] and Kunayev,[50] lavished praise on the new general secretary, ignoring Andropov almost completely. Kunayev was the most blunt, referring to Andropov only in a sentence in which he praised Chernenko as Andropov's (and of course Brezhnev's) "loyal collaborator." Tikhonov, on the other hand, shrewdly linked Chernenko's election with the concept of party unity:

> In the days of grief when we saw Yuriy Vladimirovich Andropov on his last journey—a man who devoted all his life to serving the interests of the working people, to the cause of peace and communism—our ranks grew even closer and the unity of the party and the people became even more indestructible.
>
> At the Central Committee extraordinary February Plenum Konstantin Ustinovich Chernenko, an outstanding figure of the Communist Party and Soviet State and leader of the Leninist type, was unanimously elected general secretary of the CPSU Central Committee.[51]

Shevardnadze (at that time still a candidate member of the Politburo) and Grishin[52] referred to Chernenko as "head of the Politburo," something which even Tikhonov and Kunayev did not venture to do. The other Politburo members, including Ustinov and Gromyko, in an even-handed approach divided their praise more or less equally between Chernenko and Andropov. Gorbachev himself, speaking in his election district—the Ipatovo Electoral District in Stavropol kray—balanced his treatment of Chernenko and Andropov, although he referred to Andropov as "the outstanding figure of the CPSU and the Soviet State" and refrained from according Chernenko similar praise, merely calling him "a proven Leninist leader."[53]

Thus, two weeks after his election Chernenko evidently had still not been universally acknowledged as the undisputed head of the CPSU. Contradictory signals indicated that the Soviet military and some of the Politburo members had difficulty accepting that Brezhnev's personal aide and "man for all seasons" had become general secretary of the CPSU Central Committee. Consequently, at the beginning of March no firm conclusions could be drawn regarding his success in establishing himself in his new post. A report by the Chinese news agency Xinhua that Chernenko had been named chairman of the USSR Defense Council could not be confirmed until several weeks later, even though Xinhua attributed this report to Marshal Nikolay Ogarkov, chief of the General Staff of the Soviet Armed Forces.[54]

Chernenko as Chairman of the Presidium

Despite the paucity of reliable data and clear signals on the Kremlin situation, a clearer picture began to emerge in early April. The forthcoming Central Committee plenum and Supreme Soviet session were expected to clarify the situation, at least on the question of whether Chernenko had gathered sufficient support to ensure his election as chairman of the USSR Supreme Soviet Presidium. The official announcement on the Politburo meeting preceding the Central Committee plenum was published by *Pravda* on 6 April and naturally contained no startling revelations. (The practice of publishing an announcement of the Politburo meeting was introduced by Andropov. Such announcements merely reported the fact that the meeting had taken place, with a list of the matters ostensibly discussed and/or decided. To date no announcement of this type has revealed any vital or sensitive information, let alone views expressed by members at the meeting.) The meeting had approved the slogans for the 1 May celebrations, noted that party membership had risen to 18.5 million members, discussed some matters of party education, and approved the results of the meetings of various Soviet leaders with foreign dignitaries.[55]

The information report on the 10 April 1984 Central Committee plenum[56] reported that the only central event at the plenum had been Chernenko's speech, which dealt with economic matters, the work of the Supreme Soviet, the schools reform, and so on, but contained nothing of special interest;[57] no organizational matters (personnel changes) had been discussed at the plenum. At its morning meeting on 11 April, the Supreme Soviet elected Avgust Voss, hitherto the first secretary of the Latvian Communist party, chairman of the Soviet of Nationalities, and Lev Tolkunov, formerly editor in chief of *Pravda,* chairman of the Soviet of the Union.[58]

The main event took place at the afternoon meeting of 11 April. "On the instruction of the CPSU Central Committee," Mikhail Gorbachev proposed the election of Chernenko to the chairmanship of the Presidium:

> This issue was examined at the plenary meeting of the CPSU Central Committee yesterday. Relying on the experience of party and state construction in the past years, proceeding from the supreme interests of

the Soviet society and state, the plenum of the Central Committee unanimously found it necessary that the General Secretary of our party Central Committee Konstantin Chernenko should concurrently hold the post of the President of the Presidium of the USSR Supreme Soviet.[59]

Having disclosed where the real decision was adopted, Gorbachev listed the reasons for electing Chernenko.

Simultaneous performance by the general secretary of the CPSU Central Committee of the functions of president of the Presidium of the USSR Supreme Soviet is of great importance for pursuing foreign policy of the Soviet Union.

The representation of our supreme state interests by the general secretary of the CPSU Central Committee in the international arena convincingly reflects the fact that the Soviet Union's foreign policy is inseparable from the course of the Communist Party, whose fundamental principles were formulated in the Peace Programme worked out by the 25th and 26th CPSU Congresses, by subsequent plenary meetings of the party Central Committee.[60]

Gorbachev also had kind words for Chernenko, describing him as a "steadfast fighter for communism and peace, tested leader of the Leninist type, possessing remarkable political and organizational abilities and vast life experience."[61]

Looking remarkably healthy and tanned (he never again looked as well), Chernenko took the floor, thanking the deputies "on the high level of trust," stressing the "immense responsibility" of the new post, and briefly outlining the issues upon which he would focus his attention.[62] During the same session Tikhonov was reappointed chairman of the USSR Council of Ministers.[63] Needless to say, Chernenko and Tikhonov were both elected unanimously, as was Gorbachev, who became chairman of the prestigious Foreign Affairs Commission of the USSR Supreme Soviet.[64]

Gorbachev's Increasing Status

The developments at the Supreme Soviet session permitted a number of interesting observations, which in turn suggested important conclusions. On the basis of Gorbachev's nomination speech, the combination of the two top Soviet posts in the hands of one person seemed to have become a necessity and even a convention. (Only one year later, Gorbachev would argue precisely the opposite in proposing Gromyko for the post of chairman of the USSR Supreme Soviet Presidium.)

The session offered conclusive proof of Gorbachev's firm position as number two in the Soviet leadership. Whereas Tikhonov had proposed Chernenko's election to the general secretaryship of the Central Committee, thus giving the procedure a factional character, now Gorbachev proposed Chernenko, offering him the appropriate praise. (Chernenko responded in kind by including in his acceptance speech issues with which Gorbachev was becoming increasingly identified—improving productivity and raising living standards.[65]) Since Chernenko had proposed Andropov in June 1983 for the post of presidium chairman, the logical conclusion is that this position was reserved for the second most powerful person in the leadership, namely, the second secretary.

The post of second secretary does not officially exist in the CPSU, and it is not mentioned in the party statutes. Nevertheless, practically speaking, the post does exist and is constantly referred to by scholars of the Soviet political system. The CPSU Secretariat includes a number of secretaries, in addition to the general secretary, each of whom supervises a particular area, such as agriculture or heavy industry. However, the importance of two areas of control—the supervision of cadre policy and of ideology—transcends the boundaries of a specific area of responsibility and affects party activities in all other areas. The secretary in charge of cadre policy has an unrivaled opportunity to consolidate that position by engineering the promotion of supporters to key party posts or simply by creating new vassals through promoting obscure party officials. The secretary for ideological matters is involved in defining policy in every area and providing the ideological formulations or interpretations needed to justify actual events and measures. Furthermore, the ideological duties require heavy involvement in relations with foreign Communist and workers' parties, international relations, and broad propaganda campaigns even though other secretaries are formally in charge of these areas. Therefore, the secretary for ideological matters is traditionally also the chairman of the USSR Supreme Soviet Foreign Affairs Commission, which further increases the authority of the position. Finally, because of involvement in so many crucial areas concerned with foreign policy the secretary is afforded broad international exposure, making the positionholder one of the most visible and best known Soviet leaders. The secretary in charge of ideology is often referred to as the second secretary. However, the personal qualities of a secretary can also result in elevation to this unofficial status. Thus, when Suslov controlled the area of ideology, Kirilenko was occasionally referred to as the second secretary. Nevertheless, when the areas of cadre policy and ideology are both concentrated in one person's hands, as they were with Chernenko at the end of Brezhnev's rule and with Gorbachev under Chernenko, no doubt obscures the identity of the second secretary.

Gorbachev's election to the post of chairman of the USSR Supreme Soviet Foreign Affairs Commission further increased his status and provided him with much needed foreign exposure. After years of involvement with agriculture and the economy, Gorbachev was now also directing foreign affairs, the party's cadre policy, and apparently ideology, as confirmed by subsequent events. For example, he was the only Politburo member at the 23 April ceremony marking the sixtieth anniversary of the party's ideological journal *Kommunist*.[66]

On the following day, when the CPSU Central Committee Commission entrusted with preparing the new party program met, Gorbachev spoke along with Chernenko, Gromyko, Ponomarev, and Mikhail Zimyanin.[67] On 28 April he met the Hungarian ideological secretary Miklos Ovari.[68] Although each of these signals in isolation was not sufficient grounds to establish that Gorbachev was now acting as the Central Committee secretary in charge of ideology, taken in combination with certain other pointers they provided a clear pattern. Especially important was Gorbachev's meeting with Ovari because the strict unwritten protocol of the Communist world, under which a guest must be hosted by a counterpart.

Gorbachev's position entailed an immense range of responsibilities, many more than previously held by Suslov or even Chernenko when they were the party's second-ranking secretaries. It can only be assumed that these developments resulted from the deal struck between the two factions, which cut the Gordian knot of dissension within the Politburo, enabled Chernenko to be elected general secretary, and secured for Gorbachev the second most powerful position in the Central Committee Secretariat with the promise of a future election to the post of party leader. The unavoidable conclusion is that at the session not only was Chernenko elected but part of Gorbachev's future inheritance was transferred to him.

Chernenko in Power

Whatever the details of the deal were, it was remarkable that Chernenko took two whole months to win the triple crown for himself. By mid-April he was already general secretary, president, and (apparently) chairman of the Defense Council, thus removing all doubt as to who was in charge. Furthermore, Chernenko seemed to have patched up his differences with the Army. On 10 April, one day before Chernenko's election as chairman of the Supreme Soviet Presidium, *Krasnaya Zvezda*, the Soviet Army organ, published a long letter from Lt. Gen. V. Donskoy, chief of the troops of the Red Banner Eastern Front Military District. This letter, accompanied by a photo of a youthful Chernenko with other soldiers from his unit in Kazakhstan in 1930, described Chernenko's (hitherto unknown) military service in the border troops:

> K. U. Chernenko was unanimously elected secretary of the party cell, and he fully justified his comrades' trust. Konstantin Ustinovich enjoyed great respect both in the unit and among the local population. Times were tense then, and the border guards had to wage a constant struggle against the enemies of the Soviet power. Konstantin Ustinovich Chernenko showed courage and bravery in clashes with bandits. He was an accurate shot with a rifle or a submachine gun, and did not miss when throwing hand grenades at targets. He was a good horseman and, as senior detail

officer, always rode out on border patrol. Comrade Chernenko often spoke at the village club, delivering reports and conducting talks on political subjects with the local population. His free time was devoted to self-education and he read extensively. Even at that time, as we were told by his fellow serviceman, G. A. Konev, you could feel that party work was to become a lifelong vocation for this man.[69]

No doubt the Army was lending a helping hand in establishing a military record of sorts for the general secretary to enhance his image.

By mid-April 1984 Chernenko was clearly enjoying center stage. He missed no opportunity to speak at public events, making at least one major speech every week; in April alone the Soviet press reported ten speeches by Chernenko for various occasions. The newspapers carried unusual photographs of Chernenko at leisure, amid his family. The message was evident: An active and vigorous leader was at the helm.

Chernenko's speeches during these weeks were more remarkable for their confident tone than their content. The motif of "moving forward" became the central theme in each address, although often he did not clearly state who was to move forward and in what direction. For example, in his acceptance speech at the 13 February Central Committee plenum he advocated "moving forward without stopping," urging the economic leaders to "take risks." In his election speech on 2 March he declared that "we can and want to move forward faster." In his 26 March address on agricultural issues Chernenko called for a "new approach,"[70] and in his 29 April speech at the Moscow metallurgy plant he demanded "quick changes in the system."[71] His clear intention was to project a fresh image of an innovator. To a large degree, this new approach was a tactical move; the leader of the old guard had donned a youthful mask, posing as a vigorous leader with bold ideas. Other probable reasons for this artificially projected energy and activity were more human: Chernenko realized that the sand in his hourglass was running out and that to leave his mark in the short period left to him he had to move quickly.

One of Chernenko's favorite topics was the preparation and publication of a new party program. In his speech at the 25 April meeting of the Program Drafting Commission,[72] Chernenko seemed to view the new party program in the same light as Brezhnev viewed the new USSR Constitution introduced by him—as a means of asserting authority and influencing the party's life. This issue, apart from accelerating the preparations for the 27th Party Congress, assured Chernenko of high public prominence and intense involvement in the party's daily debates and activities. In his 29 April speech at Moscow's Hammer and Sickle metallurgy plant he demanded that "preparations for the Congress should begin now!"[73] A *Pravda* editorial of 23 April used almost identical words in advocating "immediately beginning preparations for the Congress." Given the situation in the Politburo, where Chernenko could not expect to move anything forward without difficulty, the general secretary, a great expert in internal party machination and activation of the party machine, was attempting to initiate changes from the grass roots through the local accountability-election meetings that would precede the Congress, as well as through the projected new party program.

Allocation of resources was another theme often raised by Chernenko. In his 2 March election speech, he asserted that although the international situation made it necessary "to devote considerable resources" to strengthening the country's defense capability, "we did not even think of curtailing social programs" to do so.[74] Chernenko touched upon the same issue in his 29 April speech at the Moscow metallurgy plant: He pledged to raise the standard of living, promising that the existing plans for social and economic development would be implemented and underlining that the adoption of extraordinary measures (such as longer working hours)[75] was not necessary to strengthen the country's defenses. Although the Army no doubt disapproved of Chernenko's assertion that no extraordinary sacrifices were required for defense, there was no visible reaction from military circles.

The Kremlin power struggle involved a third man—Grigoriy Romanov. Romanov was the third Politburo member, in addition to Gorbachev and Chernenko, who also was a Central Committee secretary. Immediately after Andropov's death and Chernenko's installation as general secretary, Romanov became increasingly involved in military affairs. On 21 February he attended the funeral of Marshal Batitskiy, together with Defense Minister Ustinov and Moscow's party boss Grishin.[76] On 22 February he and Marshal Ustinov represented the Politburo at the main festive meeting marking the Day of the Soviet Army and Navy.[77] At the birthday anniversary of the first (and deceased) cosmonaut Yuriy Gagarin on 9 March, Romanov once again was the Politburo representative.[78] Finally, on 27 April he met the head of the Hungarian Central Committee Administrative Organs Department,[79] which traditionally supervises the activity of the military and paramilitary forces in Hungary. These indications, as well as Romanov's past involvement with the defense industry, suggested that his takeover of new responsibilities for military matters within the Secretariat was another item in the deal struck between the factions before Chernenko's election.

Toward the end of April 1984 the two rival factions within the Politburo were more or less equally matched, blocking any attempts to implement important changes in Soviet policy. The deadlock was resolved by an agreement by which Chernenko was allotted the post of general secretary (and subsequently allowed to become chairman of the Defense Council and of the Presidium) but only at the cost of recognizing Gorbachev as number two in the Soviet leadership—a quite extraordinary and unprecedented concession. Moreover, crucial areas of Soviet domestic and foreign policy were handed over to Gorbachev to supervise, and unofficial recognition of him as heir apparent was confirmed by transferring to him an important part of the political power while the incumbent general secretary was still alive and active.

Evidently, Chernenko was principally interested in obtaining the outward and visible symbols of supremacy referred to as the triple crown—the posts of general secretary, chairman of the Supreme Soviet Presidium, and chairman of the Defense Council. To achieve this goal, he was prepared to delegate some of the power vested in these posts to Gorbachev, provided that the titles remained in his hands. He was probably motivated not only by a desire to accomplish the succession as soon as possible, almost regardless of the price, but also by the hope of using these posts in the future to curb Gorbachev and return full power to himself. Thus his deal with Gorbachev involved a division of real power and responsibilities, while retaining for himself the posts that outwardly signified the possession of supreme power. This technique of splitting or sharing power was quite different from Brezhnev's approach: Brezhnev delegated power but only after he had concentrated it completely in his hands; Chernenko, on the other hand, surrendered parts of his power before he had acquired the leadership, as the price for securing his ascent.

The agreement between the factions probably involved other issues and personalities, such as the entrusting of party secretary Romanov with responsibility for the Soviet Armed Forces and further increasing Gromyko's independence in conducting foreign affairs, a matter analyzed (in Chapter 6). At the same time, a false impression of the continuity of Andropov's policies was created simply because the Politburo, deadlocked by the rivalry of the two factions, was unable to initiate any bold strokes in any vital area of Soviet politics. Consequently, forced by necessity to maintain a pretence of continuity, Chernenko tried to dissociate himself from Andropov and his policies by promoting an image of himself as a vigorous and active leader (in contrast to Andropov's erratic performance, marred by months of illness that kept him out of public view) and to assert his authority through his old power base of the party apparatus by accelerating the debates of the new party program and the preparations for the 27th CPSU Congress. By the end of April Chernenko appeared to be trying to fight the battle with his Politburo rivals through the lower party echelons, as well as by activating intense party debates from the grass roots.

6

Too Late, Too Short:
Chernenko Rules

Soon after Chernenko's election as chairman of the Supreme Soviet Presidium, it was semiofficially disclosed that he also held the post of chairman of the Defense Council. Although as far back as February the Chinese press agency Xinhua had quoted Marshal Ogarkov as announcing this news,[1] there had been no further mention of the matter. On 9 May in his Victory Day anniversary speech, Deputy Defense Minister Semen Kurkotkin identified Chernenko as the chairman of the Defense Council.[2]

Media Evidence of Kremlin Strife

Other signals indicated that the idyll in the Kremlin was over and that, notwithstanding any agreement, the struggle between the two factions was continuing, although sotto voce. Two articles in the CPSU's ideological journal *Kommunist,* no. 6, April 1984, suggested that not all was proceeding as smoothly as the publicized atmosphere of harmony among the top CPSU leaders should indicate. Both articles used historical examples to demonstrate that factionalism was an extremely harmful phenomenon that can inflict great damage on the party, in order to warn of the dangers ahead.

The author of the first article, "Unity, Organization, and Discipline," was Yevgeniy E. Bugayev, doctor of history and a member of the *Kommunist* editorial board. Again Lenin's life was used as a safe pretext for discussing sensitive aspects of current party affairs while ostensibly referring to past history. Bugayev produced his article for the occasion of the eightieth anniversary of the publication of Lenin's book, *One Step Forward, Two Steps Back.* He pointed out that although the book had been published eighty years ago, it remained "instructive" for those wishing to learn "how to strengthen and consolidate the unity of the party."[3] Quoting Lenin that "the unity of the proletariat is impossible without the unity of the party"[4] and stressing that "the monolithic ideological and organizational unity of our party is one of the most important conditions of its leading role in the Soviet society,"[5] Bugayev pointed out that "unity of action also requires unity in *organizational matters*" (Bugayev's italics).[6]

When listing the preconditions for maintenance of party unity, Bugayev gave prominence to "maintaining the unity of the party leadership."[7] He quoted Lenin on the dangers of opportunism in organizational matters (in Communist parlance this term implies personnel issues), emphasizing that this proposition "is relevant even today as then, because the multifaced forms of opportunism have not become less dangerous."[8] Bugayev concluded that "the party must have a single uniform and authoritative center" and that "this center must be composed of persons who firmly conduct the line determined by the Congress and that no personal qualities of this or that member of the center should serve as a source of discord or even split."[9]

Besides using Lenin as his authority, Bugayev quoted Chernenko on the fact that "the cohesion of Soviet Communists is the inexhaustible source of their power."[10] Repeatedly harping on the "topicality" of these thoughts on party cohesion and personal opportunism and quoting Chernenko again on the need for enhancing Communists' moral purity and sense of responsibility,[11] Bugayev added: "This applies first of all to Communists entrusted with responsible positions."[12]

The message could hardly be clearer: Personal discord and opportunism at the very top were endangering the unity and cohesion of the entire party. Since Chernenko was the only current leader quoted as an authority by Bugayev, no doubt his opinions had inspired the article.

The second article, signed by Valentin Chikin, carried the somewhat evangelical title, "We Go to Lenin." The same author had published a significant article in *Sovetskaya Rossiya* on 21 January 1983, devoted to Lenin's thoughts on the age and state of health of the members of the Central Committee and maintaining that Lenin advocated including more young blood in the party leadership to provide continuity. Chikin had developed the same idea in another piece in *Kommunist,* no. 6, April 1983, entitled "V. I. Lenin: 'These are the Lofty Tasks of Which I am Dreaming'" (mentioned in Chapter 2). Finally, revealing his political allegiance, on 13 February 1984—the very day of Chernenko's election as general secretary—Chikin published an article in *Sovetskaya Rossiya,* praising Andropov in warm, almost personal terms.

Chikin used the hackneyed ploy of referring to risky topical issues while ostensibly writing on Lenin. In his April 1984 article in *Kommunist* Chikin focused on Lenin's recovery from his stroke, describing his efforts to resume normal activity and his concern with the "danger of split" and "factional manifestations," which placed the vital unity of the party at risk.[13] "The dangers of opportunism" were also prominently mentioned. Chikin went even further than Bugayev, quoting Lenin's wife Krupskaya on the dangers of artificially dividing the leadership between young and old factions, thus plainly pinpointing the source of the current danger to party cohesion.

> Our party has not known until now a division between old and young members, age has not been a factor in our party until now. This division would have perhaps significance if the elders, while leaving their activity, would turn into "ikons", but our elders' generation remained in the very center of the struggle and work, and it had no less revolutionary and postrevolutionary experience than the new party members. This is so because the elders have a good Marxist training, which allows them to analyze well the past experience, and the old party traditions. . . . The slogan of placing the emphasis on the youth . . . is basically incorrect, and consequently, it is easy to use it in a demagogic fashion.[14]

Repeatedly stressing the slogan of "placing the emphasis on youth," Chikin also pointed out the importance of unity and "united party work."[15] "The egotistic 'I' did not exist for Lenin,"[16] he concluded plaintively.

Thus, although Bugayev implied that there was a danger of a split because of the opportunistic preoccupations of certain leaders, Chikin showed that the real problem causing the division at the top of the party was age. He suggested that certain top leaders were undermining the authority of others, who were correctly implementing the decisions of the party Congress (the country's elected leaders) by the use of irrelevant and harmful arguments—such as the age of the elected leaders—and thus threatening unity and cohesion in the party ranks. It was strange to see Chikin, a firm Andropov supporter, helping Chernenko's faction by acting with Bugayev as the mouthpiece of the old guard in the Politburo. The two articles could be interpreted as expressing a protest by Chernenko against the contract with the "young Turks" in the Politburo on the grounds that the very contract that brought about his election was now blocking his further moves and undermining his authority as party leader.

In addition, the articles were an attempt by Chernenko and his faction to inform the party apparatus (which still consisted mostly of Brezhnev's appointees) of the situation in the Politburo and to recruit the support of the nomenklatura. The specific way in which the articles delivered their messages and indicated the nature of the struggle (Bugayev's warning that opportunists were undermining the authority of the leaders elected by the Congress and Chikin's asserting that the younger leaders were trying to push the old guard aside) was bound to appeal to the nomenklatura members. The latter had strengthened their positions at the 26th CPSU Congress (against the decisions of which the "opportunists" were now struggling), and many were from Chernenko's own generation. Chernenko undoubtedly was using all means available to recruit further support, block Gorbachev's faction, and win back the power he had surrendered to Gorbachev in the deal preceding his own election.

Kommunist was not the only Soviet journal to suggest the existence of strife within the leadership. *Voprosy Istorii,* a scholarly journal with no obvious connection with the party leadership, published in its April 1984 issue an editorial that reassessed Khrushchev's era.[17] Although pointing out "certain mistakes" committed by Khrushchev in his economic policies, which were said to have arisen from his "subjectivism and voluntarism," the article focused mainly on the positive achievements of Khrushchev's rule. (Under Brezhnev mention of Khrushchev's name was anathema, and on the few occasions that his name was publicly mentioned, it was invariably in connection with a criticism of his reign.) The *Voprosy Istorii* editorial not only mentioned Khrushchev's name several times but even positively assessed some aspects of his era, such as the general improvement in living standards, the increases of wages, and the expansion of social services. Khrushchev's efforts to increase public participation in policymaking and overcome the "negative consequences of Stalin's personality cult" were cited, clearly implying that many of Brezhnev's achievements were in fact the results of initiatives originated under Khrushchev. One needed little imagination to perceive that the editorial's aim was to attack Chernenko, who was so closely associated with Brezhnev. The repreated references to collective leadership could also be interpreted as an admonition aimed at the general secretary.

The tension in the leadership was also revealed by the media treatment of the leaders' lineup at the May Day ceremony in Red Square. Although Gorbachev stood on the Lenin Mausoleum tribune in his official fifth place, Baku's *Bakinskiy Rabochiy*[18] and the Minsk daily *Byelorusskaya Pravda*[19] showed him in the third position, immediately after Chernenko and Tikhonov (this was also the order of these leaders' election speeches). Since the first secretaries of Azerbaijan (Kyamran Bagirov, elected 3 December 1982)[20] and of Belorussia (Nikolay Slyunkov, elected 13 January 1983)[21] obtained their elections under Andropov, this favoritism toward Gorbachev was easily explained. The newspapers of the other republics adhered to the official version of the leaders' lineup.

Evidence of Chernenko's Limited Power

The problem of youth continued to haunt Chernenko. On 28 May almost the entire Politburo showed up at an All-Army Conference of Komsomol Organizations' Secretaries;[22] past conferences had only required the attendance of a single Politburo member or Central Committee secretary. This time, however, Chernenko himself expressed his dissatisfaction with the work of the Komsomol in the Army and listed a number of shortcomings but praised the performance of the Soviet troops in Afghanistan. Chernenko did not miss the opportunity to point out publicly his participation in a youth forum and to associate himself with the military. Indeed, this occasion was the first time that Chernenko had spoken at a military forum (though a mere Komsomol conference), and he cleverly exploited the chance to remind the Soviet public of his only military record with the border guards. He had done the same two days earlier when he greeted his old border guards unit in Kazakhstan on the occasion of the Border Guards National Day.[23] Incidentally, Marshal Ustinov, who naturally also attended the conference, well understood the significance given by Chernenko to the affair and duly rose to the occasion, introducing Chernenko as "chairman of the Defense Council."[24]

Despite the apparent harmony between Chernenko and the military, he continued to be blocked in the Politburo by Gorbachev's faction. Nothing illustrated the situation better than the COMECON (Council for Mutual Economic Assistance) economic summit that opened in Moscow on 12 June 1984.[25] The delegations from all other socialist countries were composed of their party first (or general) secretaries, premiers, and necessary economic specialists. In sharp contrast, the Soviet delegation included Chernenko, Tikhonov, Gorbachev, Gromyko, Romanov, Ustinov, Dolgikh, Konstantin Rusakov, Nikolay Baybakov, and Nikolay Talyzin—six Politburo members, almost the entire secretariat (six secretaries, including Chernenko), and two deputy premiers, in addition to Premier Tikhonov, plus the foreign and defense ministers.[26] No other East European delegation was composed of foreign or defense ministers, nor had previous Soviet delegations. This composition demonstrated that because the Politburo factions did not trust one another the Soviet delegation included the most prominent representatives of both groups, plus Gromyko and Ustinov, who had no clear responsibilities at the economic summit but were perhaps there to monitor Chernenko's performance. Rather than demonstrating collective leadership, the composition of the delegation pointed up the mistrust and suspicion rampant in the Politburo and also indicated that Chernenko's authority was totally undermined, especially in the foreign affairs field.

When Ustinov visited India (5–10 March 1984) and Aliyev visited Syria (10–13 March), they conveyed greetings from Chernenko, Tikhonov, and Gromyko, whereas on previous occasions such greetings had been conveyed in the name of either the general secretary alone or the entire leadership, without singling out specific names. Chernenko himself, when meeting the FRG's SPD (German Socialist Party) leader Vogel on 12 March 1984, referred several times to the Soviet domestic and foreign policies "collectively worked out and conducted by the Soviet leadership."[27] Neither the occasion nor the guest's rank merited such a statement. These signs suggest that the contract between the two factions, though conferring the top posts on Chernenko, severely curbed his freedom of action in all important fields and in fact subjected every important decision to the agreement of both factions. The situation at the COMECON Council meeting showed that Chernenko and Tikhonov could not safely be left alone to deal with the East European partners; Gorbachev, Romanov, Gromyko, and Ustinov all had to be there to ensure fair play.

On 15 June the Soviet press marked the seventieth birthday anniversary of former leader Yuriy Andropov. *Pravda* published an unattributed article, "A Life Devoted to the People: On the 70th Anniversary of Yuriy Andropov's Birth," which was reprinted by other Soviet dailies. The article pointed out Andropov's concern for "observance of Leninist norms and principles of party life and ensuring collectiveness in the work of party organs—from the CPSU Central Committee to local party committees."[28] Chernenko did not figure very prominently in the article; in fact, there were only two quotations from him, concerning the importance of collective leadership.

Three weeks earlier *Sovetskaya Rossiya,* which seemed to be acting as the harbinger of Nemesis for Chernenko, published an editorial dealing with the age of the top leaders. Stressing in unequivocal terms that power should be handed over to the next generation, the editorial asserted that "young people do not carry the burden of obsolete habits" and "grasp with greater ease progressive ideas and bold concepts"[29]— extremely unusual ideas in the USSR. Hinting that the old guard should pass on the baton to the younger generation although this step would not be easy, the editorial insisted that the decision "to step aside of one's own accord" (virtually unknown in the Soviet political hierarchy) was evidence of a "very keen sense of duty." Finally, the editorial succinctly pointed out that the need for a younger leadership was felt "in every area."[30] Although no mention was made of the Politburo in the article, let alone of Chernenko and Gorbachev, every perceptive reader would understand to whom the anonymous article was directed. (Against this background, it will be remembered that *Sovetskaya Rossiya* had published the two articles by Valentin Chikin that pointed out that Lenin was seriously concerned with the age and state of health of the Central Committee members[31] and stressed the need for bringing "fresh forces" into the leadership.[32]

Chernenko's Health Deteriorates

Evidently *Sovetskaya Rossiya,* or at least someone on the newspaper's staff, was well informed on Chernenko's condition because soon after the publication of the editorial Chernenko's health visibly deteriorated. On 4 July he attended a Kremlin ceremony at which distinguished workers and various party and state figures received awards. The Soviet "Vremya" television program carried a videorecording of the ceremony in which Chernenko gave the impression of being a very sick man.[33] His shortness of breath when speaking was obvious. Nevertheless, for several days after he continued his normal activities and on 13 July met UN Secretary General Perez de Cuellar, who was visiting the Soviet Union.[34] Two days later, TASS published the following brief announcement: "General Secretary of the CPSU Central Committee and President of the Presidium of the USSR Supreme Soviet, Konstantin Ustinovich Chernenko, left Moscow today for holidays."[35]

This marked the starting point of Chernenko's seven-week absence from public view. Although Soviet leaders customarily spend much of the summer in the Crimea, they normally make public appearances during this period; indeed, Brezhnev customarily received all the East European leaders while vacationing in the Crimea. Chernenko, however, made no such appearances: Instead he made the same sort of phantom appearances that were so characteristic of Andropov's absence from public view from August 1983 until his death in February 1984. He signed obituaries, including that of Academician Georgiy Boreskov, and sent a signed photo of himself to the Penza Museum of Revolutionary Combat and Labor Glory.[36] Chernenko also replied to a letter from the Irishman Sean McBride, holder of the Lenin and Nobel Peace Prizes,[37] and to the appeal of the International Conference on Nuclear-Free Zones held in Manchester in April 1984.[38] The British press pointed out that the reply to the Manchester conference was incorrectly addressed to the lord mayor of Manchester, evidence that it had been concocted in haste without the usual punctilious attention to detail characteristic of the Kremlin office.[39]

The Politburo continued to hold its weekly meetings (perhaps already chaired by Gorbachev?), and although the short reports on these regular meetings[40] did not list Chernenko among those who spoke, a clear attempt was made to suggest that Chernenko was present. For example, one announcement read: "In connection with the preparations for the 27th Party Congress, the CPSU Central Committee Politburo considered at its routine meeting Comrade Chernenko's proposals concerning the possible introduction of certain changes in the CPSU Statute."[41] This announcement failed to state explicitly that Chernenko was actually present. Incidently, during this same period the Presidium of the Supreme Soviet appointed Andropov's son Igor, Soviet ambassador to Greece.[42] The official announcement omitted to mention who had signed the appointment document.

Chernenko's return to relatively normal and visible activity was revealed in an interview that he gave to *Pravda,* published on 2 September. No details of time or place were given, nor were there any accompanying pictures of the interview (if it indeed took place), and the headline, "K. U. Chernenko's Replies to Questions Put by the Newspaper *Pravda,*"[43] could mean that the so-called interview was merely written replies to questions posed by the daily. Only three days earlier a routine Politburo meeting had "discussed and approved the proposals by Comrade Chernenko for strengthening the material and technical base of the construction industry, further industrializing it, and assisting its development."[44] Once again, the report failed to confirm Chernenko's actual attendance.

On 5 September 1984, after a seven-week absence, Chernenko finally surfaced to give awards to Soviet cosmonauts Svetlana Savitskaya, Igor Volk, and Vladimir Dzhanibekov for their space flight.[45] In a video-recording of the ceremony shown on television, Chernenko looked sick and tired and completed his brief four and one-half minute speech with difficulty, his gaze often wandering into the distance. Instead of personally pinning the orders on the lapels of the recipients, Chernenko deviated from the usual custom and merely handed over the boxes containing the orders.[46] On the next day Chernenko did not take part in the ceremony (in which Gorbachev played the main role) at which the Politburo and Central Committee secretary paid their respects to the deceased Leonid Kostandov, deputy chairman of the Council of Ministers.[47] He was also absent from the Red Square funeral ceremony on 7 September.[48]

During summer 1984 Moscow started an intensive propaganda campaign against West German so-called revanchism.[49] The campaign was clearly prompted by the marked improvement in relations between East and West Germany, as well as by the intentions of Erich Honecker of the GDR, Bulgaria's Todor Zhivkov, and Romania's Nicolae Ceausescu to visit Bonn. Virtually hundreds of articles, commentaries, and analyses in the Soviet media warned against the "revanchist activities of the FRG authorities."[50] Soviet leaders used visits abroad to point out the dangers of West German militarism and revanchism, the most notable examples before the end of August being Tikhonov's 21 July speech to the Polish Sejm marking the fortieth anniversary of Poland's liberation[51] and Marshal Ustinov's speech at the Banska Bystica rally marking the fortieth anniversary of the Slovak uprising.[52] The verbal attacks fitted into the pattern—already established under Andropov—of pressing the East European countries to align themselves more closely with Soviet foreign policy. Under heavy Moscow pressure, on 4 September Honecker announced the cancellation of his trip to Bonn.[53]

Gorbachev Moves to the Forefront

On 9 September Bulgaria celebrated its own fortieth liberation anniversary. Moscow was represented at the ceremonies by Mikhail Gorbachev, who exploited the occasion to express his views on the ultrasensitive issue of the socialist states' unity of action. Speaking at the 8 September meeting in Sofia, Gorbachev stressed the importance of the socialist community's "firmness" and of the "purposefulness and coordinated nature" of the community's action. He strongly emphasized the "unity of national and international interests," rejecting the notion that national interests should take precedence. This was in sharp contrast to the tentative steps being made by Hungary, Romania, and more recently Bulgaria and the GDR to promote their own national interests. However, Gorbachev also showed his liberality, by stating that there was no "universal recipe" for building socialism and underlining the sovereignty and equality of all the members of the socialist community.[54]

Gorbachev's remarks on the unity of the socialist bloc were more emphatic than Tikhonov's and Ustinov's statements. He seemed to project a much stronger authority than either the Soviet premier or the defense minister, and he did not hesitate to touch upon another sensitive issue—relations with Albania. Speaking in Sofia, Gorbachev offered to normalize relations with Albania, the first statement on this issue by any Soviet leader for many years.[55]

Before he left for Sofia, Gorbachev attended a very important Politburo meeting. On 6 September TASS announced that Marshal Nikolay Ogarkov, chief of the General Staff of the USSR Armed Forces and first deputy minister of defense, had been "relieved of his post in connection with a new appointment."[56] This announcement aroused great surprise: Ogarkov had gained worldwide fame exactly one year earlier from his tough performance at the press conference following the downing of the South Korean Boeing 747 by Soviet fighters. There had been no indication that this dismissal was forthcoming. On 4 September *Krasnaya Zvezda* carried a photograph of Ogarkov together with Marshal Ustinov at a meeting with a Finnish military delegation. On the following day there was a report of Ogarkov seeing off the Finns at Moscow Airport.[57] Thus it is logical to assume that the dismissal decision was taken on the very day of its publication—6 September. Furthermore, since the Politburo met on that day,[58] the decision was probably reached at the meeting. (The announcement on the meeting, naturally, mentions nothing on such a decision.)

Another interesting aspect was the absence of certain Politburo members from the meeting. Grigoriy Romanov, closely connected with the military, had departed the day before to visit Ethiopia.[59] Dinmukhamed Kunayev was reported touring Kazakhstan on 6 September, so probably also failed to attend.[60] Gorbachev, Grishin, Gromyko, Ustinov, Solomentsev, and Vorotnikov had been reported as attending the lying-in-state of Deputy Premier Kostandov earlier on the day of the Politburo meeting, so probably did attend.[61] Chernenko was apparently in Moscow, having attended the cosmonauts' award ceremony on 5 September, but whether he attended or not is not certain since he failed to make an appearance at the funeral ceremony for Kostandov. The whereabouts of the Ukraine's party chief Shcherbitskiy on 6 September are not known. There was also no word on Tikhonov or Aliyev, who had not been seen in public for weeks. Accordingly, the Politburo meeting that decided Ogarkov's fate was probably not attended by Romanov or Kunayev and may have also been missed by other members.

The absence of Romanov was most significant. As Romanov was the supervisor of the Soviet military-industrial complex, a decision to replace the USSR chief of general staff was difficult to take without his prior agreement—if he was present. This leaves two possible explanations: Either the decision was made before 6 September (which seems unlikely in view of Ogarkov's meeting with the Finnish military delegation on 4 and 5 September) or the other Politburo members, knowing Romanov's views, decided to wait until his trip to Ethiopia to reach the decision to dismiss Ogarkov. No hard evidence is available to support either hypothesis, but the second appears more likely.

A further question is why Ogarkov was removed. *Pravda*'s editorial on 5 September was devoted to the issue of improving the people's welfare and implied that no additional funds would be diverted to defence. Furthermore, it contained the statement that "despite the tense international situation which forces the diversion of considerable resources to strengthening the country's security, we do not permit even the idea of cutting the broad social programs of the 26th CPSU Congress."[62] On the same day, the Soviet Army organ *Krasnaya Zvezda* devoted its own editorial to this topic. (Given that coincidences do not happen in the Soviet Union, this meant that a party decision has recently been reached on the matter and that the propaganda organs had received their appropriate instructions.) *Krasnaya Zvezda* used words and phrases almost identical to those in *Pravda,* asserting that the idea of cutting the welfare program "was not justified."[63]

Chernenko himself had raised the same issue several times in the past, most notably in his 2 March election speech and his 29 April address at the Moscow Hammer and Sickle plant. In the election speech he stated: "During the past five years the complexities of international life compelled us to divert considerable resources to the needs connected with the consolidation of the country's security. But we did not even think of curtailing social programs, since the ultimate goal of all our work is improving the well-being of the Soviet people."[64] On 29 April he said: "We shall consistently implement the programs planned for the social and economic development of the country, and for raising the living standard of the Soviet people."[65]

The mood of the *Pravda* and *Krasnaya Zvezda* editorials, as well as Chernenko's recorded views, differed from that held by Ogarkov. Ogarkov had repeatedly advocated extreme measures, such as the development of new weapons (which would clearly require the allocation of vast resources), a larger role for the professional military in political decisionmaking, and the creation of wartime command and control organs to prepare for the conduct of the next war. These opinions, which Ogarkov continued stubbornly to press, together with his recently enhanced prestige, were probably enough to bring about his dismissal. It is more difficult to determine a link between the dismissal and the Kremlin power struggle. His partial rehabilitation by Gorbachev in 1985 could indicate that not all the Politburo members agreed with the dismissal decision; again however there is no firm evidence. Finally, at the time rumors were circulating that Ustinov, realizing that his own political end was approaching, pressed his political colleagues to remove the ambitious and dangerous Ogarkov before he could make his bid for Ustinov's seat.

Chernenko Returns Briefly

Upon his return from his seven-week absence, Chernenko was eager to revive his image as the active, dynamic leader. On 21 September the anniversary of the Soviet-Finnish armistice was marked. In the past this routine event had never been an occasion for a major statement by a top Soviet leader. But Chernenko badly needed public exposure and grabbed the chance to make a public appearance. Soviet television viewers saw a videorecording of an old and visibly sick Chernenko delivering a message to the Finnish people.[66] The seated Chernenko struggled to deliver the text of his address (the film clearly had been spliced) and showed signs of his well-known respiratory problem. The background was neutral and nondescript, giving no hint as to where the recording had been made. Chernenko's performance lasted a scant five minutes.

Two days later on 23 September, the eve of Chernenko's seventy-third birthday, a Supreme Soviet decree was promulgated, awarding Chernenko a third star for his Hero of Soviet Labor order.[67] This was a throwback to Brezhnev's last years, when the conferring of successive awards on Brezhnev seemed to be used to build up his stature and improve his image. The normal practice was to award leaders on their round birthdays, so Chernenko's seventy-third birthday was not a usual occasion for such an award. In announcing the decree, *Pravda* stated that it had been conferred on Chernenko for "his exceptional service in leading the party and state," as well as for "strengthening the Soviet defensive capability" and "strengthening peace and security."[68]

The award ceremony took place on 27 September.[69] This was a further break with tradition, since such ceremonies normally were held immediately after promulgation of the award or on the birthday itself. The television videofilm showed Chernenko in poor physical shape. Standing stiffly, he managed to deliver a short speech. This time he tried to get through the speech as fast as possible in an attempt to shorten the ordeal. The sight aroused pity in the viewers.[70] The other speaker at the award ceremony was Marshal Ustinov. He attempted to boost his colleague's prestige, referring to him as "chairman of the Defense Council and supreme Commander in Chief."[71] No leader since Stalin had been accorded the last title.

On 25 September Chernenko took part in another event that did not require his presence—the public meeting to celebrate the fiftieth anniversary of the USSR Writers' Union.[72] In the report of the event in the "Vremya" television program[73] viewers could see Gorbachev's improved rating; he now occupied the official third place in the lineup, after Chernenko and Tikhonov and in front of Ustinov.

Gorbachev's Temporary Setback

On 29 September *Pravda,* in reporting Gorbachev's meeting with a British Communists' delegation, identified A. P. Lushchikov as "an assistant to the CPSU Central Committee secretary." The public identification of a personal assistant is a sign of great prestige and personal status in the USSR. This, along with other signs, would normally indicate an enhancement of Gorbachev's status. Yet at the 23 October Central Committee plenum, which dealt with agriculture—an area in which Gorbachev had specialized for many years—he was not listed among the speakers and apparently played no active part in the proceedings.

Chernenko read the introductory report at the plenum, and Tikhonov, himself an industrial expert, read the main report, which outlined future improvements in Soviet agriculture. Tikhonov did not fail to pay homage to Chernenko, crediting him with being the "leading force behind the plenum" and stating that the new program had been introduced "on Chernenko's initiative."[74] Although other figures, mostly regional leaders, took the floor, Gorbachev remained silent and impassive throughout the plenum.

Observers were puzzled by this agricultural plenum: Traditionally during such plenums the two main speakers are the general secretary and the person specializing in the theme of the plenum. For example, at the Central Committee ideological plenum in June 1983 the main speakers were Andropov and Chernenko, whereas at the April 1984 plenum on the subject of educational reform Chernenko and Zimyanin were the speakers. No Politburo member was more closely associated with agriculture than Gorbachev. Observers recalled that a few weeks earlier, at the award ceremony for Chernenko, Ustinov was the speaker instead of the senior Central Committee secretary (traditionally called upon to speak on such occasions), which would have been Gorbachev. Furthermore, at the agricultural plenum meeting of the Central Committee, Chernenko ignored Gorbachev's advocacy of greater efficiency as the best way of improving the wretched situation in Soviet agriculture and instead emphasized increasing investment in agriculture, a policy pursued by Brezhnev. He pointed out that "we will continue to increase capital investments in agriculture, saturating it with machinery and other materials."[75]

As already suggested, an attempt by Chernenko to undermine Gorbachev's position and retrieve the power surrendered to him in the deal preceding Chernenko's election was to be expected. Such an attempt might well entail stripping Gorbachev of his prominence as second secretary by limiting the public exposure resulting from the ceremonial functions usually performed by the second secretary (e.g.,

Ustinov's prominent role in the award ceremony) and by undermining Gorbachev's authority in one of his own areas of responsibility, such as agriculture. When these moves were accompanied by a boost in the status of the other younger leader regarded as a potential contender for the next succession—Romanov—Chernenko's tactics became obvious.

Consequently, the leader who seemed to benefit most from Gorbachev's temporary eclipse was Romanov. As the only other Central Committee secretary (apart from Gorbachev and Chernenko) who was also a Politburo member, Romanov was expected to bid for the leadership in the succession struggle following Chernenko's death and therefore was regarded as a potential rival for Gorbachev. In his speech at the plenum, Chernenko diverged from the theme of agriculture to give Romanov an unexpected boost by praising an industrial initiative taken in Romanov's home base of Leningrad. In addition, Romanov's improved position in the leaders' lineup at the 18 October award ceremony for Gromyko suggested that his career had taken an upturn.

Meanwhile, Chernenko continued to bask in the public gaze and demonstrate his new lease of life. On 17 October Soviet television showed him giving a rare face-to-face interview to a *Washington Post* reporter.[76] In the interview Chernenko, unlike in his *Pravda* interview on 2 September, projected an authoritative but moderate image, contrasting with Gromyko's tough (and last) speech on 27 September at the UN General Assembly. Incidentally, Gromyko also spoke at the 6 November meeting for the October Revolution anniversary. His speech differed in tone and content from Chernenko's *Washington Post* interview and contained unrestrained attacks against current U.S. foreign policy.[77]

In general the events celebrating the October Revolution that year demonstrated that the older generation was still very much in charge in the Kremlin. Gorbachev seemed unable to assert himself against Romanov, who seemed to have the upper hand during this period. No younger Politburo member played a significant part in the celebrations, and Ustinov, who was absent from the proceedings (and never appeared in public again), was represented by Deputy Defense Minister Marshal Sergey Sokolov, who was not much younger than Ustinov himself.

The choice of Gromyko to deliver the major address at the 6 October ceremony was unusual (see Table 6.1), as he had not read a major address at a public holiday for more than ten years. On the other hand, other signs indicated that the foreign minister enjoyed special status. On the day of his 6 October speech, it was announced that he had received the USSR State Prize for a book published in 1982.[78] (Chernenko, despite several published books of his speeches and various writings, had never received this prize.) On 26 October Chernenko, Grishin, and Gromyko were presented with awards by the Mongolian party leader Jambyn Batmonh. Although Chernenko attended the ceremony, Gromyko made the speech of thanks on behalf of the Soviet recipients of the awards.[79] Previously, on 18 October, at the ceremony

TABLE 6.1 Speeches by Soviet Leaders on Main Soviet Holidays

Year	Lenin Day	October Revolution
1978	Solomentsev	Kosygin
1979	Kapitonov	Kirilenko
1980	Ponomarev	Tikhonov
1981	Chernenko	Ustinov
1982	Andropov	Grishin
1983	Gorbachev	Romanov
1984	Dolgikh	Gromyko

in which Gromyko received the Lenin Order on his seventy-fifth birthday, full coverage was provided on Soviet television and in *Pravda*.[80]

The prominence accorded Gromyko was further accentuated by comparison with the very modest ceremony on 19 April[81] when Marshal Ustinov received an award on his seventy-fifth birthday. Whereas Gromyko was the only leader awarded at his ceremony, Ustinov shared the limelight with Solomentsev and Chebrikov, and his acceptance speech was not published in the media. *Pravda* carried no picture of the ceremony, and Soviet television showed only a still shot of the proceedings. All this, in addition to Gromyko's marked independence in his conduct of Soviet foreign policy and his visible special status in the Politburo, suggested that perhaps his special position was also a result of the accord that led to Chernenko's election in the previous February. Gromyko may have agreed to Chernenko's election only after demanding and receiving assurances on his independent and special status, which in fall 1984 became very evident.

Gorbachev, on the other hand, continued to show signs indicative of reduced status. Although the 7 November parade on Red Square found him in his customary fifth place after Chernenko, Tikhonov, Grishin, and Gromyko, on the previous day at the 6 November festive meeting he had slipped down the line. Romanov and even the lightweight Solomentsev preceded him in the lineup.

The revolution celebrations of 1984, especially the central Red Square parade, were exceptional in that for the first time in Soviet history the defense minister was not present. Marshal Ustinov, nearing his death, was represented by the First Deputy Defense Minister Marshal Sergey Sokolov. The selection of the seventy-three-year-old Sokolov was remarkable in that the more senior ranking Marshal Sergey Akhromeyev, sixty-one years old, had been passed over. In addition to being a first deputy defense minister, like Sokolov Akhromeyev was also chief of the Soviet Army General Staff. The unofficial protocol demanded that Akhromeyev should act in Ustinov's absence—which he had done during the visit of Syrian President Hafiz al-Asad to Moscow from 15 to 18 October.[82] (Asad, in need of new weapons as always, had brought along his own defense minister.)

Similarly, during Marshal Ustinov's twelve-week absence in spring 1980, Chief of General Staff Marshal Ogarkov substituted for him on various occasions, including the May Day parade in Red Square.[83] Sokolov also evidently replaced Ustinov during the two-day visit of the Indian defense minister on 30–31 October. On this occasion the Soviet delegation included both Sokolov and Akhromeyev, but *Krasnaya Zvezda,* in reporting the Indian delegation's arrival[84] and departure,[85] listed Sokolov's name before Akhromeyev's, an accepted sign of seniority. In contrast, in other *Krasnaya Zvezda* reports of joint appearances of these two leaders on 15 September and 3 October, Sokolov's name appeared after those of Akhromeyev and Kulikov.

The conclusion that must be drawn is that between 18 and 30 October the Politburo, realizing that Ustinov would never return to work, had appointed Marshal Sokolov to take his place as USSR minister of defense. This hypothesis is supported not only by the sudden change in Sokolov's status near the end of October but also by the unusual speed with which Sokolov's appointment was announced after Ustinov's death.

The signs of Gorbachev's temporary decline continued to appear. On 15 November a highly unusual Politburo meeting took place. In contrast with tradition, the Soviet press on the following day gave a detailed report of Chernenko's speech at the meeting.[86] This was the first hard evidence for a long time of the general secretary's participation in a Politburo meeting. The custom of issuing scanty reports of the routine Politburo meetings, it will be remembered, was initiated by Andropov in December 1982: Details of speeches at the meetings were never given.

The tradition was also broken in another way. Although the Politburo often invites experts to assist at the meetings, the identities of such persons are never divulged. However, the report of the 15 November meeting stated that it had been attended by the Central Committee secretaries and the republican party leaders.[87] The list of participants did not include the names of Gorbachev, Vorotnikov, Ustinov, Dolgikh, Demichev, and Chebrikov. Dolgikh was on a visit to Southeast Asia at the time;[88] Demichev was in Algeria[89] and Chebrikov was visiting Czechoslovakia.[90] Ustinov's absence needs no explanation; he had not been seen since the end of September, and his final illness was an open secret. However, the absenses of Gorbachev and Vorotnikov remained unexplained. Gorbachev's failure to attend was especially puzzling because the main subject of discussion was the Soviet economy, with particular emphasis on the 1985 plan and budget. Gorbachev's proven expertise in economic management made his attendance imperative. No official explanation of the absences was given, but Gorbachev's fits into the pattern of reduced public visibility clearly demonstrated at the 23rd October Central Committee plenum on agriculture.

Although Chernenko's speech offered no clues as to the reason for Gorbachev's absence, he went out of his way to praise Geydar Aliyev's role in heading a commission on consumer goods, as well as the activities of Shcherbitskiy of the Ukraine. In the past, Chernenko had avoided praise of individual leaders. Was he attempting to cement the alliance with Shcherbitskiy and to attract Aliyev into his faction?

Chernenko's high profile in November was evident also in his 18 November interview given to the U.S. National Broadcasting Company (NBC) network.[91] He continued to project the moderate image established by his *Washington Post* interview in mid-October, assuming a nonpolemical tone toward the U.S. administration and avoiding the most sensitive issues in the bilateral relations with the United States. In addition, he repeatedly emphasized the USSR's willingness to open a dialogue with the United States.

Somewhat surprisingly, Marshal Ogarkov, who since his dismissal had only been reported on a visit to the GDR (by the CSSR and GDR press only, on 12 October), reappeared in the Soviet press as the author of an article in *Kommunist Vooruzhennykh Sil,* no. 21, November 1984.[92] Like Chernenko, Ogarkov put foward a moderate view, stressing that a buildup of nuclear forces would not strengthen Soviet security.[93] Asserting that it was impossible for one of the two superpowers to destroy all the strategic weapons of its opponent in a single attack, Ogarkov pointed out the significance of the "immediate crushing response," which would inevitably follow the first strike.[94] Since then Ogarkov has made several public appearances and evidently continues to hold a high-ranking position within the Soviet Army. In March 1986 at the 27th CPSU Congress he even succeeded in retaining his seat in the CPSU Central Committee.

Gorbachev's Reappearance

Toward the end of November the period of Gorbachev's eclipse ended. On 29 November he delivered a report to a meeting of the Supreme Soviet Foreign Affairs Commission[95] of which he was the chairman. On 3 December he was reported meeting Dwayne Andreas, a visiting U.S. businessman,[96] and on 6 December he attended an award ceremony in the Kremlin[97] at which Chernenko was present.

On 10 and 11 December Gorbachev played the leading role in a conference called to evaluate the party's ideological activities since the June 1983 Central Committee plenum.[98] In his speech, Gorbachev echoed the main points made by Andropov at the June 1983 plenum. He pointed to the need for wide economic reforms, accused economists of being hampered by "dogmatic ideas" that prevented the introduction of new developments, and attacked Soviet social scientists as being "still too slow and timid" in developing Marxist-Leninist theory. Gorbachev also appealed for greater public participation (a theme developed by Andropov at the same June 1983 plenum) and demanded that more attention be paid to different group interests within the Soviet political system. Gorbachev pointedly referred to Chernenko as "the head of the Politburo,"[99] the first time he had done so. His renewed public appearances and central role at the ideology conference (he also made the short closing speech),[100] plus his tribute to Chernenko, all signaled the end of the period out in the cold. (Incidentally, the conference also sent a message to Chernenko, published in *Pravda* on 12 December, pledging to "improve the effectiveness" of ideological activity.)

Nothing showed Gorbachev's new status better than his visit to Great Britain as head of a Soviet parliamentary delegation, which began on 15 December.[101] Gorbachev was accompanied by his wife, Raisa, who attracted equal attention from the British public. The couple greatly impressed their British hosts, who did not hide their admiration. "I like Mr. Gorbachev. We can do business together!"[102] Prime Minister Margaret Thatcher stated. Former defense minister Denis Healey described Gorbachev as "a man of exceptional charm," "full of inner strength," and "genuinely nice and human."[103]

Gorbachev himself, avoiding polemics and propaganda cliches, emanated moderation and good will. Playing the gracious guest, he refrained from any direct attacks on Margaret Thatcher's policies, even on the delicate issue of the deployment of cruise missiles on British territory. After his 16 December meeting with Thatcher, he defined their talks as "businesslike and constructive," acknowledging that "different opinions" were registered on "a number of questions,"[104] without specifying the areas of disagreement.

The same moderate image emerged from Gorbachev's 18 December meeting at the British Parliament. He spouted no propaganda slogans, no Marxist-Leninist formulations; instead, he stressed that "the Soviet Union is prepared to go as far toward the Western partners in the talks as they will come to meet us."[105] (He repeated this statement three times in slightly different versions.) He also emphasized that "there is always room for reasonable compromise in politics and diplomacy." Nevertheless, he did remind the British of the strength of the Soviet Union:

> I would like to stress once again that the Soviet leadership stands for forthright and honest talks to help us, on a mutually acceptable basis, to limit and reduce arms, primarily nuclear weapons, and eventually eliminate them.
>
> We are ready to go as far as our Western partners in the talks. Naturally enough equality and equal security will underlie any agreements in this field. And, of course, any course that seeks military superiority over the USSR and its allies is unacceptable and has no prospects.[106]

The visit was immensely important. Gorbachev and his wife received unprecedented worldwide (and positive) exposure; flattering reactions were extensively reported by the Soviet media. Gorbachev was accorded honor far in excess of his official status as the head of a fairly ordinary Soviet parliamentary delegation. The visit often seemed like that of a head of state.

Gorbachev's visit to the United Kingdom was unexpectedly interrupted by the death of Marshal Ustinov, first reported at noon on 21 December.[107] Gorbachev even revealed the fact before the official announcement, while speaking to reporters at Edinburgh Airport: "We have had a great and tragic loss. The Minister of Defence, our old friend and Comrade Dmitriy Fyodorovich Ustinov, has passed away."[108] In an unusual display of frankness for a Soviet leader, Gorbachev went on to explain that he was cutting short his visit because his presence in Moscow was required.

Ustinov's Death

According to the official medical report, Ustinov caught pneumonia in late October,[109] which explained his prolonged absence from all public events after that time. He died on 20 December, lay in state on 22 and 23 December, and was buried on Christmas Eve. After cremation, his ashes were placed in the Kremlin wall. Those honors were also accorded to Pelshe on his death in 1983, Kosygin in 1980, and Grechko in 1976 and were in accordance with Ustinov's status as a Politburo member. Chernenko visited Ustinov's bier on 22 December[110] but did not attend the funeral,[111] which took place on a bitterly cold day.

Ustinov's death was officially announced on 21 December: The medical bulletin published by TASS at 2108 Moscow time gave the time of death as 1935 on 20 December. However, in the interval between the official time of death and its announcement, the Soviet media gave several indications that a top leader had died (all times quoted are Moscow time on 21 December):

- Beginning from approximately 1700: Unscheduled departures from normal programming on radio and television.
- 1800: Radio newscast did not include Ustinov's name with those of the other Politburo members when reporting nominations for the Republican Supreme Soviet elections.
- 1805: TASS reported that an international chess tournament being held in the hall traditionally used for the lying-in-state ceremonies of top Soviet leaders was being interrupted.
- Approximately 2000: Gorbachev tells reporters in Scotland that he is cutting short his trip because of Ustinov's death.
- 2054: TASS announced Ustinov's death; the report was broadcast on the Moscow television Vremya program at 2100.
- 2108: TASS disseminated the medical report on Ustinov's death.

The medical report stated that Ustinov caught pneumonia late in October 1984, which was then complicated by sepsis. It continued that, while recovering from the pneumonia, severe circulatory problems appeared, requiring surgical intervention. After this operation, malfunction of the liver and kidneys occurred, accompanied by blood coagulation problems, which failed to respond to intensive treatment. The liver and kidney problems caused dystrophic changes, and death finally resulted from cardiac arrest.

Marshal Sokolov was appointed to succeed Ustinov on 22 December, two days before Ustinov's funeral.[112] The timing of this appointment was in sharp contrast with past practice. When Andrey Grechko died in 1976, the Politburo waited until after the funeral before appointing Ustinov his successor. When Marshal Rodion Malinovskiy died in 1967, two full weeks elapsed before the successor was appointed, apparently amid strong dissension. A lag of several days or even a few weeks is not unusual in the USSR after a minister's death. Sokolov's speedy appointment showed that Ustinov's long illness had given the Politburo enough time to discuss and choose his successor. Sokolov was clearly a short-term appointee because of his advanced age and unimpressive record of service. In fact, Sokolov had been acting as defense minister for several weeks before Ustinov's death, although Marshal Akhromeyev was selected to lead the Soviet military delegation to the 3–5 December meeting of the Warsaw Pact defense ministers in Budapest.[113] Sokolov commanded the 7 November parade in Red Square, played the main role at the funeral of Air Force commander Marshal Kutakhov on 5 December,[114] and received a number of foreign delegations. The transitional nature of his appointment, however, was further indicated by his appointment to candidate membership of the Politburo in contrast to Grechko and Ustinov, who had both been full members.

The death of Marshal Ustinov not only removed one of the most powerful figures in the Kremlin but also left Romanov as the only full Politburo member with direct responsibility for the military. He played a central role at Ustinov's funeral, being appointed chairman of the funeral commission[115] (which at the time aroused speculation that he would be appointed the defense minister) and led the funeral ceremony, being the first leader to deliver a eulogy in memory of Ustinov.[116] However, at the 22 December lying-in-state ceremony, Gorbachev clearly outranked Romanov, who was in fifth position after Chernenko, Tikhonov, Gorbachev, and Gromyko.[117] At the funeral itself Romanov was placed higher, which was his due as the funeral commission chairman.

An interesting question is why Romanov was not appointed minister of defense. One possible answer is that Romanov, who had never concealed his ambitions, did not want the post, preferring to bide his time to run for the greater prize, Chernenko's own position. Romanov was well aware that Chernenko's seat would soon fall vacant, and if he was to compete successfully against Gorbachev, the defense minister's post would be a great hindrance. Although the minister of defense is clearly intimately connected with the military establishment, even if he is a civilian like Romanov, the party apparatus—which always plays the major role in the succession decisionmaking process—would certainly view with suspicion the efforts of a strong defense minister to secure for himself the top party and state position. Accusations of Bonapartism immediately spring to mind. Romanov, well aware of this, may have decided to wait for the crucial struggle and try his luck then.

On the other hand, his colleagues in the Politburo may have denied him the defense ministry leadership for exactly the same reason, fearing that he would exploit the post to build up strong military support and force his way into the position of general secretary. The fact that Romanov was removed by Gorbachev so soon after the latter's own election shows that Romanov was feared and regarded as a potential source of danger.

Finally, the military may have rebelled against the prospect of yet another civilian defense minister, preferring to revert to the tradition of having a professional soldier in the post. The question naturally follows, Why was Sokolov chosen? Sokolov, the deputy minister in charge of finance, administration, and logistics at the Defense Ministry, seemed unimpressive in comparison with other prospective candidates, such as Chief of General Staff Marshal Akhromeyev, the Warsaw Pact Forces Commander Marshal Viktor Kulikov, or even Mashal Ogarkov, who apparently still held a very senior position in the military establishment. His signature appeared on Ustinov's obituary ahead of the military district commanders, and he showed up at the lying-in-state ceremony. A highly controversial figure, whose military views were often at variance with official Soviet policy, Ogarkov clearly could not take up the post of defense minister so soon after his dismissal from the post of chief of the General Staff. His appointment would have opened a Pandora's box of dissension between the party and the military, something that the Politburo could hardly afford.

Marshal Akhromeyev had been appointed chief of General Staff only three months before Ustinov's death. Born in 1923, and marshal only since 1983 (when he also became a full member of the Central Committee),[118] Akhromeyev may have been considered too inexperienced at the time of Ustinov's death for the ministerial post. Marshal Kulikov, who became commander in chief of the Warsaw Pact Joint Armed Forces in 1977,[119] was far more experienced and outspoken than Akhromeyev. With him as defense minister, the Army would have a powerful and tough spokesperson in the Politburo, who would have constantly demanded increases in the military allocations; both Chernenko and Gorbachev had frequently declared that military funding was not one of their first priorities. When Kulikov failed to be included in Ustinov's funeral commission, it was clear that his appointment was not being considered.

Given the prevailing circumstances, Marshal Sokolov seems an ideal candidate for defense minister. A professional soldier (thus appealing to the Army), too old and unambitious to be a dangerous competitor in the succession struggle, and devoid of a power base in the party, his appointment was the ideal compromise solution: It provided a safe outcome from a potentially tricky situation and left no doubt that military policy would continue to be defined by the civilians in the Politburo.

Ustinov's death destroyed the Gromyko-Ustinov axis that had been responsible for Andropov's election as general secretary. Being members of the old guard (as far as age) Gromyko and Ustinov in 1982 threw their weight behind Andropov's candidacy. Chernenko's own election could not have taken place in 1984 without their consent, which was probably given on the understanding that Gorbachev would fulfill the function of second secretary during Chernenko's tenure. It is noteworthy that Gorbachev's temporary eclipse in October occurred precisely when Ustinov disappeared from public view, though there is no other evidence of a connection between the two events. One fact is certain, however: Ustinov's death deprived the military-industrial complex of a strong representative in the Politburo and destroyed the powerful link between the defense and foreign ministries, which played a decisive role in the infighting.

Meanwhile, the situation in the Politburo seemed to be calm. In an article entitled, "On the Level of the Developed Socialism's Needs" (*Kommunist*, no. 18, December 1984), Chernenko hinted that major changes were imminent in domestic policy. He stressed that "we have reached the time when we can and must move forward."[120] On the Soviet economy, Chernenko asserted that "our economy has reached a frontier at which qualitative changes and improvements have become what might be termed an imperative necessity."[121] He also hinted at changes in political participation ("freedom of discussion and criticism")[122] and indicated that there was a need to reorganize the state apparatus, as well as to strengthen discipline ("without discipline and firm public order democracy remains an empty phrase").[123]

The *Kommunist* issue with Chernenko's article had been signed to press on 17 December, only one week after the 11–12 December ideological conference. The article was similar in tone and spirit to Gorbachev's speech at the conference and dealt with the same issues, expressing identical positions: Both Chernenko and Gorbachev stressed the need for ideological flexibility, encouraged the idea of greater political participation, and complained that "dogmatic ideas" made it difficult to solve economic problems. These similarities suggest that Gorbachev's return to the public limelight after his "retreat" may have been preceded by a renewal of the accord with Chernenko. The identity of views and priorities could be interpreted as a manifestation of unity and a promise of continuity in the future. Thus by the end of the year Gorbachev and Chernenko were speaking with one voice.

Campaign for the Supreme Soviet

The year's end was also the peak period of the election campaign for the RSFSR Supreme Soviet. The nomination process commenced on 19 December and ended on 19 January, when each Politburo member would announce which nomination he accepted. On the first day of the nominations, Chernenko was nominated for twenty constituencies, Tikhonov for four, and Gorbachev for two.[124] On the next day, Chernenko continued to be nominated for many more constituencies than the remainder of the Politburo, but Tikhonov received two nominations and Gorbachev three.[125] From then on until the end of the drawn-out process Tikhonov and Gorbachev received equal numbers of nominations. The final outcome was Chernenko, sixty-two; Tikhonov and Gorbachev, twelve each; the remaining Politburo members, six each.[126] A year earlier at the Supreme Soviet elections, Andropov received fifty-eight nominations, and Tikhonov and Chernenko won fourteen each. Gorbachev, like the other members of the Politburo, obtained seven nominations.

Since the whole nomination process was a transparent manipulation, it serves as a reliable guide of the leaders' relative strength at the time. The latest result eloquently confirmed Gorbachev's status as heir apparent and acting second secretary. However, his enhanced status was demonstrated by something more than the number of nominations obtained. At the 1981 RSFSR elections, Gorbachev "accepted" the nomination of a district in the Altay in Siberia; at the 1984 USSR Supreme Soviet elections, he became the candidate for his home district of Stavropol. At the 1984-1985 RSFSR Supreme Soviet elections, Gorbachev ran for a Moscow district, an honor he shared only with Chernenko, Tikhonov, and the Moscow party boss Grishin.[127]

The number of nominations each Soviet leader receives, as well as other semiofficial signs such as the reverse order of their election speeches, serves as an accepted indication of the relative strength of the leaders and their positions in the leadership lineup at a given time. Such indicators are explained in Appendix A.

Some unexplained inconsistencies suggested a degree of confusion or perhaps even resistance to the efforts to build up Chernenko. For example, the second edition of *Krasnaya Zvezda* of 15 January replaced a laudatory sentence in its editorial relating to Chernenko ("an outstanding figure of the Communist party and Soviet state, leader of the Leninist type, and tireless fighter for peace and cooperation among the peoples") with a more neutral sentence, that omitted all praise and mentioned the other party and state leaders. This interesting editorial change indicated uncertainty and may have been a result of Chernenko's absence. He had participated in a 27 December Kremlin ceremony at which "a group of prominent writers" had received awards, and he had made a very brief congratulatory speech to the honored writers, who included Georgiy Markov, then first secretary of the Board of the USSR Writers' Union.[128] From that time he did not appear at a public event and was apparently unable to prevent the removal of Brezhnev's son-in-law Yuriy Churbanov from the Ministry of Internal Affairs. Churbanov was the first deputy minister but had not been mentioned for several months. On 29 December *Moskovskaya Pravda* reported the nomination of Vasiliy Trushin, "first deputy minister of internal affairs," for the RSFSR Supreme Soviet. Since the same daily had announced on 20 December that Trushin had been released from his post of secretary of the CPSU Moscow City Committee, it can safely be assumed that between 20 and 28 December he had received his internal ministry appointment. Whether Churbanov was removed at the same time is not known, but Chernenko evidently was powerless to help his patron's relative. On the other hand, since Trushin had served under Moscow's Grishin between 1976 and 1979 and again in 1984, he may have enjoyed the support of the Moscow party boss.

Chernenko was not seen throughout the election campaign. A report on a routine Politburo meeting of 7 February included a vague reference to him that implied that he had actually taken part in the meeting: "Reliable support for the spring sowing, as Comrade Chernenko stressed when he addressed the CPSU Central Committee Politburo session, acquires particular urgency this year."[129] The press continued to print various statements and routine greetings messages ostensibly signed by Chernenko, as it had during his seven-week absence in July-August 1984 and during Andropov's disappearance from the public arena from August 1983 until his death in the following February.

Obvious differences can be seen in the treatment Chernenko received from the different leaders in their election speeches. Predictably, the old guard once again provided the strongest support. Tikhonov,[130] Grishin,[131] and Kunayev[132] offered fulsome praise, Grishin outdoing the others in describing Chernenko as "a purposeful, principled, and highly industrious person and an outstanding party and state figure"[133] and glorifying his contributions to Soviet domestic and foreign policy. All three, as well as Aliyev[134] and Solomentsev,[135] referred to Chernenko as "head of the Politburo," although Aliyev and Solomentsev were more restrained in their praise. Romanov,[136] although recognizing Chernenko as "head of the Politburo," was lukewarm in his praise, merely noting that Chernenko was "an outstanding leader."

Gromyko[137] and Vorotnikov[138] were the only Politburo members who failed to refer to Chernenko as the head of the Politburo and were grudging in the praise they accorded him. Central Committee secretaries Ligachev[139] and Ryzhkov[140] were remarkably cool, and the KGB Chief Chebrikov was by Soviet standards insultingly moderate—refraining altogether from praise and merely noting Chernenko's "constant interest" in the peoples of the Far East and his "constant attention" to the defense of Soviet interests against foreign subversion.[141]

Gorbachev was both gracious and diplomatic in his mentions of Chernenko. In an unprecedented remark he referred to Chernenko as the "soul of the Politburo."[142] Although this could have been interpreted as a compliment, it also carried the implication that like the soul Chernenko was not physically involved in the world around him. In a Russian context, the reader would perhaps also be reminded of Nikolay Gogol's famous novel *Dead Souls,* in which the term *souls* referred to landowners' (deceased) serfs. In any case, Gorbachev praised Chernenko's "multifaced activity" and "great contribution" to Marxist-Leninist theory but also emphasized the collective essence of the leadership.

Gorbachev was again the third-ranking speaker with only Tikhonov and Chernenko (again in absentia) speaking after him. In addition, his speech was attended by Grishin, Ligachev, and Ryzhkov[143]—an imposing audience. Only Tikhonov's and Chernenko's election speeches were attended by a more distinguished group of leaders. However, by that time, Gorbachev's prominence aroused no surprise; for all practical purposes, he had already succeeded Chernenko, and Tikhonov's number two ranking was purely honorary. All political rivals (real and potential), including Romanov, trailed far behind him in authority and influence. Finally, Gorbachev's unprecedented and exceptionally favorable international exposure during his visit to the United Kingdom in December 1984 had made him a prominent international figure, a distinction he shared only with Gromyko. No matter how many Politburo members paid obeisance to Chernenko as "the head of the Politburo," Gorbachev was almost in the driver's seat, and the succession drama that had begun almost three years previously was fast approaching the end.

However, several bizarre events preceded the end, as they did during the final days of the preceding three geriatric Soviet leaders. On 22 February Chernenko was scheduled to meet his constituency members in the last and central preelection meeting. However, the participants in the meeting encountered only the "soul" of the Politburo. The chairman of the meeting, Moscow's mayor Grishin, informed the audience that the general secretary was not taking part in the meeting "on his doctor's recommendation."[144] This brought back memories of Grishin's explaining on a previous occasion to foreign reporters that Ustinov's absence from the 7 November parade was the result of "a sore throat."[145] Chernenko's speech was read by someone else (another precedent in this amazing three-year period), and Soviet citizens were asking whether the programming of Radio Moscow had been changed in recent hours (preempting regular programming with solemn music—a harbinger of an official death).

The citizens were soon surprised by the ingenious party propaganda apparatus. While everyone was taking with a pinch of salt the statements or published greetings messages allegedly signed by Chernenko, the general secretary made a ghostly "appearance." But first, let me lead into this story with a joke. A popular Moscow anecdote concerned the 1980 Olympic Games during which the authorities tried to create an impression of prosperity and abundance by stocking Moscow stores with foods that the citizens had forgotten existed. One citizen was reported to have asked a local party official whether that food really could now be ordered by telephone. "It is true," was the solemn reply, "and you will receive it over the television!" This in fact was how Chernenko cast his election vote—by television. On 24 February Soviet television showed a poorly staged report on Chernenko casting his vote.[146] The screen showed a severely restricted Chernenko, gasping for air, receiving his ballot while seated, casting his vote (standing but not walking to the ballot box), receiving flowers, and posing for photographs. The so-called polling station did not resemble any other: No ordinary citizens were in sight, merely a group of officials and photographers. (By comparison, at the 1984 USSR Supreme Soviet elections Chernenko was seen arriving in his official car, shaking hands and waving at the polling station, walking to the ballot box, and so on.) The entire show, obviously staged, aimed at assuring the Soviet people that their leader was still alive and kicking, if barely so.

On 28 February television viewers again saw Chernenko, this time receiving his credentials as a member of the RSFSR Supreme Soviet, as well as a gift from a local industrial plant.[147] He even tried to read a short statement, pausing after almost every phrase to catch his breath. Once again the background gave no clue as to the location of the event; the small, unimposing room was a far cry from his luxurious Kremlin offices, but the wall color and curtain pattern were similar to those of the room in which he supposedly cast his vote. Grishin, the only other leader to take part in the event, acted not unlike a movie director, issuing instructions as to who was to speak or move.

If these two television appearances were meant to demonstrate that Chernenko was alive and well, they clearly failed in their purpose. The viewers saw a pathetic and very sick old man, indifferent to his surroundings and indeed barely alive. Perhaps this was the real purpose of the whole affair. Perhaps Chernenko's final television appearances were to serve as the final curtain for a strange and complex period of Soviet political life, as a representation of a dying generation of leaders who were soon to hand over their place to a younger and more capable leader of a new breed.

The period of Chernenko's rule has often been described as "Brezhnevism without Brezhnev." Although it was impossible to revive all the elements of Brezhnev's system and reestablish the conservatism and associated stagnation that characterized the latter period of Brezhnev's tenure, Chernenko's rule represented a period of relative political inactivity within the era of aspiration for reform initiated by Andropov and continued by Gorbachev.

Plagued by poor health and limited authority, Chernenko can claim no significant or lasting achievements. The deal by which he shared power with Gorbachev in exchange for holding exclusive title to the posts that represented supreme power proved extremely costly and not especially gratifying to him. The compromise no doubt satisfied Chernenko's ego and probably temporarily reassured the members of the nomenklatura, but that was all. Chernenko never achieved the status of absolute and undisputed leader (in contrast to his patron Brezhnev) and indeed failed to reach Andropov's position. He was unable to make any new appointments to the dwindling ranks of the Politburo or to the Secretariat, probably because of the deadlock between the two factions.

Unable to complete the first stage of the power struggle cycle (complete acquisition of power), Chernenko accordingly could not proceed to the next stages—expanding and protecting his power. He had no real power to delegate to his supporters and the nomenklatura members, so could not consolidate his own position. Apart from routine propaganda appeals for disarmament and détente, his only apparent achievement in the field of foreign affairs—an area in which he lacked experience and which was completely dominated by Gromyko—was the U.S.-Soviet agreement to resume the Geneva disarmament talks in 1985. However, he did establish the precedent that, under certain conditions, a second chance can exist in the USSR for a leader who fails to achieve the supremacy in his first attempt. Otherwise, his brief period of leadership will remain no more than a footnote to Soviet history.

7

The Smooth Succession:
Gorbachev at the Helm

Several hours before the announcement of Chernenko's death on 11 March 1985, the Soviet populace knew that their leader had died. They needed neither secret sources nor inside knowledge because the events of the past three years had made them experts at interpreting the signals. When Soviet radio and television altered their program schedules and began broadcasting documentary films and somber classical music, everyone knew what to expect.

At 1100 GMT Chernenko's death was gravely announced by the now familiar television news reporter, who had the leader's portrait draped in black and red material on the wall behind him.

> From the CPSU Central Committee, the USSR Supreme Soviet Presidium, and the USSR Council of Ministers.
>
> The CPSU Central Committee, the USSR Supreme Soviet Presidium, and the USSR Council of Ministers inform the party and all Soviet people with profound grief that on 10 March 1985 at 1920 (1620 GMT) Konstantin Ustinovich Chernenko, chairman of the USSR Supreme Soviet Presidium, died after a grave illness.
>
> The name of Konstantin Ustinovich Chernenko, outstanding figure of the Communist Party and the Soviet state, staunch fighter for the ideal of communism and for peace, will remain forever in the hearts of the Soviet people and all progressive mankind.[1]

The subsequent announcements added to the sense of déjà vu—the feeling of viewing the same drama for the nth time. Less than thirty minutes after the first announcement, TASS issued the routine CPSU "Address to the People," which, as for Brezhnev and Andropov, surveyed the career of the deceased leader, reaffirmed the basic principles of Soviet domestic and foreign policies, and pledged continuity.[2] Several minutes later the composition of the funeral commission was announced; as was to be expected, the chairman of the commission was Mikhail Gorbachev.[3] The commission immediately declared that the funeral would take place on 13 March in Red Square[4] and that Chernenko's coffin would be placed in the Hall of Columns of the House of the Trade Unions "for the working people to bid farewell to Konstantin Ustinovich Chernenko."[5] The Mourning Decree[6] and the official obituary[7] duly followed. The medical report, signed by Dr. Yevgeniy Chazov (who in December 1985 was awarded the Nobel Peace Prize for his work as one of the leaders of the Medical Doctors for Peace organization) and other specialists determined the cause of death as "emphysema of the lungs, complicated by pulmonary-cardiac insufficiency" and "concomitant chronic hepatitis turning into cirrhosis."[8]

From this point on, however, developments ensued at a pace rarely observed in Soviet political history. Some four hours after the initial announcement of Chernenko's death, TASS announced that "Mikhail Gorbachev was unanimously elected general secretary of the CPSU Central Committee at a pre-term plenary meeting of the CPSU Central Committee that was held here today."[9] The next day *Pravda* published a longer report on the Central Committee plenum, revealing that Foreign Minister Gromyko had proposed Gorbachev as general secretary[10]— clearly a departure from the usual transition pattern. After Stalin's death in 1953 and Brezhnev's in 1982, the Central Committee plenum convened on the day following the death announcements, whereas in Andropov's case three days passed before the plenum was held.

This unusual speed clearly showed that the decision to elect Gorbachev as general secretary had already been adopted before Chernenko's death evidently without any serious opposition. During the final months of Chernenko's life there had been indications that Gorbachev had been chairing the regular Politburo meetings intead of Chernenko. Gromyko confirmed this in his nomination speech (see text in this section). Thus, the Central Committee was not an important factor in the selection of the general secretary, merely acting as a rubber stamp on a decision already adopted by the Politburo. Furthermore, the plenum was called so hastily that at least three dozen members were unable to attend.[11] Even Politburo member Shcherbitskiy, who was leading a parliamentary delegation to the United States, returned to Moscow only on 12 March, a day late for the plenum.[12]

The Central Committee plenum session was remarkable because of Gromyko's extraordinary nomination speech. His speech differed so sharply from the stiff and formal nomination speeches read by Chernenko and Tikhonov at the plenums held after the deaths of Brezhnev and Andropov that the Soviet press, apparently unable to digest this novelty immediately, did not carry the full text of the speech on the day following the plenum in accordance with the normal practice. However, the speech, as included in a brochure containing the speeches made at the plenum, was signed to press on 14 March 1985.[13] Even after editing, it retained its personal and colorful style and evident lack of organization, suggesting that Gromyko did not deliver a prepared text but rather gave an informal extemporal address.

Gromyko's Nomination Speech

Comrades! I have been instructed to present a proposal for the examination of the CPSU Central Committee plenum on the question of the candidacy for CPSU Central Committee general secretary. The Politburo has come out unanimously in favor of recommending the election of Mikhail Sergeyevich Gorbachev as general secretary. [Prolonged applause]

I would like to convey to the members of the CPSU Central Committee, candidate members of the Central Committee, members of the Central Auditing Commission, and all those present the content of the discussion of this question and the atmosphere in which the discussion took place.

First of all, the idea was emphasized that all Mikhail Sergeyevich's activity in implementing our domestic and foreign policy confirms that he is worthy of election as CPSU Central Committee general secretary. It was stressed that he has tremendous experience in party work. First at the kray level, then here, centrally, on the Central Committeee: first as secretary, then as Politburo member, he led [vel] the Secretariat, as is known. He also chaired Politburo sessions in the absence of Konstantin Ustinovich Chernenko. He conducted himself brilliantly, without exaggeration.

What else was stressed? Alongside his party experience—and this is an invaluable gift—it was stressed that he is a man of principle, a man of strong convictions. Anyone who has met with him and discussed the relevant questions can confirm this. I personally can confirm it. He always keeps attention focused on the nub of the question, its content, on the principles; he states his position frankly, whether or not it is to the liking of his interlocutor. He states it with directness, Leninist directness, and it is up to his interlocutor whether he goes away in a good mood or not: If he is a real Communist, he should go away in a good mood; incidentally, that did happen, and this too was stressed.

During the discussion of this question in the Politburo, it was stated that Mikhail Sergeyevich is a person of keen, profound intelligence, and anyone who knows him or has met with him even once will confirm this. After all, it often happens that it is difficult to examine questions, domestic or foreign, if you are guided by the law of "black and white." There can be in-between colors, in-between levels, and in-between decisions which accord with the party line. This was stressed unanimously. And for him, this has been and is the main criterion in assessing the position of this or that comrade or this or that institution, or in assessing whatever problem is at issue.

And this must also be said. Perhaps this is rather clearer to me, by virtue of my service, than to certain other comrades. He grasps very well and rapidly the essence of the processes taking place outside our country, in the international arena. I myself have often been struck by his ability to rapidly and accurately grasp the essence of the matter and draw conclusions—the correct, party conclusions.

Mikhail Sergeyevich—this is also well known—is a man of broad erudition both in education and in work experience. Of course, all this makes it easier for him to find the correct solutions. And another illustration: If what was taking place in this auditorium now was, say, a scientific forum, most likely everyone would say: This man knows how to approach problems analytically. That is the absolute truth. He has brilliant ability in this respect—he can divide a question into all its component parts before drawing a conclusion. Not only does he analyze problems well, he makes generalizations and draws conclusions. Politics sometimes requires not simply the ability to analyze a question or subdivide it—it will then just stand still—but also the ability to draw conclusions, so that our politics can then adopt these conclusions. He demonstrated this many a time at Politburo sessions and sessions of the Central Committee Secretariat.

Moreover, the comrades unanimously stated that Mikhail Sergeyevich has a party-minded approach to people and a great ability to organize people and find a common language with them. This is not given to everyone. Whatever you want to call it, a gift of nature or a gift of society, or rather, a gift of both—it is not given to everyone. In any case, not to everyone to the same degree. He has this quality.

Moreover, we are living in a world in which, figuratively speaking, various telescopes are trained on the Soviet Union, and there are many of them—big, small, over short and long distances. And perhaps more long-distance than short-distance ones. And people look to see if they can eventually find cracks of some kind in the Soviet leadership. I assure you that on many, many occasions we have come across such instances and observed them. If you like, we have witnessed discussions and guesswork conducted in a whisper or half-whisper: In some cases abroad, people are eager to see differences of opinion in the Soviet leadership. Of course, this did not originate today or yesterday. This phenomenon has been observed for many years. The Politburo's unanimous opinion is: This time too, we, the party Central Committee and Politburo, will not allow our political opponents any satisfaction on this score. [Applause]

On very many occasions Mikhail Sergeyevich has expressed the opinion—and he has done so in the Politburo—that we must, so to speak, keep our powder dry. The corresponding decisions of our congresses, Central Committee plenums, and the Politburo orient the party and people toward this policy.

Mikhail Sergeyevich's opinions are always notable for their maturity and persistence, in the best sense of the word—party persistence. He always upholds the view that the holy of holies for all of us is to struggle for the cause of peace and maintain our defense at the necessary level.

The ability to perceive the main components and to subordinate what is secondary to them is a strong characteristic of his. This ability is an asset, and a great asset. So the conclusion drawn by the Politburo is the correct conclusion. We have in Mikhail Sergeyevich Gorbachev a figure on a large scale, an outstanding figure, who will fill with dignity the post of general secretary of the CPSU Central Committee. [Prolonged applause] I would like to express confidence that, like the Politburo, the Central Committee plenum will unanimously support and approve the proposal. [Prolonged applause]

An extraordinary speech, indeed. In contrast to the previous nomination speeches, it contained no praise of the previous leader: Gromyko's address was totally focused on Gorbachev. His kind and complimentary words for Gorbachev were quite different from the routine cliché-ridden praises traditionally used on such occasions. Furthermore, Gromyko disclosed that Gorbachev had already been acting as general secretary, chairing Politburo meetings in Chernenko's absence (the only time Chernenko's name was mentioned in the speech) and had "led" the Central Committee Secretariat.

"A man of principle, a man of strong convictions," "a man of keen profound intelligence," "he states his position frankly . . . with directness," "he analyzes problems well . . . makes generalizations," and is able "to draw conclusions—the correct, party conclusions"—such words do not normally appear in a speech of any Soviet leader. Gromyko clearly was stressing Gorbachev's personal intelligence and strong character above all else. Being well aware of Gorbachev's limited experience in foreign affairs, Gromyko made a point of emphasizing his ability "to grasp very well and rapidly the essence of the processes taking place outside our country," something that "is rather clearer to me [Gromyko], by virtue of my service, than to certain other comrades." This was not the speech of a Politburo member routinely proposing the election of a new general secretary but rather that of a mentor praising his brilliant student. Finally, Gromyko repeatedly underlined that his proposal was approved unanimously by the entire Politburo. (Several observers, among them Dusko Doder writing in the *International Herald Tribune* on 19 March 1985, reported that at the plenum Gromyko had depicted Gorbachev as "a man with a nice smile, but iron teeth." Doder quoted an "authoritative account" on this matter; however, the official transcript of Gromyko's speech contains no such reference.)

In his acceptance speech, Gorbachev confined himself to the pre-scribed conventional phrases, outlining the basic principles of Soviet policy and pledging his commitment to collective decisionmaking ("In the work ahead I am counting on the support and active help of the Politburo members, candidate members, and the Central Committee secretaries, and the party's Central Committee as a whole") and to strengthening the defense potential of the Soviet Army.

> In a complicated international situation it is important now as never before to maintain the defense potential of our socialist homeland at such a level that potential aggressors will know well that any encroachment on the security of our Land of the Soviets and its allies, on the peaceful life of the Soviet people, will be met with a shattering retaliatory blow. Our glorious Armed Forces will continue to have at their disposal everything necessary for this.[14]

Gorbachev was more generous than Gromyko to his predecessor, devoting several paragraphs to describing Chernenko's contribution in various areas and also not forgetting to mention Andropov's name.

The composition of the plenum (according to Gromyko, "members of the CPSU Central Committee, candidate members of the Central Committee, members of the Central Auditing Commission, and all those present")[15] suggested that some nonmembers also attended; these may have been the marshals of the USSR, who thus joined in the "unanimous" approval of Gorbachev's election. The Russian word used—*yedino-dushno*—means not simply "unanimously," but "with one spirit" or "with one soul."[16] The term used in the information reports on the plenums that elected Andropov and Chernenko was *yedinoglasno* ("by one vote"). Whether this difference implies a more enthusiastic approval—by acclamation rather than by a mechanical vote—is a matter of interpretation. Gorbachev's unprecedented quick election caused a further deviation from tradition. On the day after the election, 12 March, Gorbachev's picture adorned the front page of *Pravda,* whereas Chernenko's was relegated to page 2. Since there is no precedent for *Pravda's* reporting the death of an old leader and the election of his successor on the same day, it is a moot point whether this represented a deliberate slight of Chernenko's memory or whether it was simply a matter of the living taking precedence over the dead.

Chernenko's funeral differed little from those of his immediate predecessors. Thanks to the ample opportunities for practice offered in the past two and a half years, everything proceeded "as on oil," as the Russians like to say. As in Brezhnev's and Andropov's final rites, the deceased's family provided a touch of genuine pathos in the pompous and stiff ritual. This time the funeral orators were Gorbachev[17] and Grishin.[18] Both eulogies were routine, mostly recalling Chernenko's merits, although Gorbachev did stress Chernenko's commitment to "work purposefully for realizing the decisions of the 26th CPSU Congress and the November (1982) and subsequent plenary meetings of the Central Committee,"[19] which could be interpreted as a commitment to implementing Andropov's policies.

The only new feature of the funeral was the clearly reduced prominence of the military. Marshal Sokolov, the recently elected minister of defense, was not even a member of the funeral commission,[20] although his predecessor Ustinov took part in the funeral commissions for Andropov in 1984 and Brezhnev in 1982. Furthermore, Sokolov was not excluded from the commission because he was not a Politburo member: Marshal Vasilevskiy, the defense minister at the time of Stalin's death, was also not in the Politburo but nevertheless was a member of Stalin's funeral commission. Moreover, at Brezhnev's and Andropov's funerals Marshal Ustinov made a speech. However, on 13 March no military person eulogized Chernenko, and indeed no military figures stood on the tribune of the Lenin Mausoleum. The decline of the army's visible role began during Chernenko's tenure and included the demotion of Chief of General Staff Marshal Ogarkov and the appointment of the oldest and least prestigious deputy defense minister—Sokolov— to the post of defense minister. Thus, at least in this area, Gorbachev had the benefit of the results of Chernenko's work; the Soviet Army, at least for the time being, was no more a decisive factor in influencing political decisions, and its reduced prominence continued to be apparent in the following months.

A possible explanation of this situation can be found in the field of economics. The USSR is a superpower in one area only, namely, the military. In all other areas, and particularly in its economy, it lags far behind the West countries. One reason for the enormous economic gap between the USSR and Western countries (apart from the inherent drawbacks of the socialist economic system) is the subordination of entire economic branches to the needs of the Soviet Army. However, the growing economic gap between the USSR and the West is bound eventually to affect Soviet military power. The need to accelerate Soviet technological development, so heavily emphasized by Gorbachev, requires a certain rearrangement of priorities, which must include the transfer of at least some of the vast resources hitherto placed at the disposal of the Soviet Armed Forces to other authorities (such as the economic ministries) engaged in setting economic targets. Limiting the involvement of the Soviet Army in the political decisionmaking process by appointing a rather mediocre defense minister and depriving the Army of the full seat in the Politburo that Ustinov had held for so many years would seem to represent a step in this direction.

Gorbachev's Political Persona and Power Base

The rise of Mikhail Gorbachev's political career was truly meteoric. In six years he rose from first secretary of the Stavropol kray CPSU Committee to the very summit of the CPSU pyramid. He served for eight years as first secretary in Stavropol before being moved to Moscow in 1978 to take up the post of CPSU Central Committee secretary in charge of agriculture.[21] He had completed two courses of higher education, graduating in 1955 from the Faculty of Law of Moscow State University and in 1967 from the Stavropol Agricultural Institute.[22] His political career prior to 1978 had been restricted to the Stavropol kray, serving first as deputy chief of the Komsomol Agitation and Propaganda Department of the Stavropol kraykom (1958), then as second and later first secretary of the Stavropol Komsomol kraykom (1958–1962). He then held the appointments of organizer of the territorial production administration of the collective and state farms under the Stavropol kraykom (1962–1963); head of the Stavropol Kraykom CPSU Party Organs Department (1963–1966); first secretary of the Stavropol CPSU gorkom (1966–1968); second secretary of the Stavropol kraykom (1968–1970); and, finally, first secretary of the CPSU Stavropol kraykom (1970–1978).[23] His limitations were self-evident; for almost twenty-five years he had dealt almost exclusively with regional agriculture and organizational matters. Even as Central Committee secretary, he continued to deal purely with agriculture, surviving several disastrous harvests without any apparent personal consequences. On the contrary, in 1979 he was appointed candidate member and in 1980 full member of the Politburo.

Gorbachev's career really took off under Andropov. He was entrusted with responsibilities in new areas of domestic and later foreign policy without losing his control over agricuture. By 1983 Gorbachev's control of the party's organizational activities (personnel) became increasingly visible: He presided over the election of a new Leningrad CPSU first secretary to replace Romanov, who had been appointed a secretary of the Central Committee; he supervised the election of Vorotnikov as the RSFSR premier in June 1983; and he played a central part in the accountability-election meetings of the party, which began in August 1983. Thus under Andropov Gorbachev graduated from the position of a junior agriculture secretary to a senior Central Committee secretary with a broad range of responsibilities.

In addition to his official duties, Gorbachev was beginning to enjoy a special privileged status among the other Soviet leaders. For example, when Andropov made his last public appearance on 15 August 1983 to meet party veterans and spoke unusually frankly on the pain of old leaders' having to step down because of age or infirmity, he was accompanied by a vigorous Gorbachev, who also addressed the meeting[24] and acted as chairman for the proceedings. The symbolic nature of the event was not lost on the participants.

Gorbachev did not emerge as a loser from the succession struggle after Andropov's death. Though not elected general secretary, he won recognition as the second secretary and heir apparent. His swift, smooth election on 11 March 1983 proved the correctness of his faction's decision to concentrate on securing Gorbachev's position as number two rather than continue the internecine struggle with Chernenko's supporters. Under Chernenko, Gorbachev's areas of responsibility increased significantly to include ideology, the economy, and foreign affairs—almost every area of Soviet political life. Later, Gorbachev chaired the regular Politburo meetings in Chernenko's absence and led the Secretariat.

The expansion of Gorbachev's authority and areas of power was accompanied by the apparent stagnation of the career of the only other Politburo member (apart from Chernenko) who was also a Central Committee secretary and thus a potential rival, Grigoriy Romanov. Under Chernenko Romanov remained confined to his existing areas of responsibility—the armed forces and heavy (mainly military) industry—without gaining any foothold in the areas of ideology, foreign policy, or organizational matters, which were all firmly under Gorbachev's control. Furthermore, despite the vacancies in the Secretariat, no new secretaries were appointed, thus giving Gorbachev almost complete freedom of action, especially in the last two to three months of Chernenko's life.

Gorbachev's meteoric rise and unprecedented gains in responsibility did not always proceed smoothly. Occasionally, one could detect signs of opposition from members of Chernenko's faction. For example, during October 1984 Romanov seemed to have moved ahead of Gorbachev in the semiofficial leadership lineup. Also during this period Gorbachev assumed a lower public profile, missing several important events and playing a secondary role in others. In contrast, Romanov enjoyed a high political profile, and perhaps his ambitions to compete with Gorbachev for the supreme post of general secretary were reawakened. It has been suggested that at the time Gromyko himself attempted to start a "stop Gorbachev" campaign[25] in the fear of losing his iron grip on Soviet foreign policy. Gromyko's highly personal and unconventional nomination speech contradicts this hypothesis. Gromyko's subsequent experience of being kicked upstairs to the chairmanship of the USSR Supreme Soviet Presidium must have been galling to him and seems to be an elegant move by Gorbachev to neutralize Gromyko's power and influence. Once again, the events are susceptible to differing interpretations.

Like preceding leaders, Gorbachev utilized his control over party personnel matters to place his close associates in key posts. The most important appointments were N. Kruchina as chief of the CPSU Central Committee Administration of Affairs (December 1983);[26] Yuriy Belov as second secretary of the Tadzhik Communist party (January 1984);[27] V. Kalashnikov as Volgograd party committee first secretary (24 January 1984);[28] and A. Nikonov as president of the prestigious Lenin Agricultural Academy (29 June 1984).[29] In addition, for two to three years before his election as general secretary Gorbachev had been in a position to influence the election or appointment of scores of lower-level officials. Within a very few years the young Central Committee secretary had established a strong power base in the party on which he would be able to rely in pushing forward his radical policies.

The swift tempo of Gorbachev's career and the obvious limitations of his experience made his public record prior to his election as general secretary rather scant. In recent years he had consistently supported the encouragement of personal initiative in economic affairs. In this context, he had not hesitated to call for a reduction in centralized control and the introduction of economic incentives to increase productivity. This approach was stressed in his speech at the ideological conference on 10 and 11 December 1984, in which he touched upon another favorite theme—the need to overcome conservative opposition to new ideas and initiatives, as well as the need for an open and free exchange of views on the direction and priorities of future development.[30]

In the past, Gorbachev had used almost exactly the same arguments in expressing his views on ideology. These bold views were apparently met with a certain apprehension by some of the top leaders. For example, *Pravda* on 11 December omitted most of Gorbachev's controversial views on the need for changes and for an open exchange of opinions voiced in his 10 December speech. These views only became known some days later, when the speech was published by Partizdat in a brochure entitled, "The People's Living Creativity: A Document of the All-Union Scientific-Practical Conference on the Improvement of Developed Socialism and the Party's Ideological Work in the Light of the Decisions of the June (1983) Plenum of the CPSU Central Committee." Gorbachev had invariably been very careful with his past public statements, which contributed to the paucity of his public record. His newly developed boldness and outspokenness, as demonstrated at the December 1984 ideological conference, surely indicated that by that time he had surmounted his temporary career setback and had reestablished his status as the heir apparent and de facto leader in Chernenko's absence.

Gorbachev's speech at the ideological conference is a useful guide to his views on other important matters. However, the central theme of the speech is the need to introduce new ideas, to exchange opinions freely, and to learn how to listen to others' views. He urged social scientists to do just this and encouraged the economists "to part with outdated ideas and stereotypes." Gorbachev rejected the notion that "everything must be regulated from the center" and repeatedly urged the development of self-management skills, as well as the provision of "room for initiative by people."

Similar ideas prevail in Gorbachev's writings on agricultural topics. He had consistently endorsed the collective contract system in agriculture, that is, the setup by which small groups of farm workers are given independence in organizing their work, with the award of bonuses and other incentives for increased productivity. His 10 February 1983 *Pravda* article argued that this approach would increase productivity in the agricultural sector by 20 to 30 percent. Gorbachev repeatedly expressed his support for expanding the private plots of collective farm workers, describing them as an important source of increased output and a legitimate part of the socialist system.

Until 1984 Gorbachev's involvement in foreign affairs had been marginal and insignificant, predominantly consisting of meetings with foreign Communist delegations. After his appointment as chairman of the Supreme Soviet Foreign Affairs Commission in April 1984, his activity in the area expanded considerably (see Table 7.1). His position on the key issues of Soviet foreign policy, as reflected in his 11 March 1985 acceptance speech,[31] was in accord with the established Soviet views on peace, disarmament, and the prevention of unilateral military superiority. In the past, he had not hesitated to attack the U.S. administration and even President Reagan personally (see his December 1983 speech at the Portuguese Communist Party Congress) in a way that did not differ from the usual Soviet propaganda. He had repeatedly endorsed détente (in his 8 September 1984 speech in Sofia, his 18 December 1984 speech before the British Parliament, and elsewhere),

TABLE 7.1   Gorbachev's Trips Abroad, 1972–1985

Year	Country	Position
1972	Belgium	Head of CPSU delegation
1975	West Germany	Head of CPSU delegation
1976	France	Head of CPSU delegation
1979	Czechoslovakia	Head of Soviet Agricultural delegation
1981	Mongolia	Head of CPSU delegation to Mongolian party congress
1982	Vietnam	Head of CPSU delegation to Vietnamese party congress
1983	Canada	Head of parliamentary delegation
1983	Hungary	Head of CPSU delegation
1983	Portugal	Head of CPSU delegation to Portuguese party congress
1984	Italy	Head of CPSU delegation to Berlinguer funeral
1984	Bulgaria	Head of Soviet party and government delegation
1984	Great Britain	Head of parliamentary delegation
Oct. 1985	France	Official leader's visit
Oct. 1985	Bulgaria	Friendly visit and attendance of Warsaw Pact summit
Nov. 1985	Switzerland	Geneva summit talks with President Reagan
Nov. 1985	Czechoslovakia	Warsaw Pact leaders' meeting in Prague

usually (as in his London speech) combining the issue with stressing the need for peaceful coexistence in Europe. "We all agree that ours is a vulnerable, fragile, yet interdependent world, where we must coexist, whether we want this or not. For all that separates us, we have one planet, and Europe is our common home, not a theater of operations."[32]

On the issue of international communism, Gorbachev stated that Moscow had no "universal recipes" applicable to all countries and that socialism should develop in accordance with "the traditions and conditions of the separate countries."[33] The fact that he chose Sofia as the stage for these particular statements indicates that they were intended for East European audiences. On the other hand, he used the same opportunity to warn against any deviation from Moscow's line, stressing the importance of socialist internationalism and "the deep recognition of the unity of the national and international interests of every fraternal country."[34] Thus, one cannot perceive any substantial differences between Gorbachev's views and the official Soviet line on the issue of the East European states' conformity with the traditional line of Moscow.

Gorbachev's Friends and Foes

The supreme organ of real political power in the USSR, the Politburo, is in the unique position not only of deciding all important matters but also of being above any control, checks, or responsibility to the electorate. Therefore, the real test of Gorbachev's political power was to take place in the Poliburo. Control over its members meant a solid grip over the country's affairs and a long and stable tenure.

Immediately after Chernenko's death, Gorbachev appeared to enjoy a great advantage. The memberships of the two top party organs, the Politburo and the Central Committee Secretariat, had fallen to their lowest levels in more than twenty years. The infighting during the last two to three years had prevented quick and regular appointments so that both the Politburo and the Secretariat had several vacancies awaiting Gorbachev's appointees. Moreover, several elderly members of the Politburo and Secretariat were expected to give up their seats soon. Finally, regardless of the wishes of certain members of the leadership, once Gorbachev held a firm majority of votes in the Politburo he was free to make any changes he thought fit.

Even before Gorbachev's election as general secretary, his allies were well known. The most prominent among them was RSFSR premier and Politburo member Vitaliy Vorotnikov (fifty-nine years). Having languished in the wilderness under Brezhnev (as ambassador to Cuba), he was recalled by Andropov in mid-1982 to replace Brezhnev's crony Medunov as first secretary of the Krasnodar kraykom. After a brief, very intensive purge of corrupt officials in the area, Vorotnikov became RSFSR premier in June 1983 (nominated by Gorbachev) and a candidate member of the Politburo; in December 1983 he was made a full member.

Vorotnikov's economic views were very close to those of Gorbachev. He openly stressed the importance of using economic incentives and administrative decentralization to stimulate initiatives by the workers and managers alike. Furthermore, as the RSFSR premier he successfully applied his approach to the republic's economy, publicly calling for the transplantation of the Georgian economic experiment to other parts of the USSR.[35] Promoted by Gorbachev's patron Andropov and sharing economic views and aversion to personal corruption, Gorbachev could safely count on Vorotnikov's support in the Politburo.

Two members of the leadership with good reason to expect quick promotion to the Politburo were the Central Committee secretaries Yegor Ligachev (sixty-four years) and Nikolay Ryzhkov (fifty-five). Both had been promoted by Andropov and shared qualities and links with Gorbachev. Yegor Ligachev was head of the Central Committee Party

Organizational Work Department from April 1983, and when the December 1983 Central Committee plenum elected him Central Committee secretary, he forged a close association with Gorbachev, working under his supervision. So close was the working relationship between the two men that occasionally Ligachev appeared to stand in for Gorbachev.

Thus, at the beginning of 1985 when Gorbachev was chairing the Politburo instead of Chernenko and was familiarizing himself with new responsibilities, Ligachev demonstrated an active involvement in agriculture, the main area in which Gorbachev had previously been active. In January 1985 Ligachev visited Leningrad and its district, taking part in a "zonal conference of party and soviet workers, which examined questions of introducing financial autonomy and the collective contract into stockraising and intensifying organizational and political work among stockraisers." After the conference—at which one of Gorbachev's favorite proposals, the collective contract system, was introduced—Ligachev visited local farms, talked to the workers, and "inquired about people's working and living conditions,"[36] following Gorbachev's style of operation. Earlier in the same month Ligachev had made similar visits to Novosibirsk oblast and the Altay kray, where he had similar conversations with local workers.[37]

On 4 March 1985 Ligachev attended an All-Union Conference of Union and Autonomous Republic Ministers of Internal Affairs, Chiefs of Krayispolkom, Oblispolkom, and Transportation Internal Affairs Administrations, Internal Forces, and Teaching Establishments, and Chiefs of Political Sections of the USSR MVD System, which discussed the results of the work of the Ministry of Internal Affairs (MVD) during the 1983–1984 period.[38] Ligachev was the only representative of the leadership at the conference, and his presence there obviously undermined Romanov's authority, since Romanov was considered in charge of all the military and paramilitary organizations in the USSR, including the secret services and the MVD. Ligachev's presence also indicated Gorbachev's interest in the conference and strengthened Ligachev's own prestige, demonstrating an extension of his areas of interest.

Nikolay Ryzhkov's past career had been concerned with the economy and its management. Under Andropov he was promoted to a Central Committee secretary in November 1982 and head of the Central Committee Economic Department. During 1984 Gorbachev showed growing interest in the economy, advocating the introduction of incentives to encourage intiatives and increase productivity. In his 1 February meeting in his Novosibirsk constituency, Ryzhkov focused on the same theme, as well as underlining the importance of the "team contract, and the introduction of 'large-scale experiments.'"[39]

Ligachev and Ryzhkov (together with Viktor Grishin) attended Gorbachev's 20 February meeting in his Moscow constituency.[40] This was a visible demonstration of the bond between them and their common stance. Accordingly, at the time of Gorbachev's ascent to the post of general secretary, his closest comrades in arms were Vorotnikov, Ligachev, and Ryzhkov. Bound by common ties—their links with Andropov, their commitment to economic reforms and decentralization, and their obvious personal closeness—they formed a powerful bloc on which Gorbachev could safely rely. One of the first proofs of Gorbachev's real political power was his success in quickly promoting Ryzhkov and Ligachev to full membership of the Politburo, thus reinforcing his control of the supreme decisionmaking body.

Nevertheless, in March 1985 Ligachev and Ryzhkov were still merely Central Committee secretaries, whereas the Politburo contained several leaders who had little reason to support Gorbachev. Most notable among these were the surviving members of the Brezhnev clan: Tikhonov (now almost eighty years), Kunayev (seventy-three), and Grishin (seventy-one). All three had apparently opposed Andropov and supported Chernenko in their respective elections to the general secretaryship. Whatever their future attitude toward Gorbachev might be, their past records made them very uncomfortable partners for the new general secretary, and their political futures seemed highly uncertain. Grishin, evidently sensing this, was the first Politburo member to go on public record as referring to Gorbachev as "head of the Politburo," only one week after Gorbachev's election as general secretary.[41]

Geydar Aliyev (sixty-two years), though often unpredictable, owed nothing to Brezhnev and much to Andropov. In addition, he possessed very healthy instincts of political survival. Whatever his private opinion might be, he was certainly going to offer Gorbachev his support as long as the latter remained in control. No opposition was to be expected from his direction.

Solomentsev (seventy-one) and Shcherbitskiy (sixty-seven) were relatively independent Politburo members whose past records did not permit them to be clearly identified with either faction. Their attitudes toward Gorbachev could not be taken for granted, but they were expected to offer qualified support, subject to their own interests. Of the two, Shcherbitskiy was clearly the more outspoken, often voicing support both for accommodating the demands of the military and for maintaining a hard line in foreign affairs. His conservatism was also evident in the economic field. In his article, "The Real Democracy of the Soviet Society" (*Kommunist,* no. 17, November 1984), while stressing the importance of public opinion and of letters from the working people[42] he warned against undermining the existing system of central planning, pointing to "dangers for the vital interests of the working people" and even of "creating the danger of restoring capitalism."[43] Clearly a hard and independent man, Shcherbitskiy's future attitude toward Gorbachev remained open to speculation.

Two of the most interesting figures in the Politburo were Romanov and Gromyko. Gromyko (almost seventy-six years old) had nominated Gorbachev for general secretary in an emotional and highly personal address at the 11 March Central Committee plenum. His support of Gorbachev as a man was plainly stated there. Whether this support extended to all aspects of Gorbachev's policies was open to dispute, especially in foreign affairs. Gromyko himself had dominated this area for almost thirty years. Indeed, Soviet foreign policy abroad was identified with the dour personality of the Soviet foreign minister. If Gorbachev was to assert himself in this area, Gromyko could prove a formidable obstacle. It was difficult to envisage any far-reaching reforms or innovations in Soviet foreign policy as long as Gromyko retained his iron grip in this field. Gorbachev would find it difficult to develop new foreign contacts under the watchful eyes of the old master. Thus, the Gromyko problem was another matter that had to be settled by Gorbachev, one that would demand all his powers of diplomacy and tact. The appointment of the lord of the Soviet Foreign Ministry and supporter of the hard line as chairman of the Supreme Soviet Presidium seemed an ideal method for dealing with this delicate and potentially explosive problem.

Finally, Romanov, the highly ambitious and relatively youthful (sixty-two years) Politburo Central Committee secretary (the only other full-member secretary) was an obvious rival. Because of the military's discontent with its clearly diminished influence on political decisions, an alliance between Romanov and the Soviet armed forces was not difficult to foresee, given Romanov's long association with the defense industry and the armed forces establishment. Romanov's future attitude toward Gorbachev was likely to be dictated by tactical considerations, as the former awaited the right moment to move against Gorbachev with the support of the Army and possibly the KGB. Therefore Romanov was a real potential threat for the new general secretary, making the curbing of Romanov's power or even his removal from the Politburo a vital concern for Gorbachev. In the same vein, the promotion of the KGB Chief Viktor Chebrikov to full membership of the Politburo might have seemed an effective way of simultaneously neutralizing Romanov and gaining the full support of the KGB.

Gorbachev Consolidates

Gorbachev wasted no time in asserting his new power, effectively using the presence of all the East European leaders and many Western dignitaries in Moscow. The death of the previous leader served as a good opportunity for signaling intentions and establishing contacts.

On 13 March Gorbachev met with East European leaders.[44] The official announcement of the meeting pointed out that "in the conditions of the difficult international situation, strengthening the fraternal countries' unity and cohesion and stepping up coordination of action in the international arena assume special importance."[45] In Communist jargon, this meant that the East European leaders were called upon to cooperate more closely with Moscow and to refrain from independent initiatives in the international arena. The description of the climate of the meeting in the announcement as "an atmosphere of cordiality and unanimity,"[46] (the absence of the words *fraternal* or even *friendly* is worthy of note) indicated that hard words had been exchanged behind the closed doors of the meeting and that the proceedings were probably not to the liking of such leaders as Nicolae Ceausescu, Erich Honecker, and Todor Zhivkov, who had taken (or at least attempted) some independent steps in relations with the West.

From the first moment of Gorbachev's election, the East European countries assumed a defensive attitude, stressing their loyalty and pledging further efforts to increase their contributions to the common cause. For example, Honecker of the GDR emphasized that "the GDR and the SED [Socialist Unity Party of Germany—the East German Communist party] will continue to be a close ally, loyal friend, and reliable companion of Lenin's country."[47] In similar vein, the Polish leaders Wojciech Jaruzelski and Henryk Jablonski pledged to do "everything possible to increase Poland's contribution to our joint cause."[48] Hungarian leader Janos Kadar promised that "in the future also we will do everything to consolidate further the unbreakable friendship between our people and promote the deepening of the many-sided cooperation between our countries."[49]

Barely two weeks after Chernenko's death Gorbachev gave the first indication of future personnel changes. On 26 March 1984 the newly elected RSFSR Supreme Soviet held its first session, and Premier Vitaliy Vorotnikov, one of Gorbachev's closest allies, promptly replaced the chairman of the RSFSR Supreme Soviet Presidium M. A. Yasnov with N. M. Gribachev.[50] The formula in the official announcement—"retired for health reasons"—was used very frequently in the following months. Three of the ten RSFSR deputy premiers were replaced by younger officials closely linked with Vorotnikov.[51] First Deputy Premier Vladimir Orlov, who had been appointed deputy premier when Vorotnikov was sent without explanation as ambassador to Cuba, was kicked upstairs to the largely honorary post of chairman of the RSFSR Supreme Soviet Presidium.

Vorotnikov, apparently too impatient to wait for the RSFSR Supreme Soviet session, began his ministerial changes even earlier. Since the beginning of the year he had appointed four new ministers and two new heads of republican state committees. One of these, N. Golub, the new minister of procurement, had been chairman of the Krasnodar soviet in 1982–1983, when Vorotnikov was first secretary of the Krasnodar kraykom.[52] The same links existed with other new appointees; all were younger people with personal associations with Vorotnikov. Vorotnikov did not lack support in his undertakings. The RSFSR Supreme Soviet session was attended by Gorbachev, Aliyev, Gromyko, Solomentsev, Grishin, Chebrikov, Ligachev, and Ryzhkov. However, Tikhonov, Kunayev, and Shcherbitskiy played no part in the session.[53]

The close association of Gorbachev's faction with the session's proceedings was further demonstrated by the participation of Ligachev and Ryzhkov (the only top leaders present) in the session of the RSFSR Supreme Soviet Council of Elders. This session actually works out the agenda for the Supreme Soviet session and prepares the final resolution (the composition of the bodies ostensibly to be elected two days later). In reporting their participation, Soviet television used the unusual expression, "Comrades Ligachev and Ryzhkov conducted the session,"[54] leaving little doubt about their role. Finally, at the Supreme Soviet session itself, Ryzhkov nominated Vorotnikov for reelection as RSFSR premier under the benevolent gaze of Gorbachev, who attended the session.[55] One had to admire the clean, coordinated, and effective team work of the four musketeers, Gorbachev, Vorotnikov, Ryzhkov, and Ligachev, in completing a neat operation only weeks after Gorbachev's election as general secretary. And of course, the events at the RSFSR Supreme Soviet session indicated what lay in store later for the rest of the country.

Gorbachev had never concealed his intention to renew and rejuvenate the entire state and party leadership. *Pravda* of 2 April, in an editorial entitled, "Improving Work with Cadres," pointed out that from then on "practical results" would be "the main criterion by which the standard of leadership is assessed." The party organs demanded "initiative" and "innovation" from the leaders and associated this demand with the March 1985 Central Committee plenum[56] making it crystal clear who the initiator of the new policy was.

The issue of improving the work with the cadres and introducing a new policy in this field had been discussed at a 18 October 1984 Politburo meeting, which adopted a decision on the matter.[57] According to the report of this meeting, the Politburo had called for the promotion of "younger leaders, women, and rank-and-file workers." However, this call had been balanced by an admonition that younger leaders should "learn from the experienced cadres of the older generation," so that they could acquire "experience and the necessary tempering."[58] One month later on 19 November, *Pravda* again addressed the issue of cadre policy, strongly condemning the selection of cadres on the basis of personal ties or family relations and attacking party organizations that continued to tolerate leaders' weaknesses and shortcomings. One may speculate that the 18 October decision had been initiated by Gorbachev, whereas the proviso on following the older generation had been added by Chernenko, who was still active at the time.

Other leaders also addressed the issue of a new cadre policy. Speaking at the 13th Hungarian Party Congress in Budapest, Romanov stressed that the CPSU was demanding from the cadres "greater responsibility" and more "creativity and initiative."[59] Even Chernenko himself reiterated the formula of "skillfully combining the experienced cadres of the older generation with younger and promising officials."[60]

Gorbachev, apparently unimpressed by Chernenko's desultory efforts, began implementing his new cadre policy while Chernenko was still alive (but already inactive). On 12 February Soviet television announced:

> The Presidium of the USSR Supreme Soviet has appointed Vasiliy Aleksandrovich Dinkov minister of the USSR oil industry, relieving him of his duties as minister of the USSR gas industry.
>
> Nikolay Aleksandrovich Maltsev is relieved of his duties as minister of the USSR oil industry in connection with his retirement on pension.
>
> Viktor Stepanovich Chernomyrdin has been appointed minister of the USSR gas industry.[61]

Since Maltsev was only fifty-six years old when he was "retired on pension" whereas his successor Dinkov was sixty-one, this change clearly was not the result of age considerations. Central Committee Secretary Vladimir Dolgikh, speaking three days later at a plenum of the Tyumen party obkom, sharply criticized the performance of the Ministry of the Oil Industry,[62] thus disclosing the real reason for Maltsev's "retirement." Other replacements followed. On 2 April France Press reported that since Gorbachev had assumed the post of general secretary six obkoms had received new leaders; this figure rises to fourteen if changes made during the final weeks of Chernenko's tenure are included.[63] Changes at the ministerial level also continued; on 23 March Petr Neporozhniy, the eighty-five-year-old minister of power and electrification, was replaced "because of poor health and was succeeded by Anatoliy Mayorets, the minister of the electrical equipment industry.[64] The fact that the Politburo did not deem it necessary to thank Neporozhniy for his long service (as minister since 1962) suggests that the real reason for the retirement was not old age but incompetence and poor performance.

During the early stages of Gorbachev's tenure, his new policy apparently encountered resistance. On 8 April a Central Committee conference of leading economic and management personnel dealt with "urgent questions pertaining to successful implementation of plans for this year and the entire 5-Year-Plan Period, ways and methods of tackling the most important economic and social tasks."[65] The conference was attended by Gorbachev, Romanov, Dolgikh, Kapitonov, and, of course, Ligachev and Ryzhkov,[66] whose promotion to full membership of the Politburo seemed to be merely a matter of time. At the conference Gorbachev outlined his plans for an extensive economic reform. Both the brief TASS and *Pravda* (9 April) reports appeared to be aimed at obscuring the scope and intensity of Gorbachev's demands for revolutionary changes in the Soviet economy. One can only suppose that persons who felt that Gorbachev's new policy was endangering their own positions were attempting to hide the true proportions of Gorbachev's plan.

The attempt misfired, however. The unusually lengthy report on deliberations at the 11 April Politburo meeting[67] revealed that it had dealt mainly with economic issues, making it "incumbent on the heads of ministries and departments, as well as local party, administrative, and economic bodies, to take measures to eliminate existing short-comings; to efficiently tackle matters affecting the timely execution of spring sowings . . . ; to steadfastly raise the level of organization and mass political work . . . , and to mount socialist competition." Various ministries were asked to improve the effectiveness of their performance and encourage workers' initiative.[68] On the next day all Soviet central newspapers carried the full text of Gorbachev's speech at the conference, revealing the full scope of his proposed reforms to all.

The main idea permeating the expanded version of the speech was that a decentralization of economic power was required, which would give more rights and responsibilities to plan managers and reduced the interference by the central ministries and planning bodies. Fur-thermore, Gorbachev invited attacks on the economic leadership, calling for a thorough discussion on improving economic management, stressing that "this is the time" to start removing "obstacles to forward movement." He pointed out that "frank conversations" were to be encouraged to find out what was preventing the growth of efficiency and what needed to be changed or corrected.[69]

The entire speech revealed not only the scope of Gorbachev's plans for economic reforms and improved efficiency—to be achieved if nec-essary by the dismissal of poor managers—but also the resistance that his reforms were still meeting from some influential persons, who were at least temporarily capable of preventing the full publication of his speech. In this case, Gorbachev needed only seventy-two hours (and, perhaps, a tough Politburo meeting) to neutralize the opposition. It was also clear that Gorbachev urgently needed additional support at the highest level, in the Politburo. To press forward with his new cadre policy and his economic reforms, he needed the solid support of his Politburo colleagues. Since some of them were evidently resisting his policies, the appointment of new supporters (notably Ligachev and Ryzhkov) became not only a test of his power but also a first priority and precondition for implementing his plans.

On 16 and 17 April Gorbachev revealed another facet of his new approach—his highly informal and personal style of leadership. He toured Moscow's Proletarskiy District, visiting the Likhachev Automotive Plant and the "residential development area" of the district, where he "was invited by a young couple" to visit their flat and where he visited a hospital.[70] Gorbachev talked freely with the workers, asked about their plans for the future, and, when speaking at the Likhachev plant, "called on the personnel of the assembly plant to more widely use economic incentives to intensify production, to show creative initiative, and to develop independence in solving major technical and organi-zational problems."[71]

A number of reasons for Gorbachev's visit are possible. It could have been prompted by genuine interest in the living and working conditions of Moscow's citizens. He could have been demonstrating his personal style (reminiscent of Andropov's at the very beginning of his brief tenure) or perhaps he was testing his popularity with the masses, or even trying to enhance it, on the eve of the crucial 23 April Central Committee plenum.

The April Plenum—Gorbachev in Control

Since Andropov's death, no new Politburo appointments had been made; following the deaths of Marshal Ustinov and Chernenko, membership had dropped to ten, giving Gorbachev the opportunity to elect his supporters to vacancies. His power to do so was demonstrated on 23 April, when TASS distributed the first short communiqué on the Central Committee plenum: Ligachev and Ryzhkov had been elected full members of the Politburo, KGB Chief Chebrikov had been promoted from candidate to full member, Defense Minister Sokolov had been made a candidate Politburo member, and V. Nikonov a Central Committee secretary.[72] These were the most extensive changes in the Politburo membership since 1973 and an irrefutable demonstration of Gorbachev's authority.

The direct promotion of Ligachev and Ryzhkov to full membership without passing through the candidate member stage was not unprecedented (both Gromyko and Grechko had been directly elected to full membership in 1973) but was unusual, especially in view of their relatively brief careers at the top of the party. Both were junior secretaries of the Central Committee and received this promotion over the heads of several more senior leaders, such as Dolgikh. Marshal Sokolov was not given similar treatment. He merely became a candidate (nonvoting) member of the Politburo—a further indication of the decline of the Army's influence on political affairs and a measure of Sokolov's own puny stature in the political arena.

The promotion of KGB Chief Viktor Chebrikov to full membership restored the tradition of having the KGB chief in the Politburo as a voting member. Although not as closely associated with Gorbachev as Ligachev and Ryzhkov, Chebrikov was nevertheless a previous close associate of Andropov, who had appointed him KGB chief and candidate member of the Politburo. It seemed that he too would be a loyal supporter of Gorbachev.

Viktor Nikonov, the new Central Committee secretary, was an agricultural specialist and evidently was to assume Gorbachev's old position as the secretary in charge of agriculture. His past record indicated that his career, which obtained a strong impetus during Gorbachev's tenure as agricultural secretary, had brought him into close contact with Gorbachev. In 1979 Nikonov was appointed USSR deputy minister of agriculture and in 1983 the RSFSR minister of agriculture,[73] revealing a close link with RSFSR Premier Vorotnikov, one of Gorbachev's allies.

These extensive changes suggested that Gorbachev had clearly consolidated his power and that he would find it easier to push through his economic reforms with the election of his allies to full Politburo membership. He could now expect a firm majority in the supreme organ of real political power, making further outbreaks of acute infighting unlikely. The promotion of Ryzhkov (an industrial specialist) implied that some of Romanov's responsibilities were going to be taken away; the future would show if Romanov was to be given new areas of activity, in addition to security matters and the defense industry, or whether he was on the way out of the Politburo. Gorbachev, however, had not removed any member from the Politburo, indicating either that he was not yet powerful enough to take such a step or that he saw no urgent need to expel any of his former rivals. In the field of foreign policy, Gorbachev still had to consider the whims and conservative stance of Andrey Gromyko, the grey eminence in Soviet diplomacy. The new appointments confirmed a trend that had become apparent earlier— Gorbachev's tendency to promote officials whose careers had started in his own home base of Stavropol or in Western Siberia. Gorbachev doubtless was aware of his bases of power and was actively exploiting them.

Besides personnel changes the plenum set the date for the 27th CPSU Congress (25 February 1986) and adopted the Congress's agenda.[74] It also set the dates for the accountability-election campaign that was to precede the 27th CPSU Congress[75] and heard an extensive report from Gorbachev on the tasks of the forthcoming party congress. Incidentally, Gorbachev used this report to stress the importance of his economic policy and to emphasize that he expected the forthcoming accountability-election campaign to contribute to the plans for increasing the productivity and efficiency of the Soviet economy.[76] Most of all, however, the plenum demonstrated that Gorbachev was firmly in control of the party and its main organs, permitting him to proceed with his reforms and to change the composition of the party's main organs even before the convening of the 27th CPSU Congress.

8

Clearing Away the Debris; The Second Front

After the 23 April 1985 CPSU Central Committee plenum, Gorbachev began to demonstrate his increased self-confidence. Not only did he continue to make new appointments at an increasing tempo, but occasionally he allowed himself to make surprising statements, which produced an unusual impact and astounded reaction. On 8 May 1985 Gorbachev was the chief speaker at a festive meeting at the Kremlin Palace of Congresses held to mark the fortieth anniversary of the Soviet victory over Nazi Germany. After reviewing the stages of the war and praising the heroism of the Soviet soldiers, he said: "The gigantic work at the front and in the rear was guided by the party, its Central Committee, and the State Defense Committee headed by the General Secretary of the CPSU Bolshevik Central Committee, Iosif Vissarionovich Stalin."[1]

The people in the audience gasped, caught completely by surprise. They needed several seconds to recover from their astonishment, and then they burst into spontaneous and prolonged applause. Gorbachev balanced this statement by referring to "the miscalculations" at the beginning of the war and by stressing that "for various reasons we were unable, and did not have the time, to fully accomplish everything that was necessary."[2] Gorbachev not only had mentioned Stalin by name (a very rare and unusual occurrence in the modern Soviet Union) but also had not hesitated to emphasize Stalin's contribution to the final victory. Not coincidentally other East European leaders, such as Erich Honecker of the GDR (in his 7 May *Pravda* article on the VE [Victory in Europe] Day anniversary) and Bulgaria's Defense Minister Army General Dobri Dzhurov in his 8 May speech in Sofia[3] mentioned Stalin's contribution in almost identical terms.

Gorbachev continued his impromptu meetings with Soviet citizens. Obviously aimed at projecting an image of concern for the opinions of the people, these meetings undoubtedly contributed to Gorbachev's popularity. The Soviet media, evidently unused to reporting such meetings, had difficulty adjusting to the new leadership style. On one hand, perhaps following explicit instructions, the coverage of Gorbachev's informal meetings and impromptu conversations with ordinary citizens was full and comprehensive. On the other hand, the media continued to have difficulty digesting Gorbachev's hard-hitting speeches.

Both sides of the coin were visible during Gorbachev's visit to Leningrad on 16 and 17 May. Soviet television carried long film reports on Gorbachev's informal meetings with citizens on the streets of Leningrad[4] and with the students of the Leningrad Polytechnic Institute.[5] Soviet viewers had a rare opportunity to see unusual and animated exchanges between Gorbachev and the people on the street.

> Woman's voice in the crowd: "You should be closer to the people!"
> Gorbachev: "How can I be any closer?"[6]

When one of the participants in the interchange mentioned "indolent and drinking people," Gorbachev replied: "As for drunkards, if any one of you at this conversation of ours has indulged, I tell you that on 17 May measures are going to be introduced: drastic measures to fight drunkenness will be published."[7] Television viewers could even hear the comment of one of the bystanders following Gorbachev's words: "It should have been done long ago. . . ."[8]

Sure enough, on the next day, 17 May, *Pravda* published on its front page a decision of the CPSU Central Committee, "On Measures to Surmount Drunkenness and Alcoholism." The decision pointed out that previous decisions on this matter "are being implemented unsatisfactorily" and instructed all party organizations to adopt strict measures to combat alcoholism and "make drinking absolutely unacceptable at enterprises, organizations, establishments, educational institutions, banquets, and receptions."[9] Severe measures, "including expulsion from party membership," were envisaged for Communists who continued to drink.

On the same day Gorbachev spoke before the leading members of the Leningrad party organization at the Smolnyy Institute assembly hall. Soviet radio and television on that day and the press on the next day disseminated only brief, bland summaries of Gorbachev's speech. Four days passed before the radio broadcasted a fifty-minute (obviously edited) recording of Gorbachev's speech, which allowed astonished Soviet listeners to hear his hard-hitting statements concerning the unacceptability of the "quiet, tranquil life," the fiction of plan fulfillment, the fact that Soviet citizens were forced to spend "75 percent, if not 80 percent" of their wages on poor-quality consumer goods, on the inadequate and outdated machinery used in Soviet industry, and so on. Never before had a Soviet leader mentioned in public such subjects.

> Try and get your apartment repaired. You will definitely have to find a moonlighter to do it for you. He will steal the materials he needs from a construction site. They come from the state anyway. So, the question

arises: Why are we unable to make a realistic evaluation of the situation? Or, take a simple example. As you have noticed, we have discussed, and now adopted, a decision on the allocation of land and necessary resources for the establishment of market gardens and plots, not for dachas, but for small summerhouses and market gardens. In the first place, the facilities we have already enable 20 million people to spend their leisure during the summer. Another 15 million people are asking us for gardens and plots of this kind. We have been terribly afraid that this is something akin to private enterprise. How can you call it private enterprise when a family possesses a garden and travels to it? So we have now decided to earmark land sufficient for at least 1 to 1.2 million families. The resources, goods, and services which are available must expand to meet cash demands. Here we must use our brains, and that's a fact. Mathematically, our approach to this problem is fundamentally weak, Comrades. It is very weak.[10]

Evidently the press was again unable immediately to stomach the highly controversial issues raised by Gorbachev. The speech received very similar treatment to that given to Gorbachev's 8 April speech at the Central Committee conference with economic managers; again Gorbachev's statements were only published three days after the conference. Nevertheless, it should be noted that such occurrences were characteristic of only the first three to four months of Gorbachev's tenure; later he had the Soviet press firmly under his control.

Romanov's Decline; New Appointments

The political fortunes of Grigoriy Romanov, the former party boss of Leningrad, began to decline immediately after Gorbachev's ascent. He lost his privileged position at the 23 April 1985 Central Committee plenum when Ligachev and Ryzhkov were elected full members of the Politburo; Ligachev assumed supervision over matters of ideology, and Ryzhkov (and Gorbachev himself) encroached upon Romanov's old area of supervision—heavy industry. Indeed, following the April plenum, it became apparent that Romanov no longer held any responsibilities in the area of the economy. For example, at the 20–21 May 1985 meeting of the economic secretaries of the CEMA member-states' Central Committees, the CPSU was represented by Ryzhkov, Central Committee Secretary Rusakov, and Deputy Premier Talyzin.[11]

On 19 April *Pravda* announced the retirement of Vasiliy Frolov, the seventy-one-year-old director of the Central Committee Machine-Building Department, which had been under Romanov's control since 1983. For almost a month no new head was appointed. When the appointment was finally announced on 16 May, the first deputy head Valeriy Pimenov, who had been Romanov's protégé since his Leningrad days, had been passed over, and A. Volskiy appointed instead,[12] further indicating Romanov's decline. Volskiy had been Andropov's aide in the field of domestic affairs and had worked under the supervision of Ryzhkov, the overseer of planning under Andropov.

Gorbachev's visit to Leningrad on 16 and 17 May 1985 further underlined Romanov's eclipse. Leningrad was Romanov's home base. Despite the fact that after his election as a Central Committee secretary in 1983 he was obliged to relinquish his position of first secretary of the Leningrad City CPSU Committee, Romanov had continued to maintain close relations with the city's leadership, making visits and sending greetings messages on diverse official occasions. However, not only did Gorbachev not take Romanov with him, but the general secretary completely ignored the former party boss of Leningrad in his 17 May speech at the meeting with the city's party aktiv. Gorbachev did, however, refer to economic policies introduced in Leningrad during Romanov's tenure as the first secretary of the city's party organization.

The signs of Romanov's decline were accompanied by further appointments of Gorbachev people to key positions. Although these appointments are too numerous to list, the case of Georgiy Razumovskiy, who was appointed head of the CPSU Central Committee Party Organizational Work Department, is characteristic. On 4 June *Pravda* reported that Razumovskiy (forty-nine years old) had been relieved of his post as first secretary of the Krasnodar CPSU kraykom and appointed head of the Central Committee department, replacing Yegor Ligachev, who had assumed wider responsibilities arising from his appointment as a full Politburo member. As in many top level appointments, Gorbachev had evidently been involved in advancing the new person's career. As first secretary of the Stavropol party organization (until 1978), Gorbachev had been closely connected with the neighboring Krasnodar party organization. During this period he apparently had developed a good working relationship with Razumovskiy in Krasnodar, since when Gorbachev was moved to Moscow, Razumovskiy soon followed him.

In 1981 Razumovskiy was appointed head of the Department for Agricultural Complexes at the USSR Council of Ministers' Administration of Affairs—a position that clearly involved frequent contact with Gorbachev (at the time the Central Committee secretary for agriculture). When Gorbachev took over supervisory duties in the area of cadres in June 1983, Razumovskiy became first secretary of the Krasnodar kraykom, replacing Vitaliy Vorotnikov, upon the latter's election as the RSFSR premier.[13]

One year later, Gorbachev selected Krasnodar as the site for a major agricultural experiment, a sign of favoritism. Razumovskiy himself attracted the public eye through an article published in the March 1984 issue of *Kommunist,* in which he described the purge of local party officials in his area, which had been started by Vorotnikov. The article implied that Razumovskiy had been personally involved in this campaign.[14] The fact that Razumovskiy managed to get an article published in the chief theoretical publication of the CPSU indicated the patronage that he enjoyed.

The main idea put forward in the article was that encouragement should be given to the development of cadres with "business-like, political, and moral qualities," as well as to the advance of young cadres and women.[15] Corruption and other negative qualities of certain cadres had been repeatedly attacked by Razumovskiy, echoing the policy that Gorbachev had tried to implement when leading the Stavropol party committee. It was hardly accidental that *Sovetskaya Rossiya* in its editorial on 19 April 1985 highly praised the achievements of the party organizations in Stavropol and Krasnodar in the area of cadre policy: "Of course, not even the most perfect system for selection and placing leading personnel can guarantee against errors. However, that the number of errors can be dramatically reduced is graphically demonstrated by the experience of the Stavropol and Krasnodar Kray party organizations, which practice open selection of cadres."[16]

It is also noteworthy that Ivan Polozkov, the newly appointed first secretary of the Krasnodar kraykom,[17] had worked as a section head of the CPSU Central Committee Party Organizational Work Department while the department was headed by Ligachev. Thus, the importance of the Gorbachev-Vorotnikov-Ligachev connection and the geographical Krasnodar-Stavropol factor in many of the new appointments made by Gorbachev is clearly illustrated.

The personnel changes initiated by Gorbachev were accompanied by pressure for economic reforms, combined with sharp criticism of the performance of certain economic ministers and party officials. This was manifested at the 11–12 June Central Committee All-Union Conference on issues relating to the acceleration of scientific and technical progress. The conference was attended by all Politburo members and Central Committee secretaries except for Grigoriy Romanov,[18] an ominous sign that his dismissal from his posts was imminent.

Gorbachev spoke at the conference, and Soviet television broadcast a videorecording of his speech on the same day.[19] In his now familiar style, Gorbachev attacked "the lack of change for many years" and pointed out that "experiments are carried out but nothing changes,"[20] implying that this situation could no longer be tolerated. Gorbachev recommended specific steps to deal with the situation: improving investment policy to produce a higher return from investments; a major shift of resources to new construction projects; sharply increasing investment in the engineering industry; initiating a process of decentralization by reducing the role of Gosplan and the central economic ministries; and giving greater independence to individual enterprises. The Ministry of Ferrous Metallurgy was sharply criticized for the misuse of funds; the Ministry of the Electrical Industry, for holding up the production of basic materials; the Ministry of the Chemical Industry, for "delaying scientific work"; the State Committee for Science and Technology, for not completing experiments; and the State Committee for Labor and the Ministry of Finance, for "interpreting the decisions of the Central Committee and the Government in such a way that, after application and all the recommendations, nothing is left of the principles."[21] The audience's mechanical applause for the general secretary's words prompted a sarcastic response from Gorbachev: "If the ministers are applauding too, the ice has begun to shift."[22]

Gorbachev's attack was specifically aimed at certain economic ministries, even at named ministers who were responsible for shortcomings, such as Aleksey Yashin, minister of the construction materials industry, and Ivan Kazanets, minister of ferrous metallurgy, whose "incorrect policy," according to Gorbachev, had led to the ministry not fulfilling "either the 10th or 11th 5-Year Plans."[23] Incidentally, the ministers, as well as several of their peers, were succeeded soon after by Sergey Voyenushkin and Serafim Kolpakov.[24]

Two other figures were also criticized by implication. Central Committee Secretary Vladimir Dolgikh, a survival from the Brezhnev era, was an economic specialist who had supervised heavy industry since 1972. From 1976 to 1983 he had been in charge of the Central Committee Department of Heavy Industry.[25] A native of the Krasnoyarsk kray (Chernenko's native region), Dolgikh had been closely associated with Brezhnev and Chernenko. Since so many of the ministries under his direct supervision had attracted severe criticism from Gorbachev, it could be assumed that Dolgikh himself was an implied target at the criticism.

The second figure who was clearly targeted by Gorbachev was Premier Tikhanov. Once Chernenko's chief ally and himself an economic specialist who had headed the Soviet government for the past five years, Tikhonov clearly shared in the responsibility for the Soviet economy's poor performance. His unqualified loyalty to Brezhnev and Chernenko also made him a natural candidate for retirement. (Since he was eighty years old, one could not speak of an early retirement.) In any case, Gorbachev could not long continue the early retirement and resignation due to poor health formulas used in the dismissal of scores of economic ministers, deputy ministers, and other officials, without replacing the chairman of the Council of Ministers himself. So in June 1985 Tikhonov's time as the Soviet premier was fast running out.

Meanwhile, Gorbachev continued his practice of paying impromptu visits and holding informal meetings with Soviet citizens. On 25 June during a visit to Kiev, Soviet television once again showed Gorbachev chatting with people on the streets, answering their questions, and evidently enjoying their admiration and good wishes.[26] Both in Kiev and in Dnepropetrovsk, where he delivered a major speech touching upon economic and foreign policy issues, Gorbachev was accompanied by the Ukraine party boss Shcherbitskiy, and in his Dnepropetrovsk speech he made a point of stressing his relationship with Shcherbitskiy, showing that, at least for the time being, Shcherbitskiy was not another candidate for early retirement: "In mapping out a trip to the Ukraine—

Vladimir Vasiliyevich and I discussed this question in detail; I have visited the Ukraine many times before, many parts of it, but I have never before been to Dnepropetrovsk—we decided that it was essential to visit Dnepropetrovsk this time."[27] (The contrast between this treatment and that which Gorbachev accorded Romanov during his visit to Leningrad is striking.)

July 1985 Central Committee Plenum

If the political position of Shcherbitskiy seemed secure, other personnel issues were waiting to be settled—Romanov's fate and the appointment of a new chairman of the USSR Supreme Soviet Presidium. Since the presidium was due to meet on 2 July, the Central Committee was expected (on the basis of past record) to convene to decide the choice of the new Soviet president. Although the usual speculations appeared on this issue, it was generally assumed that Gorbachev himself would be elected to the post. After all, as he had pointed out in nominating Chernenko for the post,

> Simultaneous performance by the general secretary of the CPSU Central Committee of the functions of president of the Presidium of the USSR Supreme Soviet is of great importance for pursuing the foreign policy of the Soviet Union.
> The representation of our supreme state interests by the general secretary of the CPSU Central Committee in the international arena convincingly reflects the fact that the Soviet Union's foreign policy is inseparable from the course of the Communist Party, whose fundamental principles were formulated in the Peace Programme worked out by the 25th and the 26th CPSU Congresses, and by subsequent plenary meetings of the party Central Committee.[28]

The Central Committee convened on 1 July. As usual, the brief information report on its meeting did not reveal the name of the presidential candidate, although it did report that Gorbachev "had delivered a speech on questions related to the Supreme Soviet plenum."[29]

The information report also confirmed the long-expected dismissal of Romanov ("retirement on health grounds") and announced a number of major new appointments:

> The plenum of the CPSU Central Committee examined organizational issues. G. V. Romanov's request to relieve him of the duties of member of the Political Bureau and secretary of the CPSU Central Committee in connection with retirement on health grounds was satisfied. The plenum made alternate member E. A. Shevardnadze a full member of the Political Bureau of the CPSU Central Committee and elected B. N. Yeltsin and L. N. Zaykov secretaries of the CPSU Central Committee.[30]

Romanov. Romanov's dismissal was expected. The only potential (though weak) rival of Gorbachev, he had not been seen in public for almost two months. His political fortunes had markedly declined under Gorbachev, and his fields of responsibility were encroached upon, or simply transferred to, other leaders, such as Ryzhkov. His close connection with the military establishment clearly did not help him, as the Army itself had lost much of its former political influence. The retirement on health grounds formula had been used so often in the last three months that it had lost all real meaning. Furthermore, the fact that the Politburo did not thank Romanov for his past service indicated that his dismissal was peremptory.

Shevardnadze. The promotion of the Georgian party leader to full membership of the Politburo seemed a logical reward for Shevardnadze's past efforts to root out personal corruption and poor economic management in Georgia. As first secretary of the Georgian CP Central Committee he had initiated economic innovations and reorganized the republic's management of agriculture. These actions brought him into close contact with Gorbachev, who visited Georgia in December 1982 and January 1984. In addition, Shevardnadze's effective measures against corrupt local officials, which amounted to a local purge, were fully in accord with Gorbachev's own style. Shevardnadze's relative youth (fifty-seven years in 1985) was a further strong asset that recommended him to Gorbachev. It is doubtful that anyone besides the insiders in the Central Committee knew that Shevardnadze's promotion to full Politburo membership was only the first step in his ascent. On the next day he took up the post of the Soviet minister of foreign affairs.

Yeltsin. The promotion of the fifty-four-year-old former first secretary of Sverdlovsk region fully confirmed the pattern established by Gorbachev—the promotion of younger, well-trained officials eager to carry out economic and administrative reforms whose careers had been associated personally either with Gorbachev and his home region of Stavropol or with one of his top allies, Ligachev and Ryzhkov, and their home base of Western Siberia.

Zaykov. The promotion of the first secretary of the Leningrad party organization was a somewhat different case. Zaykov's career had been linked with Romanov, whom he succeeded as the Leningrad party chief when Romanov was appointed Central Committee secretary on 15 June 1983.[31] Romanov and Gorbachev attended the Leningrad party plenum meeting that elected Zaykov on 21 June,[32] reflecting Gorbachev's newly assumed responsibility for cadres and Romanov's involvement in, or at least approval of, Zaykov's election as his own successor. Romanov's political decline seemed to have no effect on Zaykov's prospects: During Gorbachev's 16–17 May visit to Leningrad Zaykov was constantly at his side, and the two clearly enjoyed an excellent working relationship.

The personnel changes not only demonstrated Gorbachev's consolidation and the scope of his authority but also provided valuable support for pushing his economic reforms through the party and administrative hierarchy. Indeed, Khrushchev, Brezhnev (or rather Kosygin), Andropov, and even Chernenko had tried to introduce major changes in the Soviet economy; none of them had succeeded. In most cases, the reforms were foiled by party officials at all levels, desperately clinging to old practices and procedures in an (effective) effort to preserve their own positions. Evidently with his eye on the forthcoming February 1986 27th CPSU Congress, Gorbachev was laying the groundwork from which to launch a decisive attack during the CPSU Congress, based on broad party support at all levels and aimed at fundamentally transforming the Soviet economic system by improving its efficiency and increasing productivity. As part of this campaign, by September 1985 Gorbachev had replaced 23 of the 157 regional party leaders.[33]

July 1985 Supreme Soviet Session

On 2 July 1985 the USSR Supreme Soviet held its regular third session. The most important issue on the agenda was the election of a new president for its presidium. Since the assembled deputies assumed that the post would go to Gorbachev, they were amazed when Gorbachev himself rose to speak. Gorbachev began his speech by justifying the past policy of combining the two posts in the person of the general secretary (a principle he had strongly endorsed when nominating Chernenko for the USSR Supreme Soviet Presidium presidency):

> As you know, starting from 1977, the general secretary of the CPSU Central Committee simultaneously held the post of president of the Presidium of the USSR Supreme Soviet. One should say that it was justified in the conditions of that time to combine in one person the highest posts in the party and the state. The past period saw an invigoration of legislative and other actions of the USSR Supreme Soviet, an improvement in the work of the soviets at local level and an intensification of control over administrative bodies.[34]

Listing the important new tasks facing the country—"the intensive development of the economy, restructuring of production, introduction of effective forms of management, organization and stimulation of labor, further improvement of the well-being of the Soviet people and consolidation of the country's defensive capability—Gorbachev stressed that these tasks "demand greater intensity in the work of the CPSU Central Committee and its Political Bureau."[35] He then came to the heart of his speech:

> Under these concrete conditions and with due account taken of the present stage, the plenum of the CPSU Central Committee found it advisable that the general secretary of the CPSU Central Committee should concentrate to the maximum on organizing the work of party

central organs and pooling the efforts of all party, state, and public organizations for a successful implementation of the charted course.

In this connection the CPSU Central Committee, the Presidium of the Supreme Soviet of the USSR, and the party group of the Supreme Soviet instructed me to submit for your consideration a proposal, supported by the Council of Elders of the two chambers, for electing Comrade Andrey Andreyevich Gromyko president of the Presidium of the Supreme Soviet of the USSR.[36]

Gromyko was "unanimously" elected chairman of the USSR Supreme Soviet.[37] Eduard Shevardnadze became the new minister of foreign affairs,[38] and Gorbachev himself was unanimously elected a member of the Supreme Soviet Presidium, having been nominated by Ligachev.[39] In addition, Ligachev and Ryzhkov assumed two key posts: Ligachev became chairman of the influential Foreign Affairs Commission of the Soviet of the Union, and Ryzhkov was elected chairman of the Legislative Proposals Commission of the Soviet of the Union.[40]

Gromyko's election was a major surprise. He had served as Soviet foreign minister for twenty-eight years, during which he had made the Foreign Ministry a fortress of personal power, acquired worldwide exposure as the most widely recognized official spokesperson of Soviet foreign policy, and became the permanent (though grim and ostensibly humorless) implementer and symbol of this policy. Some forty years before, when Gorbachev was still in the children's Pioneer organization, Gromyko was helping to decide Europe's future at the Yalta Conference. Whatever Gromyko's true attitude toward Gorbachev was—and judging from his nomination speech proposing Gorbachev as general secretary at the 11 March 1985 Central Committee plenum, he seemed to pledge his full support to Gorbachev—the new general secretary could not introduce any new initiatives into Soviet foreign policy without Gromyko's approval.

The old foreign minister was clearly an awe-inspiring colleague, who could no longer be tolerated as the chief implementer of Soviet foreign policy but could not be peremptorily dismissed like Romanov. His election as chairman of the Supreme Soviet Presidium was an ideal face-saving solution for all concerned. Moreover, Gromyko remained in the Politburo as a full (voting) member, so that his vast experience, wise advice, and well-founded views would continue to be available, without hindering Gorbachev's foreign policy initiatives. Incidentally, in his nomination speech Gorbachev devoted only a single paragraph to praise of Gromyko, describing him as "an eminent politician, one of the oldest party members, making a considerable contribution to formulating and implementing our home and foreign policies."[41]

Shevardnadze's appointment as foreign minister was a further surprise. Compared with this predecessor, who had served under Stalin, Khrushchev, Brezhnev, Andropov, Chernenko, and Gorbachev and whose track record and towering presence had inspired awe throughout the world and within the Politburo, Shevardnadze appeared a lightweight parvenu. Shevardnadze had no diplomatic record, having made his career in party and state posts in the Georgian Republic, and he had only occasionally traveled abroad, mainly to meet other party leaders. His foreign visits prior to his appointment included ones to Algeria (1984), Austria (1974), Brazil (1980), Bulgaria (1974), Czechoslovakia (1981), Hungary (1975, 1981), India (1982), Portugal (1979, 1983), and Tunisia (1960).[42]

Virtually no statements by Shevardnadze were on record regarding current international issues. Apart from the routine and mandatory attacks on the U.S. administration and imperialism in general, nothing in his speeches gave clues about his real opinion or future line. Thus he appeared to be the ideal candidate for the post of foreign minister— a figure with no track record in the area, a newcomer who first had to learn the ropes, and a foreign minister who would be little more than a mouthpiece for his master and the implementer of his policy. Since the policy he would carry out would be Gorbachev's, there was no urgent need to make deep-cutting personnel changes in the Ministry of Foreign Affairs.

During his September 1985 trip to Washington and New York, Shevardnadze depended on the advice of Georgiy Korniyenko, Viktor Komplektov, Sergey Tarasenko, and Albert Chernyshov—all members of the "American Mafia" (specialists in U.S. affairs) and all appointed by Gromyko.[43] Furthermore, during the first two months of his tenure as foreign minister, Shevardnadze replaced only three ambassadors,[44] another indication that the sole reason for his appointment was to remove Gromyko from the Ministry of Foreign Affairs. Everything else, such as the appointment of new foreign affairs advisers or ambassadorial changes, was of secondary importance.

Another interesting change introduced by Gorbachev and connected with the situation in the Kremlin during the past three to four years concerned the diminished role of the general secretary's personal aides. The duties of these aides had steadily expanded under Brezhnev, Andropov, and Chernenko, mainly because the failing health of these leaders made them increasingly dependent on assistance. Brezhnev's chief assistants—Andrey Aleksandrov-Agentov (who continued to work as one of Gorbachev's chief aides in foreign affairs), Anatoliy Blatov, Viktor Golikov, and Georgiy Tsukanov—became members of the CPSU Central Committee and enjoyed increasing public exposure. Andropov also employed the services of Aleksandrov-Agentov and added Victor Sharapov, Arkadiy Volskiy, and Pavel Laptev to his personal staff. Aleksandrov and Sharapov invariably took part in Andropov's meetings with foreign dignitaries. Chernenko, on the other hand, did not make many personnel changes. He continued to rely on Andropov's team of advisers, merely adding two more experts, Viktor Pribytkov and Vadim Pechenev. As a result Gorbachev inherited a somewhat overloaded team of advisers.

In the ensuing shakeup, most of Andropov's aides were retained. Two of them, Aleksandrov-Agentov and Viktor Sharapov, even became members of Gorbachev's inner circle of foreign policy advisers. Aleksandrov-Agentov accompanied Gorbachev both to France[45] and to the Geneva summit,[46] and he and Sharapov could be seen hovering near the general secretary during the visits of foreign delegations to Moscow. A. Volskiy was appointed head of the CPSU Central Committee Machine-Building Department.[47]

Chernenko's advisers received somewhat different treatment. Gorbachev wasted little time in dispensing with their services. V. Pribytkov was appointed chief of the Main Administration for Safeguarding State Secrets in the Press on 20 March,[48] and Vadim Pechenev became deputy editor of *Politicheskoye Samoobrazovaniye*.[49] This was only the first stage of their downfall. On 2 September both V. Pribytkov and V. Pechenev lost their respective seats in the USSR Supreme Soviet[50] and the RSFSR Supreme Soviet.[51] (Terminating a person's membership of the Supreme Soviet of the USSR or RSFSR is a rare occurrence and invariably implies disgrace.) Although no official explanation was given for the public disgrace of Chernenko's aides, one may assume that a measure· of vengeance was involved in treating them so differently from the aides of Andropov and even of Brezhnev.

Gorbachev Sweeps Away the Debris

After the July Central Committee plenum and Supreme Soviet session, Gorbachev's focus had shifted from Kremlin infighting to sweeping away the debris. One of the last reverberations that might be interpreted as a sign of opposition to Gorbachev was an article in *Pravda* of 21 June signed by O. Vladimirov, which ostensibly dealt with ideological deviations in Eastern Europe and within the USSR. O. Vladimirov (also G. Aleksandrov) is a pseudonym, a name without an individual's face behind it. No observer or commentator answering to either name has ever made a public appearance on any occasion. It is therefore generally assumed that each pseudonym conceals a high official or even a group of officials who choose not to publicize their real identity. During Brezhnev's period some of the articles signed by G. Aleksandrov were assumed to be written by Suslov himself.

O. Vladimirov's article, though concerned with preserving the purity of political positions in Eastern Europe and denouncing attempts to undermine or reinterpret Marxism-Leninism, attacked certain formulations clearly identified with Gorbachev. Reducing the role of central planning, increasing the role of private agriculture, and developing ideological flexibility—all ideas put forward repeatedly by Gorbachev—were defined as harmful in the article. The author did not name Gorbachev in connection with the "harmful policies," but the implication was clear.

Personnel Changes

Meanwhile, the pace of personnel changes accelerated. One of the main targets continued to be the Council of Ministers, where both separate ministries and the body as a whole had repeatedly been subjects of Gorbachev's criticism. Consequently, ministers and deputy ministers, especially those concerned with economics, were dismissed from their positions with increasing frequency. By the beginning of August 1985 Gorbachev had dismissed seven ministers and one deputy premier, Ivan Bodyul; most were removed under the formula "retired for reasons of health" without any expression of gratitude or recognition of their services.

The only exception was Ivan Sosnov, the minister of transport construction. His retirement was announced on 7 May 1985,[52] and in his case the announcement was ornamented with an expression of gratitude. Interestingly, Gorbachev avoided the practice of appointing former deputy ministers to replace their dismissed chiefs; he preferred to appoint people from outside or from other ministries, strengthening the impression that the changes were assuming the proportions of a full-scale purge of the Council of Ministers. Perhaps this fact prompted *Rude Pravo,* the organ of the Czechoslovakian Communist party, to assure its readers that the changes in economic personnel were not a purge but merely the continuation of the old-established practice of providing youthful reinforcement to the more mature economic leadership.

> A replacement [obmena] of ranking personnel in all components of the national economy, beginning with enterprises and ending with ministries, is currently under way in the Soviet Union. However, one must stress that this is not a "campaign of reshuffling cadres," as some Western commentators rushed to depict the current changes. Citing the names of individual—formerly well-known—economic figures and state and party officials, who are leaving their posts in connection with their retirement, can in no case serve to confirm speculation about "veterans being pushed out by the young." The practice of complementing mature leading personnel with young reinforcements, which has always acquitted itself well, remains unchanged today. However, the new accentuation in the cadre policy of the CPSU, which is developing preparations for its Congress more and more actively, is attracting attention.[53]

Rude Pravo also pointed out that "the CPSU Central Committee is directing party organizations to a position whereby the path up the hierarchical ladder must be open to competent, creative, honorable, and uncompromising people, who are concerned with the general good."[54]

Gorbachev followed the same pattern in replacing regional party secretaries, that is, the appointment of mostly younger officials from outside. Although only one regional secretary was actually fired—A.

Askarov, first secretary of Kazakhstan's Chimkent region, was dismissed for "serious shortcomings in his work"[55]—and eight other first secretaries were retired, by the beginning of August Gorbachev had replaced twenty-one regional secretaries, twelve of them by outsiders.

An interesting appointment was that of Aleksandr Yakovlev, a former ambassador to Canada, to the key post of chief of the CPSU Central Committee Propaganda Department. He succeeded Boris Stukalin, who was appointed ambassador to Hungary, a move interpreted as a form of political disgrace for Stukalin (who had been appointed by Andropov).[56] Gorbachev first met Yakovlev during his visit to Canada in May 1983 and reportedly was impressed by him. Upon his return to Moscow, Yakovlev became head of the Soviet Institute for World Economy and International Relations and one of Gorbachev's closest associates.[57] The appointment was evidently connected with Gorbachev's attempt to tighten his control of the Soviet mass media. Yakovlev was the sixth new appointee among the twenty-three chiefs of the CPSU Central Committee departments,[58] which were evidently another target in Gorbachev's drive to rejuvenate the party and state leadership. Around this time Leonid Zamyatin, head of the CPSU Central Committee International Department, officially confirmed in a meeting with foreign journalists that Gorbachev was also chairman of the USSR Defense Council,[59] a fact never officially published in the USSR.

Throughout August and September the wave of new appointments continued. Dzherment Gvishiani, the fifty-seven-year-old nephew of former premier Kosygin and a noted proponent of decentralization and modernization, was appointed deputy chairman of the USSR main planning organ Gosplan.[60] It was assumed that the Gosplan chairman, Nikolay Baybakov (seventy-four), a firm supporter of strict centralism, would soon vacate his desk. Ministers, deputy ministers, first secretaries of regional party committees, and other officials were retired, dismissed, or transferred to other posts. Sometimes a new appointment was made by a straight transfer to another post, as in the case of Kenes Aukhadiyev, the former first secretary of the Alma Ata obkom, who was "transferred to economic work."[61] On other occasions all niceties were dispensed with: Akhmatilla Rustamov, chairman of the Fergana Oblast Soviet Executive Committee, "was removed for deficiencies in his work and irregularities in the way he used his position."[62]

In the climate of intensive and continued criticism of the performance of many Soviet ministries and of the Council of Ministers itself, Premier Tikhonov was in an extremely awkward position. Furthermore, the close personal relationship of the eighty-year-old premier with Brezhnev and Chernenko made him an obvious target for early removal. By September 1985 the question only remained whether Tikhonov would retire at the 27th CPSU Congress in February 1986 or would depart earlier from the scene. On 27 September, a TASS announcement, read on Soviet television and reprinted by *Pravda* on 28 September, stated that Tikhonov had been "relieved of his duties as chairman of the USSR Council of Ministers, in connection with his retirement on pension in view of his state of health."[63]

Pravda also revealed that Tikhonov had submitted a letter to Gromyko at the 27 September regular meeting of the USSR Supreme Soviet Presidium, in which he explained the reason for his wish to retire. This letter was addressed to Gorbachev, leader of the CPSU, rather than to Soviet President Gromyko, as protocol demanded. The letter was couched in highly personal terms and was thus rather unusual for Soviet political practice:

> Dear Mikhail Sergeyevich: The state of my health has deteriorated considerably of late. The physicians' consilium is urgently raising the question of ending my active work and, consequently, of my retirement on pension.
>
> No matter how difficult it is for me to address this request to you, I am forced to ask you, Mikhail Sergeyevich, and the Central Committee Politburo to retire me on pension for health reasons.
>
> I am infinitely grateful to the beloved Communist Party for everything it has done for me. I would particularly like to mention the warm, comradely atmosphere established within the Politburo recently. If I could only work and work now.
>
> I assure our Leninist party's Central Committee, the Politburo, and you personally, Mikhail Sergeyevich, that, to the extent my strength allows, I will remain ready to perform any tasks that may be assigned to me. Thanks for everything. N. Tikhonov.[64]

Tikhonov's resignation was accepted, and the presidium noted "the major contribution made by Comrade Nikolay Tikhonov to the cause of managing the country's economic and sociocultural development and his great services to the party and the state."[65]

This letter has several interesting aspects. First, the phrase "I am forced to ask you . . . to retire me" might connote that the resignation was not completely voluntary. Second, Tikhonov did not resign from the Politburo, although this move was expected in the very near future. (Tikhonov in fact retired from the Politburo at the 15 October Central Committee Plenum.) Third and most important was the sentence referring to "the warm, comradely atmosphere established within the Politburo recently." Was Tikhonov signaling the end of the infighting or the fact that the remaining members of the former Brezhnev-Chernenko faction had reconciled themselves to Gorbachev's undisputed leadership? Or perhaps he was simply noting a fact, which implied that the atmosphere within the supreme party council chamber had been less than warm and comradely in the past. In any event, Tikhonov's letter, like so many other phenomena connected with Gorbachev's tenure, was an extraordinary document, which showed a new style and spirit, a break with old customs and practices.

Tikhonov's resignation, whether voluntary or not, was an important political act. A leading member of Brezhnev's Dnepropetrovsk clan and a staunch supporter of Chernenko, Tikhonov never went on record as a supporter of Gorbachev's economic reforms. Moreover, the fact that the Council of Ministers (headed by him during the last five years) had been the subject of continual harsh criticism from Gorbachev and the rumors concerning his imminent dismissal added pure political overtones to the medical reasons ostensibly prompting his resignation. Although absent from public view during the second part of August and the beginning of September (the normal period for many Soviet leaders to take their summer vacations), Tikhonov continued fulfilling his regular functions, attending for example the 25 September luncheon for Hungary's Janos Kadar.[66]

Predictably enough, one of Gorbachev's closest allies, Nikolay Ryzhkov, replaced Tikhonov as chairman of the USSR Council of Ministers.[67] Born in 1929 and a party member since 1956, Ryzhkov was a graduate of the S. M. Kirov Urals Polytechnical Institute. According to *Pravda* of 28 September, which published Ryzhkov's official biographical details, Ryzhkov began his career as a shift foreman in the S. Ordzhonikidze Heavy-Machine-Building Plant in the Urals (1950), where over fifteen years he had progressed through the posts of section chief, shop chief, chief welder, and deputy director and finally in 1965 was appointed chief engineer. In 1970 he was appointed director of the plant and later became general director of the Uralmash Production Association. In 1975 he was appointed deputy minister of heavy and transport machine building and in 1979 first deputy chief of Gosplan. At the November 1982 Central Committee plenum Ryzhkov was elected a Central Committee secretary, simultaneously carrying out the duties of head of the Central Committee economic section. The April 1985 Central Committee plenum elevated him to full membership of the Politburo.

Ryzhkov had evidently been groomed for some time to replace Tikhonov. Even though his main field of responsibility had always been the economy (as the senior Central Committee secretary in charge of economic affairs), prior to his appointment as premier he took part in such events as the August 1985 visit of Grisha Filipov, then Bulgaria's premier, which did not necessarily call for his participation. (Ryzhkov greeted Filipov at the airport,[68] together with Tikhonov took part in the official talks,[69] and saw off Filipov at the airport.[70])

Ryzhkov's identification with Gorbachev's economic policy was total and unquestionable. On 28 June 1985 he was the main speaker at the graduation ceremony of the USSR Council of Ministers Academy of the National Economy. In his speech, he emphasized the importance of "the new economic trends of management," the need to "improve the investment policy and structural policy," as well as the "need to shift the center of gravity toward modernization." Later in his speech, Ryzhkov dwelt on the importance of using "organizational and economic levers and incentives" and stressed:

> Increasing the role of production and science-and-production associations and extending their rights, economic autonomy, and responsibility naturally means a substantial restructuring of the work of ministries, the simplification of the sectors' management structure, and the elimination of excessive overlaps. . . .
>
> It was stated at the CPSU Central Committee conference that we will continue to strengthen democratic centralism, combined organically with the expansion of enterprises' economic autonomy and with the economic methods of management. The party says this quite clearly.
>
> It is important that we continue to increase the effectiveness of planned management and make full use of financial autonomy, developing the masses' initiative in every way.[71]

These ideas were a virtual paraphrase of Gorbachev's speech at the 11 June Central Committee conference on accelerating scientific and technological progress.[72] No doubt Ryzhkov's election was aimed at facilitating and accelerating the application of Gorbachev's economic reforms, and as such it contributed enormously to the further consolidation of the general secretary.

Foreign Affairs

At the same time, Andrey Gromyko was reduced to a largely ceremonial figure as chairman of the Supreme Soviet Presidium, although retaining his Politburo membership. His future activities were limited to the performance of routine ceremonies, such as the presentation of awards (to Soviet pilots, navigators, and parachutists on 13 September[73] and to outstanding workers on 20 September[74] or the receiving of foreign parliamentary delegations (such as those from Luxembourg on 23 September[75] and Japan on 24 September[76]). Although he took part in the 16 September meeting that considered the opening round of the Soviet-U.S. Geneva talks on nuclear and space arms, together with Gorbachev, Chebrikov, Shevardnadze, Marshal Sokolov, and the leaders of the Soviet delegation to the talks, Karpov, Kvitsinskiy, and Obukov,[77] there was no other visible evidence of his involvement in foreign affairs.

Gorbachev played a much more prominent part in foreign affairs than either Foreign Minister Eduard Shevardnadze or President Gromyko. An interview with *Time* magazine on 28 August (composed of written questions and a face-to-face meeting with *Time* reporters) and published in both *Time* and *Pravda* on 2 September provided Gorbachev with valuable international exposure. Although criticizing the U.S. administration along the familiar lines followed by the Soviet propaganda machine, Gorbachev pointed out that the Soviet Union "has not lost hope." "Points of contact" and "areas of common or parallel interests" could serve as a basis for future agreements, Gorbachev stated. He reaffirmed his desire that the Geneva summit should yield positive results and restated the "serious hope" he attached to the conference. As expected, Gorbachev underlined the great significance of disarmament and attacked the U.S. Strategic Defense Initiative (Star Wars), demanding the renunciation of this program.

During this interview, Gorbachev was flanked by three aides: Georgiy Arbatov, the chief Soviet specialist on U.S. affairs (and the person rumored to have played the role of President Reagan in the simulation games conducted in the Kremlin as part of Gorbachev's preparations for the Geneva summit meeting); Andrey Aleksandrov-Agentov, already serving as the fourth-ranking general secretary in foreign policy matters; and Leonid Zamyatin, head of the Central Committee International Information Department.

Although the versions of the interview in *Time* and *Pravda* were somewhat different—*Pravda* omitted Gorbachev's references to God and Khrushchev, as well as the joke about the RSFSR finance minister who regularly dozed during meetings of the Council of Ministers— they both clearly reflected Gorbachev's highly personal style. Gorbachev's interview differed from similar routine interviews granted by Chernenko to the *Washington Post* and by Andropov to *Der Spiegel* both in its great length (over two hours of face-to-face question and answer) and in the general secretary's unusual and disarming frankness accompanied by jocular remarks. Against the background of Gorbachev's December 1984 visit to the United Kingdom, his extraordinarily frank speeches, and his ostensibly spontaneous meetings with citizens, the *Time* interview showed a Soviet leader with a distinctly personal and direct style, who was not afraid to face Western journalists and answer questions on issues considered tabu by the Soviet mass media.

Exactly the same style and image were projected by Gorbachev at his 3 September meeting with a group of U.S. senators led by Senate Democratic leader Robert Byrd[78] and during his subsequent visit to France. In the course of his address to members of the French National Assembly,[79] Gorbachev confirmed the rumor that the USSR had proposed a 50 percent reduction of Soviet and U.S. strategic weapons, linked with a proposed agreement banning "space strike arms." He enumerated the various Soviet disarmament proposals and initiatives and for the first time suggested that the INF (intermediate-range nuclear missiles) issue could be successfully resolved without a parallel agreement on space weapons. He also stated that the Soviet Union was ready to hold separate disarmament talks with Great Britain and France and repeatedly stressed the need for cooperation between the USSR and Western Europe in various areas—"we all must become aware of the continent's common destiny."[80]

Gorbachev made an obvious effort to project the image of a realistic, moderate, and approachable leader, which was already an integral part of his personal style:

I know that by far not everybody in this hall accepts our world outlook, our ideology. Being a realist, I am not trying to convert anyone to our creed. Any philosophy is approached by individuals and peoples themselves, only achieving it through much suffering, only by accepting it with their minds and hearts. But despite all differences in political and philosophical views, in ideals and values, we must remember one thing: we are all keepers of the fire of life handed on to us by the previous generations.

Each has its own mission and each in its own way enriched world civilization. The giants of the Renaissance and the great French Revolution, the heroes of the October Revolution in Russia, of victory and resistance— they have all fulfilled their duty to history.

And what about our generation? It has made great discoveries, but it has also found recipes for the self-destruction of the human race. On the threshold of the third millennium we must burn the black book of nuclear "alchemy." May the 21st century become the first century in life without fear of universal death.

We will fulfill this mission if we unite our efforts. The Soviet Union is prepared to make its contribution to ensuring a peaceful, free, and flourishing future for Europe and all other continents. We shall stint nothing for this.[81]

The Western media and the French leaders were impressed. *Le Monde* called Gorbachev's visit Operation Seduction,[82] and François Mitterrand, "a charm offensive."[83] Furthermore, Gorbachev once more demonstrated his skill in goodhumoredly sidestepping tough and awkward questions on human rights in the USSR and on the numbers of political prisoners by dismissing them as "Goebbels-like propaganda."[84] Surprisingly, Soviet television carried an uncensored videorecording of the interview, probably to demonstrate to the Soviet public Gorbachev's deft handling of the Western reporters. Gorbachev showed that he was familiar with French history and culture, quoting Charles de Gaulle, Victor Hugo, and Antoine Saint-Exupéry. Last, as during the United Kingdom visit in December 1984, Gorbachev's wife, Raisa, drew as much attention as her husband, and *Time* dubbed her "Gorbachev's 'secret weapon.' "

Party Apparatus

Upon his return to Moscow, Gorbachev resumed his remodeling of the Soviet leadership. On 14 October Nikolay Baybakov, the seventy-four-year-old chairman of the USSR State Planning Committee, was replaced by Nikolay Talyzin.[85] Once again the formula was retirement on pension, with no expression of gratitude for his past long service.[86] This step was long expected. Baybakov, who had been appointed by Brezhnev in 1965,[87] was clearly an obstacle to Gorbachev in fulfilling his commitment to reform state planning. Indeed, Baybakov's days as chief of Gosplan had been shown to be numbered several weeks earlier when economic reformist Dzherment Gvishiani was appointed Gosplan deputy chairman. A strong opponent of decentralization in planning and of the introduction of modern practices (based on computer technology and mathematical models), Baybakov had frequently resorted to dry Marxist sophistry to defend his ultraconservative views on planning policy.

Gorbachev repeatedly criticized the Soviet planning apparatus; these attacks reaching a climax in his televised 6 September speech in Tyumen. Gorbachev made many critical remarks about the work of Gosplan, while Baybakov, sitting on the platform near him, squirmed with discomfort: "Above all, we have to ask what kind of an economic mechanism we have, Nikolay Konstantinovich, that makes it possible for both leaders and labor collectives to carry on unperturbed while resources are being used in such a way?"[88]

Baybakov's successor, fifty-six-year-old Nikolay Talyzin, was a graduate of the Moscow Electrical Engineering Institute of Communications (1955), a Doctor of Technical Sciences (1970), and a professor (1975).[89] He had served as USSR deputy minister of communications (1965–1971), first deputy minister of communications (1971–1975), minister of communications (1975–1980), deputy chairman of the USSR Council of Ministers (from 1980), and the USSR's permanent representative in COMECON (from 1980).[90] Talyzin was a deputy premier for economic affairs and therefore a member of the Soviet economic establishment. His record showed no reformist tendencies, and no statement by him on such matters is on record. His appointment suggested that Gorbachev, though eager to implement his economic reforms, did not wish to overly antagonize the economic establishment by bringing in someone from outside its circle to head the chief Soviet planning organ.

The appointment of Gvishiani as Gosplan deputy chief indicated Gorbachev's long-range strategy. Gvishiani was an outspoken proponent of reforms in planning and administration, and he had demanded reductions in the numbers of centrally planned projects, cutting across branch and territorial lines in planning and increasingly relying on long-term planning assisted by the territorial planning bodies. The establishment of the Gvishiani-Talyzin combination, not merely the appointment of Talyzin, appeared to be the important personnel change effected in the central Soviet planning apparatus. This impression is strengthened by reports that Gvishiani had brought with him several close associates, who assumed various posts within the Gosplan organization.

On 15 October a plenum of the CPSU Central Committee was held. Apparently, Gorbachev did not want to wait four more months for the 27th CPSU Congress, and accordingly the plenum decided that former President Tikhonov was "relieved of his duties as Politburo member in connection with his retirement on pension on health grounds."[91] Premier Ryzhkov was also relieved of his duties as Central Committee secretary, as a result of his appointment as chairman of the Council of Ministers (a normal procedure), and the new Gosplan chief Nikolay

Talyzin was elected a candidate member of the Politburo,[92] thus giving Gosplan an unprecedented high status within the party leadership.

The two new vacancies (Tikhonov's seat in the Politburo and Ryzhkov's place in the Secretariat) were not filled by the same Central Committee plenum, creating an interesting gap that needed to be filled in the near future. Yegor Ligachev, who was in charge of ideological matters, was now the sole Central Committee secretary, apart from Gorbachev, who was also a Politburo member. Vladimir Dolgikh, who was not a member of Gorbachev's inner circle, remained the senior Central Committee secretary for economic affairs (although only a candidate member of the Politburo), whereas the other Central Committee secretaries with economic responsibilities (Kapitonov, Nikonov, Yeltsin, and Zaykov) had no Politburo status.

Drafts of Party Documents

The 15 October plenum of the Central Committee concentrated on adopting the drafts of three fundamental party documents, which were to be publicly discussed before the 27th CPSU Congress, where they would be adopted in their final form. These were a new version of the CPSU program, revisions to the CPSU statutes, and guidelines for the 12th 5-Year Plan and for the fifteen-year period until the year 2000.[93]

The CPSU program, adopted under Khrushchev, was long overdue for modification. In it Khrushchev had boasted of overtaking the West in the economic field and of completing the establishment of communism in the USSR—claims that, according to Gorbachev's speech at the plenum, were "groundless fantasy and bookish pedantry," which "have not stood the test of time."[94] (Although Gorbachev did not specify any person, it was clear whom he had in mind in speaking of "groundless fantasy.") On the subject of the CPSU statutes, he said that the draft amendments were aimed at "expanding democracy within the party" and enhancing the party organizations' "responsibility for resolving common concerns."[95] Although he did not elaborate, Gorbachev seems to have intended to use the amended party statutes as an instrument for introducing more initiative and democracy in internal party life to vitalize the activity of the local party organizations. In short, he was stressing democracy in the sense of the basic Leninist principle of democratic centralism.

Finally, the guidelines for the 12th 5-Year Plan and the period to the year 2000 were envisaged as a component part of Gorbachev's efforts to transform fundamentally the Soviet economy by increasing labor productivity and "almost doubling" Soviet economic output over the next fifteen years.[96]

The 17 October editorial in *Izvestiya*, while stressing (as Gorbachev did in his plenum speech) the principle of continuity embodied in the new draft documents, pointed out:

These are documents of tremendous historical importance. They concern the Soviet Communists' program aims, focal questions of the party's general line and economic strategy, and forms and methods of work among the masses at the present, at an exceptionally complex and crucial period of history, which in many respects—from both domestic and international viewpoints—is in the nature of a turning point.[97]

Only four days after the Central Committee plenum two more ministers—Nikolay Patolichev, minister of foreign trade,[98] and Viktor Fedorov, minister of the petroleum-refining and petrochemical industry[99]—"retired for health reasons." Patolichev (seventy-seven years) and Fedorov (seventy-three) were succeeded by sixty-year-old Boris Aristov (formerly ambassador to Poland during the Solidarity period) and fifty-six-year-old Nikolay Lemayev.[100]

Gorbachev's Overall Position

Although at the end of October, four months before the convening of the momentous 27th CPSU Congress, the Kremlin infighting was almost completely over, and Gorbachev was engaging in the initial skirmishes on another, crucially important front—the transformation of the entire Soviet economic system by bold reforms designed to increase productivity and improve product quality. Every Soviet leader since Stalin had failed miserably in this battle, mainly because of the extremely stubborn (and effective) resistance of the whole economic establishment, from the Council of Ministers to the regional party organizations. As a result, the USSR, one of the two military superpowers, had a third-rate production economy that sooner or later was bound to affect its military capability.

Gorbachev appeared to be pursuing a two-fold strategy on this second front. By effecting a quick succession of key economic appointments, he intended to remove the strongest (and oldest) opponents of economic reform, thus rejuvenating the Council of Ministers and the economic establishment and influencing what he often referred to as "the human factor." Most of Gorbachev's new appointments were in the economic field; he removed the main opponents of his reforms to facilitate their introduction. This tactic would ensure the achievement of the more strategic goal: winning the crucial battle at the 27th CPSU Congress, which would adopt the guidelines for national economic development until the end of the century.

En route to the congress Gorbachev had to cross a number of potentially dangerous minefields. First, despite the numerous new economic appointments, his reforms still encountered significant resistance. As late as the close of 1985 Ryzhkov's former position as Central Committee secretary for economic affairs (with full membership in the Politburo) had still not been filled. Perhaps Gorbachev was waiting for the dust to settle, or perhaps no agreement could be reached on the person to control the Soviet economy and supervise the implementation of Gorbachev's reforms. Second, a big question mark hung over the stance of the military establishment. Its influence seemed to have fallen to a historically low point, and its support of Gorbachev's relatively moderate foreign policy was at the best lukewarm. At the end of October the Army was awaiting with apprehension the results of the forthcoming Geneva summit to define its position toward Gorbachev. The KGB, on the other hand, with its chief Chebrikov and two former high officials (Aliyev and Shevardnadze) as full Politburo members, appeared to be firmly behind Gorbachev.

Finally, there was the human factor, namely, Gorbachev's closest allies in the Politburo. Political loyalties are notoriously inconstant in the totalitarian society of the USSR. Furthermore, in such a small and closed body as the Soviet Politburo, where an alliance of seven or eight persons can be crucial and indeed fatal for the leader, unexpected moves and extreme surprises are possible at any moment. At the end of November Gorbachev enjoyed the loyalty of the Politburo members whom he had appointed. However, as the record shows, after becoming members of the Politburo (especially if they are also Central Committee secretaries) such allies often developed independent ambitions, sometimes diametrically opposed to their former loyalties. Khrushchev discovered this the hard way. Brezhnev, naturally, was aware of this, and he kept an iron grip on the Politburo members, immediately removing any potential rivals. Gorbachev initially removed his obvious opponents with no great difficulty. It remained to be seen what the attitudes (and destinies) of his friends and allies would be.

9

Closing the Circle—
The Congress

At the beginning of November, when the world's attention was focused on the summit meeting between Ronald Reagan and Gorbachev, internal developments in the USSR showed that Gorbachev was unrelentingly following the patterns established during the previous months of his tenure. The almost daily new appointments, many of which were at the ministerial level, and the rejuvenation of the top levels of the party and state apparatus continued to confirm his new policies, along with the nationwide discussion of the draft CPSU program and statutes and the preparations for the 27th CPSU Congress.

Gorbachev Continues Party Overhaul

On 1 November the Supreme Soviet Presidium announced the appointment of Vsevolod Murakhovskiy as first deputy chairman of the Council of Ministers, releasing seventy-year-old Ziya Nuriyev from this post "in connection with his retirement on pension."[1] On the following day Ivan Silayev was relieved of his post as minister of the aviation industry (replaced by Apollon Systev) and appointed deputy chairman of the USSR Council of Ministers.[2] One day later Deputy Premier Aleksey Antonov was appointed the permanent Soviet representative to COMECON, replacing Nikolay Talyzin.[3] On 14 October, Talyzin had been named Gosplan chairman, replacing Nikolay Baybakov.[4]

On 2 November a plenum of the Kirghiz Communist Party Central Committee was held. It relieved Turdakun Usubaliyev of his duties as first secretary of the republic's Central Committee "in connection with his retirement on pension" and elected the former first secretary of the Issyk-Kul obkom, Absamat Masaliyev, as the new first secretary of the republican Central Committee.[5] These are merely a few examples of the appointments made during the first part of November 1985.

The appointment of Murakhovskiy was an interesting and characteristic example of Gorbachev's personnel changes. Murakhovskiy had held the posts of first secretary of the Stavropol City Party Committee from 1970 to 1974, secretary of the Stavropol kraykom between 1974 and 1978, and first secretary of the Stavropol kraykom since 1978.[6] He had served as a secretary during the period when Gorbachev was first secretary of the Stavropol kraykom, replacing him in that post when Gorbachev was moved to Moscow to become a candidate member of the Politburo in 1978.

More important than Murakhovskiy's personal connection with Gorbachev was the assumption that this appointment signaled the start of the reorganization of the agricultural administration proposed by Gorbachev, notably in his speech in Tselinograd on 7 September. Since the retired deputy premier Nuriyev had supervised the country's agricultural ministries, agriculture was expected to also be Murakhovskiy's main area of activity. He revealed his ideas on managing the country's agriculture in a June 1985 article in *Partiynaya Zhizn.*[7] Relying on his experience in Stavropol, he pointed out that the staff of the kray agricultural administration apparatus could be reduced by "no less than one third" and that "the number of various kinds of conferences and meetings could be reduced to a minimum."[8] He recommended cuts in the number of "central governmental departments," as well as in the number of reports and quantity of information produced. Finally, he advised that detailed day-to-day supervision should be cut back and that performance evaluation should be based on the end results—an approach that "would facilitate the formation of economic thought and developing the creative initiative of the leaders."[9] Because Murakhovskiy's opinions were very close to Gorbachev's own views, the appointment of the former to the post of top agricultural administrator undoubtedly was intended to further the implementation of Gorbachev's agricultural reforms.

The routine ceremonies marking the October Revolution anniversary offered no indication of any important new developments. KGB chief Chebrikov was the main speaker at the 6 November festive meeting in the Kremlin Palace of Congresses;[10] Marshal Sokolov reviewed the 7 November parade in Red Square and delivered the main speech;[11] and Gorbachev himself spoke at the subsequent reception in the Kremlin.[12] The official leadership lineup at the 7 November parade showed that President Gromyko had moved into the number two position. Since 1977 the general secretary of the CPSU Central Committee had also held the post of chairman of the Supreme Soviet Presidium (president), and accordingly the status of a president who was not at the same time the general secretary was unclear. Gorbachev now appeared to have returned to the practice followed during Nikolay Podgorniy's tenure as Soviet president—of reserving the second place in the official lineup for the Soviet president—which did not imply that Gromyko enjoyed any greater political power than Premier Ryzhkov, who was placed third. Ligachev was in the fourth position, thus completing the new troyka of Gorbachev, Ryzhkov, and Ligachev.

Meanwhile the rejuvenation of the USSR Council of Ministers continued at an unrelenting pace. (Occasionally, the process was furthered by nature itself, as when seventy-five-year-old finance minister Vasiliy Garbuzov died on 12 November.[13]) On 15 November Lev Voronin became deputy premier and chairman of the USSR State Committee for Material and Technical Supply, replacing seventy-five-year-old Nikolay Martynov "in connection with his retirement on pension because of poor health."[14] On the next day sixty-nine-year-old Deputy Premier Leonid Smirnov "retired on pension," making way for forty-eight-year-old Yuriy Maslyukov, a former deputy chief of the USSR State Planning Committee.[15]

Thus, within a scant six weeks after the replacement of eighty-year-old Tikhonov as premier by sixty-five-year-old Ryzhkov, five younger men had been appointed deputy and first deputy premiers: Talyzin (fifty-six years), Murakhovskiy (fifty-nine), Silayev (fifty-five), Voronin (fifty-seven), and Maslyukov (forty-eight). The trend was unmistakable. It is also worth noting that the two new deputy premiers Voronin and Maslyukov had previously worked together in Gosplan (both as deputy chairmen) and as deputy ministers of the defense industry. Furthermore, the careers of both officials, especially Voronin's, were associated with Ryzhkov, who in 1979 was appointed the Gosplan first deputy chairman for heavy industry.[16] Their appointments, as indeed virtually all appointments made after July 1985 (with the exception of Tikhonov's retirement) had little connection with the power struggle in the Kremlin.

Well aware of the tremendous difficulties involved in introducing his reforms, Gorbachev was preparing the ground for major battle by quickly and efficiently replacing most of the top economic leaders with younger officials. He was relying on persons with defense industry backgrounds (such as Voronin, Maslyukov, and Sergey Afanasyev, the new machine-building minister) to improve the country's economic management and facilitate the introduction of his economic reforms. The belief that defense industry managers were better qualified than civilian industrialists was reflected in an article by Academician Vadim Trapeznikov entitled, "Once More About Quality, Technical Progress, and Incentives," in *Pravda,* 2 October 1985. Repeatedly stressing the advantages of the defense industry, Trapeznikov stated: "The technology and output quality of our defense industry are far higher than in civilian fields. It is essential to make extensive use of the experience of the defense industry workers, particularly in the sphere of quality control and the exertion of powerful influence on quality by the consumer."[17]

De-Brezhnevization

Although the mass retirement of older officials appointed by Brezhnev, or even by Khrushchev, could not be described as a purge—mainly because the bloody and violent connotations that that concept acquired under Stalin's rule did not apply to Gorbachev's campaign—by mid-November the process bore the overt character of a de-Brezhnevization campaign. Although Brezhnev was not attacked personally (until *Pravda* did so on 19 December in an article noting his eightieth birthday), many of the phenomena associated with his rule consistently came under fire. There could be no difficulty in correctly interpreting Chebrikov's words at the 6 November festive meeting in the Kremlin to mark the sixty-eighth anniversary of the October Revolution:

> Soviet society is now going through a period that is exceptionally rich in content and is crucial. We have all felt that over a certain period of time, although progressive movement did continue, problems accumulated in the country, and delays in their solution resulted in economic and social difficulties. The growth in labor productivity and the overall rate in development of production have dragged. Negative phenomena, such as narrow departmental interests, playing safe, and falsification of reports have made themselves felt at various levels of management. A certain sector of cadres has lost the taste for the timely implementation of reforms and innovations dictated by life. They have started to manifest a fear of brave solutions, bureaucratism, and conservatism. Let us say straight out: This has had an unfavorable effect on the situation.[18]

Other developments indicated the anti-Brezhnev emphasis of Gorbachev's campaign. During November Moscow's Komsomol Theater staged a new play, *Noah and His Song,* that featured a president with dragging feet, trembling hands, and a strong Ukrainian accent—a cruel, but rather accurate parody of Brezhnev in the winter of his life. Needless to say, the senile president was not the positive hero of the very successful play.

Furthermore, on 10 November 1985 *Pravda* carried an article by V. Kozhemyako, "Reflection on Letters: Against Flattery and Fawning." The article quoted letters from party members criticizing cases of flattery and toadyism, pointing out the consequent "impossibility of developing healthy criticism and self-criticism" and naming a number of local officials in this context. Since the article was published on the third anniversary of Brezhnev's death, the proper conclusions were evidently drawn by all.

Thus the third anniversary of Brezhnev's death was marked by a total silence about the man himself, yet with widespread criticism of phenomena associated with his rule and the mass retirement of his associates and appointees. By mid-November, only Grishin, Kunayev, Shcherbitskiy and Gromyko of the old Politburo membership remained, apart from Gorbachev himself. Death, old age, and political manipulation had taken care of the rest.

Restructuring of Agro-industrial Complex

Toward mid-November it also became evident that the appointment of Vsevolod Murakhovskiy to the post of deputy premier in charge of agriculture was merely an initial stage in the restructuring of the Soviet agro-industrial complex. On 14 November TASS reported that during its regular weekly meeting the Politburo "considered proposals for further improving the management of the country's agro-industrial sector. In order to ensure a faster growth of agricultural production and to meet the population's requirements for food, it is provided to proceed to planning, financing, and managing the agro-industrial sector as a single entity at all levels."[19]

The meaning of this decision was explained a week later in a further TASS announcement: A State Agro-Industrial Committee was established "with a view to improving the management of the agro-industrial complex."[20] Murakhovskiy was appointed the chairman of the new body, which was charged with directly administering all agricultural production and processing, replacing and assuming the responsibilities of no fewer than five ministries—those of agriculture, fruit and vegetable growing, rural construction, and the meat and dairy industry—as well as the State Committee for Production and Technical Servicing of Agriculture.[21]

The formation of the new organ and the appointment of Gorbachev's protégé from Stavropol—Murakhovskiy—as its chairman were major steps toward weakening the entrenched ministerial bureaucracy and centralist administrative power at the top. Indeed, Gorbachev had repeatedly stated that he intended to reform the agricultural administration and eliminate the ministries that presented major obstacles to efficiency and change. The reorganization provided Gorbachev with the opportunity not only to appoint his own person (and thus maintain personal control) but also to remold the entire Soviet agricultural administration from top to bottom according to his liking.

Geneva Summit

The second half of November was dominated by the Geneva summit meeting between President Reagan and General Secretary Gorbachev, the central political event of 1985. Although important in its own right, the summit had little direct effect on the political struggle (or rather its dying skirmishes) in the Kremlin or certainly no immediate effect. Nevertheless, a number of interesting aspects related to the summit and its results should be mentioned.

D. Kunayev and V. Shcherbitskiy were not present at the airport to see off the Soviet delegation.[22] Since the two "provincial" members of the Politburo seldom attend such events in Moscow, their absence did not necessarily have any political connotations. The third Brezhnevist— Viktor Grishin—was reported to have been present at the airport.[23] The composition of the delegation itself revealed Gorbachev's concern with world public opinion. Many of its members were propaganda experts of long standing. The chief official members, in addition to Gorbachev himself, were Foreign Minister Shevardnadze; G. M. Korniyenko, first deputy minister of foreign affairs; A. Dobrynin, then the Soviet ambassador to the United States; A. N. Yakovlev, head of the CPSU Central Committee Propaganda Department; L. M. Zamyatin, head of the CPSU Central Committee International Information Department; and A. M. Aleksandrov, one of Gorbachev's chief foreign policy assistants.[24] Scores of other advisers and assistants, notably Vladimir Lomeyko, the spokesperson for the Ministry of Foreign Affairs, were also in Geneva.[25]

On the eve of the summit, Western observers evaluated its prospects as "dim."[26] Yet when the summit ended with rather insignificant overt results (its main achievement was establishing a "chemistry" between the two leaders and a favorable atmosphere in the two superpowers' relations), the Soviet spokespersons without exception depicted the summit as a huge, initial success. (On this point, they were in agreement with their Western colleagues.) For example, in a BBC interview the main Soviet expert on U.S. affairs, Academician Georgiy Arbatov expressed a qualified satisfaction with the summit's results.[27] Other Soviet commentators were more enthusiastic. Novosti commentator Valentin Zorin made this statement for Moscow television:

> The meeting . . . has been held, and the leaders had the opportunity to exchange views and to state their points of view frankly and in a business-like fashion. That is important in and of itself. Both leaders have achieved a better understanding of the positions of the other. They have agreed on the need to improve the international situation as a whole. . . . A start has been made on a large and important matter.[28]

Another Soviet commentator, Farid Seyful-Mulyukov, accused Western journalists of "becoming gloomy" about the summit's prospects and described the results as "evoking good hopes," regarding pessimism as "inappropriate." "Nothing gives grounds for being in a sombre mood,"[29] Seyful-Mulyukov concluded.

The same optimistic mood prevailed at the subsequent meeting on 21 November in Prague of the Warsaw Pact member states' leaders, which was an unusual event and another innovation introduced by Brezhnev. At the meeting Gorbachev reported on the results of the summit. (On similar previous occasions such reports had been made indirectly and certainly not immediately after the event). The forum explicitly noted Gorbachev's contribution to the summit's success. The official communiqué stated:

> The leaders of the fraternal parties and countries voiced full support for the constructive stand presented by Mikhail Gorbachev at his talks with U.S. President Reagan, in the spirit of the joint line put foward in a statement of the Warsaw Treaty member countries on 23 October 1983.
> The top leaders of the Warsaw Treaty member countries spoke highly of the exceptionally important contribution made by the general secretary

of the CPSU Central Committee at the Geneva meeting to the advancement of the jointly developed peace positions of the countries of the socialist community. It was unanimously noted that the direct and frank discussion which had taken place at the meeting had been needed and that its results were useful.[30]

The central concept, which appeared in all Soviet commentaries, articles, and assessments, was "results." This concept seems to be the key to understanding the truly unexpected change of tone and mood on the Soviet side. After nine months of extensive personnel changes and continued hammering of the theme of the changes and reforms in every area, Gorbachev had maneuvered himself into an awkward position from which he urgently needed to produce some positive results. Since it was too early to expect such results in the economic sphere (where the main battle was still to be fought), the Geneva summit offered a golden opportunity for producing positive results in international relations and of giving Gorbachev the credit for achieving them or at least promoting their achievement.

The CPSU Central Committee Politburo, by now completely dominated by Gorbachev's people, shared the enthusiasm of the Warsaw Pact leaders:

> The results of the talks in Geneva can have a positive effect on changing the political and psychological climate in present-day international relations and their improvement, and lessen the risk of outbreak of nuclear war. The meeting has marked the beginning of a dialogue with a view to achieve changes for the better in Soviet-American relations and in the whole world. . . .
>
> The Political Bureau of the CPSU Central Committee fully approved the work done by Mikhail Gorbachev. . . .
>
> The Political Bureau of the CPSU Central Committee noted with satisfaction that the top leaders of the Warsaw Pact member-states at their meeting in Prague on November 21, assessed M. S. Gorbachev's work in Geneva as an exclusively important contribution to advancing the joint peaceful positions of the countries of the socialist community, of the foreign policy programme adopted at the Sofia, October 1985 meeting of the Political Consultative Committee.[31]

At the 26–27 November session of the USSR Supeme Soviet, which dealt primarily with the 1986 plan and budget, Gorbachev assessed the summit's results in very positive terms. Although he modestly stated that "at the meeting we did not succeed in finding solutions for the very important questions connected with ending the arms race," Gorbachev rated the meeting as "undoubtedly a significant event" and gave a high evaluation to the "personal contact with the U.S. President." The dialogue was described by Gorbachev as a "stabilizing" factor, and he also stressed positive assessment of the Warsaw Pact leaders.[32]

The Supreme Soviet adopted a resolution which "fully approved the activity of M. S. Gorbachev, secretary general of the CPSU Central Committee and member of the USSR Supreme Soviet Presidium, in implementing the Leninist peaceloving foreign policy of the Soviet Union at the meeting with President Ronald Reagan of the United States, held in Geneva on 19–21 November 1985."[33]

Despite general satisfaction with the results, some dissident voices were heard, most notably that of chief of the General Staff Marshal Sergey Akhromeyev, who stated at the session:

> However, the talks [in Geneva] showed that the United States is not prepared to resolve this task [the danger of nuclear war], the main task of today. The United States is not prepared—this has been confirmed by speeches by the U.S. leadership even since the Geneva talks—to give up its "Star Wars" plans. The commitment adopted by the United States at the Geneva meeting not to seek military superiority over the Soviet Union is as yet only words. The so-called counterproposals put forward by the U.S. side at the talks are basically designed to undermine the strategic equilibrium in favor of the United States, and lead not to a lowering, but to a raising of the level of military confrontation. . . . These problems are far from solution. That is why we must not rest on our laurels, but must continue to struggle against the threat of war in all avenues.[34]

The opinion offered by the party leader of the Ukraine, Vladimir Shcherbitskiy (one of the few remaining Brezhnev appointees in the Politburo) also differed from the generally expressed enthusiasm with the summit's results. After admitting half-heartedly that the results of the summit had shown "in principle" that it was possible to normalize relations between the USSR and the United States, he warned that "the U.S. Administration will continue to make efforts to achieve military-strategic superiority over us and will try to deal with us, proceeding not from the principle of equality but from a position of strength."[35] The fact that Marshal Akhromeyev and Shcherbitskiy expressed dissenting opinions meant that Gorbachev could expect somewhat less than total support from the Soviet military establishment and from a few Politburo members.

Anticorruption Campaign

Apparently unperturbed, Gorbachev forged ahead with his anticorruption campaign, which by December had been extended throughout the country. The Soviet press continued to publish almost daily reports on corrupt officials, sometimes even at the ministerial level, who had been ousted, reprimanded, or otherwise punished. For example, Talgat Khuramshin, chairman of the USSR State Committee for the Supply of Petroleum Products, was released from his post "for abusing his official position for personal gains."[36] The older officials continued to be retired; in December Boris Bratchenko, minister of the coal industry, "retired for health reasons" and was replaced by the fifty-eight-year-old Mikhail Shchadov.[37] Even the venerable Marshal Sergey Gorshkov (seventy-five years), chief of the Navy since 1956, was sacked without a word of thanks for his long service and was succeeded by the fifty-seven-year-old Admiral Vladimir Chernavin.[38] On 21 December another deputy chairman of the USSR Council of Ministers, Veniamin Dymshits (seventy-five years, the highest-ranking Soviet official of Jewish origin and a deputy premier since 1962), went into retirement.[39] His successor was Yuriy Batalin, fifty-eight years, a graduate of the Urals Kirov Polytechnical Institute and former chairman of the State Committee for Labor and Social Problems, a post to which he had been appointed in 1983 during Andropov's tenure.[40]

In addition, the accountability-election campaign preceding the 27th CPSU Congress was picking up speed. Although it was to reach its peak in January and February, in December cases were already appearing of officials accused of various transgressions and even crimes during the accountability-election conferences of their particular party organizations. For example, A. Koychumanov, first secretary of the Alma-Ata City CPSU Committee and a protégé of Kazakhstan's party chief D. Kunayev, was replaced for "falsification of his official biography, immodesty, and abuse of power."[41] His replacement was interpreted as an attempt to undermine the authority of Kunayev himself, who had been one of Brezhnev's closest collaborators.

Ouster of Grishin

The most important replacement in December was the long-expected ousting of Viktor Grishin from the post of first secretary of the Moscow City CPSU Committee. The campaign against Grishin began in summer 1985. On 21 July *Sovetskaya Rossiya,* followed by *Pravda,* carried articles that criticized Moscow's housing program, the quality of construction, the distribution of products in the city, and so on. The obvious target was Moscow's mayor Vladimir Promyslov, and the implied target was the city's party boss Viktor Grishin, the longest-serving member of the Politburo (as candidate member since 1961 and full member since 1971).[42] Grishin, whose affiliation with Brezhnev and subsequently with Chernenko has already been noted, was thought to have opposed Andropov's election in 1982, instead supporting Chernenko's candidature. Furthermore, various sources linked him with a caucus within the Kremlin that opposed Gorbachev's election,[43] based on a "testimonial recommendation of Chernenko," the assertion being that Grishin had claimed the top party post for himself.[44]

On 18 August Promyslov responded to the criticism.[45] However, *Sovetskaya Rossiya,* which carried his reply, added an editorial note stating that the mayor's response was inadequate and evasive, accusing him of sanctioning abuses, and adding that such abuses had continued even after the critical article of 21 July. On 20 October, Grishin himself broke his silence and in a letter to *Sovetskaya Rossiya* conceded that there had been problems in housing construction and distribution but stated that the responsible officials had been punished.[46] On 24 December a plenum of the Moscow City CPSU Committee, which Gorbachev attended, "relieved Viktor Grishin of his duties as first secretary of the Moscow City CPSU Committee, due to his retirement" and appointed Boris Yeltsin as his successor.[47] It was widely assumed that Promyslov's "retirement" would also follow shortly and that Grishin's ousting from the Politburo was also only a matter of time. Promyslov's "retirement on pension" was announced on 3 January 1986. He was succeeded by Valeriy Saykin, forty-nine years, formerly general director of the Likhachev Automobile Works.[48]

Grishin's successor, fifty-four-year-old Boris Yeltsin, was one of the most prominent Western Siberians in Gorbachev's leadership (which by this time practically represented a Western Siberian and Stavropol mafia). Yeltsin had been first secretary of the Sverdlovsk Oblast CPSU Committee in the Urals until April 1985, when he was brought to Moscow to become first chief of the CPSU Central Committee Construction Department and then in July 1985 a secretary of the CPSU Central Committee.[49] His political career had been closely associated with the two most prominent Western Siberians, Premier Ryzhkov and Central Committee Secretary Ligachev.[50]

Boris Yeltsin, Moscow's new party boss, immediately adopted Gorbachev's style of unannounced face-to-face meetings with ordinary citizens. Soon after his election he toured the city's industrial plants, visiting the number two Clock and Watch Plant,[51] the Zarya shoe factory,[52] and various Moscow districts,[53] where he conducted spontaneous and ostensibly unstaged conversations with citizens. Yeltsin also demonstrated his style at the 24–25 January accountability-election conference of the Moscow party organization, where he sharply criticized various practices—poor organization, fallacious corrections of the annual plan, poor-quality production, inertia, poor discipline, and other negative phenomena—naming many city party officials who were responsible for these weaknesses and subjecting the city party committee itself to withering criticism.

> Of course, it is first and foremost the bureau of the party gorkom which is responsible for this. . . . The fact that Moscow and its city party organization were virtually beyond the sphere of criticism contributed to this situation in many respects. . . . The gorkom itself had frequently not fulfilled the CPSU Central Committee's demands that the misdemeanors of the leaders be subjected to party evaluation.[54]

Although Grishin was not mentioned by name, there was no doubt who was the target of this tirade.

Yeltsin's speech even included the assertion that Moscow's old administration had delayed the implementation of reforms initiated by Gorbachev's regime—implying that Grishin had resisted Gorbachev's policies. This was the first such indication since Gorbachev assumed office.

Grishin (still a Politburo member) attended the conference in person, sitting at the end of the row reserved for the Politburo members, according to the photograph in *Moskovskaya Pravda* on 25 January, but did not take the floor either to reply to the charges or to perform the rites of self-criticism. In fact there was very little he could say. Yeltsin was already purging the city party apparatus of Grishin's supporters and appointees, retiring on pension the long-serving second secretary R. Dementyeva, secretary L. Borisov, and other officials. Furthermore, Yeltsin's support at the highest level was reconfirmed on 30 January, when the Politburo at its weekly meeting gave a high assessment to the work of the conference of the Moscow city party organization and granted its leadership a mandate for "decisively reshaping the style, forms, and methods of party work and for eradicating examples of a carefree attitude and ostentation. . . . Implementation of these measures will be kept under the constant supervision of the CPSU Central Committee Politburo."[55] The Politburo was thus signaling to Yeltsin that he had a free hand in dealing with Grishin's political machine.

In January 1986 the accountability-election campaign preceding the 27th CPSU Congress entered its decisive stage. During this period the crucial role of CPSU Central Committee Secretary Ligachev in the building up of the new party apparatus became plain. He utilized the unusually high turnover rate of the oblast secretaries (by 15 February, 46 of the 157 oblast secretaries had been replaced under Gorbachev's tenure,[56] and a further 31 had been replaced under Andropov[57] to install people associated with him in the vacant posts. Many of the new appointees came from the CPSU Central Committee Cadres Department that Ligachev headed. Some appointees, such as G. Rudenko, who became first secretary of the Kiev Oblast CPSU Committee,[58] and A. Smolsky, who was appointed first secretary of the Ryazan Oblast CPSU Committee,[59] had served as deputy chairmen of the CPSU Central Committee Cadres Department, whereas others, such as V. Grigoryev, the new first secretary of the Vitebsk Oblast Committee,[60] had previously worked as inspectors in the same department.

Ligachev personally attended many of the oblast accountability-election conferences, occasionally making speeches in which he attacked various phenomena associated with Brezhnev's rule. For example, in his speech in Chelyabinsk on 12 October he lamented the past practice, "when trust in cadres was frequently not linked with high exactingness toward them."[61] In December, at the Baku city party conference, Ligachev attacked "nepotism, flattery, and careerism," stressing that "Communists, even those in leadership positions, must answer for their misdeeds."[62] Ligachev, who was also the Central Committee secretary in charge of ideology, thus demonstrated his practical abilities for organizing a solid power base within the party apparatus. Although at this time he was one of Gorbachev's closest allies, this base could also prove very useful to him in the event of a change in the political equilibrium of the Kremlin leadership.

Continued New Appointments

The accountability-election campaign did not affect the pace of new appointments, which continued unabated during January and February. Although the usual practice continued of replacing older bureaucratic officials with younger technocrats, some of the changes at the top were very surprising. On 26 January *Pravda* announced that the Supreme Soviet Presidium "has relieved Comrade Vitaliy Vasilyevich Fedorchuk of his duties as USSR minister of internal affairs, in connection with his reassignment."[63] He was replaced by Aleksandr Vlasov, fifty-four years old, and formerly first secretary of the Rostov Oblast CPSU Committee.[64]

Fedorchuk's new post (if any) was not disclosed so it was impossible to conclude whether he had been promoted or demoted. Some observers thought that the replacement was a prelude to a promotion, pointing out that because of Fedorchuk's age (sixty-seven), Gorbachev could have removed him by simply retiring him on pension. There was even a suggestion that Fedorchuk, a native of the Ukraine, might replace the Ukrainian party boss Shcherbitskiy at the 27th CPSU Congress.[65]

On the other hand, some observers maintained that Fedorchuk's reassignment meant a partial disgrace for the former KGB chief. This opinion was based on the simultaneous ousting of a relatively large number of KGB and MVD (Ministry of Internal Affairs) officials within a three-week period at the start of 1986. These included the Georgian internal affairs minister Guram Gvetadze, who was "retired on pension,"[66] the Tadzhik minister of internal affairs I. Kurbanov, who was "retired on health grounds,"[67] and Nikolay Lomov, the KGB chief of Kirgizia, who was "transferred to another post."[68] In addition, in the course of his 24 January speech the new Moscow party chief Yeltsin called upon Moscow's MVD chief V. Borisenko to be "more energetic in fighting abuses."[69] Other KGB and MVD officials were criticized at the republican party congresses. Since the ousting and criticisms could hardly be coincidences, one could infer that the MVD and KGB apparatuses had undergone a mild purge.

The anti-MVD campaign was probably linked with the broad anti-corruption campaign launched by Gorbachev, the most obvious targets of which were the Central Asian republics. The wave of retirements struck these republics harder than any other area of the USSR. Many of the top Soviet Central Asian officials even suffered public disgrace, being charged with abusing their official positions. For example, at the Turkmenian Communist Party Congress first secretary Sapamurad Niyazov attacked the already deposed first secretary M. Gapurov for cultivating "kinship," "personal loyalty," "flattery," and "careerism" and hinted at other abuses committed by the deposed leader.[70] At the Kirgizian Communist Party Congress, the former (ousted) first secretary T. Usubaliyev was accused by his successor A. Masaliyev of "creating a fertile soil for gross violations of collective leadership" and "encouraging servility and intrigue."[71] Rakhman Nabiyev, the deposed first secretary of the Tadzhik Communist party, was attacked at the republican party congress in similar terms.[72]

The worst criticism was reserved for the former first secretary of the Uzbek Communist Party Central Committee, Sharaf Rashidov, who died in November 1983 after twenty-four years of service in this post. At the Uzbek congress he was accused of "creating a cult around the top leader" and of "creating an atmosphere of selfglorification, far-fetched success stories, flattery, and servility." The new republican party leadership hastened to engage in self-criticism: The first secretary, I. Usmankhodzhayev, admitted that "he and a number of other senior personnel had been unable to act in a principled manner against Rashidov's erroneous practices and had sometimes humored him. All this was a breeding ground for violation of the rule of law and moral principles and for all manner of abuses of official position."[73]

Not only top leaders were criticized at the Central Asian congresses: Economic mismanagement of overwhelming proportions and abuse of power at all levels of the party structure were revealed. As a result the campaign against corrupt party officials, which had commenced under Andropov, was intensified in these republics. In Uzbekistan alone 300 top party officials and 200 members of the Uzbek Supreme Soviet had been ousted during the preceding two years.[74]

The congress of the Communist party of Kazakhstan drew the main attention of observers, chiefly because of the personality of Dinmukhamed Kunayev, one of Brezhnev's closest friends. Moscow hoped to see Kunayev removed by his own party organization, something that would naturally be followed by his ousting from the Politburo. Indeed, the very fact that almost one year after Gorbachev's election as general secretary Kunayev was still clinging to his membership of the highest party organ tended to place a question mark over the true extent of Gorbachev's power. To Moscow's great vexation, however, the Kazakh congress "unanimously approved the report of the Kazakh Central Committee"[75] and accordingly reelected Kunayev as the first secretary of the republican central committee.[76]

On 9 February *Pravda* published a report on the Kazakh congress entitled, "The Times Require," signed by deputy editor D. Volovoy and reporter A. Petrushov. The report amounted to an indictment of Kunayev. It quoted Yerkin Auyelbekov, first secretary of the Kzyl-Orda Oblast

CPSU Committee and member of the CPSU Central Committee, on the fact that the republican Central Committee Bureau and first secretary D. Kunayev "could not fail to know" of a long list of malpractices, including "conniving, promoting cadres on the basis of personal loyalty, kinship, common place of origin [zemlyachestvo]," and adding that "economc failures have been deliberately passed over in the ideological work." According to Auyelbekov, these shortcomings had been encouraged "by an atmosphere of toadyism and servility" that had continued "over a period of years."

Pravda also mentioned criticisms made by other congress participants, including Premier Nazarabayev, who attributed the failures to "unfounded praising of the leaders," "silencing of criticism and self-criticism," "violating the principle of collegiality in promoting cadres," and "unworthy methods of leadership." *Pravda* reported that "more than 500 leading officials have been removed recently." However, the authors asserted that "the work has only just begun," since "crimes by officials and violations of cadre policy principles have still not been eliminated."[77]

Moscow's dissatisfaction with Kunayev's reelection was thus unmistakable: For the first time since his election Gorbachev did not appear to enjoy total control and the Kazakh party organization had successfully resisted the Politburo's wishes. The criticism against Kunayev represented the first such instance in many years. Since Khrushchev's time incumbent members of the Politburo had never been publicly criticized. Romanov and Tikhonov, the two Politburo members who lost their seats under Gorbachev, had not been subjected to public criticism; even Grishin (who lost his Politburo seat on 18 February) had received no public rebuke. Thus the report on the Kazakh congress constituted a precedent.

The Ukrainian Communist Party Congress, which was held from 6 to 8 February and reelected V. Shcherbitskiy, the other Brezhnevist in the Politburo, received a somewhat different treatment in *Pravda*. The newspaper's report on the congress, entitled "Attuned to Tasks" and signed by Deputy Editor E. Grigoriev and others, contained general criticism but did not reproach Shcherbitskiy specifically and even praised his report to the Congress.[78]

Grishin paid the price for Gorbachev's disappointment with Kunayev's survival and reelection at the Kazakh congress. In a move clearly aimed at reasserting his authority, Gorbachev engineered Grishin's removal from the Politburo at the 18 February precongressional CPSU Central Committee plenum. This plenum discussed and approved the Central Committee's report to the forthcoming congress and summed up the results of the nationwide discussion of the new CPSU statutes and program, as well as the Trends for the USSR's Economic and Sociopolitical Development in 1986–1990 and Until the Year 2000 (matters routinely approved). The plenum then "relieved Comrade V. V. Grishin of his duties as a member of the Political Bureau of the CPSU Central Committee in connection with his retirement on pension."[79] The plenum also "relieved Comrade K. V. Rusakov of his duties as a secretary of the CPSU Central Committee in connection with his retirement on pension for health reasons."[80]

Even though the retirements of Romanov, Tikhonov, and Rusakov had all been stated as "due to health reasons," this face-saving formula was denied to Grishin—in an apparent attempt to single him out for humiliation. His successor as chief of the Moscow City party organization, Boris Yeltsin, was elected a candidate member of the Politburo.[81] Although these changes were expected, there was no pressing need to effect them one week before the 27th CPSU Congress, at which a reshuffle of the memberships of the Politburo and Secretariat was generally expected. Past precongressional plenums had merely approved the Central Committee report and other congressional documents and not dealt with organizational (personnel) matters. So close to the congress, such matters were usually held over for the first plenum of the new Central Committee (called on the last day of the Congress), whose main task was to elect the new top party organs.

Apparently, Gorbachev urgently needed to demonstrate his strength on the eve of the congress to counteract the effect of his failure to achieve Kunayev's removal by the Kazakh congress. However, precisely because the personnel changes on the eve of the congress were conceived as a show of strength, the fact that no other leaders apart from Yeltsin were appointed to the vacancies in the Secretariat and the Politburo indicated that Gorbachev's freedom to mold the party leadership according to his liking could not be taken for granted. Rusakov's retirement and Yeltsin's transfer from the Secretariat to the Politburo as a candidate member had opened two additional vacancies in the Secretariat, which was evidently about to undergo extensive changes at the congress. By mid-February the Secretariat contained only two senior secretaries—Gorbachev and Ligachev—and no one was available to take over Premier Ryzhkov's former functions as the senior secretary on economic matters.

The 18 February Central Committee plenum was the last major organizational event before the congress, which was widely expected to produce a reliable picture of the extent to which Gorbachev had succeeded in consolidating his authority, as well as of his ability to mold the party's long-term economic and political strategy into the twenty-first century. Extra spice was added to the forthcoming congress by the fact that during the two to three weeks preceding it Gorbachev evidently must have realized the limitations of his power. For the first time since he assumed office, his drive to renew the top Soviet party and state leadership had met a barrier. Kunayev and Shcherbitskiy were reelected by their respective republican congresses, whereas the removal of Grishin took several long weeks to organize after his removal from the leadership of the Moscow party organization.

The Congress

The delegates who started gathering in Moscow several days before the congress immediately noted one major change from previous congresses. The numerous external signs of the Byzantine personality cult that developed under Brezhnev had disappeared from Moscow's streets. No portraits of the Politburo members adorned the streets; only the pictures of the deceased high priests of communism—Marx, Engels, and Lenin—were in evidence. Furthermore, the wearing of medals had gone out of fashion. The leaders who followed Brezhnev's example (and penchant for gold stars) and proudly pinned their medals to the lapels of their business suits were now only wearing the modest insignia of the congress. Most of the delegates who followed the practice of previous congresses and ostentatiously displayed their decorations in Moscow were obliged to assume a more modest appearance.

The 27th CPSU Congress opened on 25 February at 10 A.M. Moscow time. The 4,993 delegates (7 delegates were reported "absent because of justifiable causes"[82]) and 152 guest delegations from 113 countries[83] quickly disposed of the prescribed and perfunctory election of the congress's leading organs (the Presidium, Secretariat, Editorial Commission, and Mandate Commission), and the floor was given to Mikhail Gorbachev, who for five and one-half hours read the fifty-thousand-word report of the Central Committee to the assembled congress.

Gorbachev's speech followed the traditional format. It consisted of six parts: Basic Tendencies and Contradictions in the Contemporary World; Accelerating the Country's Socioeconomic Development—A Strategic Course; Further Democratization of Society, Deepening the People's Socialist Self-Governing; The Basic Goals and Directions of the Party's Foreign Policy Strategy; The Party; and, finally, On the Discussion of the New Edition of the Party Program and Changes of the Party Statutes.[84]

The foreign policy section of the report contained no surprises, except perhaps the very tough tone adopted toward the United States. Employing every rhetorical cliché in the Agitprop manual, Gorbachev described the United States as "the metropolitan center of imperialism," a place where "immorality and hatred of all that is democratic . . . is practised on an unprecedented scale." Quoting Karl Marx, he referred to capitalism as a "hideous pagan idol, who would not drink but from the skulls of the slain." The U.S. response to his nuclear disarmament initiative was denounced, and the forthcoming summit meeting with President Reagan was put in question by the statement that "there is no sense holding empty talks." No specific international conflicts were discussed, apart from a brief reference to Afghanistan, and Gorbachev did not indicate that there was any change in the traditional Soviet view of world affairs. In short, he conveyed no new message: The foreign policy section of Gorbachev's speech gave no reason whatever to assume that Gorbachev differed from his predecessors in his orthodox Marxist-Leninist outlook.

The economic section of the speech was awaited with great interest since Gorbachev was expected to finally outline his economic innovations in plain terms. For the first time since assuming office, Gorbachev used the concept of reform (even radical reforms). He sharply criticized the Brezhnev era (without naming Brezhnev), stressing that a "radical reform was necessary to overcome the inertia, stagnation, and conservatism of the 1970's and 1980's." Gorbachev pointed out that during that period the Soviet economy registered "a sharp drop in the rhythm of productivity growth." He stressed that "for years the practical action of the party and state organs was subjected to delay in relations to the needs of the time and life itself." "The situation demanded change," he said, but "a particular psychology took hold: To improve things without changing anything." Nevertheless, Gorbachev stopped short of criticizing the system itself or calling into question the principle of centralized planning. On the contrary, he stressed that there will be "no tactical retreat from the principles of socialism."

The remedies he proposed could have been taken from any of his predecessors' speeches: "strengthening the central role of the communist party in the implementation of the economic strategy," "intensification of production," "innovation and creativity through genuine revolutionary transformations," "strengthening the role of the center in carrying out the communist party's economic strategy," "stepping up the fight against 'parasites,'" improving the quality of production, modernizing industrial and agricultural production, introducing modern equipment in every area of life, and so on. Furthermore, not only did Gorbachev fail to specify the exact nature of the radical reforms or to question the system's characteristics that had helped produce the situation that he was now attempting to remedy but none of the subsequent seventy-nine speakers, including Premier Ryzhkov and Central Committee Secretary Ligachev, used the term *reforms* in their speeches. Although these contained much introspective self-criticism and criticism, as well as pledges to eliminate various weaknesses and shortcomings, only Boris Yeltsin, Moscow's new party boss, came close to criticizing the system, voicing pregnant rhetorical questions from the congress rostrum:

> Why is it that from congress to congress we are dealing with the same problems? Why is it that our party vocabulary now includes a word obviously alien to it—stagnation? Why is it that over so many years we have been unable to pull out the roots of bureaucracy, social injustice, and abuse? Why is it that even now the demand for radical change is stuck among the inert section of timeservers with party cards?[85]

Rather than in the economic or the foreign policy sections of his speech, Gorbachev's innovation could principally be found in the area of his style (which was self-assured and occasionally even arrogant), in promoting greater openness of discussion and in eliminating various manifestations of the personality cult. When on 1 March L. Kulidzhanov, first secretary of the Union of USSR Cinematographers, began his speech at the congress by expressing his enthusiasm for Gorbachev's speech, stressing "his sorrow that the secretary general's speech has ended," Gorbachev abruptly interrupted, saying, "Let us stop declining the name of Mikhail Sergeyevich. . . ." Kulidzhanov retorted: "This is a lesson we must implement." *Pravda* of 2 March carried both Kulidzhanov's speech and the exchange with Gorbachev, illustrating the "modesty cult" promoted by the general secretary.

Otherwise the congress proceeded in the well-established routine pattern and differed in no respect from those at previous party congresses. Semantic fodder and rhetorical fireworks were produced without a single expression of political realism coming from the congress rostrum. The speakers' basic approach appeared to be to criticize everything open to criticism but to praise everything else, especially the "advantages of the socialist system." The issues of the supremacy of the party, the importance of central planning, and the infallibility of Marxism-Leninism were sacrosanct. Obsolete Leninist jargon permeated every statement delivered at the congress. Little was new, and indeed nothing new could be expected without renewing the elements of the system itself, something ruled out on the very first day of the congress. Although accusing Brezhnev (in effect) of wanting to improve things without changing anything, Gorbachev actually signaled that he wanted to improve everything while changing nothing of consequence. His emphasis was on better utilizing existing reserves, cutting down waste, corruption, and fraud, and strengthening discipline but not touching the system itself.

Thus the radical reforms heralded by Gorbachev boiled down to tentative changes in working habits and personal responsibility not even approaching reforms in centralized party control, central planning, and the other prime characteristics of the system that had produced the mess that Gorbachev was eager to change. Possibly Gorbachev did not want to say too much at this stage of the congress, preferring to obtain his voice of confidence and then proceed to implement discrete, but genuine, "radical reforms." However, on the basis of his speech and subsequent debates the prevailing impression was that the major direction would be to make the existing system work better without changing its substance.

Judging from Gorbachev's past record, he proposed to make the system work better mainly by replacing the old leaders with younger and more capable managers. To paraphrase Bertold Brecht's much quoted remark, "The government has lost the confidence of the people, so it has to elect a new people." Gorbachev, disillusioned with the existing system but unable to change it, had decided to change the people who managed the system in an attempt to improve it. This approach has the merit of preserving the system's immunity by accusing individual leaders of responsibility for the system's shortcomings. Even in this area Gorbachev broke no new ground; every single Soviet leader before him had employed the same tactic.

Because the congress debates had produced a sense of déjà vu, the expectations of the observers focused on the final day, on which the new Central Committee was to elect the new Politburo and Secretariat, thus providing a clearer picture of Gorbachev's power and authority. The membership of the new top party organs elected at the Congress reflected the situation that had emerged on the eve of the congress—the strong but somewhat restricted power of the general secretary. The extent of his power was demonstrated by the extensive changes in the membership of the Central Committee and particularly in the Secretariat, whereas its limitations were shown by the minimal changes in the Politburo, where Kunayev and Shcherbitskiy held their seats while some of Gorbachev's favorites who had been expected to gain full membership of the top organ failed to do so.

The Politburo

The new Central Committee elected at the congress did not drop any of the old Politburo's full members.[86] However, Vasiliy Kuznetsov, the eighty-five-year-old first deputy chairman of the USSR Supreme Soviet Presidium and the eighty-one-year-old Central Committee Secretary Boris Ponomarev, who for over thirty years had supervised relations with other Communist parties, lost their positions as candidate members.

Lev Zaykov (sixty-two years), a Central Committee secretary, was the only new full Politburo member, thus raising the membership to twelve full members, whereas Belorussia's first secretary Nikolay Slyunkov (fifty-eight years) and the Leningrad City party organization first secretary Yuriy Solovyev (sixty years) became candidate members. Zaykov's promotion was significant: He became the third senior Central Committee secretary, in addition to Gorbachev and Ligachev, and thus one of the most important figures in the new leadership. Earlier in his career Zaykov had been a favorite of Romanov, who selected him as first secretary of the Leningrad City party organization when Romanov moved to Moscow to take up the post of Central Committee secretary; however, Zaykov's previous political ties did not prevent him from winning Gorbachev's confidence. His area of supervision was reported to be heavy industry, including the defense industry.[87]

Defense Minister Marshal Sokolov remained merely a candidate member of the Politburo. Observers associated him and Petr Demichev, who also remained a candidate member, with the group of top leaders whose thinking differed from that of Gorbachev.[88]

An interesting question is why Gorbachev's close allies, Moscow's party chief Boris Yeltsin (Moscow first secretary had always been a full Politburo member) and Nikolay Talyzin, failed to obtain the status of full members of the Politburo, and the top agricultural administrator Vsevolod Murakhovskiy failed to win election either to the Secretariat or even to candidate membership of the Politburo. After all, Yeltsin had even outdone Gorbachev in his criticism of negative phenomena at the congress, and as one of Gorbachev's closest allies, a strong reformist, and first secretary of the Moscow City Committee, he was considered a certain candidate for full Politburo membership. The chances of Talyzin and Murakhovskiy were also considered very good. Perhaps Gorbachev's failure to gain their promotion reflected the limitations of his power and the concessions he had had to make to improve his chances of carrying out his economic program. Furthermore, the fact that Shcherbitskiy and Kunayev remained full members of the top party organ indicated that Gorbachev had to reconcile himself to further compromises. Nevertheless, Gorbachev lost no ground in the Politburo, and Zaykov's appointment may be considered a moderate success for the general secretary.

The Secretariat

Even though the minimal changes in the Politburo indicated the limitations of Gorbachev's power, the extensive changes in the membership of the Central Committee Secretariat demonstrated that his power was nevertheless impressive. Five new members were added to this organ, bringing its membership to eleven. Two secretaries were dropped: Boris Ponomarev, who had supervised the relations with foreign Communist parties, and Ivan Kapitonov, who had been responsible for the consumer goods area and was appointed chairman of the CPSU Central Auditing Commission.[89] The new members of the Secretariat included two noted Gorbachev protégés—Georgiy Razumovskiy, head of the CPSU Central Committee Cadres Department, and Aleksandr Yakovlev, head of the Central Committee's Propaganda Department, as well as Anatoliy Dobrynin (sixty-six years), the former ambassador to the United States, whose responsibilities were clearly to be in the foreign policy area, Vadim Medvedev (fifty-six), head of the CPSU Central Committee Science and Educational Institutions Department, whose responsibilities were evidently to cover science and technology, and Aleksandra Biryukova (fifty-seven), deputy chairman of the USSR Trade Union Central Council.[90] Biryukova, the first woman member of either of the two top party organs since the former minister of culture Yekaterina Furtseva (who lost her post in 1961), was apparently due to take over supervision of Kapitonov's former area of consumer goods. Her promotion was evidently intended to raise the standing of the trade unions, as well as to demonstrate the improved status of women in the party. Like Yakovlev and Razumovskiy, her career received a powerful impetus under Gorbachev.

Dobrynin had been a career diplomat for more than forty years, and his previous career had no connection with Gorbachev. The new secretary Vadim Medvedev had been promoted to the Central Committee Science and Educational Department in June 1983 under Andropov. Known as a proponent of unorthodox and flexible economic thinking, he was another representative of the new breed of reform-minded technocrats favored by Gorbachev.

Ligachev was one of only three members of the Secretariat elected by the 27th CPSU Congress who were also full Politburo members; he not only dealt with the crucially important and sensitive areas of cadres and ideology but also supervised the activity of several secretaries (Yakovlev, Razumovskiy, Zimyanin, and Medvedev). Among the other secretaries, Nikonov would continue to supervise agriculture, Zaykov would oversee the heavy and defense industries, and Vladimir Dolgikh would continue to be in charge of certain sectors of heavy industry and power supply, under Zaykov's oversight. The area of construction (which Yeltsin covered before his election as the Moscow City first secretary) remained vacant, suggesting that further changes in the Secretariat membership were expected in the near future.

The Central Committee

The membership of the new Central Committee[91] was extensively changed. Some 125 of the 307 full members (over 40 percent) and 116 of the 170 candidate members (63 percent) are newcomers. Although every party congress alters the Central Committee membership, the changes effected by the 27th CPSU Congress were unusually widespread. The 26th Congress had, for example, replaced only 25 percent of the full members and less than 60 percent of the candidate members.

The composition of the new Central Committee reflects intensive bargaining and compromise by both Gorbachev's faction and the conservative wing of the party. The following changes indicate possible gains for Gorbachev's faction: The liberal philosopher Ivan Frolov (fifty-six years), long a target of criticism from the conservatives, became a full Central Committee member, suggesting a possible transfer from the academic field to direct involvement in implementing Gorbachev's economic program. Valentin Chikin (fifty-three), the conservative former first deputy editor *Sovetskaya Rossiya,* whose articles in 1983–1985 (arguing for the removal of the old leaders and the promotion of younger cadres) provided clues to the power game in the Kremlin, was elected a candidate member of the Central Committee. (*Moskovskaya Pravda* on 23 April was the first to reveal that Chikin had also been appointed chief editor of *Sovetskaya Rossiya.* This appointment was probably made on the eve of the CPSU Congress and might be regarded as a reward for Chikin's regular and staunch advocacy of Gorbachev's policies of cadre renewal and economic reform, by which one of Gorbachev's strongest propagandists was made a member of the top leadership of the central Soviet press.) Richard Kosolapov (fifty-five years), chief editor of *Kommunist* and a prominent supporter of the orthodox party line, was dropped from Central Committee membership. As chief editor of the party's main ideological publication, his conservatism was a clear obstacle in Gorbachev's path.

The conservative faction could also boast of a number of successes. The noted liberal commentator Aleksandr Bovin failed to gain Central Committee membership and even lost his place in the Central Auditing Commission. Nikolay Glushkov, an outspoken opponent of reforms, particularly in the price system (and thus no friend of Gorbachev) was promoted out of the Central Auditing Commission to candidate membership of the Central Committee. Nikolay Baybakov, former deputy premier and Gosplan chief, a close friend of Brezhnev and a firm believer in central planning and opponent of reforms, retained his full Central Committee membership.

Several other leaders who had lost their top posts under Gorbachev retained their membership in the Central Committee. Among these were the former premier and Politburo member Nikolay Tikhonov, former Central Committee secretary Boris Ponomarev, former vice president Vasiliy Kuznetsov, and the former Navy Commander, Admiral Sergey Gorshkov. On the other hand, Grigoriy Romanov, Viktor Grishin, and Konstantin Rusakov all lost their seats in the Central Committee. The reelection of Tikhonov, Ponomarev, and the other ousted leaders could be interpreted as a shrewd signal by Gorbachev that former opponents could expect to retain some rank and status if they reconciled themselves to the loss of their real political power.

Vitaliy Fedorchuk, formerly the KGB chief and minister of internal affairs, lost his Central Committee seat. Agence France Press, quoting "reliable sources," reported that he had been transferred to the Inspectorate of the Soviet Army,[92] a body composed of semiretired highranking officers and devoid of any significance or influence. Fedorchuk's removal from the Internal Affairs Ministry on 25 January 1986 had aroused speculation on whether this was a prelude to a dramatic promotion or marked the end of his career as a result of the disclosures of widespread corruption among the ministry's cadres. His disappearance from the Central Committee's ranks provided the clear answer. In contrast, Marshal Ogarkov, who had been unceremoniously removed from his post of commander of the General Staff in September 1984, retained his Central Committee seat, showing that he still preserved a measure of political influence.

The list of the new Central Committee members also shows that Gorbachev had carried out a thorough shake-up of the Central Committee apparatus. Seven former departmental heads failed to be reelected to the new Central Committee, including Vasiliy Shauro, head of the Culture Department; Ivan Sakhnyuk, head of the Agricultural Machine

Building Department; and Kiril Simonov, head of the Transport Department. The removal of these officials had not been announced before the congress, but their nonelection to the new Central Committee inevitably implied that they had lost their responsible posts in the central party apparatus.

A number of Gorbachev's top assistants were elected to the Central Committee, among them Anatoliy Lushchikov, Gorbachev's chief aide, as a full member, and agricultural expert Valeriy Bodin, as a candidate member. Another close aide, foreign policy adviser Viktor Sharapov, was elected to the Central Auditing Commission. The long-serving foreign policy adviser Andrey Aleksandrov-Agentov was dropped from the Central Committee, confirming previous rumors of his retirement. His position was apparently taken over by Anatoliy Chernyayev, deputy head of the CPSU Central Committee International Department, who was promoted from candidate to full member of the Central Committee.

The KGB deputy chief Georgiy Tsinev was not reelected to the Central Committee, a fact that indicated the retirement of this seventy-eight-year-old protégé of Brezhnev from Dnepropetrovsk. Since another deputy chief of the KGB—Vladimir Pirozhkov—also failed to gain reelection, it may be assumed that a shake-up of the KGB leadership had taken place on the eve of the congress. On the other hand, Nikolay Yemokhanov, who was appointed first deputy chief of the KGB in 1984, became a full member of the Central Committee.

The extensive changes in the compositions of the Secretariat and the Central Committee, notwithstanding the moderate adjustments within the Politburo, justified the expectations expressed prior to the congress. However, the epithets like "historic" that were widely used by the Soviet media to describe the congress proved grossly exaggerated. The congress was hardly a "turning point" (another cliché favored by the media). Some aspects were indeed unusual: the extensive self-criticism and criticism, the departure from manifestations of a personality cult and its replacement by a modesty cult, and the urgent call for changes and even "radical reforms" by Gorbachev and his supporters. However, nothing in the work of the congress, which was carried out in a routine and orthodox manner, indicated any break with past practices or real reforms, let alone changes in the system.

The general secretary does project a sincere and dynamic persona, which in itself is a refreshing change in Soviet political life, but sooner or later the novelty will wear out. The congress converted the Central Committee and the Secretariat into fortresses of Gorbachev's power, but no clear signs showed that the roadblocks erected by the orthodox nomenclatura had all been removed. The only congress speaker who actually used the term *reform* was Gorbachev himself. No one seconded him. Perhaps many of the party officials were reluctant to abandon their stance of "wait and see" or even their opposition to Gorbachev's drive and continued doggedly to cling to their sinecure posts, now in jeopardy at the hands of the general secretary. Finally, Gorbachev himself is undoubtedly basking in the limelight of his popularity and enjoying extensive power and authority. However, his insistent drive for reforms and his removal of thousands of party officials have encouraged expectations of practical results, which he has to deliver soon; to disappoint these expectations could be dangerous or even politically lethal. Therefore, not the period of the congress but the next two or three years will prove crucial for Gorbachev and the implementation of his program.

10

Conclusions

Biology played an overwhelmingly important role in the crucial 1982–1985 succession drama in the USSR. Its importance was the natural consequence of a number of inherent characteristics of the Soviet system, which in their turn produced the extremely unusual situation of a succession of old and ailing leaders who, though physically incapable of ruling the largest country in the world, could not be removed from their posts.

1. The first such characteristic is the absence of any recognized rules of succession, based on genuinely democratic elections, a choice between alternative leaders, or a prescribed term of office. Unlike the political setup in Western democracies, no constitutional means exist for replacing leaders through a vote of no confidence nor is there any provision for the free existence and legal activity of a political opposition. The Soviet general elections involve no real contest, no freedom of choice, and no privacy. The organs elected through this process have no political power and their authority is fictitious. Power and genuine authority in the USSR are concentrated in the hands of a small elite group of leaders who make up a self-perpetuating organ—the Politburo—whose composition cannot be affected by the electorate. It rules over the country and over the elected organs of state power, and its members decide all matters of importance, including their own positions.

2. Although members of the Politburo sometimes lose their seats, the mechanism for terminating the tenure of Politburo members is obscure, erratic, and unaffected by the citizens or any other organ, apart from the Politburo itself. Although the Central Committee ostensibly transfers people to and from the Politburo, it does so in a rubber-stamp fashion, executing a recommendation by the Politburo, which has already decided the matter before the Central Committee members are convened to implement the decision.

3. The top leader—the general secretary of the Central Committee— invariably comes from the ranks of the Politburo and usually before election as general secretary holds the post of a Central Committee secretary. His election is decided by the Politburo, occasionally with the participation of the members of the Secretariat and the top Army

command. The subsequent approval of the Central Committee is a matter of course. This process produces a strange situation: In a democratic regime the leader chooses his team; in the Soviet Union the team chooses the leader. Accordingly, at least during the initial stages of his rule, the new leader is largely dependent on the other members of the Politburo. Indeed, the peril of being removed as soon as a majority vote is taken against him in the Politburo (which entails collusion by only six or seven members) haunts every Soviet leader. Consequently, the personal power of the top leader largely depends on his ability to control his peers in the Politburo, usually through promoting his allies to membership in the organ and ousting or at least neutralizing potential rivals in the Politburo by building up and effectively using a considerable majority within the organ. Obviously, this process is very delicate and complex, and can continue for several years.

The fact that both Andropov and Chernenko were prevented by their failing health from effectively engaging in this process added significantly to the uncertainty and drama of the 1982–1985 succession struggle. However, the reluctance of their peers to remove them reflected the rather surprising permanency of the general secretary's tenure.

4. Since the USSR has only one political party—the CPSU—the real political struggle cannot take place between different political parties as it does in Western countries but must occur within the CPSU itself. The struggle can take different forms, focus on different issues, and engage different opposing groups (reformers versus conservatives, supporters of heavy industry versus advocates of consumer goods production, the Army leadership against the civilians). Although the Politburo is the main stage for the struggle, the support of the party apparatus or nomenklatura is also essential. Therefore every new leader wishing to establish authority must make a pronounced and sustained effort to extend power over the party apparatus. The conservatives in the nomenklatura became the main targets of Gorbachev's drive to consolidate his position and promote the implementation of his reforms. During the 1982–1985 period control over the party apparatus was demonstrated to be more important than the additional posts held by the general secretary. Although Brezhnev, Andropov, and Chernenko made great efforts to concentrate the titles of chairman of the Defense Council and chairman of the Supreme Soviet Presidium in their hands (for both Andropov and Chernenko their acquisition of the post of chairman of the Supreme Soviet Presidium was regarded as a test of their ability to assert their power), Gorbachev did not hesitate to arrange for Gromyko to be elected as Supreme Soviet Presidium chairman, preferring to concentrate on party work, which at least during the first stages of his tenure meant his struggle against the conservatives in the party apparatus.

5. Despite these perils and hazards and the watchful eyes of the other Politburo members, the general secretary is relatively secure in

the position. The totalitarian government is poor in traditions. Since no rules of inheritance of power exist, no official heirs are designated by law or tradition, and no mechanism for removing the leader is recognized or tested, death is the most likely reason for succession in the USSR. Any method for removing the leader except natural causes necessarily involves conspiratory activity by at least some of the Politburo members (including the delicate job of securing the support of the Soviet Army leadership and the KGB). Such activity could prove highly dangerous and politically or even physically lethal if the attempt to overthrow the leader fails. Even if the plot succeeds, one can never predict the attitude of the new leader, even toward those who have obtained the crown for him. The result is a marked reluctance of the Poliburo members to remove the top leader, even when patently incapable of carrying on the duties. This reluctance explains why the Politburo members preferred to retain a clearly senile Brezhnev and a physically incapacitated Andropov and Chernenko rather than to remove them in favor of a physically fitter and younger leader. In the cases of Brezhnev and Chernenko, the members of the party apparatus enjoyed their sinecures established under Brezhnev and refused to jeopardize their positions by lending a helping hand in the selection of a more vigorous leader.

Nevertheless, one may assume that a united Politburo could overcome the resistance of the nomenklatura. However, no such unity existed in the Politburo successively led by Brezhnev, Andropov, and Chernenko. Split into contrary factions and composed of members who (with the exception of Gorbachev) were as old as or older than the top leader, it refused to establish the precedent of using considerations of age and poor health as bona fide reasons for removing the leader. After all, establishment of such a precedent would endanger its members own positions. Consequently, they preferred to let biology and old age run their course, tolerating leaders incapable of exercizing their powers rather than having to grapple with a complex equation of succession with many unknowns. The election of Andropov as Brezhnev's successor indicated that a powerful group of Politburo members, perhaps even a majority, was embarrassed by the corruption and stagnation during the latter period of Brezhnev's tenure. Yet it chose to act by electing Andropov after Brezhnev's death and not by removing Brezhnev while Brezhnev was still alive but unable to rule.

*   *   *

Andropov, not Gorbachev, fired the first salvos in the struggle against corruption, stagnation, and alcoholism, which had become endemic in the Soviet system under Brezhnev. Although his drive failed to produce significant results immediately (Andropov ruled effectively for only a few months), it sufficiently scared many of the Politburo members so that on Andropov's death they chose to return to Brezhnevism without Brezhnev—by electing his acolyte and right-hand man Chernenko. By so doing, they committed the country to another (mercifully short) period of immobility and stagnation but also apparently contracted to elect their youngest colleague to the leadership when Chernenko died. This contract explains the extraordinary speed and determination with which Gorbachev assumed office, especially when compared to the uncertainty and hesitation surrounding the elections of Andropov and Chernenko. In addition, by the time Gorbachev's turn came, the procedure for replacing the deceased leader had become sufficiently practised and smooth, so that the Central Committee could execute its ostensible prerogatives with great efficiency.

The very essence of the Soviet political system precludes any open official election campaigning. Although in the West leaders gain offices mainly through successful campaigning, in the USSR their election is dependent on the blessing of a few Politburo members, who form a sufficiently large majority to anoint the new leader. Therefore, the real campaign program of the new Soviet leader largely begins after his election: It involves winning over to the leader's side the uncommitted members of the Politburo, ousting opponents and potential rivals, and, most important, establishing control over the party apparatus. (Since the new leader's election would have been impossible without Army and KGB support, they can be assumed to form part of the leader's coalition at least during the initial stages of the tenure.)

Although Gorbachev apparently assumed many of the top leader's prerogatives while Chernenko was still alive, his real work began after his election. Moving with lightning speed and with some assistance from Mother Nature, in less than a year Gorbachev removed almost half of the country's political leaders,[1] including three senior Politburo members (Romanov, Tikhonov, and Grishin), several candidate members and secretaries, almost one-third of the 157 oblast CPSU first secretaries, 40 of the 113 officials with ministerial rank (including Premier Tikhonov and several deputy premiers), and thousands of lesser officials.[2] He set about a gigantic task—to eliminate the inherent contradictions and inertia of the system—by striking against the system's most privileged elite, the nomenklatura, and by initiating a powerful drive against corruption, flattery, ostentatious living, alcoholism, privilege, and various manifestations of the personality cult. His declared goal was to make the Soviet system more efficient and productive by radically modernizing and streamlining its administration.

Very soon it became apparent that the renewal of the party apparatus was Gorbachev's first priority—a goal that he clearly considered an essential precondition for implementing his reforms. Thus the profound personnel changes initiated by Gorbachev should not be regarded only as an instrument for asserting his authority but also as an essential first step for carrying through any radical reform in the USSR. In his campaign against the party apparatus Gorbachev was once again assisted by biology. A large number of party apparatus members had held their posts throughout Brezhnev's tenure (during which period there had been five U.S. presidents and six United Kingdom governments), and they had sunk into complacency and indulgence. The cadres were reluctant to give up the good life and agree to radical reform. By utilizing the advanced ages of an unusually large number of party officials, Gorbachev could effectively but graciously ease them into retirement, occasionally even thanking them for their past services. One cannot help but compare Gorbachev to the other great Soviet reformer—Stalin. Like Stalin, Gorbachev is building up a new apparatus to effect great economic and social reform; however, unlike Stalin, he is using the civilized instrument of retirement to remove even his strongest opponents. There has been no trace of a purge even remotely resembling those of Stalin's days.

The new persons appointed by Gorbachev have similar backgrounds and usually have had extensive managerial experience, most often in the areas of heavy industry and planning (with a predominance of technocrats from the defense industry). A geographical factor also plays an important role, with many of the newcomers at the top originating from the Stavropol area or Western Siberia. The success of Gorbachev's reforms mainly depends on this relatively youthful and vigorous team.

At the April 1985 CPSU Central Committee plenum Gorbachev declared that Moscow's claim to world leadership would lose credibility without a Soviet economic revival. He realized that far more than its credibility was at stake. He saw clearly that a further period of economic stagnation could result in a deterioration of Soviet military power (the only area in which the USSR is a world power) and thus in the long run create political instability. Thus for him economic revival—no matter how gigantic the task—is a matter of vital necessity. Gorbachev has the personal prestige, energy, and support at the very top of the party leadership, without which this undertaking would be impossible. However, these vital preconditions do not guarantee the final success of the venture. Real and effective reforms are unlikely to succeed if the inherent characteristics of the Soviet system are not changed. Yet at the 27th CPSU Congress Gorbachev clearly stated that changes in the system itself are not to be expected. Apparently, at this stage at least, he realizes that reforming the system is tantamount to opening a Pandora's box, a hazardous risk that could lead to a loss of economic and political control by the CPSU.

Gorbachev seems for the moment to have reconciled himself to reforming the Soviet economy, not by changing the system but by making it work better. He is attempting to eliminate some of the worst phenomena created by the system and to streamline the administration. In so doing he exposes himself to the accusation (which he himself leveled against Brezhnev) of attempting to improve things without changing anything really important. In fact, many of his calls for strict discipline and scientific progress differ very little from those of his predecessors. Like them, he remains an orthodox Marxist-Leninist who supports strong centralized power in combination with greater autonomy of decisionmaking at the economic base. In this respect he has broken no new ground. Indeed, he has maneuvered himself into a rather precarious position: Soon he will have to produce some results; yet at the moment these seem highly questionable unless he has not so far revealed the full extent of his intentions, which may include tacit, discrete, and slow tentative changes in the system itself.

Nevertheless, during his first year of rule Gorbachev has asserted himself beyond even the aspirations of his immediate predecessors. On 11 March 1986, a few days after the 27th CPSU Congress, fell the first anniversary of Chernenko's death; the event passed unnoticed even by the Soviet press. Even Andropov, Gorbachev's mentor, does not seem to have fared much better during the reign of his protégé. Andropov's name was mentioned only once during the ten days of the CPSU Congress, in sharp contrast to 1985, when Gorbachev referred to him on frequent occasions. After a triumphant year, crowned by the congress that endorsed Gorbachev's extensive personnel changes and his economic program, the general secretary could dispense even with the person who had initiated many of the campaigns and plans that he was now trying to carry through.

Finally, Brezhnev has apparently become a nonperson. His name was not mentioned during the congress, and his period and his image were the main targets of Gorbachev's criticism. The leader of the Soviet Union for eighteen years, during which time he played an active part in shaping world history, has become a symbol for stagnation, immobility, and decay.

Although western observers occasionally compare Gorbachev to Stalin (in the extent of his economic plans and the creation of a new party machine) and to Khrushchev (as being younger and more dynamic than his predecessors, projecting the image of the man of the people who is keen on economic change, and as using the party congress as a vehicle for asserting himself and a launching platform for a new era), the names of Stalin and Khrushchev are mentioned very rarely in the Soviet media, and the taboo on praising their political achievements is still in force.

Gorbachev, disclaiming continuity with any Soviet leader since Lenin, has effectively established himself as the direct descendant of the founder of the Soviet Communist regime. Nothing else—not even the extensive personnel changes and the ambitious economic plans—better reflects the enormous power he has amassed during two years of power. The USSR has changed: Citizens now have more freedom to attack those areas of Soviet life open for constructive criticism. There seem to be less drinking, harder work, less corruption, and more discipline.

The ruling class in the classless Soviet society has lost some of its privileges (such as job tenure and sinecure), and more sacrifices are being demanded. However, these changes are tentative and a poor reflection of Gorbachev's ambitious plans. His major battles still lie ahead. Although the power struggle inside the Kremlin was decided soon after Gorbachev assumed office, his struggle against the party apparatus is yet to be won. Gorbachev, currently the unquestioned and unrivaled leader of the USSR, may discover that in future battles friends and allies can become foes and that power and authority won quickly and effectively within a few months can easily be lost or substantially weakened by new political alliances and opposition within the ranks of the Soviet Communist party.

—— Appendix A ——
Indicators for Ranking of Soviet Leaders

According to an old witticism, Sovietologists are fantastic scholars because they deal with fantasy. This comment seems especially appropriate for cases in which Soviet scholars attempt to assess the personal power of individual Soviet leaders and to create a table of ranks for a given period of Soviet history. (A table of ranks is the semiofficial order of precedence of the Soviet leaders, according to their real power and importance; it does not necessarily correspond to their official posts.)

In the Soviet Union there is no certainty about when or how a change of leadership will occur. Although the last three successions have demonstrated that a Soviet leader has a very good chance of dying in office, the possibility of his removal at any moment by his closest colleagues is constantly present. Since an underlying power struggle appears to be continuously waged within the Politburo, it is important for Western observers and the Western public to be as well informed on the relative strength of each member of the Soviet leadership and his precise position in the table of ranks.

Attempts by Sovietologists to establish tables of ranks have often failed to be convincing and have prompted derogatory allusions to dealing in fantasy or political astrology. Secrecy and suspicion permeate the Soviet political system: No information on the inner workings of the system is available, and certainly no data on the relative strength of the different leaders. This official secrecy applies to almost every area of life in the USSR and especially to matters that could embarrass the Soviet Union or damage its interests. The tragic accident at the Chernobyl nuclear power plant, which Moscow attempted to conceal for several days and admitted only when the truth could no longer be hidden, is an excellent example of the officially imposed secrecy. Consequently, Sovietologists are often obliged to use unorthodox methods to derive information on topical developments in the USSR and to determine the table of ranks for Soviet leaders at any given moment. (This table is subject to continuous change and a leader, though still retaining his official post, may move up or down the table as a result of developments in the political struggle within the Politburo or for other reasons.)

Throughout the book I have tried to determine the tables of ranks of the Soviet leadership during the different stages of the tenures of Brezhnev, Andropov, Chernenko, and Gorbachev. On each occasion I have indicated the method used to determine the order of precedence in the particular table.

The following is a list of the more important indications used to assess the relative strength of the Soviet leaders.

The Official Lineup

No dictatorship, not even the dictatorship of the proletariat, can have a collective leadership. Sooner or later the authoritarian and unconventional manner of ruling the country produces a specific pecking order that encompasses all top leaders. The system indicates the relative prominence of the leaders by their official posts. This official lineup is revealed at the formal parades in Red Square, when the leaders stand on the tribune of the Lenin Mausoleum in an order determined by their official positions. Center stage is reserved for the general secretary, followed by the president (if this post is not also held by the general secretary) and then by the chairman of the Council of Ministers. Thus, the order at the 1 May 1986 parade was Gorbachev, Gromyko, Ryzhkov. (This official order does not imply that in this case Gromyko really was the second most powerful person in the USSR.) The fourth position attracts most attention because it is reserved for the leader who is actually the second most powerful figure in the leadership. Not surprisingly, on 1 May 1986 this place was occupied by second secretary Ligachev. The leaders who followed him in the lineup were, according to their positions on the tribune: Solomentsev, Zaykov, Vorotnikov, Chebrikov, Aliyev, Shevardnadze, and Yeltsin, followed by the members of the Secretariat.[1]

The official lineup, after the first three places which are determined by protocol, serves as one way to determine the relative strength, or the semiofficial ranking, of the top leaders. Unfortunately, the picture presented is often only partial since those members of the Politburo who also head regional or republican organizations usually attend the parades held in their own republics. For example, on 1 May 1986 two Politburo members, whose statuses were subject to much speculation, Shcherbitskiy and Kunayev, attended the parades in Kiev and Alma Ata,[2] respectively, making it impossible to determine their relative places in the official lineup.

Order of Appearance

The order of appearance at public meetings, funerals, and so on closely follows that on the tribune of the mausoleum and is accordingly merely a variant of the first method. Incidentally, the official photographs of these events, and indeed of the main parades themselves, are often the subject of manipulation. Retouching is often needed to restore a leader to his normal place in the lineup or to show him present at an event that he did not attend (as in the case of the Kunayev photograph). Incidentally, the order in which the Soviet press lists the leaders attending events is no help for determining the real positions of the leaders, since, with the exception of the name of the general secretary, the list is always in alphabetical order; the full members of the Politburo are listed first, then the candidate members, and finally the members of the Secretariat.

Obituaries

Obituaries often provide surprisingly up-to-date and correct information on developments in the Politburo. The obituaries of major figures are usually signed by all top Soviet leaders, but the names are given in alphabetical order after the general secretary. However, when the obituary concerns a less prominent personality or even a noted expert, it is signed by the leader or leaders who supervise the specific area in which the deceased was active. For example, the secretary in charge of light industry signs the obituaries of officials in this field, the minister of defense sign those for highranking officers, and so on. Consequently, when a leader who has been known to supervise the area of agriculture begins to sign the obituaries of army officers, unsigned by other Politburo members, this indicates either a change in his area of control or an extension of his power to more than one area. I have used this technique on several occasions to demonstrate Gorbachev's progress toward the position of second secretary under Chernenko. Although this method cannot provide new facts on the general leadership lineup, it can disclose vital information on the positions of individual leaders at a given moment.

Number of Nominations

The number of nominations obtained by each leader during the election campaigns preceding the USSR and RSFSR Supreme Soviet elections, as well as the precise date of the first nomination, provides reliable information covering the entire Soviet leadership. Like everything else relating to these elections, the number of nominations and the dates are predetermined, and these data are meticulously recorded and published by the Soviet press. The general secretary always receives many more nominations than any of his colleagues; he is always followed by the chairman of the Council of Ministers and the second secretary, who receive an equal number of nominations, and they in turn are followed by the remaining Politburo members, who also receive an equal but smaller number of nominations. This is a reliable tool for identifying the second secretary.

A further indication of relative prominence is the specific nomination that each leader decides to accept. For example, only the general secretary, the chairman of the Council of Ministers, the second secretary, and the first secretary of the Moscow City CPSU organization accept the nominations of Moscow City constituencies. The number of nominations received by Gorbachev before the 1984-1985 RSFSR Supreme Soviet elections (twelve, the same as by premier Tikhonov), as compared with seven only one year earlier during the USSR Supreme Soviet election campaign, combined with the fact that he accepted the nomination of a Moscow City constituency (as compared to Stavropol in the 1983 and Altay in the 1981 RSFSR Supreme Soviet elections), was a clear indication of his elevation to the position of second secretary.

Order of Election Speeches

The reverse order of the leaders' election speeches is another accurate tool for determining the table of ranks at the time these speeches are delivered. Although the first two positions are again a matter of protocol (the general secretary speaking last and the chairman of the Council of Ministers one day before him), the other Politburo members speak in the reverse order of their respective placings in the leadership. The positions of the Soviet leaders before the 1984 USSR Supreme Soviet election are shown in Table A.1.

TABLE A.1   Relative Positions of Soviet Leaders Before 1984 USSR Supreme
Soviet Election

Name	Post	Date of Speech (1984)
1. Chernenko	General secretary	2 March
2. Tikhonov	Prime minister	1 March
3. Gorbachev	Second secretary	29 February
4. Ustinov	Politburo member and Defense minister	28 February
5. Gromyko	Politburo member and Foreign minister	27 February
6. Grishin and Romanov	Politburo members and heads of the Moscow and Leningrad City CPSU organizations	25 February
7. Shcherbitskiy and Solomentsev	Politburo members and heads of the Ukrainian and RSFSR party organizations	24 February
8. Aliyev and Kunayev	Politburo member Politburo member and head of Kazakhstan party organization	23 February
9. Vorotnikov	Politburo member	22 February

Gromyko's position in Table A.1 is the one he held before his appointment as chairman of the USSR Supreme Soviet Presidium, or Soviet president, as the title is usually rendered in the West. Since the three general secretaries who preceded Gorbachev also held the post of USSR president, one will have to wait for the next election campaign to obtain an indication of Gromyko's current position as president by this method.

The techniques outlined here are unofficial. On occasion a misleading picture can be obtained from employing any one method in isolation without considering the other indicators. However, when these methods are used in combination over a short time span, such as during a major election campaign, they can yield a reasonably accurate picture of the relative strength of the Soviet leaders at a given moment.

Notes

1. Moscow Television Service in Russian 0550 GMT, 1 May 1986, Daily Report (USSR), National Affairs Supplement, 1 May 1986.

2. Moscow Domestic Service in Russian 1000 GMT, 1 May 1986, Daily Report (USSR), National Affairs Supplement, 1 May 1986.

Notes

Chapter 1

1. Shlomo Avineri, *The Social and Political Thought of Karl Marx* (Cambridge: Cambridge University Press, 1968), p. 189.
2. Karl Marx, Letter to W. Blos, 10 November 1877, in Karl Marx and Friedrich Engels, *Selected Works,* vol. 1 (Moscow: Foreign Languages Publishing House, 1955), p. 687.
3. Karl Marx, *The Civil War in France* (New York: International Publishers, 1940), p. 67.
4. Friedrich Engels, "On Authority," in Karl Marx and Friedrich Engels, *Selected Works,* vol. 1, pp. 635–638.
5. Georgiy Plekhanov, *The Role of the Individual in History* (New York: International Publishers, 1940), p. 41.
6. Ibid.
7. Ibid., pp. 59–60.
8. Alfred G. Meyer, *Leninism* (Cambridge, Mass.: Harvard University Press, 1957), p. 53.
9. Alfred G. Meyer. "Historical Developments of the Communist Theory of Leadership," in R. Barry Farrell, *Political Leadership in Eastern Europe and the Soviet Union* (Chicago: Aldine Publishing, 1970), pp. 14–15.
10. Although no official announcement is made in the USSR of the appointment of the Defense Council chairman, it is generally assumed that the new general secretary is automatically elected to this post.

Chapter 2

1. TASS International Service in Russian to Europe, 0815 Moscow Time, 4 March 1953.
2. Governmental report on Stalin's condition, Moscow *Pravda,* 4 March 1953.
3. Ibid.
4. Ibid.
5. Moscow *Pravda,* 5 March 1953.
6. Moscow Domestic Service in Russian 0630 Moscow Time, 6 March 1953.
7. Moscow *Pravda,* 6 March 1953.
8. Ibid.

9. Moscow Domestic Service in Russian 2030 Moscow Time, 6 March 1953.

10. Moscow *Pravda,* 7 March 1953.

11. Ibid., 8 March 1953.

12. Ibid., 10 March 1953.

13. Ibid., 16 March 1953.

14. Ibid., 21 March 1953.

15. Ibid., 16 April 1953.

16. Ibid., 15 October 1964.

17. TASS in English and Russian 2000 Moscow Time, 15 October 1964.

18. Stephen Cohen, "Gorbachev: How Strong He Is," *Chicago Tribune,* 12 September 1985.

19. Moscow *Pravda,* 17 October 1964.

20. TASS International Service in English 2400 Moscow Time, 16 November 1964; also Moscow *Pravda,* 17 November 1964.

21. Editorial, "Loyal to the Leninist Principles of Organization," Moscow *Pravda,* 18 November 1964.

22. George Breslauer, "Political Succession and the Soviet Political Agenda," *Problems of Communism,* May-June 1980, pp. 34–35.

23. Ibid.

24. Jerry F. Hough, "Soviet Succession—Issues and Responsibilities," *Problems of Communism,* September-October 1982, p. 38.

25. Alexander G. Rahr, "A Biographical Directory of 100 Leading Soviet Officials," *Radio Liberty Research Bulletin,* 10 February 1981, p. 207.

26. Ibid., p. 208.

27. Ibid., p. 158.

28. Ibid., p. 160.

29. Ibid., pp. 68–69.

30. Ibid., pp. 190–191.

31. Ibid., p. 170.

32. Ibid., p. 108.

33. Ibid., p. 8.

34. Ibid.

35. Ibid., p. 225.

36. Ibid.

37. Ibid., p. 37.

38. Ibid., p. 214.

39. Ibid., p. 62.

40. Ibid., p. 63.

41. Ibid., p. 33.

42. Ibid., pp. 33–34.

43. Ibid., p. 34.

44. Moscow *Pravda,* 24 February 1981.

45. Boris Meissner, "The 26th Party Congress and Soviet Domestic Policy," *Problems of Communism,* May-June 1981, p. 1.

46. Ibid.

47. Alexander Rahr, "A New Man in Power," in *Soviet/East European Survey, 1983/84,* edited by Vojtech Mastny (Durham, N.C.: Duke University Press, 1985), p. 114.

48. Ibid.

49. Moscow *Pravda,* 18 December 1980.

50. Sofia *Rabotnichesko Delo,* 31 March 1981.

51. Moscow *Pravda,* 23 April 1981.

52. Ibid., 2 May 1981.

53. Ibid., 25 September 1981.

54. Ibid.

55. Moscow *Pravda,* 8 September 1981.

56. K. Chernenko, "The Leninist Strategy of Leadership," *Kommunist,* 13 September 1981, pp. 3–22.

57. Moscow Domestic Television "Vremya" program 1700 GMT, 6 November 1981.

58. Moscow *Pravda,* 29 October 1981.

59. Ibid., 27 November 1981.

60. Ibid., 24 November 1981.

61. Moscow Domestic Television "Vremya" program 1700 GMT, 18 December 1981.

62. Moscow *Pravda,* 20 December 1981.

63. Moscow Domestic Television "Vremya" program 1700 GMT, 6 November 1981.

64. Ibid., 4 December 1981.

65. Moscow *Izvestiya,* 15 December 1981.

66. Moscow Domestic Television "Vremya" program 1700 GMT, 28 January 1981; also Moscow *Pravda,* 29 January 1982.

67. Moscow *Pravda,* 27 January 1982.

68. Ibid., 30 January 1982.

69. Ibid., 4 February 1982.

70. "Two Scandals Have All Moscow Abuzz," *New York Times,* 27 February 1982.

71. Vladimir Solovyov and Elena Klepikova, *Yuri Andropov—A Secret Passage into the Kremlin* (New York: Macmillan, 1983), pp. 224–225; also *Newsweek,* 22 November 1982, p. 39.

72. *Neue Zuericher Zeitung,* 17 March 1982; *Frankfurter Allgemeine Zeitung,* 20 April 1982; Christian Schmidt-Heauer, *Michail Gorbatschow* (Zurich: Piper, 1985), pp. 89–90.

73. Moscow *Pravda,* 22 February 1982.

74. Ibid., 1 March 1982.

75. Ibid., 12 March 1982.

76. Ibid., 14 February 1982.

77. *Pravda Ukrainy,* 23 January 1982.

78. Ibid.

79. Paris Agence France Press (AFP) in English 1401 GMT, 15 April 1982, Daily Report (USSR), 16 April 1982.

80. Paris Domestic Service in French 1700 GMT, 4 September 1982, and Hamburg German Press Agency (DPA) in German 1520 GMT, 6 September 1982, both in Daily Report (USSR), 7 September 1982.

81. Moscow *Pravda,* 23 April 1976.

82. Moscow Domestic Service in Russian 1304 GMT, 22 April 1982, Daily Report (USSR), 23 April 1982.

83. Moscow *Krasnaya Zvezda,* 8 April 1982.

84. Moscow *Pravda,* 2 May 1982.

85. *Bakinskiy Rabochiy,* 8 November 1979.

86. Moscow *Pravda,* 23 April 1982; Konstantin Chernenko, "The Leading Role of the Party of Communists an Important Condition of its Growth," *Kommunist,* no. 6, April 1982, pp. 25–43.
87. Moscow TASS in English 1642 GMT, 24 March 1982, Daily Report (USSR), 25 May 1982.
88. Elisabeth Teaque, "Signs of Rivalry Between Andropov and Chernenko," *Radio Liberty Research Bulletin,* RL 214/82, 25 May 1982; also "Andropov and Chernenko: Who's Ahead," RL 350/82, 30 August 1982.
89. Moscow *Krasnaya Zvezda,* 12 May 1982.
90. Ibid., 28 May 1982.
91. Ibid., 27 May 1982.
92. Boris Meissner, "Transition in the Kremlin," *Problems of Communism,* January-February 1983, p. 10.
93. Moscow TASS in English 1642 GMT, 24 May 1982, Daily Report (USSR), 25 May 1982.
94. Moscow *Pravda,* 3 June 1982.
95. Ibid., 23 June 1982.
96. Ibid., 16 June 1982; also Moscow Domestic Service in Russian 1100 GMT, 15 June 1982, Daily Report (USSR), 17 June 1982; TASS in English 1203 GMT, 15 June 1982, Daily Report (USSR), 17 June 1982.
97. Moscow *Pravda,* 3 June 1982.
98. *Voprosy Istorii KPSS,* no. 5, May 1982, p. 160.
99. Prague *Rude Pravo,* 29 May 1982.
100. Moscow *Pravda,* 3 June 1982.
101. Ibid., 1 June 1982.
102. Ibid., 27 June 1982.
103. Ibid., 22, 23, 24 June 1982.
104. Ibid., 1 June 1982.
105. Ibid., 23 June 1982.
106. Ibid., 22, 23, 24 June 1982.
107. Moscow Domestic Service in Russian 1000 GMT, 18 June 1982, Daily Report (USSR), 21 June 1982.
108. Moscow *Trud,* 26 June 1982.
109. *Sovetskaya Rossiya,* 17 June 1982.
110. Moscow Domestic Service in Russian 0900 GMT, 4 June 1982, Daily Report (USSR), 8 June 1982.
111. Moscow Domestic Service in Russian 1230 GMT, 23 July 1982, Daily Report (USSR), 28 July 1982.
112. Solovyov and Klepikova, *Yuri Andropov,* p. 191ff; also Jonathan Steele and Eric Abraham, *Andropov in Power* (Garden City, N.Y.: Anchor Press/ Doubleday, 1984), pp. 148–149.
113. Moscow *Pravda,* 27 September 1982; Moscow Domestic Television "Vremya" program 1700 GMT, 26 September 1982; also Zhores Medvedev, *Andropov* (New York: Norton, 1983), pp. 16–17.
114. *Zarya Vostoka,* 4 May 1982.
115. On 31 August 1982 Andropov and other leaders greeted Brezhnev at Moscow's Vnukovo Airport on Brezhnev's return from the Crimea where he had spent his summer holiday. The ceremony was carried by Moscow Domestic Television "Vremya" program at 1700 GMT, 31 August and by Moscow Domestic Service in Russian 0930 GMT, 31 August 1982, Daily Report (USSR), 31 August 1982 and 1 September 1982.

116. Moscow *Krasnaya Zvezda,* 28 October 1982.

117. Moscow Domestic Service in Russian 1800 GMT, 14 October 1982, Daily Report (USSR), 15 October 1982.

118. Ibid.

119. Moscow TASS in English 1152 GMT, 27 October 1983, Daily Report (USSR), 27 October 1982; also Moscow Domestic Television in Russian 1400 GMT, 27 October 1982, Daily Report (USSR), 28 October 1982.

120. Moscow Domestic Service in Russian 1600 GMT, 29 October 1982, Daily Report (USSR), 1 November 1982.

121. Moscow Domestic Service in Russian 0938 GMT, 2 November 1982, Daily Report (USSR), 2 November 1982.

122. Alexander Rahr, "A Bibliographic Directory of 100 Leading Soviet Officials," *Radio Liberty Research Bulletin,* Munich, August 1982, p. 215.

123. Moscow Domestic Service in Russian 0938 GMT, 2 November 1982, Daily Report (USSR), 2 November 1982.

124. Moscow Domestic Television in Russian 1355 GMT, 5 November 1982, Daily Report (USSR), 8 November 1982.

125. Ibid.

126. Moscow Domestic Television in Russian 1600 GMT, 5 November 1982, Daily Report (USSR), 8 November 1982.

127. Moscow Domestic Television in Russian 0650 GMT, 7 November 1982, Daily Report (USSR), 8 November 1982.

128. Ibid.

129. Paris AFP in English 0805 GMT, 7 November 1982, Daily Report (USSR), 8 November 1982.

130. Moscow Domestic Service in Russian 1030 GMT, 7 November 1982, Daily Report (USSR), 8 November 1982.

131. Moscow TASS in English 1106 GMT, 7 November 1982, Daily Report (USSR), 8 November 1982.

132. Moscow Domestic Television in Russian 0800 GMT, 11 November 1982, Daily Report (USSR), 11 November 1982.

Chapter 3

1. Moscow *Pravda,* 13 November 1982.

2. Zhores Medvedev, *Andropov* (New York: Norton, 1983), pp. 20–21.

3. Ilya Zemtsov, *Andropov* (Jerusalem: Irices Publishes, 1983), p. 241.

4. Ibid., p. 94.

5. Moscow Domestic Service in Russian 1600 GMT, 12 November 1982, Daily Report (USSR), 15 November 1982.

6. Moscow Domestic Television in Russian 1345 GMT, 12 November 1982, Daily Report (USSR), 15 November 1982.

7. Moscow Domestic Television in Russian 0930 GMT, 14 November 1982, Daily Report (USSR), 15 November 1982.

8. Moscow Domestic Television in Russian 0725 GMT, 15 November 1982, Daily Report (USSR), 15 November 1982.

9. See Jerry F. Hough, "Soviet Succession: Issues and Personalities," *Problems of Communism,* September-October 1982, p. 31.

10. Moscow *Pravda,* 13 November 1982.

11. Myron Rush, "Succeeding Brezhnev," *Problems of Communism,* January-February 1983, p. 6.

12. Ibid.

13. Zemtsov, *Andropov,* p. 95.

14. Ibid.

15. Moscow *Pravda,* 13 November 1982.

16. Ibid.

17. Ibid.

18. Moscow Domestic Service in Russian 0901 GMT, 15 November 1982, Daily Report (USSR), 15 November 1982.

19. Moscow Domestic Service in Russian 0910 GMT, 15 November 1982, Daily Report (USSR), 15 November 1982.

20. Ibid.

21. Moscow Domestic Service in Russian 0919 GMT, 15 November 1982, Daily Report (USSR), 15 November 1982.

22. Moscow Domestic Television in Russian 0725 GMT, 15 November 1982, Daily Report (USSR), 15 November 1982.

23. Tbilisi *Zarya Vostoka,* 30 October 1982, Daily Report (USSR), 9 November 1982.

24. Moscow *Pravda,* 13 November 1982.

25. The bibliographical data on Andropov included in this chapter are taken from Alexander G. Rahr, "A Biographical Directory of 100 Leading Soviet Officials," *Radio Liberty Research Bulletin,* Munich, 1981, pp. 7–9.

26. Archie Brown, "Andropov: Discipline *and* Reform," *Problems of Communism,* January-February 1983, p. 21.

27. Ibid.

28. Ibid., p. 24.

29. Rahr, "Biographical Directory" (1981), p. 172.

30. Ibid., p. 173.

31. Moscow *Pravda,* 3 March 1964.

32. A. Rahr, "A Biographical Directory of 100 Leading Soviet Officials," *Radio Liberty Research Builletin,* Munich, 1984, p. 14.

33. Ibid.

34. Otto Kuusinen, *Osnovy Marksizma-Leninizma* (Moscow: Partizdat, 1960).

35. Moscow *Pravda,* 17 November 1982.

36. CPSU Central Committee Plenum Communique, Moscow TASS in English 1606 GMT, 22 November 1982, Daily Report (USSR), 22 November 1982.

37. Ibid.

38. Moscow Domestic Service in Russian 0930 GMT, 31 August 1982, Daily Report (USSR), 31 August 1982.

39. CPSU Central Committee Plenum Communique, 22 November 1982.

40. Rahr, "Biographical Directory" (1984), pp. 9–10.

41. Ibid., p. 52.

42. Jerry F. Hough, "Andropov's First Year," *Problems of Communism,* November-December 1983, p. 58.

43. Moscow Domestic Service in Russian 1330 GMT, 24 November 1982, Daily Report (USSR), 24 November 1982.

44. Moscow TASS in English 1339 GMT, 24 November 1982, Daily Report (USSR), 24 November 1982.

45. Moscow TASS in English 1540 GMT, 24 November 1982, Daily Report (USSR), 24 November 1982.

46. "On the Draft USSR Law on the USSR State Border," report by Deputy V. V. Fedorchuk, chairman of the USSR KGB, Moscow *Izvestiya,* 25 November 1982.

47. Tbilisi *Zarya Vostoka,* 18 November 1982.

48. Ibid, 20–21 October 1982.

49. Kiev *Pravda Ukrainy,* 30 November 1982.

50. Frunze *Sovetskaya Kirgiziya,* 3 December 1982.

51. Alma-Ata *Kazakhstanskaya Pravda,* 1 December 1982.

52. Leningrad *Leningradskaya Pravda,* 4 December 1982.

53. Moscow *Pravda,* 24 November 1982.

54. Minsk *Sovetskaya Belorussiya,* 3 December 1982.

55. Riga *Sovetskaya Latviya,* 3 December 1982.

56. Frunze *Sovetskaya Kirgiziya,* 3 December 1982.

57. Ibid.

58. Leningrad *Leningradskaya Pravda,* 4 December 1982.

59. Moscow Domestic Service in Russian 1530 GMT, 31 January 1983, Daily Report (USSR), 1 February 1983.

60. Moscow TASS in English 1557 GMT, 17 December 1982, Daily Report (USSR), 20 December 1982.

61. Ibid.

62. Moscow TASS in English 1526 GMT, 16 December 1982, Daily Report (USSR), 16 December 1982.

63. Moscow Domestic Service in Russian 0930 GMT, 13 January 1983, Daily Report (USSR), 13 January 1983.

64. Rahr, "Biographical Directory" (1981), p. 97.

65. Moscow Domestic Service in Russian 0930 GMT, 13 January 1983, Daily Report (USSR), 13 January 1983.

66. Moscow *Pravda,* 16 October 1980.

67. Ibid., 20 April 1982.

68. First announcement: Moscow TASS International Service in Russian, 1555 GMT, 24 March 1983, Daily Report (USSR), 24 March 1983; text of the decree in Moscow *Pravda,* 26 March 1983.

69. Tikhonov talks in Yugoslavia, reported by *Pravda,* 23 March 1983.

70. Moscow *Pravda,* 7 March 1983.

71. Ibid., 10 July 1983.

72. Moscow TASS in English 1519 GMT, 11 April 1983, Daily Report (USSR), 12 April 1983.

73. Moscow Domestic Service in Russian 1500 GMT, 29 April 1983, Daily Report (USSR), 3 May 1983.

74. Rahr, "Biographical Directory" (1984), p. 126.

75. Stockholm *Dagens Nyhetter,* 27 February 1983, Daily Report (USSR), 4 March 1983.

76. Moscow *Pravda,* 4 December 1982.

77. Ibid., 9 December, 1982.

78. Ibid., 11 December 1982.

79. Ibid., 22 December 1982.

80. Moscow Domestic Television "Vremya" program 1400 GMT, 5 January 1983, Daily Report (USSR), 5 January 1983.

81. K. Chernenko, "Sixty Years of Peoples' Fraternal Friendship," *Problemy Mira i Sotsializma,* no. 12, December 1982, pp. 21–28.

82. Moscow *Izvestiya,* 24 November 1982.

83. Moscow *Pravda,* 28 December 1982.

84. Prague *Rude Pravo,* 5 January 1983.

85. Moscow *Pravda,* 18 January 1983.

86. Ibid., 30 January 1983.

87. *Voprosy Istorii Kpss,* no. 1, January 1983, pp. 21–28.

88. Ibid., p. 28.

89. Moscow Domestic Television in Russian 1300 GMT, 4 April 1983, Daily Report (USSR), 8 April 1983.

90. "Strengthening Ties With the Masses," *Pravda,* 24 May 1983.

91. Moscow *Pravda,* 19 April 1984.

92. Moscow Domestic Television in Russian 0545 GMT, 1 May 1983, Daily Report (USSR), 2 May 1983.

93. Rome Italian National Press Agency (ANSA) in English 1510 GMT, 29 April 1983, Daily Report (USSR), 2 May 1983.

94. Paris AFP in English 1806 GMT, 1 May 1983, Daily Report (USSR), 2 May 1983.

95. Paris AFP in English 0753 GMT, 11 May 1983, Daily Report (USSR), 11 May 1983.

96. Moscow *Pravda* in Russian, 2 June 1983.

97. *International Herald Tribune,* 27 April 1983.

98. Moscow *Pravda,* 13 November 1983.

99. Ibid.

100. Editorial, "Herein Lies Our Strength," *Kommunist,* no. 18, December 1982, pp. 5–15.

101. A. Sovokin, "Ilich's Great Feat: On the 60th Anniversary of V. I. Lenin's Last Words," *Pravda,* 21 January 1983.

102. V. Chikin, "January Monologue," *Sovetskaya Rossiya,* 21 January 1983.

103. V. Chikin, "V. I. Lenin: 'These Are the Lofty Tasks of Which I Am Dreaming . . . ,'" *Kommunist,* no. 6, April 1983, pp. 48–57.

104. Rahr, "Biographical Directory" (1984), p. 73.

105. Moscow *Pravda,* 22, 23 December 1982.

106. Ibid., 8 January 1983.

107. Moscow *Krasnaya Zvezda,* 13 April 1983.

108. Moscow *Pravda,* 20 March 1983.

109. Ibid, 19 April 1983.

110. Moscow Domestic Service in Russian 1500 GMT, 22 April 1983, Daily Report (USSR), 22 April 1983.

111. Moscow *Pravda,* 23 April 1983.

112. See Toronto *Star,* 18 May 1983; Toronto *Globe and Mail,* 18, 19 May, and elsewhere.

113. Michel Tatu, "Mr. Andropov's Difficulties," Paris *Le Monde,* 19 April 1983.

Chapter 4

1. *International Herald Tribune,* 27 April 1983.

2. Moscow *Pravda,* 9 May 1983.

3. A. Rahr, "A Biographical Directory of 100 Leading Soviet Officials," *Radio Liberty Research Bulletin,* Munich, 1981, p. 160.

4. Moscow TASS in English 1528 GMT, 10 June 1983, Daily Report (USSR), 13 June 1983.

5. Moscow TASS in English 1136 GMT, 14 June 1983, Daily Report (USSR), 15 June 1983.

6. Moscow *Pravda,* 15 June 1983.

7. Moscow TASS in English 1605 GMT, 15 June 1983, Daily Report (USSR), 16 June 1983.

8. Moscow *Pravda,* 16 June 1983.

9. Ibid.

10. Ibid.

11. Moscow TASS in English 1223 GMT, 15 June 1983, Daily Report (USSR), 15 June 1983.

12. *Ogonek* (no. 42, October 1981, p. 6) carries a laudatory article by Medunov on a book by Chernenko. Shchelokov worked under Brezhnev and Chernenko in Moldavia in the 1950s.

13. Moscow *Pravda,* 18 December 1982.

14. Hamburg *Der Spiegel,* 20 June 1983, pp. 100–101.

15. Moscow Domestic Service in Russian 0800 GMT, 16 June 1983, Daily Report (USSR), 16 June 1983.

16. Ibid.

17. Moscow Domestic Television in Russian 1030 GMT, 16 June 1983, Daily Report (USSR), 16 June 1983.

18. Moscow Domestic Service in Russian 0800 GMT, 16 June 1983, Daily Report (USSR), 16 June 1983.

19. Ibid.

20. Mainz ZDF Television Network in German 1900 GMT, 5 July 1983, also 1100 GMT, 6 July 1983, Daily Report (USSR), 7 July 1983.

21. Moscow Domestic Television in Russian 1445 GMT, 6 July 1983, Daily Report (USSR), 7 July 1983.

22. Ibid.

23. Moscow Domestic Service in Russian 1730 GMT, 19 July 1983, Daily Report (USSR), 20 July 1983.

24. Moscow Domestic Service in Russian 1500 GMT, 9 July 1983, Daily Report (USSR), 12 July 1983.

25. Moscow *Pravda,* 10 July 1983.

26. Ibid.

27. *Leningradskaya Pravda,* 22 June 1983.

28. Moscow TASS in English 1322 GMT, 29 July 1983, Daily Report (USSR), 1 August 1983.

29. Moscow TASS in English 1538 GMT, 29 July 1983, Daily Report (USSR), 1 August 1983.

30. Moscow *Pravda,* 30 July 1983.

31. Ibid., 18 August 1983.

32. Ibid., 19 August 1983.

33. Ibid., 16 August 1983.

34. Ibid.

35. Ibid.

36. Ibid., 30 October 1983.

37. Moscow TASS in English 1645 GMT, 17 November 1983.

38. Intermediate-Range Nuclear Forces Negotiations, which opened in Geneva in February 1983 to discuss the limitation of nuclear missile deployment in Europe.

39. Moscow *Pravda,* 27 October 1983.

40. Moscow *Izvestiya,* 27 October 1983.

41. Moscow TASS in English 1800 GMT, 26 October 1983, Daily Report (USSR), 27 October 1983.

42. Moscow Domestic Service in Russian 1800 GMT, 26 October 1983, Daily Report (USSR), 27 October 1983.

43. Moscow Domestic Television in Russian 1800 GMT and 2000 GMT, 26 October 1983, Daily Report (USSR), 27 October 1983.

44. Moscow TASS International Service in Russian 1628 GMT, 19 December 1983, Daily Report (USSR), 21 December 1983.

45. Moscow in Serbo-Croatian to Yugoslavia 2000 GMT, 22 December 1983, Daily Report (USSR), 28 December 1983.

46. Moscow Domestic Television in Russian 1355 GMT, 5 November 1983, Daily Report (USSR), 7 November 1983.

47. Moscow Domestic Service in Russian 0645 GMT, 7 November 1983, Daily Report (USSR), 7 November 1983.

48. Moscow Domestic Service in Russian 1100 GMT, 7 November 1983, Daily Report (USSR), 7 November 1983.

49. Paris AFP in English 1335 GMT, 21 October 1983, Daily Report (USSR), 24 October 1983.

50. Belgrade Tanjug in English 1604 GMT, 6 November 1983, Daily Report (USSR), 7 November 1983.

51. Helsinki International Service in English 1600 GMT, 7 November 1983, Daily Report (USSR), 8 November 1983.

52. *Moskovskaya Pravda,* 23 November 1983.

53. Hamburg DRA in German 1456 GMT, 3 December 1983, Daily Report (USSR), 5 December 1983.

54. London *Daily Express,* 17 November 1983.

55. Moscow *Pravda,* 29 September 1983, "Statement by Yuriy Vladimirovich Andropov, General Secretary of the CPSU Central Committee and Chairman of the Presidium of the Supreme Soviet."

56. Moscow *Pravda,* 25 November 1983, "Statement of Yuriy Vladimirovich Andropov, General Secretary of the CPSU Central Committee and Chairman of the USSR Supreme Soviet Presidium,"

57. K. Chernenko, "The Cause of the Entire Party, the Duty of Every Communist," *Kommunist,* no. 15, October 1985, pp. 18–34.

58. K. Chernenko, "Ideology of Revolutionary Construction and Peace," *Problemy Mira i Sotsializma,* no. 11, November 1983, pp. 4–11.

59. Warsaw *Trybuna Ludu,* 3 November 1983.

60. Prague Domestic Service in Czech 1730 GMT, 19 October 1983, Daily Report (USSR), 21 October 1983.

61. Moscow *Pravda,* 27 October 1983.

62. Ibid., 2 December 1983.

63. Ibid., 20 December 1983.

64. Moscow *Izvestiya,* 15 November 1983.

65. Ibid.

66. Moscow TASS in English 1519 GMT, 11 April 1983, Daily Report (USSR), 12 April 1983.

67. Tokyo *Asahi Shimbun,* 13 November 1983.
68. Moscow *Literaturnaya Gazeta,* 23 November 1983.
69. Moscow *Pravda,* 28 October 1983.
70. Ibid., 19 November 1983.
71. Ibid., 22 November 1983.
72. Dusko Doder, "Soviet Military Seen Taking Stronger Role in Political Affairs," *Washington Post,* 13 November 1983.
73. Gary Thatcher, "Soviet Policy Bears a Military Stamp," *Christian Science Monitor,* 28 November 1983.
74. Vienna Austrian Radio and Television Service (ORF) Teletext in German 1834 GMT, 21 October 1983, Daily Report (USSR), 24 October 1983.
75. Moscow *Izvestiya,* 20 April 1979.
76. Marc Zlotnik, "Chernenko Succeeds," *Problems of Communism,* March-April 1984, p. 22.
77. Moscow *Pravda,* 15 January 1984.
78. Ibid., 8 January 1984.
79. Moscow Domestic Service in Russian 1600 GMT, 9 January 1984, Daily Report (USSR), 10 January 1984.
80. Moscow *Pravda,* 3 December 1983.
81. Ibid., 31 January 1984.
82. Ibid., 5 January 1984.
83. Zlotnik, "Chernenko Succeeds," p. 22.
84. Moscow *Pravda,* 27 October 1983.
85. Ibid., 15 December 1983.
86. Ibid.
87. Ibid., 17 December 1983.
88. Ibid., 27 December 1983.
89. Ibid.
90. Rahr, "Biographical Directory" (1984), p. 205.
91. Moscow Domestic Television in Russian 1130 GMT, 28 December 1983, Daily Report (USSR), 29 December 1983.
92. Moscow *Izvestiya,* 30 December 1983.
93. Moscow in Serbo-Croatian to Yugoslavia 2000 GMT, 22 December 1983, Daily Report (USSR), 28 December 1983.
94. Moscow *Krasnaya Zvezda,* 7 January 1984.
95. Moscow *Pravda,* 13 January 1984.
96. Ibid., 20 January 1984.
97. Moscow *Selskaya Zhizn,* 29 January 1984.
98. Moscow *Izvestiya,* 4 February 1984.
99. Moscow Domestic Television in Russian 1400 GMT, 12 January 1984, Daily Report (USSR), 13 January 1984.
100. Moscow *Pravda,* 16 January 1984.
101. Moscow *Pravda,* 25 January 1984.
102. Ibid., 23 January 1984.
103. *New York Times,* 25 December 1983.

Chapter 5

1. Archie Brown, "Gorbachev: New Man in the Kremlin," *Problems of Communism,* March-June 1985, p. 5.

2. Moscow *Izvestiya,* 20 January 1984.

3. Ibid., 21 January 1984.

4. Moscow *Pravda,* 5 February 1984.

5. Ibid., 3 February 1984.

6. Moscow Domestic Television in Russian 1130 GMT, 10 February 1984, Daily Report (USSR), 11 February 1984.

7. Moscow *Pravda,* 11 February 1984.

8. Ibid.

9. Ibid.

10. Moscow *Krasnaya Zvezda,* 11 February 1984.

11. Ibid., 13 November 1982.

12. Moscow Domestic Television in Russian 1237 GMT, 11 February 1984, Daily Report (USSR), 12 February 1984.

13. Ibid.

14. Moscow *Pravda* and *Izvestiya* were among the newspapers of 12 February that carried the clearly doctored photographs.

15. Moscow Domestic Television in Russian 1237 GMT, 11 February 1984, Daily Report (USSR), 12 February 1984.

16. Moscow *Pravda,* 11 February 1984.

17. Ibid., 13 February 1984.

18. Moscow *Sovetskaya Rossiya,* 13 February 1984.

19. Ibid., 21 January 1984.

20. "Communique of the Plenary Meeting of the CPSU Central Committee," *New Times,* no. 8, February 1984, p. 2.

21. Ibid.

22. Ibid.

23. "Speech of Nikolay Tikhonov, member of the CPSU Central Committee Political Bureau and chairman of the USSR Council of Ministers," *New Times,* no. 8, February 1984, p. 6.

24. Ibid., p. 7.

25. Moscow *Pravda,* 13 November 1984.

26. "Speech of Konstantin Ustinovich Chernenko, general secretary of the CPSU Central Committee," *New Times,* no. 8, February 1984, p. 6.

27. "Speech of Mikhail Gorbachev, Political Bureau Member and Secretary of the CPSU Central Committee," *New Times,* no. 8, February 1984, p. 7.

28. See the doctored photo in Moscow *Pravda,* 12 February 1984.

29. Moscow Domestic Television "Vremya" program in Russian 1400 GMT, 13 February 1984; also photographs in all Soviet dailies of 14 February 1984.

30. Moscow Domestic Television in Russian 0700 GMT, 14 February 1984; also Moscow *Pravda,* 15 February 1984.

31. Ibid.

32. Moscow TASS in English 1510 GMT, 2 March 1984, Daily Report (USSR), 5 March 1984.

33. "Speech of Mikhail Gorbachev, Political Bureau Member and Secretary of the CPSU Central Committee," *New Times,* no. 8, February 1984, p. 7.

34. Rahr, "Biographical Directory" (1984), p. 38.

35. "Speech of Konstantin Ustinovich Chernenko, general secretary of the CPSU Central Committee," *New Times,* no. 8, February 1984, p. 6.

36. Rahr, "Biographical Directory" (1984), p. 37.

37. Ibid., p. 37.

38. *Directory of Soviet Officials: National Organizations* (Washington, D.C.: National Technical Information Service [NTIS], November 1984), p. 23.

39. Moscow *Pravda,* 31 May 1985.

40. Ibid., 22 February 1984.

41. Ibid.

42. Christian Schmidt Hauer, *Michail Gorbatschow* (Zurich: Piper, 1985), p. 117.

43. Moscow *Pravda,* 19 February 1984.

44. Ibid., 15 March 1984.

45. Ibid., 23 February 1984.

46. *Leningradskaya Pravda,* 26 February 1984.

47. Moscow *Pravda,* 23 February 1984.

48. Ibid., 19 February 1984.

49. Moscow Domestic Service in Russian 1447 GMT, 1 March 1984, Daily Report (USSR), 2 March 1984. Also Moscow *Pravda,* 2 March 1984.

50. Moscow *Pravda,* 24 February 1984.

51. Moscow Domestic Service in Russian 1447 GMT, 1 March 1984, Daily Report (USSR), 2 March 1984.

52. Moscow *Pravda,* 26 February 1984.

53. Moscow *Izvestiya,* 1 March 1984.

54. Beijing *Xinhua* in English 0247 GMT, 26 February 1984, Daily Report (USSR), 27 February 1984.

55. Moscow *Pravda,* 6 April 1984.

56. Ibid., 11 April 1984; also *Partiynaya Zhizn,* no. 8, April 1984, p. 3.

57. Moscow *Pravda,* 11 April 1984.

58. Moscow TASS in English 0816 GMT, 11 April 1984, Daily Report (USSR), 11 April 1984.

59. Moscow TASS in English 1400 GMT, 11 April 1984, Daily Report (USSR), 11 April 1984.

60. Ibid.

61. Ibid.

62. Moscow Domestic Service in Russian 1500 GMT, 11 April 1984, Daily Report (USSR), 12 April 1984.

63. Moscow TASS in English 1354 GMT, 11 April 1984, Daily Report (USSR), 11 April 1984.

64. Moscow *Izvestiya,* 14 April 1984.

65. Moscow Domestic Service in Russian 1500 GMT, 11 April 1984, Daily Report (USSR), 12 April 1984.

66. Moscow *Pravda,* 24 April 1984.

67. Ibid., 25 April 1984.

68. Ibid., 29 April 1984.

69. Moscow *Krasnaya Zvezda,* 10 April 1984.

70. Moscow *Pravda,* 27 March 1984.

71. Ibid., 30 April 1984.

72. Ibid., 26 April 1984.

73. Ibid., 30 April 1984.

74. Ibid., 3 March 1984.

75. Ibid.,. 30 April 1984.

76. Moscow *Krasnaya Zvezda,* 22 February 1984.

77. Ibid., 23 February 1984.

78. Moscow *Pravda,* 10 March 1984.

79. Ibid., 29 April 1984.

Chapter 6

1. Beijing *Xinhua* in English 0247 GMT, 26 February 1984, Daily Report (USSR), 27 February 1984.
2. Moscow Domestic Service in Russian 0442 GMT, 9 May 1984, Daily Report (USSR), 10 May 1984.
3. Ye. Bugayev, "Unity, Organization, Discipline," *Kommunist,* no. 6, April 1984, p. 52.
4. Ibid., p. 53.
5. Ibid., p. 54.
6. Ibid., p. 55.
7. Ibid., p. 55.
8. Ibid., p. 56.
9. Ibid., p. 58.
10. Ibid., p. 59.
11. Ibid., p. 62.
12. Ibid., p. 63.
13. V. Chikin, "We Go to Lenin," *Kommunist,* no. 6, April 1984, p. 72.
14. Ibid., p. 73.
15. Ibid., p. 74.
16. Ibid., p. 76.
17. Editorial, "CPSU Activity in the Building of Developed Socialism in the Sixties," *Voprosy Istorii,* no. 4, April 1984, pp. 3–14.
18. Baku *Bakinskiy Rabochiy,* 2 May 1984.
19. Minsk *Byelorusskaya Pravda,* 2 May 1984.
20. *Directory of Soviet Officials: National Organizations* (Washington, D.C.: NTIS, November 1984), p. 59.
21. Ibid., p. 75.
22. Moscow *Krasnaya Zvezda,* 29 May 1984.
23. Moscow *Krasnaya Zvezda,* 27 May 1984. The issue also carried an article by Lt. Gen. I. Vertelko, first deputy chief of the USSR KGB Border Guards, which stated: "Comrade K. U. Chernenko maintains his ties with the border forces to this day, despite being extremely busy." The article also mentions Chernenko's greetings message. Moscow Domestic Service in Russian 0800 GMT, 27 May 1984, Daily Report (USSR), 31 May 1984, carried an interview with a soldier from Chernenko's border guard unit, in which Chernenko's military record was also recalled.
24. Moscow *Krasnaya Zvezda,* 29 May 1984.
25. Moscow TASS in English 0715 GMT, 12 June 1984, Daily Report (USSR), 12 June 1984.
26. Moscow TASS in English 1702 GMT, 11 June 1984, Daily Report (USSR), 12 June 1984.
27. Moscow *Pravda,* 13 March 1984.
28. Ibid., 15 June 1984.
29. Moscow *Sovetskaya Rossiya,* 23 May 1984.
30. Ibid.
31. Moscow *Sovetskaya Rossiya,* 21 January 1983.
32. Ibid., 22 April 1984.

33. Moscow Domestic Television in Russian 1430 GMT, 4 July 1984, Daily Report (USSR), 5 July 1984.

34. Moscow Domestic Service in Russian 1000 GMT, 13 July 1984, Daily Report (USSR), 13 July 1984.

35. Moscow *Pravda,* 16 August 1984.

36. Moscow *Krasnaya Zvezda,* 3 August 1984.

37. Moscow *Pravda,* 13 August 1984.

38. *London Times,* 1 September 1984.

39. Ibid.

40. Moscow TASS in English 1705 GMT, 13 July 1984, Daily Report (USSR), 23 July 1984. Also Moscow *Pravda,* 21 July, 28 July, 4 August, and 25 August 1984.

41. Moscow *Pravda,* 25 August 1984.

42. Moscow Domestic Service in Russian 1000 GMT, 31 August 1984, Daily Report (USSR), 31 August 1984.

43. Moscow *Pravda,* 2 September 1984.

44. Ibid., 31 August 1984.

45. Moscow World Service in English 1202 GMT, 5 September 1984, Daily Report (USSR), 5 September 1984.

46. Moscow Domestic Television in Russian 1700 GMT, 5 September 1984, Daily Report (USSR), 6 September 1984.

47. Ibid., 1430 GMT, 6 September 1984, Daily Report (USSR), 7 Septembrr 1984.

48. Ibid., 0855 GMT, 7 September 1984, Daily Report (USSR), 7 September 1984.

49. Moscow *Krasnaya Zvezda,* 3 August 1984, commentary by Yuriy Kornilov, "Pertinent Notes: A Strange Awareness."

50. Moscow Domestic Television in Russian 1700 GMT, 25 August 1984, commentary by Yevgeniy Grigoriyev, deputy editor in chief of *Pravda,* Daily Report (USSR), 27 August 1984.

51. Moscow Domestic Service in Russian 1500 GMT, 21 July 1984, Daily Report (USSR), 23 July 1984.

52. Moscow *Pravda,* 29 August 1984.

53. East Berlin *Neues Deutschland,* 5 September 1984.

54. Sofia *Rabotnichesko Delo,* 9 September 1984.

55. Ibid.

56. Moscow TASS International Service in Russian 1702 GMT, 6 September 1984, Daily Report (USSR), 7 September 1984..

57. Moscow *Krasnaya Zvezda,* 6 September 1984.

58. Moscow *Pravda,* 7 September 1984.

59. Moscow TASS in English 0629 GMT, 5 September 1984, Daily Report (USSR), 5 September 1984.

60. Moscow Domestic Television (in Russian 1430 GMT, 6 September 1984, Daily Report (USSR), 7 September 1984) included a report on Kunayev speaking in Pavlodan, Petropavlovsk, and Kokchetav.

61. Moscow Domestic Television in Russian 1430 GMT, 6 September 1984, Daily Report (USSR), 7 September 1984.

62. Moscow *Pravda,* 5 September 1984.

63. Moscow *Krasnaya Zvezda,* 5 September 1984.

64. Moscow TASS in English 1510 GMT, 2 March 1984, Daily Report (USSR), 5 March 1984.

65. Moscow *Pravda,* 30 April 1984.

66. The message was read by Chernenko at 1600 GMT and disseminated by TASS in English at 1716 GMT, 21 September 1984, Daily Report (USSR), 24 September 1984.

67. Moscow *Pravda,* 24 September 1984.

68. Ibid.

69. Moscow Domestic Television in Russian 1700 GMT, 27 September 1984, Daily Report (USSR), 28 September 1984.

70. Ibid.

71. Ibid.

72. Moscow *Pravda,* 26 September 1984.

73. Moscow Domestic Television in Russian, 1700 GMT, 25 September 1984, Daily Report (USSR), 26 September 1984.

74. Ibid.

75. Ibid.

76. Moscow TASS in English 0722 GMT, 17 October 1984, Daily Report (USSR), 17 October 1984.

77. Moscow *Pravda,* 7 November 1984.

78. Moscow TASS in English 1759 GMT, 6 November 1984, Daily Report (USSR), 7 November 1984.

79. Moscow Domestic Service in Russian 1600 GMT, 26 October 1984; Moscow Domestic Television *"Vremya" program* in Russian 1800 GMT, 26 October 1984, Daily Report (USSR), 29 October 1984.

80. Moscow Domestic Television *"Vremya" program* in Russian 1800 GMT, 18 October 1984, Daily Report (USSR), 19 October 1984.

81. Moscow Domestic Service in Russian 1100 GMT, 19 April 1984, Daily Report (USSR), 20 April 1984.

82. Moscow *Pravda,* 16, 17, 18 October 1984.

83. Moscow *Krasnaya Zvezda,* 2 May 1980.

84. Ibid., 31 October 1984. Also Moscow Domestic Television in Russian 1800 GMT, 30 October 1984, Daily Report (USSR), 31 October 1984.

85. Moscow *Krasnaya Zvezda,* 1 December 1984.

86. Moscow *Pravda, Izvestiya, Krasnaya Zvezda,* 16 November 1984.

87. Ibid.

88. Moscow Domestic Service in Russian 1600 GMT, 15 November 1984; also Moscow Domestic Television in Russian 1800 GMT, 15 November 1984, Daily Report (USSR), 19 November 1984.

89. Moscow *Izvestiya,* 16 November 1984; Moscow Domestic Service in Russian 1800 GMT, 17 November 1984, Daily Report (USSR), 19 November 1984, reported Demichev's return to Moscow.

90. Moscow *Pravda,* 15 November 1984; Moscow Domestic Service in Russian 2030 GMT, 16 November 1984, Daily Report (USSR), 19 November 1984, reported Chebrikov's return to Moscow.

91. Moscow *Pravda,* 18 November 1984, carried the text of Chernenko's interview given to NBC reporter Marvin Kalb.

92. N. Ogarkov, "The Undimming Glory of the Soviet Weapons," *Kommunist Vooruzhennykh Sil,* no. 21, November 1984, pp. 16–26.

93. Ibid., p. 25.

94. Ibid., p. 26.

95. Moscow *Pravda,* 3 December 1984.

96. Moscow TASS in English 1207 GMT, 3 December 1984, Daily Report (USSR), 3 December 1984.

97. Moscow Domestic Television *"Vremya" program* in Russian 1530 GMT, 6 December 1984, Daily Report (USSR), 7 December 1984.

98. Moscow *Pravda,* 11 December 1984.

99. Ibid.

100. Moscow *Pravda,* 12 December 1984.

101. Moscow Domestic Television in Russian 1530 GMT, 15 December 1984, Daily Report (USSR), 17 December 1984.

102. London *Financial Times,* 22 December 1984.

103. Dennis Healey, "Gorbachev Face to Face," *Newsweek,* 25 March 1985, p. 15.

104. Moscow *Pravda,* 17 December 1984.

105. Ibid., 19 December 1984.

106. Ibid.

107. Paris AFP in Spanish 1215 GMT, 21 December 1984, Daily Report (USSR), 21 December 1984; also Moscow *Sovetskaya Rossiya,* 22 December 1984.

108. New York *New York Times,* 22 December 1984.

109. Moscow TASS in English 1808 GMT, 21 December 1984, Daily Report (USSR), 24 December 1984.

110. Moscow Domestic Television in Russian 1130 GMT, 22 December 1984, Daily Report (USSR), 24 December 1984.

111. Moscow Domestic Television in Russian 0928 GMT, 24 December 1984, Daily Report (USSR), 24 December 1984.

112. Moscow TASS in English 1303 GMT, 22 December 1984, Daily Report (USSR), 24 December 1984.

113. Belgrade *Tanjug* Domestic Service in Serbo-Croatian 2202 GMT, 2 December 1984, Daily Report (USSR), 3 December 1984.

114. Moscow *Krasnaya Zvezda,* 6 December 1984.

115. Moscow Domestic Service in Russian 1800 GMT, 21 December 1984, Daily Report (USSR), 24 December 1984.

116. Moscow Domestic Television in Russian 1001 GMT, 24 December 1984, Daily Report (USSR), 26 December 1984.

117. Moscow Domestic Television in Russian 1130 GMT, 22 December 1984, Daily Report (USSR), 24 December 1984.

118. Rahr, "Biographical Directory" (1984), p. 2.

119. Ibid., p. 113.

120. K. Chernenko, "On the Level of the Developed Socialism's Needs," *Kommunist,* no. 8, December 1984, p. 6.

121. Ibid., p. 9.

122. Ibid., p. 17.

123. Ibid., p. 18.

124. Different Moscow Domestic Service and Television casts on 19 December 1984, Daily Report (USSR), 20 December 1984. Also Moscow *Pravda,* 20 December 1984.

125. Moscow *Pravda,* 21 December 1984.

126. Ibid., 20 January 1985.

127. Ibid.

128. Moscow Domestic Service in Russian 1100 GMT, 27 December 1984, Daily Report (USSR), 27 December 1984.

129. Moscow *Selskaya Zhizn,* 8 February 1985. Moscow TASS in English (1810 GMT, 7 February 1985, Daily Report (USSR), 8 February 1985) included the same sentence. Interestingly, the sentence appeared yet again almost verbatim in a report on the 21 February Politburo meeting published by *Pravda* on 22 February 1984.

130. Moscow *Pravda,* 22 February 1985.
131. ibid., 19 February 1985.
132. Ibid., 12 February 1985.
133. Ibid., 19 February 1985.
134. Ibid., 14 February 1985.
135. Ibid., 16 February 1985.
136. Ibid., 15 February 1985.
137. Ibid., 20 February 1985.
138. Ibid., 10 February 1985.
139. Ibid., 2 February 1985.
140. Ibid.
141. Ibid., 7 February 1985.
142. Ibid., 21 February 1985.
143. Ibid.
144. Moscow Domestic Service in Russian 1800 GMT, 22 February 1985, Daily Report (USSR), 25 February 1985. Grishin also referred to Chernenko as "leader of the party, chairman of the Defense Council, and supreme commander-in-chief," according to Moscow Television 1800 GMT, 22 February 1985, Daily Report (USSR), 25 February 1985. On the following day, *Pravda,* in reporting Grishin's opening speech, omitted this reference.
145. *Newsweek,* 31 December 1984.
146. Moscow Domestic Television in Russian 1215 GMT, 24 February 1985, Daily Report (USSR), 25 February 1985.
147. Moscow Domestic Television in Russian 1800 GMT, 28 February 1985, Daily Report (USSR), 1 March 1985.

Chapter 7

1. Moscow Television Service in Russian 1100 GMT, 11 March 1985, Daily Report (USSR), 11 March 1985.
2. Moscow TASS International Service in Russian 1122 GMT, 11 March 1985, Daily Report (USSR), 11 March 1985.
3. Ibid., 1139 GMT, 11 March 1985, Daily Report (USSR), 11 March 1985.
4. Ibid., 1150 GMT, 11 March 1985, Daily Report (USSR), 11 March 1985.
5. Ibid., 1146 GMT, 11 March 1985, Daily Report (USSR), 11 March 1985.
6. Ibid., 1158 GMT, 11 March 1985, Daily Report (USSR), 11 March 1985.
7. Moscow TASS International Service in English 1250 GMT, 11 March 1985, Daily Report (USSR), 11 March 1985.
8. Moscow TASS International Service in Russian 1245 GMT, 11 March 1985, Daily Report (USSR), 11 March 1985.
9. Moscow TASS in English 1518 GMT, 11 March 1985, Daily Report (USSR), 11 March 1985.
10. "Ein Roter Star Steigt auf im Osten," *Der Spiegel,* no. 12, 1985, p. 155.
11. Moscow TASS in English 0753 GMT, 12 March 1985, Daily Report (USSR), 12 March 1985.

12. Ibid., 0752 GMT, 12 March 1985, Daily Report (USSR), 12 March 1985.

13. "Materialy Vneocherednogo Plenuma Tsentralnogo Komiteta KPSS" (Moscow: Partizdat, 1985), pp. 6–8; also *Kommunist,* no. 5, March 1985, pp. 6–7.

14. Gorbachev's speech at the 11 March Central Committee plenum in Moscow, *Pravda,* 12 March 1985.

15. "Materialy Vneocherednogo Plenuma Tsentralnogo Komiteta KPSS" (Moscow: Partizdat, 1985), p. 6.

16. "Information Report of the CPSU Central Committee Plenum," Moscow *Pravda,* 12 March 1985.

17. Moscow TASS in English 1045 GMT, 13 March 1985, Daily Report (USSR), 13 March 1985.

18. Ibid., 1128 GMT, 13 March 1985, Daily Report (USSR), 13 March 1985.

19. Ibid., 1045 GMT, 13 March 1985, Daily Report (USSR), 13 March 1985.

20. Moscow TASS International Service in Russian 1139 GMT, 11 March 1985, Daily Report (USSR), 11 March 1985.

21. Rahr, "A Biographic Survey of 100 Leading Soviet Officials," *Radio Liberty Research Bulletin,* Munich, August 1984, pp. 73–74.

22. Ibid., p. 73.

23. Ibid.

24. Moscow *Pravda,* 16 August 1983.

25. Seweryn Bialer, "Gorbachev to the Rescue: Big Job, Big Opportunities," *International Herald Tribune,* 20 March 1985.

26. *Directory of Soviet Officials: National Organizations* (Washington, D.C.: NTIS, November 1984), p. 11.

27. *Directory of Soviet Officials: National Organizations* (Washington, D.C.: NTIS, January 1985), p. 195.

28. Ibid., p. 25.

29. *Directory of Soviet Officials: National Organizations,* November 1984, p. 275.

30. Moscow *Pravda,* 11 December 1984.

31. Ibid., 12 March 1985.

32. Ibid., 19 December 1984.

33. Sofia *Rabotnichesko Delo,* 9 September 1984.

34. Ibid.

35. Tbilisi *Zarya Vostoka,* 27 November 1984.

36. Leningrad *Leningradskaya Pravda,* 27 January 1985.

37. Moscow *Pravda,* 13 January 1985.

38. Moscow *Izvestiya,* 5 March 1985.

39. Moscow *Pravda,* 2 February 1985.

40. Ibid., 21 February 1985.

41. Moscow *Moskovskaya Pravda,* 19 March 1985.

42. V. Shcherbitskiy, "The Real Democracy of the Soviet Society," *Kommunist,* no. 17, November 1984, p. 37.

43. Ibid., p. 42.

44. Moscow *Sovetskaya Rossiya,* 14 March 1985.

45. Ibid.

46. Ibid.

47. East Berlin Television Service in German 1830 GMT, 11 March 1985, Daily Report (USSR), 12 March 1985.

48. Warsaw Domestic Service in Polish 0600 GMT, 12 March 1985, Daily Report (USSR), 12 March 1985.

49. Budapest Domestic Service in Hungarian 1730 GMT, 11 March 1985, Daily Report (USSR), 12 March 1985.

50. "Resolution on the Election of the RSFSR Leading Bodies," Moscow *Sovetskaya Rossiya,* 27 March 1985.

51. Ibid.

52. Rahr, "Biographical Directory," 1984, p. 232.

53. "Information Report of the RSFSR Supreme Soviet Session," Moscow *Sovetskaya Rossiya,* 27 March 1985.

54. Moscow Television Service in Russian 1800 GMT, 25 March 1985, Daily Report (USSR), 26 March 1985.

55. Moscow Domestic Service in Russian 1000 GMT, 25 March 1985, Daily Report (USSR), 26 March 1985.

56. Moscow *Pravda,* 2 April 1985.

57. Ibid., 19 October 1984.

58. Ibid.

59. Ibid., 27 March 1985.

60. K. Chernenko, "On the Level of the Needs of Developed Socialism," *Kommunist,* no. 18, December 1984, p. 20.

61. Moscow Television Service in Russian, 1800 GMT, 12 February 1985, Daily Report (USSR), 13 February 1985.

62. Moscow *Pravda,* 16 February 1985.

63. Paris AFP in English 1035 GMT, 2 April 1985, Daily Report (USSR), 2 April 1985.

64. Moscow *Pravda,* 24 March 1985.

65. Moscow TASS in English 1651 GMT, 8 April 1985, Daily Report (USSR), 12 April 1985.

66. Ibid.

67. Moscow Domestic Service in Russian 1700 GMT, 11 April 1985, Daily Report (USSR), 12 April 1985.

68. Ibid.

69. Moscow *Pravda,* 12 April 1985.

70. Moscow *Krasnaya Zvezda, Pravda,* 18 April 1985.

71. Moscow *Krasnaya Zvezda,* 18 April 1984.

72. Moscow TASS in English 1823 GMT, 23 April 1985, Daily Report (USSR), 23 April 1985.

73. Moscow TASS in English 1613 GMT, 23 April 1985, Daily Report (USSR), 24 April 1985.

74. Moscow *Pravda,* 24 April 1985.

75. Ibid.

76. Ibid.

Chapter 8

1. Moscow Television Service in Russian 1055 GMT, 8 May 1985, Daily Report (USSR), 9 May 1985.

2. Ibid.

3. Sofia *Narodna Armiya,* 9 May 1985.

4. Moscow Television Service in Russian 1430 GMT, 16 May 1985, Daily Report (USSR), 17 May 1985.

5. Ibid., 1700 GMT, 16 May 1985, Daily Report (USSR), 17 May 1985.

6. Ibid., 1430 GMT, 16 May 1985, Daily Report (USSR), 17 May 1985.

7. Ibid.

8. Ibid.

9. Moscow *Pravda,* 17 May 1985.

10. Moscow Domestic Service in Russian 1800 GMT, 21 May 1985, Daily Report (USSR), 22 May 1985.

11. Moscow *Pravda,* 22 May 1985.

12. Moscow *Komsomolskaya Pravda,* 16 May 1985.

13. Moscow *Pravda,* 28 June 1985.

14. Georgiy Razumovskiy, "Decisive Unit of the Party Leadership," *Kommunist* no. 4, March 1984, pp. 27–39.

15. Ibid., pp. 28–29.

16. Editorial, "Checking Efficiency," Moscow *Sovetskaya Rossiya,* 19 April 1985.

17. Moscow *Pravda,* 4 June 1985.

18. Moscow Television Service in Russian 1030 GMT, 11 June 1985, Daily Report (USSR), 11 June 1985.

19. Moscow Television Service in Russian 1700 GMT, 11 June 1985, Daily Report (USSR), 12 June 1985.

20. Ibid.

21. Ibid.

22. Ibid.

23. Ibid.

24. Moscow *Pravda,* 15 July 1985.

25. Rahr, "A Biographic Directory" (1984), p. 52.

26. Moscow Television Service in Russian 1700 GMT, 25 June 1985, Daily Report (USSR), 26 June 1985.

27. Ibid., 1700 GMT, 26 June 1985, Daily Report (USSR), 27 June 1985.

28. Moscow TASS in English 1400 GMT, 11 April 1985, Daily Report (USSR), 11 April 1984.

29. Moscow TASS in English 1040 GMT, 1 July 1985, Daily Report (USSR), 1 July 1985.

30. Ibid.

31. Moscow TASS in English 1223 GMT, 15 June 1983, Daily Report (USSR), 15 June 1983.

32. *Leningradskaya Pravda,* 22 June 1983.

33. Frederick Kempe, "Gorbachev Acts to Install Key Allies Who Will Back His Economic Plans," *Wall Street Journal,* 16 October 1985.

34. Moscow TASS in English 0915 GMT, 2 July 1985, Daily Report (USSR), 2 July 1985.

35. Ibid.

36. Ibid.

37. Moscow Television Service in Russian 0830 GMT, 2 July 1985, Daily Report (USSR), 3 July 1985.

38. Moscow TASS in English 0708 GMT, 2 July 1985, Daily Report (USSR), 2 July 1985.

39. Moscow TASS In English 0938 GMT, 2 July 1985, Daily Report (USSR), 2 July 1985.

40. Moscow Domestic Service in Russian 1200 GMT, 2 July 1985, Daily Report (USSR), 3 July 1985.

41. Moscow TASS in English 0915 GMT, 2 July 1985, Daily Report (USSR), 2 July 1985.

42. Rahr, "Biographical Directory" (1984), p. 191.

43. Celestine Bohlen, "New Chief, Old Aides," *Washington Post,* 28 September 1985.

44. Ibid.

45. Moscow Domestic Service in Russian (1500 GMT, 3 October 1985, Daily Report (USSR), 4 October 1985) mentioned Aleksandrov-Agentov as a member of the Soviet delegation, which had a meeting with deputies of the French National Assembly.

46. Moscow Domestic Service in Russian 1600 GMT, 18 November 1985, Daily Report (USSR), 19 November 1985.

47. Moscow *Pravda,* 17 June 1985.

48. *Sobraniye Postanovleniy Pravitelstva SSSR,* no. 14, 1985, pp. 261–262, Daily Report (USSR), 11 June 1985.

49. *Politicheskoye Samoobrazovaniya* (no. 4, 1985, signed to press on 22 March 1985) listed Vadim Pechenev as deputy editor.

50. *Vedomosti Verkhovnogo Soveta SSSR,* 4 September 1985.

51. *Vedomosti Verkhovnogo Soveta RSFSR,* 5 September 1985.

52. Moscow *Pravda,* 7 May 1985.

53. Prague *Rude Pravo,* 8 August 1985, Daily Report (USSR), 13 August 1985.

54. Ibid.

55. Moscow *Pravda,* 11 July 1985.

56. Paris AFP in English 1303 GMT, 6 August 1985.

57. Ibid.

58. Ibid.

59. Hamburh DPA in German 1237 GMT, 1 August 1985, Daily Report (USSR), 1 August 1985.

60. Paris AFP in English 1511 GMT, 16 August 1985, Daily Report (USSR), 19 August 1985.

61. Moscow Television Service in Russian 1430 GMT, 24 September 1985, Daily Report (USSR), 26 September 1985.

62. *Tashkent Domestic Service* in Uzbek 0115 GMT, 25 September 1985, Daily Report (USSR), 26 September 1985.

63. Moscow *Pravda,* 28 September 1985.

64. Ibid.

65. Ibid.

66. Moscow Domestic Service in Russian 1230 GMT, 25 September 1985, Daily Report (USSR), 26 September 1985.

67. Moscow *Pravda,* 28 September 1985.

68. Moscow TASS in English 0729 GMT, 9 August 1985, Daily Report (USSR), 9 August 1985.

69. Moscow Domestic Service in Russian 1230 GMT, 9 August 1985, Daily Report (USSR), 12 August 1985.

70. Ibid.

71. Moscow *Pravda,* 30 June 1985.

72. Moscow Television Service in Russian 1700 GMT, 11 June 1985, Daily Report (USSR), 12 June 1985.

73. Moscow Television Service in Russian 1700 GMT, 13 September 1985, Daily Report (USSR), 16 September 1985.

74. Moscow Domestic Service in Russian 1500 GMT, 20 September 1985, Daily Report (USSR), 23 September 1985.
75. Moscow TASS in English 1746 GMT, 23 September 1985, Daily Report (USSR), 24 September 1985.
76. Moscow TASS International Service in Russian 1621 GMT, 24 September 1985, Daily Report (USSR), 26 September 1985.
77. Ibid., 1449 GMT, 16 September 1985, Daily Report (USSR), 17 September 1985.
78. Moscow *Pravda,* 4 September 1985.
79. Ibid., 4 October 1985.
80. Ibid.
81. Ibid.
82. *Time* magazine, 14 October 1985, p. 14.
83. Ibid.
84. Ibid.
85. Moscow Domestic Service in Russian 1500 GMT, 14 October 1985, Daily Report (USSR), 15 October 1985.
86. Ibid.
87. *Directory of Soviet Officials: National Organizations,* NTIS, p. 202.
88. Moscow Television Service in Russian 1700 GMT, 6 September 1985, Daily Report (USSR), 9 September 1985.
89. Rahr, "Biographical Directory" (1984), p. 210.
90. Ibid.
91. Moscow TASS in English 1209 GMT, 15 October 1985, Daily Report (USSR), 16 October 1985.
92. Ibid.
93. Moscow TASS International Service in Russian 1245 GMT, 15 October 1985, Daily Report (USSR), 16 October 1985.
94. Moscow Domestic Service in Russian 1200 GMT, 15 October 1985, Daily Report (USSR), 16 October 1985.
95. Ibid.
96. Ibid.
97. Editorial, "Program of Acceleration," Moscow *Izvestiya,* 17 October 1985.
98. Moscow TASS in English 1748 GMT, 19 October 1985, Daily Report (USSR), 21 October 1985.
99. Moscow Domestic Service in Russian 1500 GMT, 18 October 1985, Daily Report (USSR), 21 October 1985.
100. Paris AFP in English 1210 GMT, 20 October 1985, Daily Report (USSR), 21 October 1985.

Chapter 9

1. Moscow Domestic Service in Russian 1600 GMT, 1 November 1985, Daily Report (USSR), 4 November 1985.
2. Ibid., 1530 GMT, 2 November 1985, Daily Report (USSR), 4 November 1985.
3. Moscow TASS in English 1407 GMT, 3 November 1985, Daily Report (USSR), 4 November 1985.
4. Moscow Domestic Service in Russian 1500 GMT, 14 October 1985, Daily Report (USSR), 15 October 1985.

5. Ibid., 1100 GMT, 2 November 1985, Daily Report (USSR), 5 November 1985.

6. Moscow *Izvestiya,* 3 November 1985.

7. V. Murakhovskiy, "To Effectively Use the Potential of the Agro-Industrial Complex," *Partiynaya Zhizn,* no. 11, June 1985, pp. 43–48.

8. Ibid., p. 47.

9. Ibid., p. 48.

10. Moscow Television Service in Russian 1355 GMT, 6 November 1985, Daily Report (USSR), 7 November 1985.

11. Ibid., 0649 GMT, 7 November 1985, Daily Report (USSR), 8 November 1985.

12. Moscow *Pravda,* 8 November 1985.

13. Moscow Domestic Service in Russian 1400 GMT, 13 November 1985, Daily Report (USSR), 13 November 1985.

14. Moscow TASS in English 1916 GMT, 15 November 1985, Daily Report (USSR), 21 November 1985; also Moscow Television Service in Russian 1800 GMT, 15 November 1985, Daily Report (USSR), 19 November 1985.

15. Moscow TASS in English 1515 GMT, 16 November 1985, Daily Report (USSR), 19 November 1985.

16. Rahr, "Biographic Directory" (1984), p. 172.

17. Moscow *Pravda,* 2 October 1983.

18. Ibid., 7 November 1985.

19. Moscow TASS in English 1828 GMT, 14 November 1985, Daily Report (USSR), 15 November 1985.

20. Ibid., 1311 GMT, 22 November 1985, Daily Report (USSR), 25 November 1985.

21. Ibid.

22. Moscow TASS International Service in Russian 0749 GMT, 18 November 1985, Daily Report (USSR), National Affairs Supplement, 18 November 1985.

23. Ibid.

24. Ibid.

25. Paris AFP in English 1747 GMT, 18 November 1985, Daily Report (USSR), Supplement on Geneva Summit, 19 November 1985.

26. *Newsweek,* 18 November 1985, p. 11.

27. London BBC Television Network 2315 GMT, 21 November 1985, Daily Report (USSR), Supplement on Geneva Summit, 22 November 1985.

28. Moscow Television Service in Russian 1330 GMT, 21 November 1985, Daily Report (USSR), Supplement on Geneva Summit, 22 November 1985.

29. Moscow Television Service in Russian 1545 GMT, 20 November 1985, Daily Report (USSR), Supplement on Geneva Summit, 21 November 1985.

30. Moscow *Pravda,* 22 November 1985.

31. Moscow TASS in English 1805 GMT, 25 November 1985, Daily Report (USSR), 26 November 1985.

32. Moscow Television Service in Russian 0842 GMT, 27 November 1985, Daily Report (USSR), 29 November 1985.

33. "Resolution of the USSR Supreme Soviet on the Geneva Summit," Moscow TASS International Service in Russian 1407 GMT, 27 November 1985, Daily Report (USSR), 29 November 1985.

34. Moscow *Izvestiya,* 28 November 1985.

35. Ibid.

36. Moscow Domestic Service in Russian 1900 GMT, 5 December 1985, Daily Report (USSR), 6 December 1985.

37. Moscow Domestic Service in Russian 1500 GMT, 15 December 1985, Daily Report (USSR), National Affairs Supplement, 16 December 1985.

38. Paris AFP in English 0954 GMT, 11 December 1985, Daily Report (USSR), 11 December 1985.

39. Moscow Domestic Service in Russian 1600 GMT, 21 December 1985, Daily Report (USSR), National Affairs Supplement, 23 December 1985.

40. Ibid., 1830 GMT, 21 December 1985, Daily Report (USSR), National Affairs Supplement, 23 December 1985.

41. Paris AFP in English 1328 GMT, 15 December 1985, Daily Report (USSR), National Affairs Supplement, 16 December 1985.

42. Rahr, "Biographical Directory," 1984, p. 83.

43. *New York Times,* 25 December 1985.

44. Hamburg *Der Spiegel,* no. 3, January 1986, p. 111.

45. Moscow *Sovetskaya Rossiya,* 18 August 1985.

46. Ibid., 20 October 1985.

47. Moscow TASS in English, 1212 GMT, 24 December 1985, Daily Report (USSR), National Affairs Supplement, 24 December 1985.

48. Moscow TASS International Service in Russian 1803 GMT, 3 January 1986, Daily Report (USSR), National Affairs Supplement, 6 January 1986.

49. *New York Times,* 25 December 1985.

50. London, *The Economist,* 4 January 1986.

51. *Moskovskaya Pravda,* 5 January 1985, Daily Report (USSR), National Affairs Supplement, 10 January 1986.

52. Moscow Television Service in Russian 1800 GMT, 10 January 1986, Daily Report (USSR), National Affairs Supplement, 13 January 1986.

53. Moscow *Pravda,* 18 January 1986.

54. *Moskovskaya Pravda,* 25 January 1986, Daily Report (USSR), National Affairs Supplement, 31 January 1986.

55. Moscow Domestic Service in Russian 1730 GMT, 30 January 1986, Daily Report (USSR), National Affairs Supplement, 31 January 1986.

56. Vienna *Kurier,* 15 February 1986.

57. Paris AFP in English 1249 GMT, 26 January 1986.

58. Moscow Domestic Service in Russian 1600 GMT, 4 November 1985, Daily Report (USSR), 5 November 1985.

59. Moscow Television Service in Russian 1530 GMT, 14 December 1985, Daily Report (USSR), National Affairs Supplement, 16 December 1986.

60. Moscow Domestic Service in Russian 1600 GMT, 6 January 1986, Daily Report (USSR), National Affairs Supplement, 7 January 1986.

61. Moscow *Pravda,* 13 October 1985.

62. Baku *Bakinskiy Rabochiy,* 22 December 1985, Daily Report (USSR), National Affairs Supplement, 7 January 1986.

63. Moscow *Pravda,* 26 January 1986.

64. Moscow *Izvestiya,* 26 January 1986.

65. Paris AFP in English 1705 GMT, 26 January 1986.

66. Tbilisi *Zarya Vostoka,* 23 January 1986, Daily Report (USSR), National Affairs Supplement, 3 February 1986.

67. Dushanbe *Kommunist Tadzhikistana,* 21 January 1986, Daily Report (USSR), National Affairs Supplement, 3 February 1986.

68. Frunze *Sovetskaya Kirgiziya,* 28 December 1985, Daily Report (USSR), National Affairs Supplement, 29 January 1986.

69. *Moskovskaya Pravda,* 25 January 1986, Daily Report (USSR), National Affairs Supplement, 28 January 1986.

70. Ashkhabad *Turkmenskaya Iskra,* 18 January 1986, Daily Report (USSR), National Affairs Supplement, 27 January 1986.

71. Frunze *Sovetskaya Kirgiziya,* 24 January 1986.

72. Moscow *Pravda,* 28 January 1986.

73. Ibid., 2 February 1986.

74. Paris AFP in English 1220 GMT, 2 February 1986.

75. Alma Ata Domestic Service in Russian 0200 GMT, 5 February 1986, Daily Report (USSR), National Affairs Supplement, 7 February 1986.

76. Moscow TASS International Service in Russian 1604 GMT, 8 February 1986, Daily Report (USSR), National Affairs Supplement, 10 February 1986.

77. Moscow *Pravda,* 9 February 1986.

78. Ibid.

79. Moscow TASS in English 1206 GMT, 18 February 1986, Daily Report (USSR), National Affairs Supplement, 18 February 1986.

80. Ibid.

81. Ibid.

82. Moscow *Pravda,* 26 February 1986.

83. Ibid.

84. Ibid.

85. Ibid., 27 February 1986.

86. Moscow TASS in English 0950 GMT, 6 March 1986; also Moscow *Pravda* 7 March 1986.

87. Paris AFP in English 1401 GMT, 6 March 1986.

88. Paris AFP in English 1411 GMT, 6 March 1986.

89. Moscow *Pravda,* 7 March 1986.

90. Moscow TASS in English 0950 GMT, 6 March 1986; also Moscow *Pravda,* 7 March 1986.

91. Moscow TASS International Service in Russian 1405 GMT, 6 March 1986; also Moscow ·*Pravda,* 7 March 1986.

92. Paris AFP in English 1014 GMT, 9 March 1986.

Chapter 10

1. Paris AFP in English 1242 GMT, 26 February 1986.

2. *International Herald Tribune,* 24 February 1986.

Index